INDIA BOOKVARSITY
LOTUS CHOICES
Editor: Mahendra Kulasrestha

GANDHI 3/21
Fresh Global Editions
for
the Third Millennium and
Twenty First Century

The Bhagavadgita

A Commentary by
Mahatma Gandhi

'.... a work which persons of all faiths can read.
It does not favour any sectarian view.
It teaches nothing but pure ethics.'
— Gandhi

'How Did I Read the Gita'

"I was induced to read the *Gita* by two Englishmen. I say 'induced' because I had no particular desire to read it. When these friends asked me to read it with them, I felt rather ashamed. That I know nothing about my holy books made me feel miserable.

"I did not know Sanskrit well enough to be able to read the *Gita* without help, so they gave me Sir Edwin Arnold's excellent translation of the poem. I went through the whole of it immediately and was fascinated by it. From that time till now, the last nineteen stanzas of Ch. 2 have ever remained engraved in my heart. They contain the essence of Dharma. I since then have read most of other translations and listened to many discourses .... and the impression made by that first reading, persists."

—M.K. Gandhi

The Bhagavadgita

A Commentary by

Mahatma Gandhi

4735/22, Prakash Deep Building
Ansari Road, Darya Ganj,
New Delhi - 110002

Lotus Press : Publishers & Distributors
Unit No. 220, 2nd Floor, 4735/22, Prakash Deep Building,
Ansari Road, Darya Ganj, New Delhi- 110002
Ph.: 41325510, 98118-38000
• E-mail : lotuspress1984@gmail.com
www.lotuspress.co.in

The Bhagavadgita
A Commentary by Mahatma Gandhi

ISBN: 978-81-8382-213-8 (PB)

Printed & Published by : **Lotus Press Publisher & Distributors,** New Delhi-02

Editorspeak

An Ignored Commentary

While working on this manuscript, I was struck— may I say 'hit'?— by the fact that Gandhi's commentary on the *Bhagavadgita* was an unknown entity. I myself thought so, but it was confirmed by Sh. B.B. Singh, a Civil Judge from Hazaribagh, who was visiting me that day. He is an avid reader of books on Indian philosophy and religion, thorough in Upanishads, and his first comment on looking at the proofs etc. was: 'Never heard of it.' My own interest in this particular work having not being overmuch, though I do have a general idea of the various commentaries and the material they serve to the hungry, I was again struck by the simplicity, ease and understandability of these discourses—one will even laugh at critical points—that I did not hesitate in describing it as one of the best—or even the best—among all, especially because it seemed to cater to the common man, not the scholar, which in fact it was: these discourses were given to young boys and students of his Ashram— in 1927— whom, he kept cajoling and scolding whenever needed, which his close-to-ideal secretary, Mahadev Desai, kept noting down, and later on converting to a full-fledged commentary.

My appreciation for this commentary was due to one more reason. What does the *Gita* propagate? For some it is Karma Yoga, for others Bhakti Yoga, Dvaita, Advaita and their various varieties, creating uncertainty and confusion of the highest degree, but Gandhi simply critiques it as the propounder of Anasakti, Non-Attachment, nothing else. He has surely taken the bull of the *Gita* by its horns.

My reading of this commentary cast new searchlight on the personality of the great-great-great Gandhi. I was assured that he was a deeply religious person, and his great strengths in his unexpected forays into politics as well as other fields came from his genuine religious beliefs. The Ramayana was of central importance to him (and the Congress party which he nurtured with great care, even blood, should take note of it.) Gandhi's biographers, the future ones, would do well to carefully read this commentary before taking up the pen; they would understand his heart and soul better and would be able to present certain new dimensions of his thought and work-processes.

That Gandhi, the most significant person of the last century, commented in so much detail on the *Gita*, again, the most significant as well as representative scripture of Indian philosophy and culture; is still again, the most-most-most significant work of the present day religious-philosophical literature of the world. That the Gandhi organisations so blatantly ignored it, seems unpardonable. We know about Lokmanya Tilak's commentary on the *Gita*, which Gandhi himself quotes occasionally in these discourses— he fondly calls him 'Tilak Maharaj'— and admire it as a notable work, but Gandhi's own work has been dusted under the carpet.

Returning to the main subject, the *Gita* has been widely recognised as one of the best treatises on life and its philosophy all over the world. Quotes after quotes by scholars and publicmen can be cited in its favour, but we will be content with a meaningful few. Aldous Huxley says: 'The *Gita* is one of the clearest and most comprehensive summaries of the perennial philosophy ever to have been made. Hence its enduring value, not only to Indians, but for all mankind.... The *Bhagavadgita* is perhaps the most systematic spiritual statement of the perennial philosophy.' According to Willam von Humbolt: '(It is)... the most beautiful, perhaps the only true, philosophical song which exists in any known tongue.' In the view of Schlegel: '... (the author's) oracular soul has wafted aloft into divine and eternal truth with a certain affable delight.' Its translator Sir Edwin Arnold wrote: 'English literature would be incomplete without possessing in popular form a poetical and philosophical work so dear to India.'

Dr. Radhakrishan in his well known commentary states that the *Gita* has exercised an influence that extended in early times to China and Japan and latterly to the West. Two chief works of the Mahayana Buddhism, *Mahayanasraddhotpatti* and *Saddharma Pundarika*, are deeply indebted to the teachings of the *Gita*.

He further states that "It is interesting to observe that the official exponent of 'the German Faith', J.W. Hauer, a Sanskrit scholar who served as a missionary for some years in India, gives to the *Gita* a central place in the German faith. He calls it a work of imperishable significance. He declares that the book gives us not only profound insights that are valid for all times and for all religious life, but it contains as well the classical presentation of one of the most significant phases of Indo-Germanic religious history.

"The *Gita*, unlike other books of world religions, does not propagate dogma of any kind. It asks us to find out the meaning of life before we involve in any kind of action. It bases its philosophy of action essentially on a philosophy of life. It does not advocate a fanatical devotion to the practical to the disparagement of the dignity of thought. Its philosophy of the practical is a derivative from its philosophy of spirit and ethical action is derived from metaphysical realisation." Gandhi himself at the end of his discourses, declares it as a book of ethics which men of every religion and sect should study.

I would now like to delve in a little history— though history has always been given zero importance in Indian culture— even as compared to Chinese and Japanese cultures, where every event and its date is very carefully noted— as regards Krishna, who he was, his Guru, the genesis of his chief contribution to the concept of Atman, soul, that it does not die, it is immortal, etc., a concept which won the whole world and even today wields a strong hold over it. I am sure the reader will find it interesting.

Krishna, it would seem, was a multi-talented person, a miraculous child who could kill demons, an empire-builder who traversed from Mathura to Dwarka, an intelligent diplomat who advised the Pandavas and led them to victory, a great lover since childhood, and above all, a thinker and philosopher, the propounder of the *Gita*— the subject with which we are presently concerned. In modern terminology, we could call him a Superman.

The word 'Krishna', as everyone knows, means dark, quite dark indeed, even black, therefore he may not be regarded as of Aryan origin. He, as son of Devaki, has been mentioned in the Chandogya Upanishad and is said to be the pupil of a priest named Ghora Angirasa. The word 'Ghora' is notable—it may mean very strong. He was a believer of the Sungod. This also is noteworthy because the Aryans were the believers of Agni, Sun is a minor deity in the Vedas. This is an interesting fact because all other religions of the world were worshippers of the Sun, which seems more natural. Why fire? Perhaps because as Lokmanya Tilak has propounded in his books— which Gandhi had also read; he mentions this in these discourses— the Aryans lived originally at the North Pole, for which reason fire was very important for them. Science has now come to accept this fact; not only so, the snow on the poles has once again started melting.

The Kaushitaki Brahmana gives some more details about the Angirasa. Here he is called Krishna Angirasa, and he is said to have composed two or three hymns of the Rigveda. The name Angira and Angirasa is known to the students of the Vedas. There are several

Angirasas in the Rigveda. Ghora Angirasa explained to Krishna the meaning of the word 'yajna' , and clarified that the qualities of austerity, charity, uprightness, non-violence and truthfulness were a must to fulfil it. A shloka in the 16th chapter of the *Gita* repeats these qualities exactly in the same form, which seems to establish the direct connection between both.

Ghora Angirasa, then, tells him something more which in the *Gita* is the central point of its special philosophy, and for which the *Gita* is given the prominent place in world philosophy. He told Krishna that in his hour of death one should devote himself to three thoughts: (1) that of Akshita, which means that you are not destroyed, (2) of Achyuta, that you are immovable, and (3) of Prana, that you are the very essence of life. We are all aware that the idea of the indestrutibility of the Atman is the chief idea of the *Gita* as well as its contribution to world philosophy. Around it the whole story of the *Gita* is spun.

Now this was another achievement of the Indian mind in ancient times, the first being the idea of Atman and the second being the idea of Brahman, in which the Atman submerges. Paul Deussen and others in modern times recognised the significance of these ideas and hailed them as India's major discoveries in philosophy.

So Ghora was the guru of Krishna, son of Devaki, and the latter look it upon himself to spread and popularise this idea. He opposed some ideas of the Vedic religion, especially its elaborate and bloody Yajnas and powerful priesthood and wanted to simplify it. Many others also did so and, according to Harivamsha Purana, even the almighty Indra, a major deity of the Vedas, accepted defeat from Krishna and his superiority over the cows. This story is rather well known, though this interpretation is not. Indra called him 'Govinda.'

Krishna belonged to the Satvata branch of the Yadav clan, who lived around Mathura, and taught his people the worship of the Sun. His cult acquired the name of Vasudev, the name of his father, and it grew quite fast. His elder brother was named Baldev, and he was also worshipped. The Vasudev cult was very well established by the 4th century B.C. Megasthenes as well as Buddhistic works mention it. Heliodorus the Greek became a Bhagvat and called Vasudev as 'Devadeva'— the god of gods— in his famous Basenagar inscription.

Panini the grammarian also mentions it in his famous *Mahabhashya* and calls him 'Vasudev Bhagvat'. The Gita for this reason, is called the *Bhagavadgita*. It is therefore the book of a religious sect and propounds the creed of the Bhagavata sect, a major sect of those times which had greatly influenced even the invaders. And as has been the custom of our sect leaders, Krishna declared that it was not a new religion, it was most ancient. He says in the *Gita* that it was given by him in ancient times to Vivasvan, who gave it to Manu and Manu in its turn gave it to Ikshvaku. The *Narayaniya,* which presents the Bhagvata religion in exclusive detail, clearly mentions that the religion was preached in the *Bhagavadgita*. The Shanti Parva of the Mahabharata also mentions it.

It is thus established that there was a sound tradition, supported by a strong organisation, behind the preaching of the *Gita*. The religion regarded Krishna as the supreme God or Paramatman, who creates life in all its forms and controls it. This is most clearly and powerfully described in Ch. 10 of the *Gita* where he describes himself as the best among all kinds of life. As could be expected, Arjuna was overawed and started praying, in the next chapter, in the most reverential terms. Such overwhelming descriptions of God, by himself, are not available in any other Hindu scripture.

Krishna thus acquired a position in Hindu culture which even Rama could not acquire. The temples of Krishna are many more, even in south India, than the temples of Rama. This was to some extent compensated by Ramalilas in north-India, which were started by Tulasidas in much later times. As an avatar of Lord Vishnu, he has undoubtedly been regarded as senior to Krishna, and also more idealistic, Maryadapurushottama, but in terms of popularity and influence, he has been quite far behind. Also, he did not leave behind him any new ideas or philosophy, which is Krishna's utmost contribution.

The skeletons of Krishna's history are strong enough to establish that he was a historical figure who lived on India's soil quite long ago, much before the Buddha, in Vedic times. It also looks almost certain that Ghora Angirasa and Krishna Angirasa were two different persons, the former the teacher of the latter. Krishna was a successful preacher and organiser of a new religion. His presentation of the philosophy in the Mahabharata may not have been the first, but its inclusion in the epic did give it very wide publicity and helped it in its spread, which continues till day. One doesn't know when the Vasudev sect started declining, which may have been during the first centuries of the Christian era. But the sect's book of the *Gita* did not dissolve into oblivion, it continued to be read and influence the propounders of the theory of Atman and Brahman.

They had worked out a detailed account and critique of the theory of the Brahman in the Brahma Sutra, and were organising related relevant material in the group known as Prasthana. So far the Upanishads and the Brahma Sutra had been included in the group and now the *Gita* was also given this honour, chiefly because it further clarified the concept of Atman, providing it a glow it had so far not acquired, and bccause it was a quite short, properly organized and powerful presentation of the subject. Its Vishwarupa Darshan was a very effective and sure shot for the common man, a master-stroke of the genius of Krishna. The Upanishads in comparison to the *Gita* were unmanageable stuff, scattered far and wide in every direction, and the Brahma Sutra highly intellectual and difficult to understand. Now the Prasthana was complete, enough material to present the philosophical case of the Atman and Brhaman. The group came to be known as Prasthana Traya— the trilogy of the Prasthanas—and the *Gita* not only entered the mainstream of the Atman philosophy, but became its most important book. It was a tremendous achievement for a sectarian book to have floated ahead of all its predecessors. The win has served the nation well, and to an extent the humanity at large also. If handled properly, it can provide complete service to all human beings in modern times. I venture to suggest that—**Gandhi's commentary on the *Gita* can, and should be, used as a tool for this great purpose**.

As Dr. Radhakrishnan points out in his commentary: 'The chief problem facing us today is the reconciliation of mankind. The *Gita* is specially suited for the purpose, as it attempts to reconcile varied and apparently antithetical forms of the religious consciousness and emphasizes the root conception of religion which are neither ancient nor modern but eternal and belong to the very flesh of humanity, past, present and future.'

Amen!

❑❑❑

Gandhispeak

A Book of Non-Violence

I became acquainted with the *Gita* in 1898. I was twenty years of age at that time. I had not yet fully understood the significance of non-violence as a principle of dharma. It was from Shamal Bhatt's couplet, "Let him offer water, and a good meal to eat," that I had first learnt the principle of winning over even an enemy with love. Its truth had made a deep appeal to my heart, but the couplet had not suggested to me the principle of compassion for all creatures. I had even eaten meat before that time while I was still in India. I believed that it was one's duty to kill snakes and other such creatures. I remember having killed bed-bugs and other insects. I remember killing a scorpion once. Today I think that we should not kill even such poisonous creatures. In those days I believed that we would have to fit ourselves to fight the British. I used to murmur to myself the lines of the poem beginning, "Is it any wonder that the British rule over us?" My eating meat was for the purpose of fitting myself for this fighting in future. These were the views I held before I left for England. It was my desire to keep, even at the cost of my life, the promises which I had given to my mother that saved me from eating meat and other sins. My love of truth has saved me in many difficult situations.

It was at this time that, coming into contact with two Englishmen, I was induced to read the *Gita*. From that time till now, the last nineteen stanzas of Chapter II have ever remained engraved in my heart. They embody the highest knowledge. The principles enunciated in them are immutable. The intellect, too, is active in them in the highest degree, but it is intellect, disciplined to high purpose. The knowledge which they contain is the fruit of experience. These stanzas are the key to the understanding of the *Gita*. I would even go so far as to advise people to reject statements in the poem which bear a meaning contrary to that of these nineteen stanzas. For a person who is humble there can be no question of rejecting anything. He will merely reason: "It is the imperfection of my own intellect that today other stanzas seem to me inconsistent with these. In the course of time, I shall be able to see their consistency." So he will tell himself and others, and leave the matter there.

Let us now examine the *Gita*. Its subject-matter is simply the realization of Brahman and the means thereto; the battle is only the occasion for its teaching. One can say, if one likes, that the poet used it as an occasion because he did not look upon it as morally wrong. On reading the *Mahabharata* I formed quite a different impression. Vyasa wrote his supremely beautiful epic to depict the futility of war. What did the Kauravas' defeat and the Pandavas' victory avail? How many among the victors survived? What was their fate? What was the end of Kunti, mother of the Pandavas? What trace is left today of the Yadava race?

Since the *Gita's* subject is not description of the battle and justification of violence, it is perfectly wrong to give much importance to these. If, moreover, it is difficult to reconcile a few of the verses with the idea that the *Gita* advocates non-violence, it is still more difficult to reconcile the teaching of the work as a whole with the advocacy of violence.

When a poet composes his work, he does not have a clear conception of all its possible implications. It is the very beauty of a good poem that it is greater than its author. The truth which a poet utters in his moment of inspiration, we do not often see him following in his own life. Hence the lives of many poets are at variance with the teaching of their poems. **That the overall teaching of the *Gita* is not violence but non-violence is evident from the argument which begins in Chapter II and ends in Chapter XVIII.** The intervening chapters propound the same theme. Violence is simply not possible unless one is driven by anger, by ignorant love and by hatred. The *Gita*, on the other hand, wants us to be incapable of anger and attain to a state unaffected by the three *gunas*. Such a person can never feel anger. I see even now the red eyes of Arjuna every time he aimed an arrow from his bow, drawing the string as far as his ear.

But, then, had Arjuna's obstinate refusal to fight anything to do with non-violence? In fact, he had fought often enough in the past. On the present occasion, his reason was suddenly clouded by ignorant attachment. He did not wish to kill his kinsmen. He did not say that he would not kill anyone even if he believed that person to be wicked. Shri Krishna is the Lord dwelling in everyone's heart. He understands the momentary darkening of Arjuna's reason. He, therefore, tells him: "You have already committed violence. By talking now like a wise man, you will not learn non-violence. Having started on this course, you must finish the job." If a passenger travelling in a train which is running at a speed of forty miles an hour suddenly feels aversion to travelling and jumps out of the train, he will have but committed suicide. He has not in truth realized the futility of travelling as such or of travelling by train. Arjuna was in a similar condition. **Krishna, who believed in non-violence, could not have given Arjuna any advice other than what he did.** But to conclude from this that the *Gita* teaches violence or justifies war is as unwarranted as to argue that, since violence in some form or other is inescapable for maintaining the body in existence, dharma lies only in violence. The man of discriminating intellect, on the other hand, teaches the duty of striving for deliverance from this body which exists through violence, the duty, that is, of striving for *moksha*.

But whom does Dhritarashtra represent, and likewise Duryodhana, Yudhishthira or Arjuna? Whom does Krishna represent? Were they historical personages? Does the *Gita* relate their actual doings? Is it likely that Arjuna should suddenly, without warning, ask a question when the battle was about to commence, and that Krishna should recite the whole *Gita* in reply? And then, Arjuna, who had said that his ignorance had been dispelled, forgets what he was taught in the *Gita*, and Krishna is made to repeat his teaching in the *Anugita*.

Personally, I believe that Duryodhana and his supporters stand for the Satanic impulses in us, and Arjuna and others stand for

Godward impulses. The battlefield is our body. The poet-seer, who knows from experience the problems of life, has given a faithful account of the conflict which is eternally going on within us. Shri Krishna is the Lord dwelling in everyone's heart who is ever murmuring His promptings in a pure *chitta* like a clock ticking in a room. If the clock of the *chitta* is not wound up with the key of self-purification, the in-dwelling Lord no doubt remains where He is, but the ticking is heard no more.

I do not wish to suggest that violence has no place at all in the teaching of the *Gita*. The dharma which it teaches does not mean that a person who has not yet awakened to the truth of non-violence may act like a coward. Anyone who fears others, accumulates possessions and indulges in sense-pleasure, will certainly fight with violent means, but violence does not, for that reason, become justified as his dharma. There is only one dharma. Non-violence means *moksha,* and *moksha* means realizing Satyanarayana. But this dharma does not under any circumstances countenance running away in fear. In this world which baffles our reason, violence there will then always be. The *Gita* shows the way which will lead us out of it, but it also says that we cannot escape it simply by running away from it like cowards. Anyone who prepares to run away would do better, instead, to kill and be killed.

If the verses cited by the correspondent cannot be understood even after this explanation, I cannot explain them. I am sure no one doubts that God, who is omnipotent, is, and must be, the Creator, the Preserver and the Destroyer of the Universe. He who creates has certainly the right to destroy. Even so, He does not kill, for He does nothing. God is so merciful He does not violate the law that every creature that is born will die one day. If He were to follow His fancies and whims, where should we be?

❑❑❑

CONTENTS

It was the first of books; it was as if an empire spake to us, nothing small or unworthy but large, serene, consistent, the voice of an old intelligence which in another age and climate had pondered and thus disposed of the same questions which exercise us.

— R.W. Emerson

The reader is nowhere raised into and sustained in a higher, purer, or rarer region of thought than in the Bhagavad gita.... Beside (it), even our Shakespeare seems sometimes youthfully green and practical merely.

— Thoreau

1

अर्जुनविषादयोग

धृतराष्ट्र उवाच

धर्मक्षेत्रे कुरूक्षेत्रे समवेता युयुत्सवः। मामकाः पाण्डवाश्चैव किमकुर्वत सञ्जय।। 1

सञ्जय उवाच

दृष्ट्वा तु पाण्डवानीकं व्यूढं दुर्योधनस्तदा। आचार्यमुपसङ्गम्य राजा वचनमब्रवीत्।। 2

पश्यैतां पाण्डुपुत्राणामाचार्य महतीं चमूम्। व्यूढां द्रुपदपुत्रेण तव शिष्येण धीमता।। 3

अत्र शूरा महेष्वासा भीमार्जुनसमा युधि। युयुधानो विराटश्च द्रुपदश्च महारथ।। 4

धृष्टकेतुश्चेकितानः काशिराजश्च वीर्यवान्। पुरूजित्कुन्तिभोजश्च शैब्यश्च नरपुङ्गवः।। 5

युधामन्युश्च विक्रान्त उत्तमौजाश्च वार्यवान्। सौभद्रो द्रौपदेयाश्च सर्व एव महारथाः।। 6

अस्माकं तु विशिष्टा ये तान्निबोध द्विजोत्तम। नायका मम सैन्यस्य सञ्ज्ञार्थं तान्ब्रवीमि ते।। 7

भवान् भीष्मश्च कर्णश्च कृपश्च समितिञ्जयः। अश्वत्थामा विकर्णश्च सौमदत्तिस्तथैव च।। 8

अन्ये च बहवः शूरा मदर्थे त्यक्तजीविताः। नानाशस्त्रप्रहरणाः सर्वे युद्धविशारदाः।। 9

अपर्याप्तं तदस्माकं बलं भीष्माभिरक्षितम्। पर्याप्तं त्विदमेतेषां बलं भीष्माभिरक्षितम्।। 10

अयनेषु च सर्वेषु यथाभागमवस्थिताः। भीष्ममेवाभिरक्षन्तु भवन्तः सर्व एव हि।। 11

तस्य सञ्जनयन् हर्षं कुरूवृद्धः पितामहः। सिंहनादं विनद्योच्चैः शङ्खं दध्मौ प्रतापवान्।। 12

ततः शङ्खाश्च भेर्यश्च पणवानकगोमुखाः। सहसैवाभ्यहन्यन्त स शब्दस्तुमुलोऽभवत्।। 13

ततः श्वेतैर्हयैर्युक्ते महति स्यन्दने स्थितौ। माधवः पाण्डवश्चैव दिव्यौ शङ्खौ प्रदध्मतुः।। 14

पाञ्चजन्यं हृषीकेशो देवदत्तं धनञ्जयः। पौण्ड्रं दध्मौ महाशङ्खं भीमकर्मा वृकोदरः।। 15
अनन्तविजयं राजा कुन्तीपुत्रो युधिष्ठिरः। नकुलः सहदेवश्च सुघोषमणिपुष्पकौ।। 16
काश्यश्च परमेष्वासः शिखण्डी च महारथः। धृष्टद्युम्नो विराटश्च सात्यकिश्चापराजितः।। 17
द्रुपदो द्रौपदेयाश्च सर्वशः पृथिवीपते। सौभद्रश्च महाबाहुः शङ्खान् दध्मुः पृथक् पृथक्।। 18
स घोषो धार्तराष्ट्राणां हृदयानि व्यदारयत्। नभश्च पृथिवीं चैव तुमुलो व्यनुनादयन्।। 19
अथ व्यवस्थितान् दृष्ट्वा धार्तराष्ट्रान् कपिध्वजः। प्रवृत्ते शस्त्रसम्पाते धनुरुद्यम्य पाण्डवः।। 20
हृषीकेशं तदा वाक्यमिदमाह महीपते।

अर्जुन उवाच

सेनयोरुभयोर्मध्ये रथं स्थापय मेऽच्युत।। 21
यावदेतान्निरीक्षेऽहं योद्धुकामानवस्थितान्। कैर्मया सह योद्धव्यमस्मिन् रणसमुद्यमे।। 22
योत्स्यमानानवेक्ष्येऽहं य एतेऽत्र समागताः। धार्तराष्ट्रस्य दुर्बुद्धेर्युद्धे प्रियचिकीर्षवः।। 23

सञ्जय उवाच

एवमुक्तो हृषीकेशो गुडाकेशेन भारत। सेनयोरुभयोर्मध्ये स्थापयित्वा रथोत्तमम्।। 24
भीष्मद्रोणप्रमुखतः सर्वेषां च महीक्षिताम्। उवाच पार्थ पश्यैतान् समवेतान् कुरूनिति।। 25
तत्रापश्यत्स्थितान् पार्थः पितृनथ पितामहान्। आचार्यान्मातुलान्भ्रातृन् पुत्रान्पौत्रान्सखींस्तथा।। 26
श्वशुरान् सुहृदश्चैव सेनयोरुभयोरपि। तान्समीक्ष्य स कौन्तेयः सर्वान्बन्धूनवस्थितान्।। 27
कृपया परयाविष्टो विषीदन्निदमब्रवीत्।

अर्जुन उवाच

दृष्ट्वेमं स्वजनं कृष्ण युयुत्सुं समुपस्थितम्।। 28
सीदन्ति मम गात्राणि मुखं च परिशुष्यति। वेपथुश्च शरीरे मे रोमहर्षश्च जायते। 29
गाण्डीवं स्रंसते हस्तात् त्वक्चैव परिदह्यते। न च शक्नोम्यवस्थातुं भ्रमतीव च मे मनः।। 30
निमित्तानि च पश्यामि विपरीतानि केशव। न च श्रेयोऽनुपश्यामि हत्वा स्वजनमाहवे।। 31
न काङ्क्षे विजयं कृष्ण न च राज्यं सुखानि च। किं नो राज्येन गोविन्द किं भोगैर्जीवितेन वा।। 32
येषामर्थे काङ्क्षितं नो राज्यं भोगाः सुखानि च। त इमेऽवस्थिता युद्धे प्राणांस्त्यक्त्वा धनानि च।। 33
आचार्याः पितरः पुत्रास्तथैव च पितामहाः। मातुलाः श्वशुराः पौत्राः श्यालाः सम्बन्धिनस्तथा।। 34

एतान्न हन्तुमिच्छामि घ्नतोऽपि मधुसूदन। अपि त्रैलोक्यराज्यस्य हेतोः किं नु महीकृते।। 35
निहत्य धार्तराष्ट्रान्नः का प्रीतिः स्याज्जनार्दन। पापमेवाऽऽश्रयेदस्मान् हत्वैतानाततायिनः।। 36
तस्मान्नार्हा वयं हन्तुं धार्तराष्ट्रान् स्वबान्धवान्। स्वजनं हि कथं हत्वा सुखिनः स्याम माधव।। 37
यद्यप्येते न पश्यन्ति लोभोपहतचेतसः। कुलक्षयकृतं दोषं मित्रद्रोहे च पातकम्।। 38
कथं न ज्ञेयमस्माभिः पापादस्मान्निवर्तितुम्। कुलक्षयकृतं दोषं प्रपश्यद्भिर्जनार्दन। 39
कुलक्षये प्रणश्यन्ति कुलधर्माः सनातनाः। धर्मे नष्टे कुलं कृत्स्नमधर्मोऽभिभवत्युत।। 40
अधर्माभिभवात्कृष्ण प्रदुष्यन्ति कुलस्त्रियः। स्त्रीषु दुष्टासु वार्ष्णेय जायते वर्णसङ्करः।। 41
सङ्करो नरकायैव कुलघ्नानां कुलस्य च। पतन्ति पितरो ह्येषां लुप्तपिण्डोदकक्रियाः।। 42
दोषैरेतैः कुलघ्नानां वर्णसङ्करकारकैः। उत्साद्यन्ते जातिधर्माः कुलधर्माश्च शाश्वताः।। 43
उत्सन्नकुलधर्माणां मनुष्याणां जनार्दन। नरकेऽनियतं वासो भवतीत्यनुशुश्रुम।। 44
अहो बत महत्पापं कर्तुं व्यवसिता वयम्। यद्राज्यसुखलोभेन हन्तुं स्वजनमुद्यताः।। 45
यदि मामप्रतीकारमशस्त्रं शस्त्रपाणयः। धार्तराष्ट्रा रणे हन्युस्तन्मे क्षेमतरं भवेत्।। 46

सञ्जय उवाच

एवमुक्त्वार्जुनः सङ्ख्ये रथोपस्थ उपाविशत्। विसृज्य सशरं चापं शोकसंविग्नमानसः।। 47

Arjuna's Gloom and Question

The *Mahabharata* is a *dharma-grantha,* a work treating of religious and ethical questions. In this battle, the warriors were, on the one side, the sons of Dharma, Vayu, Indra and Ashvinikumars and, on the other, a hundred brothers all born at the same instant. Duryodhana rode on the chariot of *adharma,* and Arjuna that of dharma. The battle described here is, therefore, a struggle between dharma and *adharma.* Sanjaya is a man of devotion. The battle takes place far away from where he is, and he cannot see it; Vyasa endows him with divine vision so that he can see what is happening.

What does this signify? Only this: that the epic describes the battle ever raging between the countless Kauravas and Pandavas dwelling within us. It is a battle between the innumerable forces of good and evil which become personified in us as virtues and vices. We shall say that this *dharma-grantha* was written to explain man's duty in this inner strife.

Quite a few such blind men live within us. This is not a battle which took place so many thousand years ago; it is one which is raging all the time, even today.

Duryodhana tells Dronacharya that his own pupil, Dhrishtadyumna, has planned the deployment on the Pandava side. They are, on both sides, his pupils, to whom he has imparted the same knowledge. But it depends on themselves whether they use that knowledge well or ill.

There is much in the *Gita* for anyone who, though ignorant of grammar, aspires after *moksha.* It is stated in the *Gita* itself that everyone, whether a woman, a Vaisya or a Sudra, can acquire spiritual knowledge if they have devotion to God.

The battlefield described here is primarily the one inside the human body. Does the *Gita* then prohibit physical fighting altogether? No; fighting there may well be. **But here the physical battle is only an occasion for describing the battlefield of the**

human body. In this view the names mentioned are not of persons but of qualities which they represent. What is described is the conflict within the human body between opposing moral tendencies imagined as distinct figures. A seer such as Vyasa would never concern himself with a description of mere physical fighting. It is the human body that is described as Kurukshetra, as *dharma-kshetra.* It does become that when used in the service or God. The epithet may also mean that for a Kshatriya a battlefield is always a field of dharma. Surely a field on which the Pandavas too were present could not be altogether a place of sin.

Kunti had five sons. Karna had the Sun-god as father. Everyone of the characters had a miraculous birth. Whether out of compassion for Duryodhana, or because he was generous-hearted, Karna joined the former's side. Besides Karna, Duryodhana had good men like Bhishma and Drona also on his side. This suggests that evil cannot by itself flourish in this world. It can do so only if it is allied with some good. **This was the principle underlying non-cooperation, that the evil system which the Government represents, and which has endured only because of the support it receives from good people, cannot survive if that support is withdrawn.** Just as the Government needs the support of good men in order to exist, so Duryodhana required men like Bhishma and Drona in order to show that there was justice on his side.

The pair of words *aparyapta* and *paryapta* can be interpreted in two different ways: *aparyapta* may mean (1) boundless, limitless, or (2) inadequate, insufficient; and *paryapta* may mean (1) limited or (2) adequate, sufficient. The meaning will depend on what we believe to be the feeling in Duryodhana's heart. Of the two meanings of *aparyapta,* I have accepted "inadequate", "insufficient". It has appealed to me from my earliest days. What Duryodhana felt was that their army, protected by Bhishma, was not sufficiently strong, whereas the Pandava army, protected by Bhima was; for grandfather Bhishma loved both sides and Duryodhana had, therefore, a secret fear that he might not fight with his whole heart.

Sanjaya is proceeding with his description of the conches which are being blown in the Pandava camp.

Kairmaya saha yoddhavyam: Arjuna is asking, not whether it is necessary that he should fight, but against whom he has to fight. If he did not wish to fight, he would have told Krishna so on the previous day itself. He had no aversion to fighting as such. In fact, he had obtained Yudhishthira's permission and secured weapons from Indra that he might fight. Krishna would have, in that case, asked Arjuna to go to Duryodhana and win him over. But that was not the case. Arjuna had fought even during the exile. He had fought when King Virat was attacked by Duryodhana. He was always prepared to fight. His question, therefore, was who they were against whom he would be fighting. We should always bear this in mind.

Arjuna requests Shri Krishna to station his chariot between the two armies, so that he may see the warriors on the field.

He sees that all of them are relatives and friends, whom one cannot easily bring oneself to kill.

Arjuna says: "I do not see any good in killing one's kinsmen." The stress here is on "kinsmen". He says:

> *I would not fight against them, even for the kingdom of the three worlds; how could I, then, fight against them for a few clods of earth? (35)*

... because he has asked for only five villages as the Pandava's share. He repeatedly asks how he can be happy after killing his kinsmen. All his arguments are summed up in the question; *Kairmaya saha yoddhavyam?* He is unhappy, not at the thought of killing, but at the thought of whom he was required to kill. By putting the word "kinsmen" repeatedly in his mouth, the author of the *Gita* shows into what darkness and ignorance he has sunk. Arjuna has been arguing from a practical point of view and Shri Krishna, it is hinted here, will try to meet that very argument.

The world will blame a person even for going to a court against his relations. Arjuna is shaken in his whole being, but it is not as if Shri Krishna wanted him to cast off this weakness of his forthwith. If, while seeking to follow the path of good, we do not eschew something which even in practical life we are required to eschew, dharma would cease to be dharma. In our daily life we avoid doing things out of fear of society. In this case, it is not merely a question of avoiding something which even ordinary people would avoid; it is a question of killing hundreds of thousands of men. How could Arjuna bring himself to do that? He had no need to go to Krishna for an answer to the question. If he could have approached us, even we could have told him: "Do not fight." When the dharma laid down for even this *kaliyuga* requires us to refrain from unnecessary fighting, we should ask why Arjuna thought it necessary to put the question to Shri Krishna and why the two had such a long discussion. We can, therefore, understand the teaching of the *Gita* aright only if we give careful thought to the author's aim and the attendant circumstances. These last verses, however, are of great importance, for the entire argument which follows is based on them.

What people would generally do in their common dealings is regarded as good. If we see anyone here, or elsewhere, who renounces a right in regard to wordly matters and forgives even strangers, not to speak of relations, we should think of him as a good man. If we desist from beating up a thief or any other felon, do nothing to get him punished but, after admonishing him and recovering from him the stolen article, let him go, we would be credited with humanity and our action would be regarded as an instance of non-violence; a contrary course would be looked upon as violence. How is it, then, that Shri Krishna stops Arjuna from advancing such an argument? How can we explain a plainly contrary teaching in The *Gita?* Why does Shri Krishna describe Arjuna as cowardly and weak?

The *Gita* is consistent from the first to the last verse. That is why we meditate on its teaching and hope to discover from it the path to *moksha.* We should, therefore, think whether Arjuna's argument is valid or contains some flaw.

As though he were digging up a mountain to discover a mouse, Shri Krishna describes the *Gita,* at the conclusion of each chapter, as an Upanishad, as a *Yogashastra* and as *brahmavidya* and describes this particular one as a chapter on Arjuna's despondency.

It is important to consider what Arjuna's question was and what the circumstances were in which he raised it. Having got his chariot stationed between the two armies, he said he wanted to see who those men were against whom he would be fighting. His reason is, for the time being, clouded. He has lost his nerve. All that has gone before shows that Arjuna is a great warrior and that, when starting out to fight, he does not, like Dharmaraja, hesitate and ask all manner of questions. In the past, he never hesitated even when he had to fight against relations. Even during their fourteen years' exile, he gave free expression to his hatred for the Kauravas before Dharmaraja; what is more, victory in the battle depends entirely on him. Bhima is physically strong and daring, but he lacks Arjuna's power. In their preparations for the battle during fourteen years' exile, the other brothers always placed Arjuna at their head. When there was a battle outside Viratnagar, Arjuna, who had been living there in disguise wanted to be led to the place of fighting.

Why does a man, who loves fighting to this extent, want his chariot to be stationed between the two armies and to see who the warriors are on the other side? He knows everyone of them well enough. Why does he argue with Shri Krishna and tell him all that he does? He could have left the place immediately. Arjuna has a smaller army—an army of seven *akshauhini* as against the Kauravas' of eleven. Let us suppose that Arjuna flees the battlefield. Though his enemies are wicked people, are sinners, they are his relations and he cannot bring himself to kill them. If he leaves the field, what would happen to those vast numbers on his side? If Arjuna went away, leaving them behind, would the Kauravas have mercy on them? If he left the battle, the Pandava army would be simply annihilated. What, then, would be the plight of their wives and children?

I published in *Navajivan* a narrative of the European War, and there is a reason for this. It reminds us of the battle of the *Mahabharata.* I gave the narrative so that readers may know the ruin which such a war brings on a whole people. If Arjuna had left the battlefield, the very calamities which he feared would have befallen them. Their families would have been ruined, and the traditional dharma of these families and the race would have been destroyed. Arjuna, therefore, had no choice but to fight. This is the meaning of the battle in crude physical terms; I shall discuss later what it would be if the battlefield were taken to be the human being.

2

सांख्ययोग

सञ्जय उवाच

तं तथा कृपयाऽऽविष्टमश्रुपूर्णाकुलेक्षणम्। विषीदन्तमिदं वाक्यमुवाच मधुसूदनः।। 1

श्रीभगवानुवाच

कुतस्त्वा कश्मलमिदं विषमे समुपस्थितम्। अनार्यजुष्टमस्वर्ग्यमकीर्तिकरमर्जुन।। 2

क्लैब्यं मा स्म गमः पार्थ नैतत्त्वय्युपपद्यते। क्षुद्रं हृदयदौर्बल्यं त्यक्त्वोत्तिष्ठ परन्तप।। 3

अर्जुन उवाच

कथं भीष्ममहं सङ्ख्ये द्रोणं च मधुसूदन। इषुभिः प्रतियोत्स्यामि पूजार्हावरिसूदन।। 4

गुरूनहत्वा हि महानुभावान् श्रेयो भोक्तुं भैक्ष्यमपीह लोके।
हत्वार्थकामांस्तु गुरूनिहैव भुञ्जीय भोगान् रुधिरप्रदिग्धान्।। 5

न चैतद्विद्मः कतरन्नो गरीयो यद्वा जयेम यदि वा नो जयेयुः।
यानेव हत्वा न जिजीविषाम-स्तेऽवस्थिताः प्रमुखे धार्तराष्ट्राः।। 6

कार्पण्यदोषोपहतस्वभावः पृच्छामि त्वां धर्मसम्मूढचेताः।
यच्छ्रेयः स्यान्निश्चितं ब्रूहि तन्मे शिष्यस्तेऽहं शाधि मां त्वां प्रपन्नम्।। 7

न हि प्रपश्यामि ममापनुद्यात् यच्छोकमुच्छोषणमिन्द्रियाणाम्।
अवाप्य भूमावसपत्नमृद्धं राज्यं सुराणामपि चाधिपत्यम्।। 8

सञ्जय उवाच

एवमुक्त्वा हृषीकेशं गुडाकेशः परन्तप। न योत्स्य इति गोविन्दमुक्त्वा तूष्णीं बभूव ह।।9
तमुमाव हृषीकेशः प्रहसन्निव भारत। सेनयोरुभयोर्मध्ये विषीदन्तमिदं वचः।। 10

श्रीभगवानुवाच

अशोच्यानन्वशोचस्त्वं प्रज्ञावादांश्च भाषसे। गतासूनगतासूंश्च नानुशोचन्ति पण्डिताः।। 11

नत्वेवाहं जातु नासं न त्वं नेमे जनाधिपाः। न चैव न भविष्यामः सर्वे वयमतः परम्।। 12

देहिनोऽस्मिन्यथा देहे कौमारं यौवनं जरा। तथा देहान्तरप्राप्तिर्धीरस्तत्र न मुह्यति।। 13

मात्रास्पर्शास्तु कौन्तेय शीतोष्णसुखदुःखदाः। आगमापायिनोऽनित्यास्तांस्तितिक्षस्व भारत।। 14

यं हि न व्यथयन्त्येते पुरुषं पुरुषर्षभ। समदुःखसुखं धीरं सोऽमृतत्वाय कल्पते।। 15

नासतो विद्यते भावो नाभावो विद्यते सतः। उभयोरपि दृष्टोऽन्तस्त्वनयोस्तत्त्वदर्शिभिः।। 16

अविनाशि तु तद्विद्धि येन सर्वमिदं ततम्। विनाशमव्ययस्यास्य न कश्चित्कर्तुमर्हति।। 17

अन्तवन्त इमे देहा नित्यस्योक्ताः शरीरिणः। अनाशिनोऽप्रमेयस्य तस्माद्युद्धयस्व भारत।। 18

य एनं वेत्ति हन्तारं यश्चैनं मन्यते हतम्। उभौ तौ न विजानीतो नायं हन्ति न हन्यते।। 19

न जायते म्रियते वा कदाचिन्नायं भूत्वा भविता वा न भूयः।

अजो नित्यः शाश्वतोऽयंपुराणो न हन्यते हन्यमाने शरीरे।। 20

वेदाऽविनाशिनं नित्यं य एनमजमव्ययम्। कथं स पुरुषः पार्थ कं घातयति हन्ति कम्।। 21

वासांसि जीर्णानि यथा विहाय नवानि गृह्णाति नरोऽपराणि।

तथा शरीराणि विहाय जीर्णान्यन्यानि संयाति नवानि देही।। 22

नैनं छिन्दन्ति शस्त्राणि नैनं दहति पावकः। न चैनं क्लेदयन्त्यापो न शोषयति मारुतः।। 23

अच्छेद्योऽयमदाह्योऽयमक्लेद्योऽशोष्य एवं च। नित्यः सर्वगतः स्थाणुरचलोऽयं सनातनः।। 24

अव्यक्तोऽयमचिन्त्योऽयमविकार्योऽयमुच्यते। तस्मादेवं विदित्वैनं नाऽनुशोचितुमर्हसि।। 25

अथ चैनं नित्यजातं नित्यं वा मन्यसे मृतम्। तथापि त्वं महाबाहो नैवं शोचितुमर्हसि।। 26

जातस्य हि ध्रुवो मृत्युर्ध्रुवं जन्म मृतस्य च। तस्मादपरिहार्येऽर्थे न त्वं शोचितुमर्हसि।। 27

अव्यक्तादीनि भूतानि व्यक्तमध्यानि भारत। अव्यक्तनिधनान्येव तत्र का परिदेवना।। 28

आश्चर्यवत्पश्यति कश्चिदेन-माश्चर्यश्चैव तथैव चान्यः।
आश्चर्यवच्चैनमन्यः श्रृणोति श्रुत्वाप्येनं वेद न चैव कश्चित्।। 29
देही नित्यमवध्योऽयं देहे सर्वस्य भारत। तस्मात्सर्वाणि भूतानि न त्वं शोचितुमर्हसि।। 30
स्वधर्ममपि चावेक्ष्य न विकम्पितुमर्हसि। धर्म्याद्धि युद्धाच्छ्रेयोऽन्यत् क्षत्रियस्य न विद्यते।। 31
यदृच्छया चोपपन्नं स्वर्गद्वारमपावृतम्। सुखिनः क्षत्रियाः पार्थ लभन्ते युद्धमीदृशम्।। 32
अथ चेत्त्वमिमं धर्म्यं सङ्ग्रामं न करिष्यसि। ततः स्वधर्मं कीर्तिं च हित्वा पापमवाप्स्यसि।। 33
अकीर्तिं चापि भूतानि कथयिष्यन्ति तेऽव्ययाम्। सम्भावितस्य चाकीर्तिर्मरणादतिरिच्यते।। 34
भयाद्रणादुपरतं मंस्यन्ते त्वां महारथाः। येषां च त्वं बहुमतो भूत्वा यास्यसि लाघवम्।। 35
अवाच्यवादांश्च बहून् वदिष्यन्ति तवाहिताः। निन्दन्तस्तव सामर्थ्यं ततो दुःखतरं नु किम्।। 36
हतो वा प्राप्स्यसि स्वर्गं जित्वा वा भोक्ष्यसे महीम्। तस्मादुत्तिष्ठ कौन्तेय युद्धाय कृतनिश्चयः।। 37
सुखदुःखे समे कृत्वा लाभालाभौ जयाजयौ। ततो युद्धाय युज्यस्व नैवं पापमवाप्स्यसि।। 38
एषा तेऽभिहिता साङ्ख्ये बुद्धिर्योगे त्विमां श्रृणु। बुद्ध्या युक्तो यया पार्थ कर्मबन्धं प्रहास्यसि।। 39
नेहाभिक्रमनाशोऽस्ति प्रत्यवायो न विद्यते। स्वल्पमप्यस्य धर्मस्य त्रायते महतो भयात्।। 40
व्यवसायात्मिका बुद्धिरेकेह कुरुनन्दन। बहुशाखा ह्यनन्ताश्च बुद्धयोऽव्यवसायिनाम्।। 41
यामिमां पुष्पितां वाचं प्रवदन्त्यविपश्चितः। वेदवादरताः पार्थ नान्यदस्तीति वादिनः।। 42
कामात्मानः स्वर्गपरा जन्मकर्मफलप्रदाम्। क्रियाविशेषबहुलां भोगैश्वर्यगतिं प्रति।। 43
भोगैश्वर्यप्रसक्तानां तयाऽपहृतचेतसाम्। व्यवसायात्मिका बुद्धिः समाधौ न विधीयते।। 44
त्रैगुण्यविषया वेदा निस्त्रैगुण्यो भवार्जुन। निर्द्वन्द्वो नित्यसत्त्वस्थो निर्योगक्षेम आत्मवान्।। 45
यावानर्थ उदपाने सर्वतः सम्प्लुतोदके। तावान् सर्वेषु वेदेषु ब्राह्मणस्य विजानतः।। 46
कर्मण्येवाधिकारस्ते मा फलेषु कदाचन। मा कर्मफलहेतुर्भूर्मा ते सङ्गोऽस्त्वकर्मणि।। 47
योगस्थः कुरु कर्माणि सङ्गं त्यक्त्वा धनञ्जय। सिद्ध्यसिद्ध्योः समो भूत्वा समत्वं योग उच्यते।। 48
दूरेण ह्यवरं कर्म बुद्धियोगाद्धनञ्जय। बुद्धौ शरणमन्विच्छ कृपणाः फलहेतवः।। 49
बुद्धियुक्तो जहातीह उभे सुकृतदुष्कृते। तस्माद्योगाय युज्यस्व योगः कर्मसु कौशलम्।। 50
कर्मजं बुद्धियुक्ता हि फलं त्यक्त्वा मनीषिणः। जन्मबन्धविनिर्मुक्ताः पदं गच्छन्त्यनामयम्।। 51
यदा ते मोहकलिलं बुद्धिर्व्यतितरिष्यति। तदा गन्तासि निर्वेदं श्रोतव्यस्य श्रुतस्य च।। 52
श्रुतिविप्रतिपन्ना ते यदा स्थास्यति निश्चला। समाधावचला बुद्धिस्तदा योगमवाप्स्यसि।। 53

अर्जुन उवाच

स्थितप्रज्ञस्य का भाषा समाधिस्थस्य केशव। स्थितधीः किं प्रभाषेत किमासीत व्रजेत किम्।। 54

श्रीभगवानुवाच

प्रजहाति यदा कामान् सर्वान् पार्थ मनोगतान्। आत्मन्येवात्मना तुष्ट स्थितप्रज्ञस्तदोच्यते।। 55

दुःखेष्वनुद्विग्नमनाः सुखेषु विगतस्पृहः। वीतरागभयक्रोधः स्थितधीर्मुनिरुच्यते।। 56

यः सर्वत्रानभिस्नेहस्तत् तत्प्राप्य शुभाशुभम्। नाभिनन्दति न द्वेष्टि तस्य प्रज्ञा प्रतिष्ठिता।। 57

यदा संहरते चायं कूर्मोऽङ्गानीव सर्वशः। इन्द्रियाणीन्द्रियार्थेभ्यस्तस्य प्रज्ञा प्रतिष्ठिता।। 58

विषया विनिवर्तन्ते निराहारस्य देहिनः। रसवर्जं रसोऽप्यस्य परं दृष्ट्वा निवर्तते।। 59

यततो ह्यपि कौन्तेय पुरुषस्य विपश्चितः। इन्द्रियाणि प्रमाथीनि हरन्ति प्रसभं मनः।। 60

तानि सर्वाणि संयम्य युक्त आसीत मत्परः। वशे हि यस्येन्द्रियाणि तस्य प्रज्ञा प्रतिष्ठिता।। 61

ध्यायतो विषयान् पुंसः सङ्गस्तेषूपजायते। सङ्गात्सञ्जायते कामः कामात्क्रोधोऽभिजायते।। 62

क्रोधाद्भवति सम्मोहः सम्मोहात्स्मृतिविभ्रमः। स्मृतिभ्रंशाद् बुद्धिनाशो बुद्धिनाशात्प्रणश्यति।। 63

रागद्वेषवियुक्तैस्तु विषयानिन्द्रियैश्चरन्। आत्मवश्यैर्विधेयात्मा प्रसादमधिगच्छति।। 64

प्रसादे सर्वदुःखानां हानिरस्योपजायते। प्रसन्नचेतसो ह्याशु बुद्धिः पर्यवतिष्ठते।। 65

नास्ति बुद्धिरयुक्तस्य न चायुक्तस्य भावना। न चाभावयतः शान्तिरशान्तस्य कुतः सुखम्।। 66

इन्द्रियाणां हि चरतां यन्मनोऽनुविधीयते। तदस्य हरति प्रज्ञां वायुर्नावमिवाम्भसि।। 67

तस्माद्यस्य महाबाहो निगृहीतानि सर्वशः। इन्द्रियाणीन्द्रियार्थेभ्यस्तस्य प्रज्ञा प्रतिष्ठिता।। 68

या निशा सर्वभूतानां तस्यां जागर्ति संयमी। यस्यां जाग्रति भूतानि सा निशा पश्यतो मुनेः।। 69

आपूर्यमाणमचलप्रतिष्ठं समुद्रमापः प्रविशन्ति यद्वत्।

तद्वत्कामा यं प्रविशन्ति सर्वे स शान्तिमाप्नोति न कामकामी।। 70

विहाय कामान्यः सर्वान् पुमांश्चरति निःस्पृहः। निर्ममो निरहङ्कारः स शान्तिमधिगच्छति।। 71

एषा ब्राह्मी स्थितिः पार्थ नैनां प्राप्य विमुह्यति। स्थित्वाऽस्यामन्तकालेऽपि ब्रह्म निर्वाणमृच्छति।। 72

-.

THE THEORY OF SANKHYA AND YOGA PRACTICE

Shri Krishna tells Arjuna: 'Shake off this faintness of heart and arise.' Why does Krishna say this to Arjuna, who is in fact ready to forgo everything?

When I was in London, I had talks with many revolutionaries. Shyamji Krishnavarma, Savarkar and others used to tell me that the *Gita* and the *Ramayana* taught quite the opposite of what I said they did. I felt then how much better it would have been if the sage Vyasa had not taken this illustration of fighting for inculcating spiritual knowledge. For when even highly learned and thoughtful men read this meaning in the *Gita*, what can we expect of ordinary people? If what we describe as the very quintessence of all Shastras, as one of the Upanishads, can be interpreted to yield such a wrong meaning, it would have been better for the holy Vyasa to have taken another, more effective, illustration to teach sacred truths.

He has drawn Arjuna and Shri Krishna so vividly that we are inclined to regard them as historical figures. The historian-author, moreover, gives histories of cities, communities and individual characters and claims that he is describing a battle in which the best men of his age took part. I said how much better it would have been if the revered Vyasa had not adopted the method which he did. This, you may say, was impertinence on my part. But what should one seeking to serve truth do? What must one do if one sees an error? It is not wrong to draw attention, in all humility, to what one feels to be an error.

This thought remained in my mind for many years. Then I thought I should read the *Mahabharata*. I decided to do so, that I might understand the atmosphere of the age in which the *Gita* was written and feel the good and the evil influences at work in that age. I read in jail a Gujarati version of the *Mahabharata* which

I could get there. I saw that Vyasa did not believe that fighting was wrong. The illustration which he has taken is a very beautiful one. Just as in Aesop's *Fables* and in *Panchtantra,* the authors have created conversations among birds and animals to impart moral teaching, so in the *Mahabharata* virtues and vices are personified and great moral truths conveyed through those figures. The description of the battle serves only as a pretext. The *Mahabharata* itself was not composed with the aim of describing a battle. In the *Gita,* the author has cleverly made use of the event to teach great truths. If the reader is not on his guard, he may be misled.

The very nature of dharma is such that one may easily fall into error if one is not vigilant. Anyone rashly imitating Prahlad would do something very wrong. This is the reason for the injunction against the reading of the Shastras by one without qualification. It is not easy for any person to solve the problems of dharma which may face him. He will not succeed till he has made himself fit by observing the *yama-niyamas* and similar other rules of discipline. It would be like taking up a study of botany without ever having seen plants.

The author has used the word *Gudakesha* for Arjuna. It means one who has conquered sleep, who is always vigilant. We should, therefore, think carefully about this illustration of the battle. The first thing to bear in mind is that Arjuna falls into the error of making a distinction between kinsmen and outsiders. Outsiders may be killed even if they are not oppressors, and kinsmen may not be killed even if they are. My son, even if a drunkard, would inherit my property. I would write in *Navajivan* about another's son if he was wicked, but would not treat my own son in that manner. The *Gita* says, "No, this is not right. We have no right to point an accusing finger at others. We should point out the lapses of our own people first."

Arjuna was Dronacharya's best pupil. Bhishma had actually showered love on him as if he had been his first-born. Arjuna should be ready to kill either of them. It has become his duty to non-cooperate with both, for they have joined the wrong side. Should it become necessary to cut off, with a sword, one's father's head, one must do so if one has a sword and is a Kshatriya, and if one would be ready to cut off anyone else's head in similar circumstances. Shri Krishna, therefore, asks Arjuna to free himself from ignorant attachment in this world. How should I act as editor of *Navajivan?* Would it be right for me to proclaim with the beat of a drum the theft committed by an outsider's child any say nothing about a boy of my Ashram, who may have misbehaved in the same way? Certainly not. The *Gita* permits no distinction between one's relations and others. If one must kill, one should kill one's people first.

Shri Krishna asks Arjuna: "What is this you are saying about people being your relations?" The *Gita* wants to free him from this ignorant distinction of some people being his relations and others not. He has resolved to kill. It was not right, then, that he should shrink from killing particular individuals. It was not with any selfish motive that he had gone out to kill. Ravana deserved to be killed by Rama. Why did not the latter take cover behind such wise talk? He knew well enough that Ravana could do no harm to Sita. But he did not argue with himself in that manner. We never say that he fought for the sake of Sita; we believe that he fought in order to kill Ravana.

Even if we believe in non-violence, it would not be proper for us to refuse, through cowardice, to protect the weak. If Arjuna had forgotten the difference between kinsmen and others and had been so filled with the spirit of non-violence as to bring about a change of heart in Duryodhana, he would have been another Shri Krishna. Actually, however, he believed Duryodhana to be wicked. I might be ready to embrace a snake, but, if one comes to bite you, I should kill it and protect you. Arjuna has two courses open to him: he should either kill Duryodhana and others, or else convert them. In the circumstances, Arjuna's laying down arms would mean the annihilation of an those on his side. His refusal to fight would bring on a disaster. Thus, Vyasa has taken the right illustration. A person who believes in fighting and does not regard it as violence, though it is violence, is here being asked to kill.

The question which Arjuna asks Shri Krishna is not whether it is right for him to kill. His question is whether it would be right to kill his kinsmen. This question arises out of bias. Bhishma and Drona, a kinsman and an honoured person, stand vividly before his eyes. How can he kill them? To a person whose dilemma is not concerning violence and non-violence but is only about whom he may kill, our commonsense can give only one answer. But a godfearing man like Arjuna should pause and reflect before acting. Only a person with deep understanding, can solve the rather fine problem whether he should go on with the recitation of *gayatri* or run to the help of someone who is crying out in distress.

To a godfearing man the problem would present no difficulty. The author of the *Mahabharata* has discussed such delicate issues on almost every page of the epic. He has taken instances from the lives of individual characters and drawn lessons from them. Some of the instances may well have been incidents of history, but he has treated them as poets and seers have always treated such incidents. English poets, too, have written plays and poems with historical figures as subjects. The author of the *Mahabharata* raises, for instance, the question whether the sage Vishvamitra had secretly eaten beef and whether one should accept food offered by a chamar. The author has, thus, discussed problems of three kinds.

The argument addressed to Arjuna begins with the eleventh verse, and continues right up to the last chapter. Shri Krishna starts with the distinction between the atman and the body, for that is the first step to spiritual knowledge. We must first know certain definitions, then alone can we proceed. Arjuna is represented as a seeker, as a man who believes in the atman and observes the disciplines of *yama-niyama,* and so Shri Krishna starts giving him the knowledge of the atman. One becomes entitled to ask questions and seek illumination only if one has observed *brahmacharya* and always followed truth, and only then will one's questions deserve to be answered. Arjuna has this fitness; he has the genuine spirit of submission and humility.

We have not yet fully discussed the premise on which the argument of the *Gita* is based. We were discussing Arjuna's plea that it is wrong to kill one's kinsmen, not that it is wrong to kill at all. He was asked to forget the distinction of kinsmen and outsiders. The Hindu shastras say that non-violence is the supreme dharma. The question, therefore, whether or not it is right to kill does not arise. Only an atheist would raise such a question. Arjuna has observed the disciplines of *yama-niyama,* among which ahimsa is placed first. But ahimsa is an ideal which it is impossible to realize to perfection. It may be possible to realize it in thought, but not in action. Shankaracharya has said that one seeking *moksha* should have far greater patience than one who would try to empty the sea, drop by drop, with a blade of grass. One must have equal patience for realizing the ideal of perfect non-violence.

It is impossible in this body to follow ahimsa fully. That is why *moksha* is laid down as the supreme end of life. Violence is inescapable. While the eyes wink and nails have to be pared, violence in one form or another is unavoidable. Evil is inherent in action, the *Gita* says further on. Arjuna did not, therefore, raise the question of violence and non-violence. He simply raised the question of distinction between kinsmen and others, much in the same way that a fond mother would advance arguments favouring her child.

The *Gita* traces all maladies to their one source. A physician treats different diseases with different remedies. But, on the basis of researches in medical science, physicians are now coming to the conclusion that, though diseases seem different from one another, in the final analysis they are one. The cause is one, and so is the cure. Similarly, Shri Krishna says that there is only one spiritual evil, with only one cause and one remedy. To explain this oneness, an extreme example is used. If one's kinsmen deserve to be killed, they ought to be killed; and one must not hesitate even if the entire world were likely to be destroyed in consequence. It is not only Arjuna's right but his duty to act in this manner. To his question whether one ought not to make an exception in regard to relations, he gets an unambiguous answer. The principle, thus, admits of no exception, just as there can be no exception in the matter of following truth, for truth is God and, if exceptions were admitted in regard to it, God also would be sometimes truth and sometimes not-truth. Thus the rule in this instance admits of no exception.

Shri Krishna tells Arjuna that he is talking spacious wisdom. **The *Gita* does not teach the path of action, nor of knowledge, nor of devotion. No matter how well one cultivates *vairagya* or how diligent one is in performing good actions or what measure of *bhakti* one practises, one will not shed the sense of "I" and "mine" till one has attained knowledge, One can attain self-realization only if one sheds this attachment to the ego.** It is possible only for a person who has succeeded in doing so. In English, 'i' is a vertical line with a dot above it. Only when this 'I' is done away with can one attain self-realization. A man's devotion to God is to be judged from the extent to which he gives up his stiffness and bends low in humility. Only then will he be not an impostor, but a truly illumined man, a man of genuine knowledge. The *Gita* does not advocate anyone of the three paths;

I have from my experience come to the conclusion that it has been composed to teach this one truth which I have explained. We can follow truth only in the measure that we shed our attachment to the ego.

It is to teach this that Shri Krishna has advanced the beautiful argument of the *Gita*.

As every human being passes through childhood, youth and so on to old age, so also does he or she meet death. The phrase *dehantarprapti* used here does not mean a new body or another life, for what is being discussed here is the fear of death, not that of a new life.

We feel afraid only so long as we take the rope to be a serpent. Likewise, if we know the natural stages of growth of the body, we should not grieve over death. In order to help Arjuna to overcome his agitation, Shri Krishna tries to explain to him the difference between the atman and the body.

> *O Kaunteya, contacts of the senses with their objects bring cold and heat, pleasure and pain; they come and go and are transit. Endure them, O Bharata.*
>
> *O noblest of men, the wise man who is not disturbed or agitated by these, who is unmoved by pleasure and pain, he alone is fitted for immortality. (14-15)*

Any being who is not subject to the impressions of senses will never experience fear. It is these impressions which are responsible for the feelings of happiness and misery. Someone has said that the muscles of a man who is angry become thirteen times as tense as when he is normal, and of a man who is laughing nine times as tense. That is, one spends more energy when one is angry, and one whose energy is thus wasted cannot attain to immortality. The cultivation of this state requires practice. We can even say of a person who has attained it that he is God.

Once a sannyasi, an imposter, paid a visit to Phoenix. He asked me to recite any verse from the *Gita* which I knew. I recited this one. During the early days of my legal practice, I was on one occasion very much troubled in my mind. I then went out for a walk. I was very much agitated. I then remembered this verse, and the very next moment I was almost dancing with relief. We should identify ourselves with Arjuna and have faith that Shri Krishna is driving our chariot. **Thus, the meaning of the *Gita* on**

the commonsense level is that once we have plunged into a battle, we should go on fighting. One ought not to give up the task one has undertaken. In this way, the illustration used should not read a wrong meaning in it either.

Vyasa's own intention was something different. He wanted to write the *Mahabharata* in such a way that even little boys and girls would study it, remember the virtuous characters in it and learn to keep away from people like the wicked characters in the epic. His aim was to strengthen the finer impulses in us and help to overcome the evil ones. **Before the women, too, he held up the example of Draupadi and thus taught them that they should, when threatened with danger, roar like lionesses and protect their honour.** Draupadi could do this and rouse Arjuna, Yudhishthira and Bhima.

The author of the *Mahabharata* has raised woman to a great height through his epic. The chief aim of the epic, however, is to represent the most invisible of all invisible wars. It tells of the Arjuna and other Pandavas in our minds who are battling with the Kauravas in it. The moral problems which confront one in this inner war are far more difficult than those of a physical war. An error in the sphere of practical action will at the most result in the destruction of this perishable body, but the result of an error in this inner invisible war will lead to perdition. The most painful punishment is appointed for evil intention. In the course of time, Pandavas and Kauravas are bound to be forgotten. They will most certainly be forgotten when this Age ends. We should not delude ourselves with the belief that they will continue to be remembered for ever. This Age of ours was preceded by many others. Even when all of them are forgotten, this war in our heart will go on. The *Gita* shows how we may emerge safe from it.

The Krishna of the *Gita* is not the person who when the hour of his death arrived, fell to a hunter's arrow, and Arjuna is not that person from whose hand the Gandiva bow slipped. Krishna is the atman in us, who is our charioteer. We can win only if we hand over the reins of the chariot to him. God makes us dance, like the master in a puppet show. We are smaller than even puppets. We should, therefore, trust everything to God, as children to parents. **Let us not eat uncooked stuff. Let Krishna the cook prepare and give us that food of grace. He wills for our atman.**

The *Gita* does not decide for us. But if, whenever faced with a moral problem, you give up attachment to the ego and then decide what you should do, you will come to no harm. This is the substance of the argument which Shri Krishna has expanded into 18 chapters.

This verse beginning with the phrase *matrasparsha* applied to sleeping as much as to waking. We have to make ourselves conscious machines. We should cultivate such perfect concentration that, like a man asleep, we are aware of nothing else. Hazrat Ali told his people to draw out the arrow from his body while he was praying, for at that time he would be totally absorbed in devotion to God. One cannot say that such a thing could be done when one was asleep, for one would not be able to fall asleep at all when the body was pierced with an arrow. A person who can be totally absorbed in every task on hand, as Hazrat Ali could be in prayer, who lives in such a state of self-absorption all the twenty-four hours of the day, will attain to immortality.

Shri Krishna now explains why the impressions of the senses are unreal:

> *What is non-Being is never known to have been, and what is Being is never known not to have been. Of both these the secret has been seen by the seers of the Truth. (16)*

That which never was cannot exist, and that which exists, cannot cease to exist. Even the sun is transient, coming into existence and vanishing. The candle both exists and does not exist, for, when it is burnt up, its substance dissolves back into the five elements. Everything which has a name and a form ceases one day to exist in that particular mode, though it does not cease to be as a creation of God.

The *jnanis,* the men of knowledge, have discovered what exists and what does not exist. Name and form are brittle as glass. The *jnanis* know what is implied in the difference between existence and non-existence. We only know one simple thing: God is, nothing else is.

We shall breathe life into the Ashram by laying down our own lives. Its lands and buildings may disappear, but the spirit we inform it with will never perish.

> *Know that to be imperishable whereby all this is pervaded. No one can destroy that immutable Being. (17)*

Know that this Bodiless One, which can lift many Govardhan mountains on its little finger is imperishable.

Avyaya means that which cannot be spent.

These bodies of the embodied one who is eternal, imperishable and immeasurable are finite. Fight, therefore, O Bharata. (18)

Aprameya means that for which there can be no evidence, that is, no evidence in the sense in which smoke is regarded as evidence of fire.

Therefore fight, O Bharata. If we argue that since all bodies are perishable, one may kill, does it follow that I may kill all the women and children in the Ashram? Would I have in doing so acted according to the teaching of the *Gita,* merely because their bodies are perishable? We believe the watchman to have been mad because he had killed a person; if, however, he were to cite this verse of the *Gita to* justify what he did, we would call him wicked. What, then, shall we say of a person who mouths these seemingly learned arguments and then commits wickedness? To know the answer to this, we should go back to the First Chapter. Arjuna had said that he did not want even the kingdom of gods if he had to kill his kith and kin for that. But he is bound, in any case, to kill them, for he has accepted the dharma which requires him to kill. This verse with the word *yudhyasva* applies to him, but it does not apply to others. In this verse, Shri Krishna wants to free Arjuna from his ignorant attachment. When Harishchandra was required to kill a virtuous woman like Taramati, his eyes fell on her *mangal-sutra* and, recognizing her, he held back. He would not have done so if it had been some other woman. In this case Shri Krishna would have told him that it was his duty to kill her. He would say to Harishchandra: You have lost your wits; you have killed people in the past and now you shrink from killing the woman because of your attachment for her as your wife. You would thus betray your dharma. He would tell Harishchandra that his body as well as his wife's was perishable. If a person would cut his own throat rather than another's, than Krishna would tell him that he could kill others as a duty.

Shri Krishna advances another agrument.

He who thinks of This (Atman) as slayer and he who believes This to be slain, are both ignorant. This neither slays nor is ever slain. (19)

The atman neither kills nor is killed. It is like putting the cart before the horse. As that is impossible, so the body, if it sought to drive the atman, would never succeed. If anyone says that it can, he does not know what he is talking about.

This is never born nor ever dies, nor having been will ever not be any more; unborn, eternal, everlasting, ancient. This is not slain when the body is slain? (20)

This atman was never born and will never die; it is not as though it even was not and may not be again. The author has used a separate epithet to indicate each of these several aspects. The atman is unborn, eternal and ancient. Everyone knows it. The body perishes, but it does not. One generation knows of it from another. It is a thing that all parents must have explained, or ought to explain, to their children.

He who knows This O Partha, to be imperishable, eternal, unborn, and immutable—whom and how can that man slay or cause to be slain? (21)

The *Gita* has been composed not in the form of aphorisms, but so as to be carried in the mind from moment to moment. It was written not for the learned, but for all the four castes,—rather, all the eighteen castes—to read and understand. It was written for the Sudras, the Bhangis, and for women— In fact, for all classes. If the author has used a variety of epithets for a subject, though all of them mean the same thing, it is simply in order that we may grasp what he wants us to understand—in the same way that a mother explains a point to her children over and over again in different words.

As a man casts off worn-out garments and takes others that are new, even so the embodied one casts off worn-out bodies and passes on to others new. (22)

Would I be ready to change this body for another, unless I would give up a worn-out one and have a fresh one? If the eyes cannot see, the ears cannot hear and the palate cannot relish food, would a person wish to live on bed-ridden, or die?

This no weapons wound, This no fire burns, This no waters wet, This no wind doth dry. (23)

Weapons cannot cleave it. If we strike the air with a weapon, can we hurt it? The atman is subtler even than air, Fire cannot burn it, nor can water wet it; how can air, then, ever dry it? Having described the atman thus, the author gives an appropriate epithet to indicate each of its several aspects:

Beyond all cutting, burning, wetting and drying is This— eternal, all-pervading, stable, immovable, everlasting. (24)

More epithets again: eternal, all-pervading, stable, immovable and everlasting. The verse which follows states the same thing:-

Perceivable neither by the senses nor by the mind, This is called unchangeable therefore, knowing This as such, thou shouldst not grieve. (25)

Such is the atman, Krishna says and you should not, therefore, grieve over anyone's death. Why should you, then, grieve over the death *of* your relations?

What do you call the thing which protects us against the sun? Likewise, there is a word, *aja,* to designate that which was never born, and another, *acchhedya,* to designate that which cannot be pierced.

Shri Krishna takes Arjuna slowly from darkness to light. Have you seen the atman?

It is so naughty that it dwells in us and yet we cannot see it. It is the deer that even Ramachandra would not be able to kill. Ramachandra is omnipotent, and so he could kill only that which deserved to be killed.

Having argued thus, Shri Krishna says: "But suppose that the atman has none of these attributes. What of it? What even if it is born and dies again and again? All the more reason why you should not grieve over death."

And if thou deemest This to be always coming to birth and always dying, even then, O Mahabahu, thou shouldst not grieve. For certain is the death of the born, and certain is the birth of the dead; therefore, what is unavoidable thou shouldst not regret. (26-27)

He who dies is certain to be born again. We ought not to grieve over what is inescapable, what cannot be helped.

The state of all beings before birth is unmanifest; their middle state is manifest; their state after death is again unmanifest. What occasion is there for lament, O Bharata? (28)

All beings were unmanifest before birth and will again become unmanifest after death. Birth and death are God's concern. He alone, therefore, knows their mystery. Even doctors have failed here, for they cannot create a body. "Who am I, whence do I come? Am I destined to rise to heaven?" The atman becomes incarnate in birth. We can see this, the middle stage. Men who have thought over these problems have asserted that, for bestowing and taking away life, God does not require even a fraction of the time that is required for drawing and erasing a circle on the blackboard. No mathematician can ever calculate the measure of that time.

Tatra ka paridevana. Why, then, grieve? This is the great mystery of God. As a magician creates the illusion of a tree and destroys it, so God sports in endless ways and does not let us know the beginning and the end of his play. Why grieve over this?

> *One looks upon This is a marvel; another speaks of This as such another hears thereof as a marvel; yet having heard of This none truly knows This. (29)*

Some wise men see the atman as a thing of wonder and some describe it so. Others hear it so described but cannot understand what it is. Such is our pathetic state. There can be no end to describing God's greatness, so mysterious is His part.

Finally, Shri Krishna sums up:

> *This embodied one in the body of every being is ever beyond all harm, O Bharata; thou shouldst not, therefore, grieve for anyone. (30)*

"O Arjuna, this atman which dwells in everyone's body can never be killed." The body's death is like the breaking of a piece of glass. The cycle of birth and death goes on for ever and ever.

After discussing the problem from the spiritual point of view Shri Krishna considers it from the mundane point of view. He tells Arjuna what his duty in the practical world requires.

> *Again, seeing thine own duty thou shouldst not shrink from it; for there is no higher good for a Kshatriya than a righteous war. (31)*

A Kshatriya has no duty higher than that of fighting in a righteous war. Why is the war described as righteous? Because it is not of Arjuna's seeking: he was happy enough in his home, but he was challenged by Duryodhana. The war came to him without his seeking, and had as it were opened the door of heaven to him.

Proceeding, Shri Krishna talks about one's good name in the world:

> *The world will for ever recount the story of thy disgrace; and for a man of honour disgrace is worse than death. (34)*

If a person who has accepted cleaning of latrines as his work wearied of it, saying that it was a Bhangi's work, Shri Krishna would tell him that he was betraying his dharma, that he would lose his good name, that people would for ever talk ill of him. For a man who has a good reputation in society, its loss is worse than death. Arjuna, Shri Krishna said, would give the great warrior a ground for accusing him of having fled from the battlefield in fear. He sums up this part of the agrument with the following verse:

> *Hold alike pleasure and pain, gain and loss, victory and defeat, and gird up thy loins for the fight; so doing thou shalt not incur sin. (38)*

The argument in this verse is not practical, but spiritual.

The verse about "pleasure and pain" is not addressed to Arjuna alone but to all of us. "You will incur no sin by killing your kinsmen"—this is said repeatedly in the *Gita*. If a person remains unconcerned with defeat or victory, knowing that they are a part of life, he commits no sin in fighting. But we should also say that he earns no merit. If we seek merit, we shall also incur sin. Even the best thing has an element of evil in it. Nothing in the world is wholly good or wholly evil. Where there is action there is some evil. If Harishchandra had felt any doubt in his mind, what would a holy sage have told him? "Cut your wife's throat; you will incur no sin." If a person learns to make no distinction between gain and loss, pleasure and pain, he would rarely be tempted to commit a sin.

If we had blamed the thieves and regarded them as very wicked men, we would have been filled with rage and wanted to kill them.

We can do without beating of drums over a birth, but it is difficult not to grieve over a death. If we thus cultivate an attitude of indifference and learn to check anger, we shall one day succeed in freeing ourselves from these pairs of opposites.

The argument in the *Gita* falls into three parts: (1) "Whence this weakness in you?" (2) Arjuna's questioning; (3) Krishna awakening his intellect and explaining to him how the atman and the body are separate things. Then the practical considerations.

What is one to do? How is one to proceed having known that the atman is different from the body? This is the fourth stage in the argument.

> *Thus have I set before thee the attitude of Knowledge; hear now the attitude of Action; resorting to this attitude thou shalt cast off the bondage of action. (39)*

The word *sankhya,* it has been said, is somewhat confusing. It may be so for the learned, it is not so for us. All that Shri Krishna means is this: "I explained the matter to you from a theoretical point of view. I pointed out the difference between the atman and the body. Having explained this to you, I will now put the argument with reference to yoga. Yoga means practice. After understanding this, you will have to translate your knowledge into action in the manner I shall explain." The word yoga is used repeatedly in the *Gita.* It explains how to act. "If you understand this," Shri Krishna says, "You will escape from the bondage of action."

There is much disputation concerning the meaning of the verse which we took up for discussion, as will be evident to anyone who makes a deep study of the *Gita.* I however feel that you should follow the rule that I have followed. It does not matter if that seems like making a virtue of our weakness. We should not involve ourselves in disputations about the meaning of Shastras. Bishop Butler was a man of great learning, but he took a pledge never to enter in a religious controversy. An atheist happened to be on a visit to England. The Bishop could have argued with him, but he wrote to a friend saying that he would not enter into any discussion with the atheist. It was possible, he said, that he might not be able to answer an argument of the latter on the instant. It was also possible, he added, that his reasoning might have no effect on others, in which case he would produce on them a wrong impression. It was therefore better, he said, to remain quiet. The atheist was free to question any belief. Why enter into any argument about the existence of God, which was self-evident?

A person may say about Siva: 'He may be naked, He may wear human skulls round his neck, but He is my God, I want no other.' We may say the same thing in regard to this verse. *Sankhya* may mean any number of things. I have explained the idea to the best of my understanding and I have set you thinking. Now I shall demonstrate a practical application. Its many explanations may be of interest to learned men; they are not for us. We wish to study so that we may learn to be servants and devotees of God, may see God. To see God we do not have to enter into disputes. At the moment these children make my world. I wish to awaken their thought, entertain them and explain things to them. I have no aim beyond this. Everyday we recite:

What is non-Being is never known to have been,
And what is Being is never known not to have been.

At every moment we have to decide whether a particular action will serve the atman or the body. We cannot, however, break open the cage of the body, and so we must simultaneously follow *vidya* and *avidya.*

And now follows a verse which explains how a person who tries to put this teaching into action is saved.

Here no effort undertaken is lost, no disaster befalls. Even a little of this righteous course delivers one from great fear. (40)

No sin is incurred by those that follow the path of action. A beginning made is not wasted. Even a little effort along this path saves one from great danger. This is a royal road, easy to follow. It is the sovereign yoga. In following it, there is no fear of stumbling. Once a beginning is made, nothing will stand in our way.

I wrote to a friend and told him that he suffered not from fistula but from something else. I advised him to keep repeating Ramanama. What one does in this way never goes in vain. How would it have helped him if I had advised him to have a *yajna* performed? He would not have got a genuine priest to conduct the *yajna.* There would be many other difficulties. Nor would I advise him to go to Jagannath Puri and make such and such an offering to such and such a diety. What if following my advice, he became an atheist? **If, instead, he got smitten with love for Rama, he would be saved from a great fear. He suffers from a mental disease and should become free from attachments.** He should constantly think on Rama. Doctors, too, advise us not to think of the disease from which we may be suffering.

This is a very important verse. It contains the profound idea that nothing done is ever lost, that there is no sin there, only safety. This is the royal road, the right angle. All right angles are of 90 degrees. This path is the path of truth. There is no harm, no fear of destruction, in following it. On the other hand, a person who argues whether it is right to tell a lie in order to save a cow or to eat meat to save one's life, can never be sure where he will end up.

Three points, tests or conditions are mentioned for proving that the atman is different from the body. We can act every moment on the assurance: in this path no effort is ever lost. What can we do right now which will never be lost? What can we think of? There is only one reply, that we must follow the prayers, and that too with perfect concentration.

Ramaswamy Aiyar once addressed a meeting in Bombay in the early days of non-cooperation. Khadilkar said then that among all political activities there was only one which satisfied all the three conditions. That activity yields immediate result; there is no obstacle to its progress; and there is the advantage of being saved from the fear of loss of sixty crores of rupees.

Shri Krishna explained the same thing over again in the verse which follows:

> *The attitude, in this matter, springing, as it does, from fixed resolve but one, O Kurunandana: but for those who have no fixed resolve the attitudes are many-branched and unending. (41)*

O Arjuna, the resolute intellect here is one-pointed. Along this path which I shall explain to you, one must hold one's intellect so firm that there is no wavering. The actions of a man whose intellect is not fixed on one aim, who is not single-minded in his devotion, will branch out in many directions. As the mind leaps, monkey-fashion, from branch to branch, so does the intellect. A person who clings to his life will seek help from any *vaid* or saint or witch-doctor whom he meets. Similarly, a monkey will fly from branch to branch and ultimately meet an untimely death, the victim of a sling-shot. The mind of a person of uncertain purpose grows weak day by day and becomes so uncertain that he can think of nothing except what is in his mind at the moment. In present-day politics, there is no good at all and plenty of evil, for it is full of flattery and one is not protected from dangers, but, on the contrary, surrounded by them. It does not help us to realize the atman; in fact we lose our soul. We lose our dharma, we lose the capacity for good works, lose both this world and the other. If, on the other hand, we can have faith in this spinning-wheel movement, we can serve the world, be happy ourselves, can live safe from a great danger, that is, can live without fear of those who would hold us down. We also secure, simultaneously, a means of ensuring our welfare in the other world. If a person who takes up this work does not seem to be of a fixed mind, you may conclude that he is not following the royal path.

It is only if we have the faith in our hearts that we are all one, though we exist as separate beings, it is only then that we can feel a sense of equality. Otherwise, even two leaves are not equal.

The next three verses describe the man whose intellect is not resolute.

A person who is of fixed mind in a small matter can be so even in a big matter. If he is asked to make an ellipsoid of clay and concentrate on it, he would do so. In trying to concentrate on any object, one is likely to be distracted by all manner of troublesome thoughts. A person to whom this happens may be described as one whose intellect is not fixed on one aim. One who would succeed in the yoga of works must be of a fixed mind in small matters as well as big.

Now follows the description of an intellect not fixed on one aim. In describing it, Vyasa has run down the Vedas as he has done nowhere else. So many things were interpolated into the Shastras in the course of time, but we have gone on believing that everything in them is divinely inspired. By doing this, we make ourselves mere pedants. *Veda* means to know. That which helps us to acquire the knowledge of the Brahman, which provides us the best means of acquiring such knowledge, that is the Veda.

The ignorant, revelling in the letter of the Vedas, declare that there is naught else; carnally-minded, holding heaven to be their goal, they utter swelling words which promise birth as the fruit of action and which dwell on the many and varied rites to be performed for the sake of pleasure and power; intent, as they are, on pleasure and power their swelling words rob them of their wits, and they have no settled attitude which can be centred on the supreme goal. (42-44)

Ignorant people, that is, persons who are learned and yet devoid of knowledge, utter flowery speech, that is, speech which is attractive, on which blossom new flowers everyday. Men who wrangle over the meaning of the Vedas; men filled with endless desires (men who have many wishes and teach others to be like them); men who are ever thinking of heaven (who are merely for enjoyments, who always talk of enjoying even this world thoroughly and paint glowing and attractive pictures of life in heaven) and who assert that there is nothing beyond heaven; who always say that our actions in life unfailingly bear appropriate fruits and persuade people to perform innumerable rituals to secure enjoyments and win greatness (there are people who say these things even today); who advise us to propitiate a great many gods and so make us feel helpless; who induce us to offer fanciful prayers to imaginary gods and turn us away from prayer to the God of all gods—such men push us deeper and deeper into quagmire. The fancies and thoughts which often trouble our minds are also evidence of an intellect branching out in many directions. Even in small matters, we can say, our intellect is not resolute. It will be resolute only if we fix our minds on one purpose and cling to it with discrimination, only if we work without looking for immediate results. At present, whether in politics or social reform we leap from one branch to another. I began with the illustration of a ball of earth and told you that, even if we concentrate on that, we can realize the atman.

I was once asked by someone why I had not succeeded in realizing the atman. I told him that for me the means themselves stood for such realization. The fact that such a question was asked is enough to suggest that the person who put it would not understand the humility which inspired my reply and would approach many others with the same question. This same condition prevailed in Vyasa's time. How can we expect that a person who is attached to enjoyments of the senses and possession of power, whose mind has been led away by all manner of attractive words, will have a resolute intellect? *Samadhi* means fixing the mind on God. How can one's intellect remain fixed and motionless in such a state? The mind of a person who is not satisfied with a lakh which he has earned and hopes to earn ten lakhs the next day, who addressed as a *Mahatma* this day, hopes to be so addressed ever afterwards—the mind of such a person is distracted by all manner of thoughts and attractive visions. His mind will not be plain white, like khadi; he is ever wanting to dress his mind, as fashionable women do their bodies in many-coloured saris with borders of various designs. Such a person can never be devoted to God. Only he who has a spirit of extreme humility, who has the faith of the Faithful, can be said to have a resolute intellect.

We have seen that those who hanker after enjoyments and power can never fix their intellect on one aim. Only a person like Hazrat Ali who is completely absorbed in God can succeed in doing so. Only a person whose *chitta* has become absolutely purified, whose mind has expanded and awakened to light, has become as clear as a mirror, can have in his stainless mind, a vision of God. If any sound emanates from such a person it can only be that of the name of Rama. After explaining this, Shri Krishna described the pedantic student of the Vedas. He now sums up the idea of the three verses in one:

> *The Vedas have as their domain the three gunas; eschew them, O Arjuna. Free thyself from the pairs of opposites, abide in eternal truth, scorn to gain or guard anything, remain the master of the soul. (45)*

The Vedas treat of the three *gunas;* you rise above them. (But this is not true, if it is, the Vedas would not be God's word. Shri Krishna is here talking about the Vedas as expounded by the ritualist pedants. The statement, therefore, gives only one side of the truth. The Vedas which utter *neti neti*—there is nothing except truth—those Vedas are ever the objects of reverence for us. We can cite verses from the *Gita* itself and that it tells us to accept the Vedas as thus understood.)

Arjuna is asked to be above the pairs of opposites, which means to be indifferent to happiness and suffering. He should act in the fighting between the Kauravas and the Pandavas as if he was not personally involved in it. He should be *nitya-sattvastha,* which means that his mind should always remain steadfast. He should be *niryogakshema,* that is, give up all thought of acquiring, holding and defending possessions. But one must preserve one's body, at any rate. Arjuna should, therefore, cultivate detachment in that respect. He should cease to concern himself with yoga and *kshema* and live in the atman. He should live always thinking that he is not the body, not an entity with a name and a form, that he transcends these.

> *To the extent that a well is of use when there is a flood of water on all sides, to the same extent are all the Vedas of use to an enlightened Brahman. (46)*

What may be found in a tank will also be found in a big lake. He who knows *Brahman* will know everything else. He possesses occult powers, too, for the knowledge of the *Brahman* is the perfection of these powers. The three *gunas* are dealt within the Vedas; he who rises above them attains to the knowledge of *Brahman*. The person who has the throne will not covet a position of civil or police authority. He who has reached the Gangotri has known the Ganga. We get from the former all the benefit we would from the latter, and in addition the person taking his abode near the Gangotri is away from the crowd and lives unattached to the pairs of opposites. Near the Hoogli, the Ganga water is turbid, but it is fresh and dear near Rishikesh and Hardwar. The higher one ascends towards the top, the greater the purity and cleanliness.

After this introduction, Shri Krishna tells Arjuna that the sovereign yoga which he wished to explain to the latter was this:

> *Action alone is the province, never the fruits thereof; let not thy motive be the fruit of action, nor shouldst thou desire to avoid action. (47)*

Your right is to work, and not to expect the fruit. The slave-owner tells the slave: "Mind your work, but beware lest you pluck a fruit from the garden. Yours is to take what I give?" God has put us under restriction in the same manner. He tells us that we may work if we wish, but that the reward of work is entirely for Him to give. Our duty is to pray to Him, and the best way in which we can do this is to work with the pickaxe, to remove scum from the river and to sweep and clean our yards. This, certainly, is a difficult lesson to learn. The relationship between the slave-owner and his slave is an unhealthy one. It is based on the owner's self-interest. That between the lion and the goat is of the same character. But man is ever rushing into the mouth of God. A wise man does so consciously and deliberately, and tells God that he wishes to be His slave, and not the world's. The more God seems to reject him, the more he strives to be near Him. This verse is intended to describe this peculiar relationship. The eyelids certainly protect the eyes, but they do not do so with conscious intention. They protect the eyes by reflex action. The relationship between God and man is similarly spontaneous. Mirabai has sung: "By a slender thread has Hari tied me to Him, and I turn as He pulls the thread." The relationship between us and God is of the kind described here. The thread is slender, and a single one besides.

Ma karmafala, etc., means: "Do not act so as to be the cause of your suffering fruits of action; do not be attached to action; or be over-eager to do anything. Think that everything is done by Me. What reason do you have to believe that you do things?" So if it is God's will that we must die, He will destroy us; if such is not His will, He will arrest the hand raised against us.

Ma te sangostvakarmani: In reading this, I said *karmani* instead of *akarmani,* for that is how I have always read this verse. *Akarma* means all work which falls outside the sphere of one's duty. "You should not," Krishna says to Arjuna, "feel tempted to take up such work, feel drawn to work which is not your duty."

> *Act thou, O Dhananjaya, without attachment, steadfast in Yoga, even-minded in success and failure. Even-mindedness is Yoga. (48)*

Work without attachment, being established firmly in yoga. Yoga means renouncing the fruit of action. It means not desiring the fruit of work which is *akarma.* We should do no work with attachment. Attachment to good work, is that too wrong? Yes, it is. If we are attached to our goal of winning swaraj, we shall not hesitate to adopt bad means. If a person is particular that he would give silvers to me personally, one day he might even steal them. Hence, we should not be attached even to a good cause. Only then will our means remain pure and our actions too.

Proceeding, Shri Krishna says: One should be even-minded in success and failure. In other words, one should dedicate to Krishna all that one does, surrender oneself completely to Him. The person who has an equal mind towards all things may be described as one established in yoga. Krishna explains the same idea further:

For action, O Dhananjaya, is far inferior to unattached action; seek refuge in the attitude of detachment. Pitiable are those who make fruit their motive. (49)

Work done without the yoga of intellect is extremely harmful. One should, therefore, seek refuge in intellect. "Intellect" means a resolute intellect. Having once made a decision there is no arguing the matter further. Anyone who works for reward is a *kripan,* that is, a person deserving our pity.

A person without a fixed purpose has an unsteady mind. Bhartrihari has described many forms of this weakness of mind.

Here in this world a man gifted with that attitude of detachment escapes the fruit of both good and evil deeds. Gird thyself up for yoga, therefore. Yoga is still in action. (50)

A person who is firmly yoked to his intellect, an intellect which is resolute, who is totally merged in it and who is a yogi, such a one renounces the fruit of work both good and bad, that is, disinterested towards either. Shri Krishna, therefore, asks Arjuna to be a yogi. Yoga means nothing but skill in work. Anyone who wants to decide whether he should or should not do a particular thing, should seek a yogi's advice. This is why it is said that where there is a prince of yogis like Shri Krishna and a bowman of prowess like Arjuna, prosperity and power follow as a matter of course.

For sages, gifted with the attitude of detachment, who renounce the fruit of action, are released from the bondage of birth and attain to the state which is free from all ills. (51)

Yogis renounce the fruits of work, and are freed from the bonds of birth. How can a person who has awakened to the truth about his body ever die? Such a one attains immortality.

When thy understanding will have passed through the slough of delusion, then wilt thou be indifferent alike to what thou hast heard and wilt hear. (52)

When your intellect, Shri Krishna tells Arjuna, has crossed the slough of delusion, you will become disinterested towards all that you may have heard in the past or that may seem to you worth hearing in future; that is, you will remain indifferent.

When thy understanding, distracted by much hearing, will rest steadfast and unmoved in concentration, then wilt thou attain Yoga. (53)

When your intellect, once perverted by listening to all manner of arguments, is totally absorbed in the contemplation of God, you will then attain to yoga. When a person is firmly established in *samadhi* he is filled with ecstatic love and, therefore, can be completely indifferent to this world.

Arjuna now asks how we may know the man established in *samadhi* from his speech. "Speech" means outward sign. The food which the *Gita* offers is different from what one's mother gives. Before Mother *Gita*, the earthly mother stands no comparison. He who has the *Gita* always engraved in his heart and keeps it there till the moment of death, will attain to *moksha*. A boy who gives himself to daily worship of the *Gita* will be another Dhruva or Sudhanva. We recite these verses daily so that we may understand their meaning and be guided by them.

"You are my arm," Shri Krishna tells Arjuna. "It is I who make it move." We say, likewise, in our morning prayers: "You it is that makes our sense function." One who is ever patient and works with single-minded attention to the task on hand may be described as a yogi skilled in action.

The Lord says:

When a man puts away, O Partha, all the cravings that arise in the mind and finds comfort for himself only from atman *then is he called the man of secure understanding. (55)*

This means that he who banishes all bad desires arising in his mind may be described as a *sthitaprajna*. We add the word "bad" because here in the Ashram we engage ourselves in ceaseless work and we cannot ask a cripple to get up and walk. Though, of course, ultimately we arrive at a stage when we should banish all desires, even the desire to see God, for to a person in that stage all action becomes spontaneous. After one has seen God face to face, how can the desire to see Him still remain? When you have already jumped into the river, the desire to do so will no longer be there. Our desire to see God ceases when we are lost in Him, have become one with Him.

We would be ill if we remained in a river the whole day. Anyone who sleeps all the twenty-four hours will fall ill, and so also anyone who eats all day long. There is not a single thing in the world which we can go on desiring perpetually. It is because of this that we have the problem of happiness and misery. The more often we desire a thing, the stronger our desire becomes every time. The more we satisfy desires, the more urgent they become. That is also true about our daily discussions of the *Gita.* Though I cannot make them very interesting, those who really wish to follow them will find their desire becoming daily stronger. No one, of course, will fall ill because of that. Or, maybe, we need not consciously desire a thing which we always want. The sun rises and sets everyday; we do not consciously wish that it may. He who has overcome his desires completely, should be natural in all his actions, as walking and similar movements of the body are natural.

There is only one desire in life which is good and the desire for the means to realize it is also good.

Who can succeed in banishing desires in this manner? He whose self abides content in itself is known as a *sthitaprajna.*

Whenever we hear anyone speaking about God, we should forget everything else and attend to his words. A person such as described above, if he is attending a reading of the *Ramayana* or the *Gita,* will be completely absorbed in following them. He will never feel it a strain to rise even at four in the morning.

The state in which the self abides in itself in serene content is the same as described by Narasinh Mehta in this line of a poem of his; "The *Brahman* dancing in sportive play in front of *Brahman.*" The poet here expresses the very same truth. The *Brahman* has all its joy through the *Brahman* in the company of the *Brahman.* The slave can never conceive of his existence without his master. A person who has the name of another on his lips all the twenty-four hours will forget himself in the latter. The atman becomes the *Param*atman in the same manner. The atman may be a ray of the *Param*atman, but a ray of the sun is the sun itself. Apart from God, we can have no existence at all. He who makes himself God's slave becomes one with God.

The state described here is not that of a person who lives self-satisfied, surrounding himself with possessions of all kinds. We should learn to be content in ourselves. The means and the end should become one. But who can find joy in the self through the self? One can do that by learning to work in a new spirit? One who takes opium before going to bed will not sleep well, but the man who sleeps in the natural course will sleep in peace, his mind abiding in God.

The verses which follow are by way of an explanation of this verse. Self-help does not consist merely in not seeking help from others; it consists in not needing such help.

If children have faith, they can live as a *sthitaprajna* does. They have their parents and teachers to look after their needs. They have, therefore, no need to take thought for themselves. They should always be guided by their elders. A child who lives in this manner is a *brahmachari, a muni, a sthitaprajna.* He is so in the sense that he does what he is asked to and carries out every instruction. Such a child could even become Prahlad.

The verse beginning with *prajahati* can never mean that we may remain as we are. If that were the meaning, the second line would have no place in it. The man who lives contented in the self through the self will give up all desires, but one can live in such a state only if the desire to become better, to grow spiritually awakens in one. Anyone who wants to live in such a state must give up everything which is likely to obstruct his effort. If all that we do is merely to indulge in fancies, like Shaikhchilli, the day-dreamer, it would be better not to think at all, neither good thoughts nor bad. The road to hell is paved with good intentions. That is why it is said that one may cast into a river a ton of thoughts and cling to an ounce of practice.

I have read in an English book that a boy who eats till he is full cannot preserve celibacy. One should not overload one's stomach.

> *Whose mind is untroubled in sorrows and longeth not for joys, who is free from passion, fear and wrath—he is called the ascetic of secure understanding.* (56)

The man who does not feel depressed by suffering, is not overcome by suffering—knowing that suffering is always the effect of some cause, who is indifferent amid pleasures and is no more subject to attachments, fear and anger—such a person may be described as *sthitadhi,* that is, one whose intellect remains steadfast and is never caught in a whirlpool.

> *Who owns attachment nowhere, who feels neither joy nor resentment whether good or bad comes his way—that man's understanding is secure.* (57)

The man who has withdrawn interest from all objects, given up desire for them, who is unconcerned, indifferent in good or ill chance, who is neither pleased nor annoyed by anything—such a person's intellect is steadfast. Shri Krishna gives an illustration of this:

And when, like the tortoise drawing in its limbs from every side this man draws in his senses from their objects, his understanding is secure. (58)

The man who holds in his senses to prevent them from going out to their objects, as the tortoise draws in his limbs and holds them as if under a shield, has an intellect which is steadfast. Only that man who voluntarily holds in his senses may be known as completely absorbed in God. When our senses seem to move out of our control, we should think of the tortoise. The objects of the senses are like pebbles. If we hold in the senses, the pebbles will not hurt, that is, if we hold under control our hands, our feet, our eyes, and so on.

Shri Krishna now explains how the senses may be held back from their objects.

When a man starves his senses, the objects of those senses disappear from him, but not the yearning for them; the yearning too departs when he beholds the Supreme. (59)

Only a person who denies the body the food it craves for will cease to be troubled by his senses. The senses of a well-fed man always keep awake, but they lose all their power when he stops eating. The Shastras say that, if a man's appetites are not under his control, it would be best for him to fast. We are enjoined to fast during the Ramadan and the extra lunar month of the Hindus to discipline the senses. Suppose that I have decided to go to the city and see a play; if, however, I have been fasting on that day, I would feel disinclined to go. If our senses cannot be controlled we should undertake a fast; if they cannot be controlled fully, we should give up food altogether. This is what the first half of the verse means.

And now about the second half:

The appetites subside, but our pleasure in the objects of senses remains. If a person who is fasting feels that his life is secure, he will not suffer because of the fast, but ordinarily desire for food persists. During a fast, impure desires will probably subside, but one gets impatient for the fast to end. Unless the desire for food disappears completely, the fast will not endure. The desire for sacrifice will not endure without renunciation. When we have an opportunity to enjoy anything, we find that our physical appetites become strong again. This, of course, does not mean that we should not occasionally give up things for a temporary period. We should certainly give up anything we can give up.

In the first half, we are told that we should curb impure desires by fasting; but fasting alone does not yield the required result. Something more is needed. If we see God, our instinctive desire for objects of senses will also subside. This last thing confronts us with a problem. Until one's pleasure in objects of the senses has disappeared, one cannot become established in *samadhi,* and until one has become so established one will not succeed in overcoming desires.

How to solve this problem? We should persevere in our effort. We should, slowly and gradually, learn to feel God's presence in the depths of our heart. We should, occasionally, banish the very thought of eating and feel that it would be much better that our body should perish than that we should be enslaved by pleasures. One does not, of course, achieve self-conquest by committing suicide. It is the desires which need to be conquered. Anyone who eats to keep alive his body may certainly eat, but he should stop eating if he finds that eating food rouses his appetites. If he can be patient when fasting, they will subside completely. He may, when they have subsided, ask for milk or water if he wants these for keeping himself alive. It is said about Lord Buddha that he once fainted because he had been fasting. At that time, a woman came and placed a few drops of milk on his lips. Did the milk rouse his appetites? No; on the contrary, he realized God soon after.

The purport of this verse is that we should fast for self-purification. But the Shastras tell us that, while fasting, we should wish with all our strength for freedom from desire. If, in addition, we also yearn to see God, then only will our fasting bear fruit. If we desire that our appetite should subside, it is in order that we may see God. When we are fasting, our one desire should be to see God. Our appetites stand in the way, and so we must weaken their hold on us. After a person has seen God, it is all one to him whether he eats or does not eat.

Vinoba told me a story about Chaitanya, that a lump of sugar placed on his tongue remained there undissolved, like a stone. The reason for this was that his pleasure in objects of sense had completely died away. I have said that it is not the palate, but the mind, which feels pleasure. If a man's pleasure in objects of sense has disappeared, if he has become established in *samadhi,* or if he is suffering from a disease like jaundice, nothing placed on his tongue will dissolve. Thus, the man who has turned away from pleasures and the man who is stricken with disease ultimately reach the same state, one voluntarily, the other against his will.

Chaitanyadeva felt all the time that it was God's grace which sustained him and that if he should eat all, it must be only that he may see God one day. To see Him one should completely conquer one's appetites, and even the instinctive pleasure one feels in objects of sense must subside. This verse provides the key to such a state. To curb the appetites, we should stop eating, that is, deny our senses their food. When they have no occasion to function, they will be denied their food. If, after this, we take the next step and concentrate our attention on attaining self-realisation, our instinctive pleasure in objects of sense will subside completely. The man who attains such a state will be in the same condition as Janaka.

It was a very important verse. I kept thinking on it the whole day. Four or five hundred years ago, in Europe and Arabia they attached great importance to mortification of the flesh. In the time of the Prophet, prayer, fasting and keeping awake at night were considered essential for subduing the *nafas* (this is a very good word denoting the sense-organs collectively; it also means desire). The Prophet was often awake till two or three after midnight, and was never particular when and what he ate. It was not merely that he kept the *roza* fast. That was necessary for everyone to keep, even for people engrossed in worldly affairs. The Prophet, however, undertook a *roza* fast every now and then. While one is keeping this fast, one is not permitted to take water during day-time, but after sunset it is absolutely necessary that one must drink some water.

The Prophet, however, did not apply this rule to himself, and so an associate of his told him: "Since you do not eat, we too will not eat." The Prophet's reply was: "No, you should not fast. God sends you no such food as He sends me." Silenced by the reply, the questioner slapped himself on the face and left, thinking: "We, others, observe the *roza* because he falls into ecstasies and asks us to fast, but in actual practice we only make a fuss." To the Prophet, fasting brought happiness, for it was an occasion when he could live constantly in the presence of God. His food consisted of dates. Just as in countries where people drink every home has a vineyard, so in Arabia there are date-palms near every house, and when the Prophet wished to eat he plucked a few dates from these trees. Some others who lived with the Prophet and served him also ate dates. The little flour that was ground for them was also coarse. He used to keep awake for such long hours that the Bibisaheb would wait impatiently for him to lie down to sleep. Besides keeping awake thus, he would withdraw himself into solitude so that he might subdue the senses and be blessed with a vision of God.

Jesus did likewise. He lived in solitude, fasted for forty days and subjected his body to the utmost mortification. At the end of forty days, he felt that he heard a mysterious voice, that God was talking to him and that the veil which hid God from him had lifted. Those who followed him taught the same thing. There has been a tradition of fasting and prayer in Europe right to the present day.

And then came Luther in Germany. He said that the others had misinterpreted the text, and that their lives were all deception. As the sun moves westward, darkness follows close behind it, reaching almost as far as the sun but not quite; in the same way, hypocrisy follows close behind holiness. Luther saw through all this. He plainly saw the superstitions and hypocrisies which flourished in monasteries. It is a strange law of nature that once men become accustomed to a certain thing they continue to do it through sheer inertia. In those days, they even burnt people alive. Those who believed in mortifying the flesh thought it their duty to curb the senses and to kill others who did not do so. Observing these evils, Luther went to the opposite extreme. After all, whatever the evils associated with external practices, it is only through self-control that one can see God. The Protestants, however, believed that there was nothing but hypocrisy in the Catholic practices, and so they destroyed a most potent means of realizing God. Because this means harmed some people, it does not follow that it harms all. But they believed that it did.

In India, too, this wind is blowing at present. It is often said that control of the senses is difficult to achieve, but in truth it is not so. This is not only my present belief; I held it even when I was conducting my experiments. Three things are essential for control of the senses: (1) faith; (2) a conviction of the necessity of subjugating the senses, so strong that we would persist even if we were all alone in this belief; (3) food is body's nourishment, a means of keeping it alive, but it is also the cause of the senses becoming turbulent and, therefore, when it ceases to serve the purpose of nourishing the body, eating should cease. When steam fails to make the engine run, when the pipe through which it flows is rusted, its supply ought to be stopped. A wise engineer would know that, if this supply were not stopped, the engine could burst.

The position with regard to food and the body is identical, and, therefore, if feeding the body results in the senses becoming turbulent, we should stop eating. As, however our instinctive pleasure in food will not disappear when we stop eating we should also pray for God's grace. We have a poem in which we say that we should pray for God's forgiveness for the thousand sins which we commit. We are drawn to these sins against our will, we slip into them slowly and gradually without consciously wishing to commit them. We should pray for God's mercy so that we may be forgiven the many thousand sins of this kind. Hence, if anyone is convinced that he ought to kill his physical appetites, he does nothing wrong in fasting. If he has faith, it will certainly be rewarded. If it is not rewarded, God's promise to man will be falsified; but our experience is that this never happens. One must not shrink from a fast of ten or twenty or fifty days.

Gibbon never made any statement first without verifying its truth. He has mentioned Catholics fasting for as many as fifty days. They had certainly mastered the senses to that degree. In this miserable age, people become impatient if they get no result in five days. Let no one think that our pleasure in objects can be quickly destroyed. If it is not destroyed and the man can control himself no longer, he may eat, but he should not accept defeat. He should start a fast again. This readiness to stake one's all and perish is bound to be rewarded with victory. The man will ultimately win but only if he perseveres after failing ten or even twenty times. There is such great beauty in this effort, and that is why I advise it.

What is followed in the Roman Catholic Church is also enjoined in Islam. The people who at present do evil things in the name of Islam have little understanding of it. Those, on the other hand, who go on praying in their obscure homes, certainly realize God. They give up indulgences, One cannot indulge in pleasures and live a life of renunciation at the same time. If we understand the truth that we eat only to give the body its hire, then we are fit to understand the *Gita*.

One more point. It is, that the author of the *Gita* has categorically laid down the principles. We shall find no error in them if we examine them in the abstract; but when we try to put them into practice we experience difficulties.

Having told Arjuna this with regard to cravings of the senses, Shri Krishna proceeds as in the next verse.

For, in spite of the wise man's endeavour, O Kaunteya, the unruly senses distract his mind perforce. (60)

However much an intelligent man may strive, the senses are restless, they shake his self-control and forcibly draw his mind towards their objects; they draw even a *jnani* after them. The senses are like uncontrollable horses. If the rider is not vigilant and the reins are not all right, there is no knowing where they will carry him. "A monkey, and drunk besides," that is how it will be.

Holding all these in check, the yogi should sit intent on Me; for he whose senses are under control is secure of understanding. (61)

"The *sthitadhi,* having controlled all his senses, will rest wholly absorbed in Me. Anyone who strives in this manner and succeeds in holding his senses under control, such a one is a *yogi.*"

Thus Shri Krishna shows how to become a *sthitaprajna.*

I have explained that, in order that our pleasure in the objects of senses may subside completely, fasting, *bhakti,* prayer and vigils are necessary. But the pleasure in objects will not disappear till we have realized God: The question is, can it disappear completely while the body is there? I have come to the conclusion that no one can be called a *mukta* while he is still alive; one may be said at the most to have become fit for *moksha*. When we speak of Janaka as a *muktatma,* the word *mukta* is used in a general sense and the term means that he was a man who would attain deliverance after his death, that he would not have to be born again. It is doing violence to the meaning of words to say that a man has attained deliverance even while he lives in the body, for the necessity for deliverance remains so long as connection with the body remains. A little reflection will show us that, if our egoistic attachment to ourselves has completely disappeared, the body cannot survive. If we have no wish at all to keep the body alive, it must cease to exist. If we but move our hand the mind is bound to move too.

If, now, we would completely withdraw the mind from the body, the latter should become "as the burnt silken thread, only the form surviving". Some attachment is bound to persist while our bodies are capable of motion. Scientists remove air from a bottle, but a little of it remains in it. The air becomes more and more rarefied, and only a scientist would know there was any inside. Similarly, our pleasure in objects does not disappear completely while the least degree of association with the body persists, as signified by its movements. Moreover, as long as we commit even a little violence, *moksha* is not possible, and the slightest movement of the body involves some violence. Even if the body is lying completely motionless, its functioning involves some violence, however little it may be. There is violence even in the act of thinking, and so long as that is so, man cannot attain a state of perfect self-realization, his mind cannot even comprehend such a state.

Thus, the cravings of the senses die away only when we cease to exist in the body. This is a terrible statement to make, but the *Gita* does not shrink from stating terrible truths. Truth does not remain hidden because it is not stated. *Moksha* is the supreme end, and even yogis can experience it only in contemplation. We must, therefore, say that the Dweller in the body cannot be free while He dwells in it. The prisoner is in jail and the king promises him that he will be released; but till he is actually released he cannot be said to have come out of the cage.

He can only imagine his condition after release. In the same way, if there is any waiting to receive and greet the atman on its release, he cannot do that as long as it remains imprisoned in this cage of the body.

And this cannot but be so. How can it be otherwise than that the state after releaze will be different from the state before it?

Truth is so profound and great a thing that, as we think more and more about it, we realize that to have a direct experience of it, we should completely shed our attachment to the body and yearn every moment for *moksha*. As we think of *moksha* in this light, its value in our eyes should daily increase. If it is the most important thing in life, it should be clear to us that it cannot be attained while we live in this body. Till the gate of the body-prison has opened, the fragrance of *moksha* is beyond our experience. Whether terrible or not, this is the truth.

We need not spend much thought or indulge in intellectual exercise over this problem. Once we are decided on the end, we should concentrate our attention on the means; if they are right, the end is as good as attained. If we have trust in our father, we may rest assured that we shall get our share in his property and need not ask him whether he has made a will. Similarly, we need not argue about this matter. The thing is like Euclid's straight line. No one in the world has as yet succeeded in drawing a perfect right angle, but we can construct buildings with the help of instruments which approximate to a right angle. Likewise, we can only conceive the state of *moksha*. We can conceive a perfect straight line only when we erase the straight line before us; similarly, we can attain deliverance only when we leave the body.

> *In a man brooding on objects of the senses, attachment to them springs up; attachment begets craving and craving begets wrath. Wrath breeds stupefaction, stupefaction leads to loss of memory, loss of memory ruins the reason, and the ruin of reason spells utter destruction. (62, 63)*

Dwelling constantly on objects of sense-pleasure produces attachment for them. Shri Krishna here explains the order in which withdrawal from sense-objects is to be accomplished. If we constantly think about having a certain object, the mind will become strongly attached to the thought of its possession, and this in turn will grow into a passionate desire to possess it so that the object takes still greater hold of our mind. Attachment produces impatience and passion gives rise to anger. When we fail to get the object of our desire, we become angry. As it recedes from us, we get angry with others. Anger clouds a man's vision, so that he loses his judgment and forgets what he is. "Who am I, and from whence?"—he forgets to ask. If he could but recollect, would he not realize what was proper and what was not proper for him?

The man who forgets what he is, loses his power of discrimination. Such a person is as good as dead. Quite a few persons mount the gallows witb perhaps a smile on their face. But they depart from this world and have no future in the other. Thus, through constant dwelling on objects of sense the man is ultimately destroyed. He as good as commits suicide. It is not merely that his body perishes; he will not rise from his fallen state for many lives to come. One should, therefore, crush the craving of sense the moment it arises. The first thing to do is to get over the habit of dwelling on objects of sense-pleasure in our imagination. For that purpose, one should constantly think on God, should live as it were in a state of *samadhi.*

> *But disciplined soul, moving among sense-objects with the senses weaned from likes and dislikes and brought under the control of* atman, *attains peace of mind. (64)*

He who lives with his senses and is no longer subject to attachments and aversions and perfectly under his control becomes fit for God's grace. When a man's ears, nose, eyes, and so on, go on performing their functions naturally without conscious willing on his part—the winking of the eyelids does not need to be willed, there must be some disease if it is otherwise—we say of such a person that his sense-organs, having become free from attachments and aversions, function spontaneously.

What is the natural work of the ear? We describe a man as established in *samadhi* when his atman abides in serene content in itself. His senses must be under his perfect control. The ears of a man whose mind has become one-pointed must have become the servants of his atman. Actually, however, we are the slaves of our senses. **From this slavery we must win swaraj for the atman. The ears should in fact listen only to the divine music of the**

atman. They would not, then, hear even the loud beating of drums. While the atman dwells in this body, it should live as the latter's master and god, and use the senses to do only their natural work. Such a person has no charm for Panditji's singing; he attends only to the praise of God.

As Sanjaya had been given the gift of divine vision, so there are divine eyes and ears behind our bodily eyes and ears. The person who is ruled by his atman will have the gift of inner senses and will not need the outer ones. These latter are always subject to some degree of attachment and aversion. Our hands may be cut off, but they will not move on their own—such should be the degree of our self-control. There was once a great Bishop in England who held out his hands to be burnt first. Hazarat Ali did not feel the pain of the arrow, for his mind was absorbed in the contemplation of God. The man who has not sold himself to his senses as their slave, but has made himself God's slave has no right to ask for a reward from Him in the form of His grace. He who has become God's slave will, instead of trying to be a master in this world, believe even while he suffers God's lashes that they are for his good. Why do we pray to God to breathe greater life into us? God had His own interest—a divine interest—in creating man and that is that the latter should so live that he would not seek pleasures of the senses, but would devote himself entirely to His contemplation and service.

This is the principle. In daily life, one should choose the best that is possible for one. If a man is incapable of hearing the divine song in him, he may listen to good songs sung by others. He should do work which would make him feel in tune with his atman. As long as we must use our moral judgment, we should choose what is good and shun what is evil. We shall then succeed in making the senses do their natural work. For one who lives in this way,

> *Peace of mind means the end of all ills; for the understanding of him whose mind is at peace stands secure. (65)*

When God's grace descends on us, bringing us peace, all our suffering ends. Who can harm him who is protected by Rama? He on whom God showers His grace has all his sufferings destroyed. The intellect of a man whose *chitta* has become calm and whose only thought is of God, stands secure and is protected against error. Shri Krishna now describes a condition the opposite of this:

> *The undisciplined man has neither understanding nor devotion; for, for him who has no devotion there is no peace, and for him who has no peace whence happiness? (66)*

The meaning is that the man who has not become one in God, who is not a yogi established in *samadhi,* lacks the faculty of intellect altogether. One who is unsteady has an intellect which is many-branched; of what good is such an intellect? It feels no devotion, it does not utter Ramanama. He who lacks devotion and does not meditate on God, how can he attain peace? The man who is filled with devotion sits in single-minded contemplation of God, but the other man who has no peace, how can he be happy?

Let us apply to our practical situation what we have already learnt. Today is the sixth, the day of India's awakening.[1] I look upon it as a day of religious awakening, though ordinarily it would be regarded as a day of political significance. On that day we had kept a fast, bathed in a river and gone to temples; Muslims had offered prayers in mosques and Parsis in their fire-temples. Who can say how many of them were sincere? At that time, of course, everyone seemed to be sincere. That was the day on which we started satyagraha. We commenced civil disobedience in the evening by selling copies of *Hind Swaraj.* All, Hindus, Muslims and Parsis, seemed to have gone crazy on that day. Today, too, we have kept a twenty-four hour's fast. We should understand the aim behind it. The aim is to bring about spiritual awakening in us. Our aspiration to go from untruth into truth, from darkness into light, is not something for the distant future; it is immediate. For us, non-violence and truth are symbolized in the spinning-wheel. It may be made only of wood, but if we see in it the gem *chintamani* then it becomes the *chintamani.* It is intelligent to regard the spinning-wheel to be what it is, but it is more intelligent to regard it as the *chintamani.* If even the dullest can see God in a clod of earth, what may we not see in the spinning-wheel?

What is wrong if we see swaraj in the spinning-wheel? Our idea, therefore, does not violate dharma. We should

1. Day of protest against the Rowlatt Act.

understand this when we keep a fast and spin. The Satyagraha Ashram will go on doing its work even when the rest of the country goes to sleep. And we shall, as I have said, get swaraj through the spinning-wheel. The *Gita* says that women, Vaisyas and Sudras, all classes of people, can win freedom. In the same way, all of us can do this. Whether or not we are stout and well-fed, we can do this work if we are strong in mind. Let us, therefore, cultivate firmness of mind; if we do not let the senses distract the mind, we can become fit for satyagraha.

Let us now take up the next verse.

> *For when his mind runs after any of the roaming senses, it sweeps away his understanding, as the wind a vessel upon the waters. (67)*

A pleasure-loving man wastes his time in aimless wandering he must have new suits of clothes every day, he eats and drinks what pleases his palate and goes about dressed in finery. If one of his pleasure-loving senses is so undisciplined that it seeks gratification anywhere and anyhow and if his mind is totally enslaved by this one sense, it will drag his intellect behind it as the wind drives a ship before it in the sea and wrecks it on a rock or runs it aground. Thus the man whose senses are completely out of his control and whose mind is totally enslaved by one of them will be ruined through gradual stages explained earlier as the consequences of attachment. If the mind is enslaved by even a single sense one is lost.

> *Therefore, O Mahabahu, he, whose senses are reined in on all sides from their objects is the man of secure understanding. (68)*

The man whose senses are under his control and are kept away from their objects is a man established in *samadhi*.

> *When it is night for all other beings, the disciplined soul is awake; when all other beings are awake, it is night for the seeing ascetic. (69)*

In conclusion, Shri Krishna gives the mark of a *sthitaprajna* in one verse. He is awake when it is night for other human beings, and when other human beings and all the creatures seem to be awake, it is night for the ascetic who sees.

The world will tell us that the senses cannot be controlled. We should reply that they certainly can be. If people tell us that truth does not avail in the world, we should reply that it does. The world and the man established in *samadhi* are like the west and the east. The world's night is our day and the world's day is our night. There is thus non-co-operation between the two. This should be our attitude if we understand the *Gita* rightly. This does not mean that we are superior to others; we are humble men and women, we are a mere drop while the world is the ocean. But we should have the faith that, if we succeed in crossing to the other shore, the world, too, will. Without such faith we cannot claim that the world's night is our day. If we can achieve self-realization through fasting and spinning, then self-realizsation necessarily implies swaraj.

We have learnt an important mark of the *sthitaprajna*. What seems light to other people is darkness to the yogi. For instance, we tell a great number of people that they should eat sparingly, but a man who has spent his days in devotion to God will immediately understand that, if he eats full meals every day, it will be a hindrance to his life of devotion. Such a yogi, therefore, will keep himself alive on very little food while other people go on feasting on delicacies. But he will not parade his self-control. Narasinh Mehta ridiculed in his song renunciation, knowledge, meditation, etc., and gave the palm to the *gopi's* love, but this sounds strange to people in the modern age. The truth is that those whom the world knows as yogis are not really yogis, nor what the world describes as the four modes of liberation or as spiritual enlightenment are such in fact. These phrases are used merely to deceive the world.

The man who really lives a life of contemplation will outwardly seem a man of the world. His mind may be absorbed in God all the hours of the day, but he will move in the world like other men. He will not go about trumpeting that he lives a life of contemplation. The *gopis* in their love go on dancing, for, knowing that their love is pure, they are not afraid of the world's censure. Mira said that she paid no heed to what the world said, since she had not left her husband but only wished to discover the true meaning of devotion to one's husband. Gopichand is living in a palace of gold. He is looking admiringly at his body, which is exuding the fragrance of *abir* and *gulal,* and his face is lit up with a smile of joy. And then, it happens, tears drop from the eyes of Mainavati who is watching him from the balcony above. Gopichand wonders from where the water-drops can come seeing that there are no clouds in the sky. Mainavati explains too him that his body which he so admired will one day perish, it will be covered with wrinkles, the teeth in the mouth will loosen and come out and the eyes will see no more. What will his body avail him, she asks, if he were to die just then? She has wasted her whole life, but he has time yet to escape and save himself. It is likely that a mother would give such advice? What the world prizes highly seemed of little worth to this mother, for she was a woman of spiritual wisdom.

As the earth rotates on its axis once every twenty-four hours, we are hanging with our feet up and heads down. We can move about in this position because the earth pulls us towards itself like the ants moving on the surface of a lump of sugar. We, the ants on the earth, do not know that the latter is round and is in constant motion. The spiritually enlightened man and the yogi know the hidden truth of these things and tell us what is unreal. What the world takes as real is unreal to them. What it describes as darkness, they will describe as light. The yogi has an inner vision which is different from the world's. The body should live as prisoner of the atman; It should function entirely under the latter's control.

> *He in whom all longings subside, even as the waters subside in the ocean which, though ever being filled by them, never over-flows—that man finds peace; not he who cherishes longing. (70)*

The sea, though being ever added to, remains confined within its boubds; it stands where it has always stood despite countless rivers emptying their waters into it. The man in whom evil impulses and desires subside in the same manner is a yogi. The man who is a slave of desires, whose senses are for ever being allured by their objects, such a person is not a yogi. He is a yogi who is like the sea, who is not like a rivulet or a brook which soon overflows and soon dries up. Christian, (in 'Pilgrim's Progress') too, was a yogi and a man of contemplative life. His voice sounded but one refrain. A man, whose mind is constantly absorbed in God, whether he is bathing or eating or drinking, how can he feel evil desires? Like the sea, he is ever full. Rivers and streams fall into it and come to rest, and their waters are cleansed of their dirt. If this dirt spread out in the sea-water, would the latter be as clear as it is? We actually go to a sea-coast to enjoy its fresh air. In like manner, every evil subsides and disappears in the sea of a mind.

The man who sheds all longing and moves without concern, free from the sense of 'I' and 'mine'—he attains peace. (71)

Such peace may be experienced by a man who has given up all cravings and lives untroubled by desires. He attains to it by shedding the consciousness of "I" and "mine". He alone is a true yogi who never feels "I am doing this".

This is the state, O Partha, of the man who rests in Brahman; having attained to it, he is not deluded. He who abides in this state even at the hour of death pass into oneness with Brahman. (72)

The *brahmi* state is that in which we realize the *Brahman*. Having attained it, we are never overpowered by the darkness of ignorance again. It has already been said that objects of sense lose all attraction for us when we have seen God. Similarly, here again Shri Krishna sums up the argument by saying that, having attained to the *brahmi* state, a man never falls again into delusion. A person who is in this state at the moment of his death attains *Brahma-nirvana*. This statement can mean either of two things: one, that he will attain to the *Brahman* if he is in that state at the moment of death, and, two, that he will attain eternal peace if he always lives in such a state, right up to the moment of death. If a man who has lived a wicked life till now takes to a good life from tomorrow, there is nothing he will lack. But it will not avail a man to have been good all his life if in his last days he becomes wicked. That man, then, may be said to be good who remains so till the last day of his life. That is why it is said: "Call no man good till he is dead." However good a man may have been, he may yet weaken in his old age and worry over his children and his social affairs. We may know that a man has attained *moksha* only if he died in the *brahmi* state.

The nirvana of the Buddhists is *shunyata,* but the nirvana of the *Gita* means peace and that is why it is described as *brahma-nirvana.* We need not concern ourselves with this distinction. There is no reason for supposing that there is a difference between the nirvana mentioned by Lord Buddha and the nirvana of the *Gita*. Buddha's description of nirvana and this other description of nirvana refer to the same state. A number of learned men have shown that the Buddha did not teach a doctrine denying the existence of God. But all these are pointless controversies. What can we say about a state which is so different from anything known in our life that we cannot describe it even when we have attained to it? If it is agreed that our bodily existence is not a thing to be cherished, all these other controversies are unmeaning.

❑❑❑

3

कर्मयोग

अर्जुन उवाच

ज्यायसी चेत्कर्मणस्ते मता बुद्धिर्जनार्दन। तत्किं कर्मणि घोरे मां नियोजयसि केशव।। 1

व्यामिश्रेणेव वाक्येन बुद्धिं मोहयसीव मे। तदेकं वद निश्चित्य येन श्रेयोऽहमाप्नुयाम्।। 2

श्रीभगवानुवाच

लोकेऽस्मिन्द्विविधा निष्ठा पुरा प्रोक्ता मयाऽनघ। ज्ञानयोगेन साङ्ख्यानां कर्मयोगेन योगिनाम्।। 3

न कर्मणामनारंभान्नैष्कर्म्यं पुरुषोऽश्नुते। न च संन्यसनादेव सिद्धिं समधिगच्छति।। 4

न हि कश्चित् क्षणमपि जातु तिष्ठत्यकर्मकृत्। कार्यते ह्यवशः कर्म सर्वः प्रकृतिजैर्गुणैः।। 5

कर्मेन्द्रियाणि संयम्य य आस्ते मनसा स्मरन्। इन्द्रियार्थान् विमूढात्मा मिथ्याचारः स उच्यते।। 6

यस्त्विन्द्रियाणि मनसा नियम्यारभतेऽर्जुन। कर्मेन्द्रियैः कर्मयोगमसक्तः स विशिष्यते।। 7

नियतं कुरु कर्म त्वं कर्म ज्यायो ह्यकर्मणः। शरीरयात्रपि च ते न प्रसिद्ध्येदकर्मणः।। 8

यज्ञार्थात्कर्मणोऽन्यत्र लोकोऽयं कर्मबन्धनः। तदर्थं कर्म कौन्तेय मुक्तसङ्ग समाचर।। 9

सहयज्ञाः प्रजाः सृष्ट्वा पुरोवाच प्रजापति।। अनेन प्रसविष्यध्वमेष वोऽस्त्विष्टकामधुक्।। 10

देवान् भावयतानेन ते देवा भावयन्तु वः। परस्परं भावयन्तः श्रेयः परमवाप्स्यथ।। 11

इष्टान्भोगान् हि वो देवा दास्यन्ते यज्ञभाविताः। तैर्दत्तानप्रदायैभ्यो यो भुङ्क्ते स्तेन एव सः।। 12

यज्ञशिष्टाशिनः सन्तो मुच्यन्ते सर्वकिल्बिषैः। भुञ्जते ते त्वघं पापा ये पचन्त्यात्मकारणात्।। 13

अन्नाद्भवन्ति भूतानि पर्जन्यादन्नसम्भवः। यज्ञाद्भवति पर्जन्यो यज्ञः कर्मसमुद्भवः।। 14

कर्म ब्रह्मोद्भवं विद्धि ब्रह्माऽक्षरसमुद्भवम्। तस्मात्सर्वगतं ब्रह्म नित्यं यज्ञे प्रतिष्ठितम्।। 15
एवं प्रवर्तितं चक्रं नानुवर्तयतीह यः अघायुरिन्द्रियारामो मोघं पार्थ स जीवति।। 16
यस्त्वात्मरतिरेव स्यादात्मतृप्तश्च मानवः। आत्मन्येव च सन्तुष्टस्तस्य कार्यं न विद्यते।। 17
नैव तस्य कृतेनार्थो नाकृतेनेह कश्चन। न चास्य सर्वभूतेषु कश्चिदर्थव्यपाश्रयः।। 18
तस्मादसक्तः सततं कार्यं कर्म समाचर। असक्तो ह्याचरन् कर्म परमाप्नोति पूरुषः।। 19
कर्मणैव हि संसिद्धिमास्थिता जनकादयः। लोकसङ्ग्रहमेवापि सम्पश्यन् कर्तुमर्हसि।। 20
यद्यदाचरति श्रेष्ठस्तत्तदेवेतरो जनः। स यत्प्रमाणं कुरुते लोकस्तदनुवर्तते।। 21
न मे पार्थास्ति कर्तव्यं त्रिषु लोकेषु किञ्चन। नानवाप्तमवाप्तव्यं वर्त एव च कर्मणि।। 22
यदि ह्यहं न वर्तेयं जातु कर्मण्यतन्द्रितः। मम वर्त्मानुवर्तन्ते मनुष्याः पार्थ सर्वशः।। 23
उत्सीदेयुरिमे लोका न कुर्यां कर्म चेदहम्। सङ्करस्य च कर्ता स्यामुपहन्यामिमाः प्रजाः।। 24
सक्ताः कर्मण्यविद्वांसो यथा कुर्वन्ति भारत। कुर्याद्विद्वांस्तथाऽसक्तश्चिकीर्षुर्लोकसङ्ग्रहम्।। 25
न बुद्धिभेदं जनयेदज्ञानां कर्मसङ्गिनाम्। जोषयेत्सर्वकर्माणि विद्वान् युक्तः समाचरन्।। 26
प्रकृतेः क्रियमाणानि गुणैः कर्माणि सर्वशः। अहङ्कारविमूढात्मा कर्ताऽहमिति मन्यते।। 27
तत्त्ववित्तु महाबाहो गुणकर्मविभागयोः। गुणा गुणेषु वर्तन्त इति मत्वा न सज्जते।। 28
प्रकृतेर्गुणसम्मूढाः सज्जन्ते गुणकर्मसु। तानकृत्स्नविदो मन्दान् कृत्स्नविन्न विचालयेत्।। 29
मयि सर्वाणि कर्माणि संन्यस्याऽध्यात्मचेतसा। निराशीर्निर्ममो भूत्वा युध्यस्व विगतज्वरः।। 30
ये मे मतमिदं नित्यमनुतिष्ठन्ति मानवाः। श्रद्धावन्तोऽनसूयन्तो मुच्यन्ते तेऽपि कर्मभिः।। 31
ये त्वेतदभ्यसूयन्तो नानुतिष्ठन्ति मे मतम्। सर्वज्ञानविमूढांस्तान् विद्धि नष्टानचेतसः।। 32
सदृशं चेष्टते स्वस्याः प्रकृतेर्ज्ञानवानपि। प्रकृतिं यान्ति भूतानि निग्रहः किं करिष्यति।। 33
इन्द्रियस्येन्द्रियस्यार्थे रागद्वेषौ व्यवस्थितौ। तयोर्न वशमागच्छेतौ ह्यस्य परिपन्थिनौ।। 34
श्रेयान् स्वधर्मो विगुणः परधर्मात्स्वनुष्ठितात्। स्वधर्मे निधनं श्रेयः परधर्मो भयावहः।। 35

अर्जुन उवाच

अथ केन प्रयुक्तोऽयं पापं चरति पूरूषः। अनिच्छन्नपि वार्ष्णेय बलादिव नियोजितः।। 36

श्री भगवानुवाच

काम एष क्रोध एष रजोगुणसमुद्भवः। महाशनो महापाप्मा विद्ध्येनमिह वैरिणम्।। 37

धूमेनाऽऽव्रियते वह्निर्यथादर्शो मलेन च। यथोल्बेनावृतो गर्भस्तथा तेनेदमावृतम्।। 38

आवृतं ज्ञानमेतेन ज्ञानिनो नित्यवैरिणा। कामरूपेण कौन्तेय दुष्पूरेणानलेन च।। 39

इन्द्रियाणि मनो बुद्धिरस्याधिष्ठानमुच्यते। एतैर्विमोहयत्येष ज्ञानमावृत्य देहिनम्।। 40

तस्मात्त्वमिन्द्रियाण्यादौ नियम्य भरतर्षभ। पाप्मानं प्रजहि ह्येनं ज्ञानविज्ञाननाशनम्।। 41

इन्द्रियाणि पराण्याहुरिन्द्रियेभ्यः परं मनः। मनसस्तु परा बुद्धिर्यो बुद्धेः परतस्तु सः।। 42

एवं बुद्धेः परं बुद्ध्वा संस्तभ्यात्मानमात्मना। जहि शत्रुं महाबाहो कामरूपं दुरासदम्।। 43

-.-

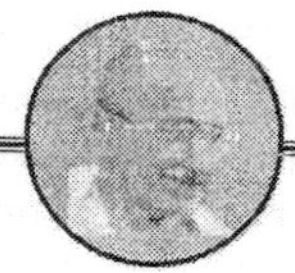

Karma Yoga: The Method of Work

The last Chapter is known as Sankhyayoga. We saw that, after discussing the distinction between the body and the atman, Shri Krishna told Arjuna that he had explained the Sankhya view, that is, analysed logically the distinction between the body and the atman. This did not help Arjuna to know it in his own experience, but he grasped it intellectually. Arjuna's duty of fighting was explained to him, but only so far as it could be done with the help of argument. Shri Krishna then explained yoga to him, that is, the method of acting in a disinterested spirit. This led to the discussion concerning the *sthitaprajna*.

From the last verse of that Chapter, it would seem that Shri Krishna had nothing further to add. Indeed, if Arjuna had not again put a question to him, there was really nothing for him to add. The *brahmi* state includes *bhakti* too. But in view of the natural tendency in everyone to let his desires rule his reason, truth has to be repeated often so that it may be made more clear. If an unenlightened man decides for himself, he usually decides in favour of worldliness. Therefore, he has to keep on repeating to himself that he is the atman, for it is not a truth experienced by him at all hours of the day. A son who has no doubt in his mind at all need not tell his mother that he is her son. The repetition of Ramanama and *dwadashmantra* are for people who have not had self-realization. After release from the body, the man who explains and the man who listens, the two will be one. So long as the body exists, the problems of the means of attaining *moksha* will remain; that is why Vyasa expanded the *Gita* this length. There is nothing in it which is not contained in the verses which we recite at the time of our evening prayers.

Vyasa has placed before readers a divine truth through the *Gita*. Whether Sankhya or yoga, sannyasa or the life of the householder, all these paths are essentially one. Action and inaction mean the same thing, this is the substance of the *Gita's* teaching. Since these different paths are so mixed up with one another, we should understand their essential identity if our one aim is to know God and realize the unreality of all else. The way to know Him is not to sit cross-legged, but to work in a disinterested spirit.

A man does not become a yogi because he is known to have performed a thousand *yajnas* or made huge gifts. We have to take into account whether he was free from attachment to the ego, whether he willingly turned in Mira's words as God pulled him with a slender thread, whether he worked accordingly, and so on. Vyasa wants to tell us that a yogi should offer up to God everything he does, whether it be good or indifferent, should look upon Him as the sole author of everything. And so he makes Arjuna ask Krishna:

Arjuna says:

> *If, O Janardana, thou holdest that the attitude of detachment is superior to action, then why, O Keshava, dost thou urge me to dreadful action.*
>
> *Thou dost seem to confuse my understanding with perplexing speech; tell me, therefore, in no uncertain voice, that alone whereby I may attain salvation.* (1, 2)

First, Shri Krishna put forward the logical argument, and then he described the marks of the *sthitaprajna.* He also explained that yoga meant *karmasu kaushalam.* Arjuna complains that Shri Krishna has confused his judgment by such contradictory advice, and requests him to tell him some one thing clearly and definitely.

The Lord Says:

> *I have spoken, before, O sinless one, of two attitudes in this world—the Sankhyas', that of Jnanayoga and the yogis', that of Karmayoga.* (3)

Arjuna tells Shri Krishna: I cannot judge what is good. At moments I feel that I should fight, and then again I feel that a *sthitaprajna* should have no work to do.

> *Never does man enjoy freedom from action by not undertaking action, nor does he attain that freedom by mere renunciations of action.* (4)

Merely by refusing to work, one can never experience the state of *naishkarmya* (freedom from experiencing results of action), or attain to *moksha*.

We shall meet this word 'karma' again and again in the *Gita*. What can it mean? It must have, of course, a restricted meaning. But it will help us to understand the relevant verses in the *Gita* if we take the word in its broadest meaning. Karma means any action, any bodily activity or motion. In the *Gita's* definition of the word, however, karma includes even thought. Any motion, any sound, even breathing, are forms of karma. Some of them we cannot avoid performing. Some of them we perform as a matter of necessity, some others are involuntary. The divine in us urges us on to the path of good, and the demoniac to that of evil. Even if the man is good the demoniac element in him drives him to evil courses. Another man may be wicked, but the divine element in him forces him to follow good. Thus action is impelled by nature, or is the result to compulsion or volition. How do you say, Shri Krishna asks Arjuna, that you will not work? You will not stop riding the horses of your fancies. Even sannyasis are helpless, let them say what they will. Even the decision to stop breathing is karma. Even the refraining from karma is karma. It will not, help one, therefore, to attain to the state of *naishkarmya*. Renunciation of action and the state of *naishkarmya* should come spontaneously.

For none ever remains inactive even for a moment; for all are compelled to action by the gunas inherent in prakriti. (5)

No one can cease from karma even for a moment. To listen and not to listen, both are forms of karma. *Sattva, rajas* and *tamas*, the three forces or modes of *prakriti*, drive everyone to action, whether he will or not. A *tamasik* man is one who works in a mechanical fashion, a *rajasik* man is one who rides too many horses, who is restless and is always doing something or other, and the *sattvik* man is one who works with peace in his mind. One is always driven to work by one or another of these three modes of *prakriti* or by a combination of them.

He who curbs the organs of action but allows the mind to dwell on the sense-objects—such a one, wholly deluded, is called a hypocrite. (6)

Anyone who curbs the organs of action outwardly but dwells all the time on the objects of senses and gives free rein to his fancies, and then believes that he has attained to *naishkarmya*, such a person is sunk in ignorance and his claim is mere hypocrisy. A person who gets his hands tied up but in his mind strikes the enemy, does in reality strike, though outwardly he does not seem to do so. He does not get the pleasure of actually striking, but certainly experiences the fruit of doing so. Please do not misunderstand what I have said. It does not mean that there is no scope for effort or striving, nor that, in that case, we had better act as we feel inclined to.

We are constantly thinking of doing something or other, but reflection also helps us in restraining our hands. There can be no hypocrisy in ceaselessly fighting the enemy who holds us in his grip. The point of the verse is that there should be no contradiction between thought and action. It is hypocrisy to yearn inwardly for an object and outwardly keep away from it. It is not hypocrisy, if, despite one's best efforts, one does not succeed in always remaining vigilant, for the evil habit has had a long hold over us. Only, one should not merely try but also wish to remain vigilant. Hence, it is wrong for anyone who mentally dwells on objects of sense and outwardly shuns them to describe himself as a sannyasi or yogi. The psychological effects of our actions in past lives cannot be wiped out all at once. Waves of desire will continue to rise. They will drench us again and again, but one day they will leave us dry.

If someone forces me to take up and hold a lamp in my hand, I can say that I did not hold it, for I was not willing to do so. If a person is forced to do anything, his action is not his. For instance, a person who is forced to let off a gun is not a murdrer. On the other hand, the man who supplied him the powder and planned everything is a murderer. If the man who actually fires the shot does so of his own free will, he too is a murderer. In this way, there should be concord between thought and action. Where this is absent, it is difficult to judge to whom to attribute intention and to whom action. We kept a fast on the sixth; if, however, we dwelt in our minds the whole day on the pleasure of eating, our fast was no fast. On the other hand, a person is not a hypocrite if, though tempted to eat, he suppresses the desire every time he feels it and so keeps struggling all the time.

The man who does evil things has no hope. But he who raggles against evil thoughts will tell himself that he would die rather than let himself do an evil thing; he will go on fighting against his evil thought. The *brahmachari* between whose thoughts and actions reigns perfect harmony and who is always pure in mind deserves the highest reverence. It is the nature of the mind to be ceaselessly active, thinking of one thing or another. He who strives ceaselessly to restrain it is sure to win the battle. It is not as if he never gratified sex-urge, but he does so with discrimination. He is a true sannyasi and yogi between whose thoughts and actions there is such complete harmony that he is not even aware that he observes *brahmacharya.* He should be a man who has made himself an eunuch. If the person is a woman, she should not be conscious at all of being a woman. The man's impotence should not be the incapacity of disease; he should have voluntarily cultivated it. He should become completely free from desire, should become incapable of doing evil. Even a vigilant man may fall, but ultimately he will win complete freedom from desire. A man who remains non-violent in action will in time become free even from the desire to strike anyone.

There is no outward difference between a fool and a wise man. The former has no pretensions. The latter wants to be taken as a fool. Outwardly, the behaviour of the two will seem alike. The man whose mind is active with intense energy will appear dull. The earth rotates with such great speed that it seems to be stationary. There is no reference here to the idea of *shunya.* Buddha's nirvana was also no *shunya.* There is only a seeming inertness.

We have seen that a man, while himself remaining in the background, may provide the means of killing and get someone else to do it and thus become guilty of the heinous sin of murder. His guilt is even greater than that of the person who actually kills. Yudhishthira went to Drona and Bhishma and asked them: 'What is this you have decided to do?' They replied that it was their stomach which had forced them. This means that a slave or servant, being unable to oppose his master's wishes, is less guilty than the latter. The person, on the other hand, who plots a murder and gets someone else to execute the plot is far more wicked than the latter. He is a hypocrite, moreover, as the verse explains—

Proceeding, Shri Krishna explains the opposite manner of acting:

But he, O Arjuna, who keeping all the senses under control of the mind, engages the organs in karmayoga, without attachment— that man excels. (7)

The first point is that one should go on doing karma through the respective organs of action, and the second is that one should hold the same organs under one's control. Shri Krishna has thus divided the physical organs into two classes. The ten organs are the sentries. Five of them function as spies and the other five carry out orders. Hands, feet, etc belong to the latter class. If the eyes, the nose and other sentries of their class do not remain under our control, we can stop using them. We can curb them every moment. Holding them under control, we make the sentries of the other class carry out orders. He is the best man who controls the functioning of his organs in this manner and works without attachment. A man who gets angry cannot be described as non-attached, he is, in truth, strongly attached.

Do thou thy allotted task; for action is superior to inaction: with inaction even life's normal course is not possible. (8)

One should do the appointed work, the task which has been assigned to one, for action is superior to inaction. No one can cease completely from action even for a moment. If that is so, it is better that we work of our own free will. Why need we consult anyone for doing *niyata* karma, that is, for doing work specially meant for us? For, we cannot even keep our bodies alive without working.

This world of men suffers bondage from all action save that which is done for the sake of sacrifice; to this end, O Kaunteya, perform action without attachment. (9)

We should now discuss the meaning of *yajna*. Some learned students of the Shastras believe that the *Gita* is not concerned with work like a cobbler's or like spinning, that is, with work which we do in our practical life. By karma, they mean such things as ritual offering of food to the masses and exclude spinning and weaving from its definition. But the *Gita* is very much concerned with practical life. A dharma which does not serve practical needs is no dharma, it is *adharma*. Even cleaning of latrines should be done in a religious spirit. A man of such spirit will ask himself, if he does the work, why there should be so much foul smell? We should realize that we are full of evil desires. The excreta of a person who is suffering from a disease or is full of evil desires is bound to emit foul smell. Another person who does not do this work in a religious spirit but shirks his duty will remove the contents anyhow, and not clean the bucket; such a man does not do the work as a religious duty. He has no compassion in him nor discrimination. Thus, dharma is certainly connected with practical life.We have, therefore, accepted a broad definition of Karma, and will accept an equally broad definition of *yajna.*

As we have the word *yajna* in our language and the practice is enjoined in our dharma, so the Bible and the holy books of the Jews too have each a corresponding word, and an idea similar to that of *yajna*. We find three things in the Koran: (1) animal sacrifices, on the Bakar-i-Id day; (2) it refers to a practice which also obtained among the Jews, a father sacrificing his son—Ibrahim does this; and (3) Ramadan, which is a form of sacrifice, that is, parting with or giving up something which is dear to us.

In the same way, **we see in the Bible the meaning of the term 'sacrifice' expanding after Jesus.** He told the people that they could not realize their aim by this sacrifice of animals, that for performing a sacrifice in the right sense of the term they would have to do much more than kill animals. **He told them that it was not a sacrifice to destroy other lives, that one should give one's own life as sacrifice. With that idea, he sacrificed his own life for the eternal welfare of the world,** for its spiritual welfare, for washing away its sins and not merely for feeding the people.

Among the Hindus, too, the practice of human sacrifice was prevalent at one time. Then followed animal sacrifice. Even today, thousands of goats are sacrificed to Mother Kali. *Yajnas* are also performed for securing the fulfillment of many worldly desires. **The root word in the English term "sacrifice" had a good meaning; it meant "to sanctify". In Sanskrit, *yaj* means "to worship". In the Old Testament, the word for *yajna* means "to renounce".** But the underlying idea, that all actions performed for the good or service of others, are forms of *yajna,* will be accepted by everyone. Maybe our motive in sacrificing an animal is that of public good, for instance, securing rainfall. The motive in this may be that of public good, but it is not a true sacrifice in which we kill other creatures. We may tell ourselves that we have made a sacrifice in paying for the goat, but the crores of other Hindus are not likely to share that belief.

In Gujarat, too, we find this practice prevails in places. A buffalo is sacrificed on the Dusehra day. Our reason, however, tells us that there is no sacrifice in this, that we do not really worship God by doing this. However, the belief underlying this practice, too, is that we serve public good through it. We should, therefore, include two points in the definition of *yajna:* it is something which is done to serve others' good but without causing suffering to any creature.

We serve the good of the world by refraining from causing suffering to other creatures, because we shall refrain from doing so only if we cherish the lives of other creatures as we do our own, only if we believe that the body is transient. If we interpret correctly the word *yajna* as it is used in the *Gita,* we shall find no difficulty in understanding its teaching and living in accordance with it. We can perform a *yajna* with the mind as much as with the body. Of these two meanings of *yajna,* we should accept that which suits the context every time.

We need not go into why in the past people performed—or even at the present time do perform—animal sacrifice. We shall answer the question in one or two sentences. Man selects for his food what is available in his environment. What objection, moreover, can there be from people's point of view to anything done for public good which is not in itself regarded as sinful? Where people believe that the rains will not come unless some person or creature is sacrificed, no hesitation is felt in performing such a sacrifice. As man's beliefs become more enlightened, the meanings, which people attach to certain words also become more enlightened. Even if Vyasa had defined the words which he used, we would ask why we should accept the meanings given by him.

For instance, non-cooperation has come to mean much more than we at first intended it to mean. There is no harm in our enlarging the meaning of the word *yajna,* even if the new meaning we attach to the term was never in Vyasa's mind. We shall do no injustice to Vyasa by expanding the meaning of his words. Sons should enrich the legacy of their fathers. Why should we object if anyone regarded the spinning-wheel with greater sentiment than what we seek to create in the people about it? It is quite possible that in future people may see harm in the spinning-wheel, may come to think that no one should wear cotton clothes at all, because they do harm. They may, for instance, believe that clothes should be made from fibres extracted from banana leaves. If people should come to feel that way, anyone who still clings to the spinning-wheel would be looked upon as a fool. **A wise man, however, will mean by the spinning-wheel not an article made of wood but a type of work which provides employment to all people.** That is also the case with regard to the meaning of the term *yajna.* Thus, we may, and should, attach to it a meaning not intended by Vyasa.

> *Together with sacrifice did the Lord of beings create, of old, mankind declaring:*
>
> *"With this may you cherish the gods and may the gods cherish you; thus cherishing one another may you attain the highest good.* (10, 11)

We should think carefully what the term god, too, means. Who are god Indra and other gods? Who is the god of water and the god of woodlands? There was an argument once over one of the verses in our morning prayers, whether it was proper to worship Saraswati conceived as a figure with hands and feet. Just as it was explained at the time that Saraswati was not a goddess living somewhere far away in the clouds, so are Indra and others not gods living in the heavens; they symbolize the forces of nature. If only we take the thirty-three crores of gods in whom we believe to stand for man, we would serve our own good and also that of the whole world, of all the creatures in it.

The gods symbolize the different forms of energy, the forces which sustain the universe. Even the belief in terrible gods does not deserve to be dismissed. The power of God in all its three aspects—creative, protective and destructive—is beneficial, but we do not understand the real meaning of these three aspects because of our limited knowledge. The *Nagapanchami* day is observed to save ourselves from harm by snakes. It is not right to observe any such day to appease snakes. And so also about ghosts and spirits. What are ghosts? They are merely creatures of our imagination. Our aim should be, instead, to worship sustaining energy of God, to worship it in all its aspects.

We cannot give any arbitrary meaning to the term *yajna.* We can adopt only a meaning which is consistent with the use of the word in the *Gita.* We may draw all possible conclusions from the principles of geometry, but they should be such as Euclid would not question or oppose. We do no injustice to the poet in going beyond his meaning. Any purpose which a well serves will be served by a lake too. If water can be used for a good purpose, it can also be used for an evil purpose. We can destroy a dam and thereby render innumerable fields useless. So the meaning which we have attached to the term *yajna*, namely, any action performed with a view to public good, is not inconsistent with the use of the term in the *Gita*.

"This world suffers bondage from work unless it is work done as *yajna;*" in this verse, the word *yajna* can also be interpreted to mean Vishnu and the worshippers of Siva may take it to mean Siva. In other words, any work dedicated to God helps one to attain *moksha*.

"Along with *yajna* the Lord created men." Which type of *yajna* is meant here? Does the term have any special meaning? I think it has. The reference here is not to mental or intellectual work. Brahma did not ask human beings to multiply and prosper merely by working with their minds; what He meant was that they would do so through bodily *yajna*, by working with the body. Scriptures of other religions enjoin the same thing. The Bible says: "With the sweat of thy brow thou shalt earn thy bread." Thus bodily labour is our lot in life; it is best, then, to do it in the spirit of service and dedicate it to Shri Krishna. Anyone who works in that spirit all his life becomes free from evil and is delivered from all bonds. Such a person is like a soldier in the King's army, who is content to carry out orders. He is as worthy as the General. Both have equal value in God's eyes, for He looks only to the attitude. Arjuna's arrows availed him not when Krishna was no longer by his side, and he was robbed by a robber.

The verse, commencing with *sahayajna* then, talks of bodily *yajna*, of a kind, moreover, through which gods and men would serve each other's needs. By gods we may understand all living beings or God's sustaining energy. Gods are the invisible forces. So long as a person has someone in sight for whom he works, he is not engaged in service; real service consists in working for those whom one does not know personally. The thirty-three crores of gods belong to the world of imagination. Children cannot even conceive this number. We cannot take in with our eyes so many beings assembled at one place, nor count them. We cannot see these gods, as we see our children, and yet we cultivate a living relationship with them. By and by, the sphere of our service will enlarge itself to embrace the whole world. We have thus left aside the word gods and interpreted the verse to mean that we would serve the humblest human beings, even those whom we never see, with respect and honour and looking upon them as gods and not as our servants; we should, in other words, serve the whole world.

This verse tells us that we should undertake bodily labour to do service. Man simply cannot live without such work. If he had not violated this law, he would not suffer as much as he does, the rich would not have become masters of immeasurable stores of wealth and the millions would not be suffering in poverty. **God is a great economist. He is omnipotent. We cannot refrain completely from storing things for future use. But God never stores, for he can destroy and create the universe with a mere thought. He wants us, therefore, to provide only for each day. If we want anything the next day, we must labour for it.** He has warned that we are doomed if we do not labour, if we do not bend the body and work with it. He has commanded that we should willingly endure every kind of suffering. If we honour this law in our life, there would be no hunger and no sin or immorality in this world.

Evil desires will never disturb a man who labours all the twenty-four hours for the good of the world—I say twenty-four hours because one keeps working even in sleep. If the labourers in the world were filled with evil desires as we are, the world could not last. The rich seek all kinds of luxuries. If the workers, too, did that, where would the world be? In the West, nowadays the idea has come to prevail that men and women are born to gratify all their desires. *Adharma* is being propagated. If people worked with the shovel or pick-axe, would they be disturbed with evil desires? We should submit ourselves, therefore, to this restraining law. If we do our bodily *yajna* properly, all will be well with us, we shall advance the good of our atman and of the world, our mind and body will be ruled by our atman and we shall be filled with serene peace. It can be said that such a person, even thought acting, does nothing.

I cannot understand the idea that one can perform a *yajna* by lighting a few sticks. It does not do to say that doing so purifies the air. There are many other ways of purifying the air. Why should we at all pollute the air? It is always pure. It is we who pollute it. But this is not the aim behind a *yajna.* **When the Aryans first came to this country, they tried to civilize the non-Aryan**

races. May be the idea of *yajna* was originally conceived for the uplift of the latter. There were big forests in those days, and it may have been regarded as everyone's duty to help in clearing these forests, for it was a social necessity. And because this work was regarded as a duty, it came to be looked upon as a means of attaining *moksha.* Innumerable ceremonies were devised, all of which required the lighting of fire.

If these *rishis* had lived in the desert of Sahara, they would have conceived of *yajna* as refraining from cutting a single twig, as planting of trees or drawing a certain quantity of water. In burning wood in this age, we misuse the capital of our forefathers, or we show ourselves witless pedants by understanding the thing in a literal sense. If we think of the matter now, we shall see that burning sticks is no longer a form of bodily *yajna.* **If we would undertake any such *yajna* in this age and in this country, it is spinning, the reason being the same as in the instance I cited of the forests.** At that time, the very thought of cutting trees for wood in a forest might have shaken a man with fear; but the man who had faith would have started the work straightway, for the person who had asked him to do it was inspired with absolute conviction. Such a man of faith would simply go on cutting trees (Recall the instance of Stevenson and the ditch near Manchester. He asked people, to go on and on filling it with earth.) If the order for cutting down trees had not gone out, snakes and poisonous air would have remained of course.

Someone has said that a true idea is born in the mind of one person who acts upon it, and thus, it starts on its career. If you employ the right means, the end is certain to follow. All that is necessary is to make a start. A man of faith will go ahead with his work, undeterred by difficulties. He knows no such thing as failure. Let the world believe in failure, he would say, I do not know what it is. This is what is meant by disinterested work. Such a person hopes for nothing, and works in patience; he resorts to no scheming and is never in too much hurry for the result.

We have discussed the meaning of the term *yajna.* Using one's limbs, labouring, working for others' good, these ideas follow from this one verse. What is meant by saying that mankind was created along with *yajna?* As we cannot escape the cycle of birth, old age and death, so also bodily labour is our lot in life from which there is no escape. But what actually happens is that man becomes self-centred and follows his own wishes in every matter, or works in order that he may be able to indulge in pleasures. But the world cannot go on thus, and if the world cannot go on, the individual who behaves in this manner also cannot live.

Man is born a helpless creature. The child needs someone—a mother-god or father-god—to look after it. Man is born dependent, and dies in dependence. Freedom is a state of the mind. A man can describe himself as *swadhin* only to the extent that he feels so for he can say that he submits himself to a law of his own free will. But there are laws disregard of which would make government impossible; a man cannot, however, commit a crime and escape its consequences. Not only that, the relations of the person committing a crime also suffer with him. A crime ultimately proves as harmful to its author as the swallowing of raw mercury. Man is, thus, dependent on others in all things. He is his own master in only a few matters. It is, therefore, best for him to do everything in the spirit of *yajna*.

Yajna was created simultaneously with us, so that we may serve the gods and the latter may serve us. If we let ourselves be ruled by them, they, too, will be ruled by us. The right *yajna* for this age is the *yajna* of spinning. We should, however, think of *yajna* only in its primary meaning which we have discussed. All other forms of *yajna* follow from that. Our most important activity is eating and drinking. Even our body is born as a slave. If we learn to keep it alive exclusively for the good of the atman, we should attain *moksha*. The body is meant to be spent for the good of the atman and of the world. Different men act in different ways, and if we believe in what the law terms "a legal fiction", that the king does no wrong, then the king also becomes good. If today the Princes are wicked, so are their subjects. In other matters too, we keep up some legal fictions. **We entertain such a fiction about the spinning-wheel, too, that through it we establish a bond with the world, having abandoned the old fiction that we establish such a bond by burning sticks and pouring ghee into the fire.**

It is not recently that I have come to attach this meaning to *yajna;* I have understood it in that sense ever since I first read the *Gita*. What I read about the Russian writer Bondoref's views on "bread labour" only confirmed my idea, but the idea was with me from the beginning and has grown stronger with years. The

Russian writer has stated one side of the truth. We understand the other side too. We now understand the idea of bread labour better, for by *yajna* we do not mean labour as a means of livelihood. Thanks to the associations which the term calls up, we do not restrict *yajna* to mean this and no more. Labour in this context means bodily labour. He alone should eat who has laboured for twelve hours. Anyone who sincerely wants to observe *brahmacharya,* to preserve purity and to be free from evil desires, must engage himself in bodily labour. People who do physical work are not subject to the sway of such desires as much as we are. Maybe they are dull in mind; but it is better to be dull in mind, than to be a prey to evil desires. The world would go on even if there were no intelligent men and women in it, but it would be nowhere if all people refused to do physical work. We have exercised our intelligence in acknowledging the law of bodily labour. The one universal form of such labour is agriculture and it should, therefore, be looked upon as *yajna.*

> *"Cherished with sacrifice, the gods will bestow on you the desired boons." He who enjoys their gifts without rendering aught unto them is verily a thief.* (12)

The gods, gratified by *yajna,* that is, by your work for the service of others and your bodily labour, will grant you the means to gratify your desires; that is, the gods in the form of society will grant them to you. Anyone who receives what they give but offers nothing to others is a thief. He is a thief who does not do bodily labour for society.

> *The righteous men who eat the residue of the sacrifice are freed from all sin, but the wicked who cook for themselves eat sin.* (13)

Those holy persons who eat only what is left behind after the *yajna* is over become free from all sins. They who first offer to society, to Shri Krishna, what they get to eat, live free from sin. But those who cook food only for themselves, who work only for selfish ends, take in nothing but sin when they eat. That is why one should regularly and daily perform *yajna,* make a sacrifice, of which body labour is the foundation. The greatest *yajna* consists in observing the very first commandment of God, the commandment with which every human being is sent into this world.

From food springs all life, from rain is born food; from sacrifice comes rain and sacrifice is the result of action. (14)

If people did nothing, there would be no rains, which means that there would be no rains if people did not perform *yajna*. Work which is necessary must be done. But people are simply not ready to exert themselves and plant trees. Rains are plentiful in forests. But there they are of no benefit to human beings; in fact they do terrible harm. They do not do that after human beings start working in those forests. Cherapunji has the heaviest rainfall in the world, but what good does all that rain do?

In this verse, the *Gita* enunciates the principle explained by scientists that there can be no rain in regions barren of vegetation.

Know that action springs from Brahman and Brahman from the Imperishable; hence the all-pervading Brahman is ever firm-founded on sacrifice. (15)

This verse is a little difficult to understand. "You should know," Krishna says to Arjuna, "that karma springs from *Brahman,* and the latter from *yajno.*" In an annotated *Gita* found in Bihar, karma is explained as *Brahman,* and a little below, the latter is explained as the source of the universe, as that which fills the entire universe, and from which arise Brahma, Vishnu and Siva, or, in other words, as that which we describe as dwelling in the hearts of all creatures, that which is the common element of belief among all faiths and sects.

It is true that *Brahman* springs from *yajna*. Wherever we find anyone filled with the spirit of renunciation, anyone whose atman abides in serene content within itself, who suffers when others suffer and who practises the supreme *yajna* of maintaining a sameness of attitude towards all, there we may be sure that *Brahman* is present. But there is one thing, whether about this *yajna* or any other, namely, that it should not be so performed as to cost the body nothing. Dharma is not to be followed with tender regard for one's body. That is dharma in following which one suffers in the body to the limit of one's endurance. There is no *yajna* for him who is not ready to mortify his body. What right does a person have who undertakes bodily labour for the sake of the world—if there are so many crores in India, there must be billions in the whole world, and if to these we add the insects and other forms of life, then each of us is but one hair on the body as compared with the total number of living creatures in the world—what right does such a person have to feel that he works for the world? If all my hairs were to be plucked off, I would die, but one hair lost means nothing. If we look a round in the world, we shall see that the whole of it is within us. If we forget which is the hair and which the world, we shall come to feel one with the world. We shall then spend this body in the service of the world all the hours of the day.

All this talk about knowledge is because of the body; otherwise, for an unembodied one, how can there be any question of knowledge? The highest knowledge of all in the world is knowledge of the self. Moreover, the idea of a human being having no body exists only in our imagination. Mortification of the body, therefore, is the only means of self-realization and the only *yajna* for everyone in this world. We are all labourers. If the rich would look upon themselves as labourers as much as the people who work with their bodies are labourers, the latter would get all that they want. They would then feel quite satisfied with their condition and devote themselves whole-heartedly to their work. If the working men, however, deliberately claim that they are the equals of their masters, they are sure to come to grief. **If we follow the methods of the British in running our government when we have swaraj, we would be behaving as masters. But we wish to give up the ways of masters and turn ourselves into workers.** If, while working as labourers, we learn to be detached and make ourselves ciphers, we would come out of the darkness of night. This is the idea in the verse containing the phrase eternally founded in *yajna*.

But, then, who is the Brahma mentioned in the first verse of this group? Who, again, are Vishnu and Shiva? I do not look upon them as distinct Beings. We may take them to represent aspects of God or His powers. They are represented in the *puranas* as being different from other gods. All that is partly right and partly wrong. They imagined all these things because they wanted to teach people dharma somehow. **In truth, there is no such Being as Brahma or Siva. The only reality is the neuter *Brahman*. But as God is conceived of as doing nothing, it was imagined that this universe comes into existence out of Brahma.** If I destroy a man's belief in a Brahma with four faces, in what way do I enlighten him? How will that profit me? If such a person asks me whether

I share his belief, I will tell him that I do not. But others who believe in a personal God should be free to do so.

And so **Brahma means the active energy of God.** In fact in Tilak Maharaj's *Gita*, Brahma is explained as *prakriti;* I will say, then, that *prakriti* is Brahma. Whatever our belief, what we have to understand from all this is that in every *yajna* God's presence may be felt, and that, where there is no *yajna* of body labour, God, too, is absent, though, of course, we believe that God is present everywhere. Human beings go on working with their bodies and that keeps the cycle going. I have no doubt at all that the Imperishable here means God.

> *He who does not follows the wheel thus set in motion here below, he, living in sin, sating his senses, lives, O Partha, in vain. (16)*

Such a person's life is a burden on others, The earth rotates ceaselessly all the twenty-four hours of the day, and anyone who merely rests on it doing nothing lives to no purpose. One who is always engaged in *yajna* is not subject to the binding effects of karma. But he who, disinclined to work, pleads *aham Brahmasmi* in justification of his idleness, is stated by the *Gita* to be living in sin. This is what Narasinh Mehta meant when he wrote that those who renounce the world will not win deliverance and those who enjoy life will. Here, "those who enjoy life" means all the people in the world who labour with their bodies and "those who renounce the world" means the incorrigible idlers.

I have explained the wheel in this verse to mean the spinning-wheel. I look upon it as the means of supreme *yajna* in this age. He who plies it will have lived worthily, will have won the battle of life.

Yajna means any activity for the good of others. A man works for the good of others when he spends his body in their service. If we look upon our body as the property of the world and use it so, we would retain our control over it but always keep it clean, would not let it be eaten up by white ants. All this, however, should be done in a spirit of dedication to God. It would give us profound happiness if in using it we act as its trustees or guardians. A watchman who serves as one who held his body as a trust may assure us that he would be constantly seen coming to our houses and that this fact by itself was enough to keep off thieves, and if we have trust in such effect of his name we might let this Rama, this watchman, go, grant him *moksha*. Similarly, we should have faith that any physical labour undertaken in the spirit of service will produce rain.

That is a poet's explanation and it is correct. The word *yajna* comes from the root *yaj,* which means "to worship", and we please God by worshipping Him through physical labour. What should we do if we want rain over a desert? We should plant trees there. We should plant trees in any region over which we want rain, and cut them down in those regions where it rains in excess.

The original intention behind the idea of *yajna* was that people should do physical work. We forgot the root and came to concern ourselves with branches and leaves, believing that by pouring oblations into fire we perform a *yajna.* In the old days, it was necessary to cut down trees and burn up the wood in order to clear the land. **What was the idea in the pupils approaching their teachers wood in hand? Cutting down trees and burning wood had become a form of *yajna.* At the present time, spinning has become a *yajna.*** If water was scarce and we had to fetch it from a distance of two miles, fetching water would be a *yajna.*

Laborare est orare—Work is worship. We can connect this dictum with the idea in this verse.

If we use our intellect for serving others, would that also not be a form of *yajna?* This verse does not say that all forms of *yajna* produce rain. It only says that without *yajna* there can be no rain. That does not mean that all forms of *yajna* can produce rain, just as it is not true that all edible things can support life.

It may be asked what connection there can be between the facts of physical life and spiritual matters? The laws which hold in the spiritual world hold also in the phenomenal world. All the rules which concern the physical body have the welfare of the atman as their aim. That should be our primary aim in all our physical activities. We must turn away from everything which does not help us to attain self-realization. One thing, of course, is true. Just as bodily labour undertaken with a view to service will produce rain, so the employment of our intellect in the service of others will promote the welfare of the world.

How do we explain the fact that sometimes *yajna* fails to produce rain? An effect follows a chain of causes, all of which are not visible to us. Besides *yajna,* many other favourable circumstances have to be present. We have no ground for believing that a given action must always produce a given effect. There may have been a thousand other factors which had contributed to the appearance of that effect on a previous occasion.

No event or action is without its effect. Was the earthquake in Japan at the end of the last war the result of Divine wrath? The explanation was that when man becomes cruel, nature too may become so. There is, however, no question of cruelty on the part of nature. How can we regard anything which is pure justice as cruelty? Man does everything through pride. Not so God. To attribute cruelty to Him is to measure Him with a yardstick which we apply to human beings. This is the point of view which produced philosophical atheism. How can we turn God into a human being? From another point of view, He certainly acts, for he bestows life and consciousness. It is He who is ever active and does everything, hears without ears and sees without eyes. It is not correct to believe that an earthquake may be punishment for sin.

Why should we believe, either, that an earthquake is a punishment? If a nation is sunk in sin and God wants to save it, He might send an earthquake with that aim. If I wish to commit an immoral act, a most heinous one, and if God sends a snake to bite me in order to prevent me from doing what I intend, would that be His wrath? He does that in order to save me. Take the story of Nala and Karkotak. Karkotak told Nala that if he did not transform him into an ugly figure, he, Nala, would perish with the advent of *Kaliyuga.* Similarly, we should not believe that possession of a kingdom is necessarily the reward of holy merit earned by our goodness. God's ways are inscrutable. We should be afraid of answering all such questions. We may answer simply that we do not know. Of course, we can know God's laws, we have a right to ask what they are. But a wise man restrains his curiosity and tries to know only as much as is necessary for attaining self-realization. Even in that sphere, there ought to be a limit somewhere. Even scientists have not been able to discover how the soul comes into being. I do not find it impossible to imagine that one day man will be able to prevent earthquakes, just as he is able to change the courses of rivers. But the power to bring about such changes is a trivial matter. The laws of physical nature pale into insignificance when compared with those of the atman, for the former concern only the world of name and form.

It is wise not to have too much curiosity regarding them. We may know what is necessary for us in order to offer praise to God, and, having acquired enough for that purpose, we should have no more curiosity in such matters.

But the man who revels atman who is content atman and who is satisfied only with atman, for him no action exists.

He has no interest whatever in anything done, nor in anything not done, nor has he need to rely on anything for personal ends. (17, 18)

There is nothing for such a person to do; not that he does nothing, but it makes no difference to him whether he does or does not do it. He is equally unconcerned in either case. He has no end to pursue through other beings,

It may seem to us that both the verses say the same thing. If we do not think carefully, we shall probably feel that they contradict the verses which precede them. It was said in one of them that anyone who refused to work the rotating wheel was a sinful and indolent man. Here, on the other hand, it is said with reference to the man living contented in the atman that there is nothing for him to do. It may seem, but it is not, a paradox to say that one who works in the spirit of service will live contented in his self and there will be nothing which he wants to do. If we place an ant on a ball and keep the latter rotating, there will be nothing for the ant to do but to rest where it is, content with itself. It will tell itself that the ball was rotating, and itself with it, and that was enough. If, now, an ant-hill was provided inside the ball and it was necessary for the ant to move and reach it, it would say that it would be moving inside a rotating ball and have to exercise no choice in doing so.

What duty can a prisoner have? He merely carries out orders. The man who lives in the self makes himself the slave of the self. He carries out the orders of the self, and therefore, has his happiness in the self and lives contented in it. If he is all the time absorbed in listening to the voice of the self and acts so as to conform to the turning wheel, what would be there for him to do? Tolstoy states somewhere this same thing, that man in his foolishness boasts that he will do this and he will do that he will relieve the suffering of people in distress and so on. But it will be enough, says Tolstoy, if this person comes down from off the backs of the people he is sitting on. The people on whose backs he is riding, they have nothing to do. We are riding on the backs of the poor. There is nothing we need do, except get off their backs—if, that is, we follow only the voice of the self inside. There is nothing for us to do because we are not even aware of doing anything when we do it spontaneously.

Thus, the man who refused to do *yajna* was described earlier as *indriyarama,* as an incorrigible idler, and another who is ceaselessly employed in work is described as one who is content in the self. He works so much, and that spontaneously, that there is nothing for him to do.

> *Therefore, do thou ever perform without attachment the work that thou must do; for performing action without attachment man attains the Supreme. (19)*

The verses here have different meanings, but it is not that one verse applies to the enlightened man and the other to the man yet striving for enlightenment. One and the same verse can be understood to apply to both, in the same way that the *Gita* as a whole can be interpreted to refer to both the types of war, the outer and the inner. This verse, therefore, means that we may say of a person whose attachment to the ego has disappeared that there is no karma for him, that he may do something and yet do nothing.

> *For through action alone Janaka and others achieved perfection; even with a view to the guidance of mankind thou must act. (20)*

When Janaka was informed that his city was burning, he merely said: what if it is burning? The man who is directing the operations of a fire brigade can go on giving directions only if he keeps himself where he is. Can he leave his place of duty if he is told that his town or his house is on fire? He has completely given up thinking about himself. The person who follows the maxim, "Honesty is the best policy," exchanges a diamond for a cowrie. If the man who follows truth does so with the hope that he will thereby succeed better in his business, his truthfulness will be a cause of bondage for him, but it will be the cause of his deliverance if he follows it for the sake of *moksha.* Anyone who acts in this manner is a yogi, for yoga means skill or wisdom in action. He who does all these things with a selfish motive is a mere stone; he who does them for the highest end is like Jada

Bharata, though, in the end, he does attain illumination. The line "Live as you like" applies to him. For that, however, the person should go on working ceaselessly. "He intends nothing to serve other ends". This can be said only of one who has cleansed himself completely of the ego.

> *Whatever the best man does is also done by other men; what example he sets, the world follows. (21)*

People will adopt the standards which such a person sets. They will always observe what the eminent do. To what extent does Gandhi follow truth in life? Even the thoughts in which a great man indulges will produce an effect. His is a lame truthfulness who speaks truth as a matter of policy, but he who is truthful in his thoughts will act right though he be dumb. Every thought of such a person is bound to come true. He is the ideal man whose actions, speech and thought are in harmony with one another. Everyone will follow him. This is the reason why I have placed the spinning-wheel before people; if there are any who devote themselves to it whole-heartedly, all will follow them. If those who worship an image of clay can realize God, why not a person who spins in this spirit?

We should learn from this verse that if young people follow the bad example of their elders, it is the elders who should be blamed.

> *For me, O Partha, there is naught to do in the three worlds, nothing worth gaining that I have not gained; yet I am ever in action. (22)*

For whom should one cook for one already full or for one fasting? For others, of course.' To Shri Krishna, the whole world is a guest, and he loves all the creatures in it—and he must, for the world is his creation! People look upon me as Purushottam, says Krishna, so I must observe proper measure in everything, otherwise the universe would perish.

> *Indeed, for were I not, unslumbering ever to remain in action, O Partha, men would follow my example in every way. (23)*

'I have to be busy every moment to see that the world goes on, for I am its ruler, I am the master of the ceremonies. Since I make the world dance as I will, I am also called Natavar.' This ruler of the world cannot afford to sleep by day or by night, nor can he rest from work.

If I were not to perform my task, these worlds would be ruined; I should be the cause of chaos and of the end of all mankind. (24)

I must, says Krishna, keep the fire burning the whole day, otherwise there would be confusion in the social order, and, I would be responsible for the destruction of society.

We work so that we may please God, and if we give up doing that the people will observe no discipline, will refuse to work and feel completely lost.

Just as, with attachment, the unenlightened perform all actions, O Bharata, even so, but unattached, should the enlightened man act, with a desire for the welfare of humanity. (25)

One must work just as ignorant people do, except that they work with attachment. We, too, must take up a pick-axe and work like them. A wise man should be as industrious and work as hard as others; only, he should work for the good of the world, disinterestedly and without attachment. If you work in this spirit, you are a man of spiritual knowledge and, though working, are doing nothing. Does a person who has kept the *ekadashi* fast commit a sin by attending to cooking? He or she cooks, in a disinterested spirit, for children and guests.

The enlightened may not confuse the mind of the unenlightened, who are attached to action; rather must he perform all actions unattached, and thus encourage them to do likewise. (26)

A wise man should not confuse the judgment of ignorant people who are attached to the work which they do, should not, for instance, ask them to go without a thing because we can do so. Shri Krishna has said a little earlier that if he did not work for the people, there would be confusion of *varnas* in society. He says the same thing in this verse in different words. If Arjuna took any unexpected step, people would not understand his intention and might do something which he had never wanted them to do. He had asked those hundreds of thousands of men to assemble there ready for battle. How could he, now, cause confusion in their minds? He should, therefore, go on doing his duty in the spirit of yoga, unattached to the fruits of his work, and inspire others to work likewise.

All action is entirely done by the gunas of prakriti. Man, deluded by the sense of 'I', thinks 'I am the doer'. (27)

The man who is sunk in ignorance believes in his pride that his actions are his, whereas they are prompted by his nature, by *sattva, rajas* and *tamas*. Anyone who says that he bats his eyelids is either a fool or suffering from a disease of the eye. He does not wink his eyes really, he harms them. But he who acts as if he were a mere witness of his actions will win admiration for everything he does. The work done by a person without much ability but also without attachment to his ego will produce better results than done by another who is attached to his ego.

Take the example of a state ruled by a king and his minister. The latter works within the framework of the administrative set-up. In just the same way, we are pilgrims in this world and obey the laws of the world. If we lay claim to what we are prompted by our nature to do, we sow confusion in the minds of the ignorant. We should realize that we are no more than servants bound to carry out another's orders, and should voluntarily act as if we were slaves. Mira described herself as being a slender thread, because she submitted to her nature. She used the phrase "slender thread" because she had submitted herself to God's will so completely that there was no question of her resisting. He who eats simply to give the body its hire will not think of pleasing his palate. Anyone who lives in accordance with this law will forget his ego completely, surrender to Krishna everything he does.

The following verse presents a problem, for its meaning has been completely perverted. It is interpreted without any reference to the context. There was a libertine in Rajkot. He used this verse to justify his dissolute life. He was a student of the shastras and could cite appropriate Sanskrit verses, on occasion, and so enjoyed a good status in society. He used to say that nature followed its own urges and that, therefore, he was not to blame, that he was untouched by either sin or virtue.

But he, O Mahabahu, who understands the truth of the various gunas and their various activities, knows that it is the gunas that operate on the gunas; he does not claim to be the doer. (28)

He who classifies *gunas* and karma into their sub-divisions, divides them into their different types and then analyses each, and so arrives at the truth about them will know that everything is the result of *gunas* acting upon one another and will not get involved in their activities through attachment to them. The impostor I mentioned used to say that *prakriti* was God's *maya*, and he was not responsible for her actions. If, however, we understand the meaning which the term *prakriti* bears in the preceding verse, we shall see that there was nothing we need to do of our own choice. Only that person who has ceased to be attached to any work can say, like King Janaka, that he is not responsible for the actions of his *prakriti*. But the man who is full of ignorant attachment and thinks little cannot take cover behind this verse.

The point of this verse is, in the extremely difficult business of running this world, in the running of this intricate machine—the very thought of which is sufficient to make one's head spin—what is there that I can do? What strength have I? I dare not touch a single part of it. Anyone who considers carefully how this world is kept going will see that the different *gunas* are ceaselessly active and doing their work. Let us take the small example of the spinning-wheel. Suppose for a moment that the spindle became conceited. Its part in the working of the wheel is quite small. It has no motion of its own, and if it believed itself or the string to be the source of the motion, it would commit a grievous error. If it decides to become bent, it would produce a discordant note while rotating. It might feel that, instead of rotating monotonously, it was now moving in a novel manner, but it would soon lose its place. When dying, it might perhaps realize that it had made a terrible mistake, that its pride had cost it its very life.

Let us suppose now that the spindle has no such pride. It will then think that its motion was not its own, that it contributed nothing to the spinning, the string did its work and the wheel did its. It might then say that the *gunas* operate on the *gunas* and that its was of no interest to itself how they worked I must work, the spindle would tell itself, as a mere slave otherwise I and my relations would be ruined. It would then feel no pride and would no longer be carried away by foolish notions. We could say of such a spindle that it had learnt wisdom. The same argument applies to human beings. No one can go on indulging himself and then argue that his conduct was the result of the *gunas* doing their work according to their nature. We would come to grief if we made wrong comparisons. If, pointing to the example of an animal, we, too, act as it does, we would become animal.

A man, on the contrary, must bear in mind that he is a human being, and that he resembles animals up to a point and no more; that is, he resembles them in respect of the physical needs of sleeping, eating, breeding, etc. The man who decides that he need not eat and sleep as animals do, that he need not, like a dog fight for a piece of bread, such a person will reflect deeply and, having discovered the truth, always live as a mere witness. The animal instincts will not have completely disappeared, but he will realize, if he has understood the law which rules human life, that he must not be a slave to sleep, food and sex, that, in other words, the laws of animal life do not apply to him. As soon as he has understood the laws of *prakriti,* he will see that they are the basis of the laws governing human life. In regard to the machine of his body his only right, he now sees, is to maintain a disinterested attitude towards it. He will not, then, touch anything unclean with his hand or see it with his eyes.

Such a person will become free from bondage to the body and be able to say that in all his actions it is the *gunas* which act according to their nature, that the ears do their work of hearing, the eyes of seeing, and so on. He will act like the spindle in our example as if he were inert matter with no will of his own. His body will function mechanically. It will then indulge in immorality no more than a log of wood does. By its nature the human body is but a corpse and, by itself, is as sinless as a log. The senses will not do evil of themselves, so long as the mind which controls them does not wish to do evil. He who has discovered the law of human life will study the working of the *gunas* and act accordingly like the man who prints after setting the types carefully. The types which have become worn out have to be melted back into metal and cast again, and then reset: in like manner, the man who is guided by the truth that in all matters it is the *gunas* which do their work will make himself completely inert, doing nothing on his own.

The senses are not just 16,000 their number is infinite. If we make them dance as we wish, instead of ourselves dancing as they wish, we would be the directors of the drama of life. In the first Chapter, even the evil minded Duryodhana asks his warriors to remain in their positions and protect the patriarch Bhishma. If, likewise, we protect the director of the drama, who dwells within us, play our part in accordance with his instructions, the director would not become weak.

> *Deluded by the gunas of prakriti men become attached to the activities of the gunas; he who knows the truth of things should not unhinge the slow-witted who have not the knowledge. (29)*

This world is *maya*, it is a rotating wheel, and, therefore, those who are sunk in darkness remain attached to *guna* and karma. Those who are under the spell of the *gunas* of *prakriti* are swayed by all kinds of desires, yield to grief and ignorant attachments. The man of knowledge should not unsettle the ignorant, he should not lift him from one place and put him in another. For instance, says Shri Krishna to Arjuna, you are on a battlefield, ready for fighting, and so are these others; you have now chanced to learn some wisdom, but you should not, because of that, shake others from their beliefs. If anyone of us should suddenly become enlightened with profound knowledge, it does not mean that he would be able to change all others immediately. He is a fool who seeks to change overnight other people who are following their own ways in life. This, of course, does not mean that, where the system itself is bad, we should not try to reform it. That would be a complete perversion of this idea.

> *Cast all thy acts on Me, with thy mild fixed on the indwelling* atman, *and without any thought of fruit or sense of 'mine' shake off thy fever and fight! (30)*

After explaining all this—after explaining what karma is and why one should do it—Shri Krishna tells Arjuna than dedicating every action to Him, having purified his mind fixed it is his atman and emptied it of all desires, and without entertaining any thought of gain, he should go on doing karma (not that, Shri Krishna explains, he should win a kingdom and enjoy it but) as a matter of duty and irrespective of whether or not he was likely to benefit. We should, for instance, get up at four in the morning as a matter of duty without thinking whether it will do us any good. You should, Shri Krishna says, shed your att. chment to the ego and work—that is, work with the thought that you are not the doer of the karma and its fruit is not meant for you to enjoy, acting as if you were a piece of inert matter like the spindle of the spinning-wheel and like the wick of a lamp which goes on burning by itself. If I did not bring into existence all the factors necessary for the burning of the lamp, how would the wick burn? The wick was shut up within the cotton pad. How did that cotton know that it would one day be made into a wick? It was spun and twisted and then made into a wick.

If Arjuna wanted to be like the wick, to think of himself as the atman within and not his body, he must learn to shed his attachment to the ego and empty himself of all desires. By first choosing good against evil and then becoming unattached to either, one can transcend both. So long as we dwell in the body, it functions according to its nature. We should live in accordance with this truth, otherwise we shall invite moral ruin. We should, therefore, aim at the highest. The same is true about our aspiration for *moksha.* One who is already in water no longer desires to jump into it. If it were true that in water we melt away, we would not at all want to jump into it. Just then, however, *moksha* was not Arjuna's goal, nor did he aspire after it or hope for it. We should have as our ideal a state unaffected by hope or desire though, of course, our present state is that of human being, full of desires.

Being in a state unaffected by desire is the same as have the absolute conviction that we shall attain *moksha.* This idea of a state unaffected by desire is to be understood both in regard to our spiritual aspiration and the needs of the body, that is, both in regard to the ultimate goal and practical concerns. In regard to the former, there is no question of being affected by desire. The man who is incapable of doing evil, what interest can he have in good and evil? It is not true that, after the evil in one is completely destroyed, one is able to do good. We only imagine that it is so. When a person never feels the urge to use a sword, how can we attribute non-violence to him? This is a scientific truth, and not poetry: it states a principle concerning the atman. Be in such a state, Shri Krishna tells Arjuna, that is, be perfectly still in your mind, and fight. This idea that one should learn to act like inert matter occurs at many places in the *Mahabharata.* Why did Shri Krishna ask them to place an iron image of Bhima before Dhritarashtra? He made everyone his instrument, and then asked them to place an iron image of Bhima—what does all this mean? He asked Arjuna to become passion-free and fight, that is, to banish all impatience and anxiety from his mind and then fight. I would kill a snake or flea or bug only if I am angry or annoyed.

Now we shall discuss what Krishna meant when he asked Arjuna to "fight".

Shri Krishna asked Arjuna to banish all impatience and anxiety and then fight. When he said "fight", he meant that Arjuna should do what he regarded as his duty. If we could know every time what we should do, if everyone's duty, in a given situation was evident to him, all of us would have the same ideas of duty. But that is not so. On the contrary, we have to reflect to discover what our duty is. We have to apply numerous tests and then only do we see what our duty is. That is why Shri Krishna asks Arjuna to be passion-free and do his duty. One can do one's duty only if one banishes all impatience and anxiety in regard to it. Anyone who has lost control over his speech-organs will seem to talk in a disconnected fashion. The fact is that all of us talk in that manner.

An Italian has described all human beings as mad. If we were not mad, we would not indulge in all this vain prattle; though, even when prattling, we prefer to prattle in one way rather than another. Since, therefore, we must make a choice at every step, Arjuna is asked to do his duty without being over-excited about it, that is, without attachments and aversions. We need not doubt the intentions behind the actions of a mother who has ceased to make any distinction between her own child and another's. Freedom from attachment and aversion is the first step towards understanding one's duty. Following this line of thinking to its logical conclusion, we would see that a non-violent man is one who is free from attachments and aversions. For instance, Harishchandra saw the auspicious necklace round Taramati's neck and recognized it. He saw that he had to cut off the dear head of her whom he adored. You will ask me how this is an illustration of non-violence. Violence does not consist in the act of cutting off someone's head; it consists in the motive behind the act. How if we knew that Harishchandra would have preferred to kill himself rather than kill Taramati? Suppose it had been the King's order that, if the *chandal* could not bring himself to kill the person before him, he could kill himself, Harishchandra would have certainly preferred to put the knife to his own throat. But he was given no such choice. He had actually brought down the knife and it was then that the gods held back his hand.

Take another instance, that of a doctor who has to carry out an operation. The doctor who operated upon me was all kindness. Even if he was not, he did not in any case wish to harm me. If the doctor was called upon to amputate someone's leg, he would certainly not derive pleasure from the operation. His only motive would be to help the patient. Not only the doctor, but the patient too knows that the amputation is for his benefit. Thus operations involve the use of all kinds of knives and lancets, but they involve no violence.

A third instance. Let us suppose that a man has had his head half cut and it is hanging loose from the neck. He signs to passers-by and requests them to kill him so that he might be spared the suffering. Most passers-by, let us suppose, take no notice and go on. One, however, stops and looks at the man, sees his suffering and realizes that his death is certain. This person, then, may surely severe the head completely and end his suffering. This, too, is non-violence. It is so because the passer-by was not prompted by any selfish motive in what he did.

We hear in our country many persons advance such arguments to justify killing but they are insincere; those, for example, who kill snakes are cowards. They are afraid of dying themselves, and their only thought in killing a snake is to save themselves from being bitten by it. The violence involved in killing a snake may be pardonable, but violence there certainly is. There is violence may be pardonable violence in killing even a person who is the most wicked of men in the eyes of the world, for killing him will not make the world a happier place, and those who kill him do not do so because they are really concerned about his welfare. If one person is out to destroy the entire world, and all the people in the world prefer to be destroyed rather than kill him, it is possible that that person will be terrified by the violence he would have perpetrated, and after that there would be no more violence in the world.

Thus, to be *vigatajvara* means to be without aversions and attachments. One may even commit violence then. If anyone, deceiving himself, commits violence in the name of non violence, of course he would not attain *moksha.* There is a possibility of *moksha* for one who commits violence but knows that he does so, but there is none for the hypocrite.

And so Shri Krishna said, "Cast all thy acts on Me." He thus asked Arjuna to fulfil a number of conditions and then to fight.

Those who always act according to the rule I have here laid down, in faith and without cavilling,—they too are released from the bondage of their actions. (31)

To do one's duty means to fight and struggle. Since every karma involves a choice, there is necessarily a struggle. Even though caught in this way between opposites, you will have transcended them if you dedicate every action to Krishna, do everything without attachment or aversion, have faith in God and present every karma as a gift to Him. If you believe God to be the author of all you do, you will be touched neither by sin nor by virtue. God comes down in the form of Vaman, with an appealing face like a mother's, and begs us to trust everything to Him. He who accepts my teaching, says Shri Krishna, and acts accordingly, without attachments and aversions and without partiality to anyone, is not bound by the effects of any karma.

But those who cavil at the rule and refuse to confirm to it are fools, dead to all knowledge; know that they are lost.

Even a man of knowledge acts according to his nature; all creatures follow their nature; what then will constraint avail? (32, 33)

This verse has been taken to mean that a wicked person can never reform himself. An instance of this is provided here by that girl; she lies there away from us, and how can we persuade her to change her ways? But, then, the aspiration to realize God is also part of human nature. The beast's nature is merely to feed and sleep. It cannot meditate on Rama every morning, but man is different. But this verse says something altogether different: all creatures follow their nature. If a person has the nature of an animal, how far will another succeed, try as long as he might, in reforming that person? How long can we keep such a person suppressed? What can we do to a person who refuses to behave better than an animal?

I could have hit that girl with my sandals, but it would have made her more obstinate still. One day, however, she may feel Rama's grace and, remembering this incident, reform herself. This verse is not intended to discourage a man from struggling against his nature. One must of course struggle to improve oneself. But should some other person tell us day in and day out that we remain as beasts and do not improve, there is bound to be a quarrel every time. Take the example of a teacher and a pupil. If the pupil himself tells the teacher that the latter should cane him or box his ears whenever he did anything wrong, the teacher should certainly do that.

We mentioned three illustrations of non-violence. This is one more instance of it. Pupils such as the one in this illustration control themselves and are also controlled by others. Our minds may be disturbed by innumerable evil desires, but we do not welcome them, as we do not welcome a disease which may attack us. Our natural desire is to get well, and the doctor, therefore, is free to put any restrictions on us; the patient will thank him for doing so. But what good will it do to punish a person who does not himself wish to change? Anyone who has ceased to be a human being and behaves like a beast cannot be reformed by others, true though it is that Rama dwells in his heart too. Of course, one should never despair of being able to improve oneself. But how can outward self-control help a man to whom wickedness has become second nature? His release can come only with death. Ravana told Mandodari that he was an enemy of Rama, that he wished to die. And die he did, through his own sins.

Nigraha means trying to control oneself or others. One may try to control a friend, or one's wife or sister or pupil if they wish to reform themselves. But what can we do if they oppose us? What can even an emperor do to a person who has abandoned all shame? No one will succeed in his efforts to reform such a person.

We can offer satyagraha only against a person who has some love in his heart. We can control another only if there is mutual love between us; where there is no such love, the only course for us is non-cooperation with the other party. Tulsidas advised non-cooperation with the wicked.

Men believe in their pride that they can imprison others and beat them into submission. But we know that thefts and murders have not stopped. What, then, should one do? Everyone should look after himself. This verse certainly does not mean that one should not try even to control oneself, for we have already read: holding all these in check, the yogi should sit intent on Me. The senses are so powerful that trying to control them taxes our energy to the utmost and involves us in violent struggle against ourselves. Shri Krishna tells Arjuna there that he who controls them—passionately beats them down into submission and reins them in, as we do a horse—we do no violence in using the whip thus—and sits meditating on Him, self-controlled, is a man established in *samadhi.* A little later, he says: therefore Mahabahu, he whose senses are reined in on all sides from their objects...

Nigraha means another person trying to impose discipline on us. Addressed to Arjuna, the verse means: "If you believe that you can control your army, you should understand that it will not obey you, for it does not think as you do, its heart is set on fighting. By ruining away from battle, you will be instrumental in the warriors forsaking the traditional duty of their caste and being guilty of conduct unwound of themselves."

> *Each sense has its settled likes and dislikes toward its objects; man should not come under the story of these, for they are his besetters. (34)*

Attachment and aversion are an inseparable pair. The sense feel either the one or the other towards their objects. We should not be swayed by them, for they are the thieves trying to rob the *purusha* within us. They are ever after us, go where we will, and rob us of all our earnings. There is thus the fullest scope for human striving; in fact, it is one's duty to strive. Having done that duty, one may console oneself with the preceding verse; struggling tirelessly, we may tell ourselves that we can go no further than our nature permits. But taking up such an attitude does not help us. We must continue to struggle ceaselessly. We should continue till we reach the breaking point and that with the conviction that we are bound to succeed. Any man or woman or child who takes cover behind the preceding verse and stops struggling will be a thief in God's eyes. The line, "seeking pearls, men plunge into the sea, reckless of their lives," describes the spirit of desperate earnestness in striving.

> *Better one's own duty, bereft of merit, than another's well-performed; better is death in the discharge of one's duty; another's duty is fraught with danger. (35)*

We should strive to the best of our ability in our own sphere of work, but waste no effort on anything which lies outside it. It would be dangerous for us to go and live in a mansion in Bombay, but it would be a sign of our being happy if we are content to live here in the Ashram.

To speak the truth is a dharma common to all. But there are special duties, that is, duties which pertain to individuals. Suppose that one's job is to clean lavatories. Such a person should not envy another whose job is to keep accounts. The man who cleans lavatories as carefully as he does the utensils in his home, observes his dharma in the truest manner. It would not be right for Arjuna to think of retiring to a forest and spending his days telling beads on the rosary. His duty was to fight and kill. Retiring to a forest may be the right course for a *rishi,* it was not so for Arjuna. Even if the dharma meant for Arjuna seemed less worthy, for him it was the best. Why should he, Shri Krishna asks him, talk egotistically, acting like the proverbial dog who believed that he was drawing the heavily-laden cart? He assures Arjuna that, if there was any sin in the latter following his dharma, the responsibility for that would be His, Krishna's. During the years which Ramachandra spent in the forest, Bharat did not himself rule the kingdom as king but acted as the former's representative. Ramachandra's sandals were placed on the throne and Bharat carried on the administration in Ramachandra's name. There was not a moment when he was not absorbed in thinking on Rama. Similarly, Shri Krishna asks Arjuna why he thought that, if he won the battle, the kingdom would be his. If he had no wish to enjoy the fruits of his effort, it was actually his dharma to fight and win the kingdom. He should act only as an instrument.

Arjuna asks:

Then what impels man to sin, O Varshneya, even against his will, as though by force compelled? (36)

How is it that a person is often driven to a wrong path against his or her will?

The Lord answers:

It is Lust, it is Wrath, born of the guna—rajas. It is the arch-devourer, the arch-sinner. Know this to be man's enemy here. (37)

The reply, according to Shri Krishna, was simple. When the child refuses to go to school, is simply unwilling to go, what is the reason? He refuses to go because he wants to run away with a bad play-fellow or because he is planning some mischief. Thus, one cause is *kama.* It is man's evil thoughts which drive him to evil deeds. The second cause is anger. We get angry when we do not get the thing we want. Anger has its source in *rajas.* These two great enemies of man drive him to sin. The reign of *kama* is different in its effect from the reign of Rama. Those who prosper under Rama's reign understand the sport of God which this creation is. Those, on the other hand, who are swayed by desire and anger will see, in the creation, not Rama's sport, but Satan's. Like Kumbhakarna *kama* is ever waiting, open-mouthed, for its prey. When its appetite is not satisfied, its victim is filled with anger. Know, Shri Krishna tells Arjuna, that this is your enemy. Since, the two are twins, He has used the singular pronoun *enam*.

> *As fire is obscured by smoke, a mirror by dirt, and the embryo by the amnion, so is knowledge obscured by this. (38)*

If there is any smoke, it stays only for a while. As soon as it has gone, the fire gives full heat. The mirror will have to be cleaned, and only then will it give service, provided of course we know that the thing is a mirror. But the foetus covered by the placenta can do nothing about it, it cannot even cry. The man who is under the sway of desire and anger passes through these three stages.

> *Knowledge is obscured, O Kaunteya, by this eternal enemy of the wise man in the form of Lust, the insatiable fire. (38)*

This *kama* harms, like an enemy, even a man of spiritual knowledge.

> *The senses, the mind and the reason are said to be its seat; by means of these it obscures knowledge and stupefies man. Therefore, O Bharat-arshabha, bridle thou first the senses and then rid thyself of this sinner, the destroyer of knowledge and discrimination.*

> *Subtle, they say, are the senses; subtler than the senses is the mind; subtler than the mind is the reason; but subtler even than the reason is He. (40-42)*

Shri Krishna now explains the various stages. It is true indeed that the senses are powerful—they control the body. The mind is stronger than the senses and the intellect stronger than the mind. But stronger still than the intellect is the atman which dwells in the body. The senses, the mind and the intellect, these three are the dwelling places of desire and anger. But the atman in you, Shri Krishna tells Arjuna, is higher than all of them. If we seize the house in which the enemy lodges, we shall be able to kill him, or he will leave the place and run away. Occasionally, one may forget Him who is the Lord over these three, but that need not worry us, since the moment we think about that Lord we shall be able to overcome all of them.

> *Thus realizing Him to be subtler than the reason, and controlling the self by the Self* (Atman), *destroy,* O *Mahabahu, this enemy—Lust, so hard to overcome.* (43)

"Subduing the atman by the atman" means overcoming the baser, the demoniac impulses in the mind through the atman, that is, through the god-ward impulses; in other words, Arjuna should, Shri Krishna tells him, master his egotistic instincts by striving for spiritual welfare and, assured that his real self was more potent than the intellect, he should storm the fort and seize it. The senses are the gate-keepers and the mind is the minister. What the senses tell the mind is reported by the latter to the intellect, and the intellect decides and issues its order. If, however, we regain the sovereignty which is rightfully ours, then we would be able to subdue the mind, the intellect and the senses whom at present we have accepted as our masters, as in our country we have accepted foreigners as our masters and believe that we get the food we eat because of them.

Our atman should be vigilant day and night. One whose atman is so awake will not have dreams in his sleep. But we are bound to have them if we are slaves of sleep. Shri Krishna thus assures Arjuna that, if he keeps constant watch, he will be reassured neither by thieves coming in from outside nor by those that dwell within. If we do not establish our rule over the body, it will yearn for things which we do not approve of and we shall forfeit our authority over it.

If we wish to deal worthily by even the most wicked person, we should assume that he has no evil intention. He is bound to have good feelings somewhere deep in his heart. The atman never gets angry. It remains unattached and unmoved. If we cannot overcome desire or anger in us even in some measure, we should tolerate them when they invade us.

No one has yet succeeded in laying down a universal rule about how we should act towards a thief. We should, however, bear in mind that however we act we should be inspired by love for him. We must think and find out how we may win him over with love. We should assume that it is not in human nature to steal. Even as rational beings we should be convinced that there is no human being in the world who is beyond all hope of change. Love is a kind of force of attraction. Science tells us that even dust has the property of attracting other things. Even a particle of dust possesses some kind of power of attraction; that is why Mirabai sings about the bond of love. That bond is much stronger than that of a slender thread can ever be. Why should we be filled with passion or get angry whenever we lose anything?

Such is the yoga described in this third Chapter. There is ceaseless movement and change. We cannot choose but work with the body as ceaselessly as the ball of this earth rotates. What is the way, then, of saving ourselves from work? The *Gita* replies that, by shedding all attachment and aversion, we escape the fruits of our actions.

❑❑❑

4

ज्ञानकर्मसंन्यासयोग

श्रीभगवानुवाच

इमं विवस्वते योगं प्रोक्तवानहमव्ययम्। विवस्वान् मनवे प्राह मनुरिक्ष्वाकवेऽब्रवीत्।। 1

एवं परम्पराप्राप्तमिमं राजर्षयो विदुः। स कालेनेह महता योगो नष्टः परन्तप।। 2

स एवायं मया तेऽद्य योगः प्रोक्तः पुरातनः। भक्तोऽसि मे सखा चेति रहस्यं ह्येतदुत्तमम्।। 3

अर्जुन उवाच

अपरं भवतो जन्म परं जन्म विवस्वतः। कथमेतद्विजानीयां त्वमादौ प्रोक्तवानिति।। 4

श्रीभगवानुवाच

बहूनि मे व्यतीतानि जन्मानि तव चार्जुन। तान्यहं वेद सर्वाणि न त्वं वेत्थ परन्तप।। 5

अजोऽपि सन्नव्ययात्मा भूतानामीश्वरोऽपि सन्। प्रकृतिं स्वामधिष्ठाय सम्भवाम्यात्ममायया।। 6

यदा यदा हि धर्मस्य ग्लानिर्भवति भारत। अभ्युत्थानमधर्मस्य तदात्मानं सृजाम्यहम्।। 7

परित्राणाय साधूनां विनाशय च दुष्कृताम्। धर्मसंस्थापनार्थाय सम्भवामि युगे युगे। 8

जन्म कर्म च मे दिव्यमेवं यो वेत्ति तत्त्वतः। त्यक्त्वा देहं पुनर्जन्म नैति मामेति सोऽर्जुन।। 9

वीतरागभयक्रोधा मन्मया मामुपाश्रिताः। बहवो ज्ञानतपसा पूता मद्भावमागताः।। 10

ये यथा मां प्रपद्यन्ते तांस्तथैव भजाम्यहम्। मम वर्त्मानुवर्तन्ते मनुष्याः पार्थ सर्वशः।। 11

काङ्क्षन्तः कर्मणां सिद्धिं यजन्त इह देवताः। क्षिप्रं हि मानुषे लोके सिद्धिर्भवति कर्मजा।। 12

चातुर्वर्ण्यं मया सृष्टं गुणकर्मविभागशः। तस्य कर्तारमपि मां विद्ध्यकर्तारमव्ययम्।। 13

न मां कर्माणि लिम्पन्ति न मे कर्मफले स्पृहा। इति मां योऽभिजानाति कर्मभिर्न स बद्ध्यते।। 14
एवं ज्ञात्वा कृतं कर्म पूर्वैरपि मुमुक्षुभिः। कुरु कर्मैव तस्मात्त्वं पूर्वैः पूर्वतरं कृतम्।। 15
किं कर्म किमकर्मेति कवयोऽप्यत्र मोहिताः। तत्ते कर्म प्रवक्ष्यामि यज्ज्ञात्वा मोक्ष्यसेऽशुभात्।। 16
कर्मणो ह्यपि बोद्धव्यं बोद्धव्यं च विकर्मणः। अकर्मणश्च बोद्धव्यं गहना कर्मणो गतिः।। 17
कर्मण्यकर्म यः पश्येदकर्मणि च कर्म यः। स बुद्धिमान् मनुष्येषु स युक्तः कृत्स्नकर्मकृत्।। 18
यस्य सर्वे समारम्भाः कामसङ्कल्पवर्जिताः। ज्ञानाग्निदग्धकर्माणं तमाहुः पण्डितं बुधाः। 19
त्यक्त्वा कर्मफलासङ्गं नित्यतृप्तो निराश्रयः। कर्मण्यभिप्रवृत्तोऽपि नैव किञ्चित्करोति सः।। 20
निराशीर्यतचित्तात्मा त्यक्तसर्वपरिग्रहः। शारीरं केवलं कर्म कुर्वन्नाप्नोति किल्बिषम्।। 21
यदृच्छालाभसन्तुष्टो द्वन्द्वातीतो विमत्सरः। समः सिद्धावसिद्धौ च कृत्वापि न निबध्यते।। 22
गतसङ्गस्य मुक्तस्य ज्ञानावस्थितचेतसः। यज्ञायाचरतः कर्म समग्रं प्रविलीयते। 23
ब्रह्मार्पणं ब्रह्म हविर्ब्रह्माग्नौ ब्रह्मणा हुतम्। ब्रह्मैव तेन गन्तव्यं ब्रह्मकर्मसमाधिना।। 24
दैवमेवापरे यज्ञं योगिनः पर्युपासते। ब्रह्माग्नावपरे यज्ञं यज्ञेनैवोपजुह्वति।। 25
श्रोत्रादीनीन्द्रियाण्यन्ये संयमाग्निषु जुह्वति। शब्दादीन् विषयानन्य इन्द्रियाग्निषु जुह्वति।। 26
सर्वाणीन्द्रियकर्माणि प्राणकर्माणि चापरे। आत्मसंयमयोगाग्नौ जुह्वति ज्ञानदीपिते।। 27
द्रव्ययज्ञास्तपोयज्ञा योगयज्ञास्तथापरे। स्वाध्यायज्ञानयज्ञाश्च यतयः संशितव्रताः।। 28
अपाने जुह्वति प्राणं प्राणेऽपानं तथाऽपरे। प्राणापानगती रुद्ध्वा प्राणायामपरायणाः।। 29
अपरे नियताहाराः प्राणान् प्राणेषु जुह्वति। सर्वेऽप्येते यज्ञविदो यज्ञक्षपितकल्मषाः।। 30
यज्ञशिष्टामृतभुजो यान्ति ब्रह्म सनातनम्। नायं लोकोऽस्त्ययज्ञस्य कुतोऽन्यः कुरुसत्तम।। 31
एवं बहुविधा यज्ञा वितता ब्रह्मणोमुखे। कर्मजान् विद्धि तान् सर्वानेवं ज्ञात्वा विमोक्ष्यसे।। 32
श्रेयान् द्रव्यमयाद्यज्ञाज्ज्ञानयज्ञः परन्तप। सर्वं कर्माखिलं पार्थ ज्ञाने परिसमाप्यते।। 33
तद्विद्धि प्रणिपातेन परिप्रश्नेन सेवया। उपदेक्ष्यन्ति ते ज्ञानं ज्ञानिनस्तत्त्वदर्शिनः।। 34
यज्ज्ञात्वा न पुनर्मोहमेवं यास्यसि पाण्डव। येन भूतान्यशेषेण द्रक्ष्यस्यात्मन्यथो मयि।। 35
अपि चेदसि पापेभ्यः सर्वेभ्यः पापकृत्तमः। सर्वं ज्ञानप्लवेनैव वृजिनं सन्तरिष्यसि।। 36
यथैधांसि समिद्धोऽग्निर्भस्मसात्कुरुतेऽर्जुन। ज्ञानाग्निः सर्वकर्माणि भस्मसात्कुरुते तथा।। 37
न हि ज्ञानेन सदृशं पवित्रमिह विद्यते। तत्स्वयं योगसंसिद्धः कालेनात्मनि विन्दति।। 38

श्रद्धावाँल्लभते ज्ञानं तत्परः संयतेन्द्रियः। ज्ञानं लब्ध्वा परां शान्तिमचिरेणाधिगच्छति।। 39

अज्ञश्चाश्रद्दधानश्च संशयात्मा विनश्यति। नायं लोकोऽस्ति न परो न सुखं संशयात्मनः।। 40

योगसंन्यस्तकर्माणं ज्ञानसञ्छिन्नसंशयम्। आत्मवन्तं न कर्माणि निबध्नन्ति धनञ्जय।। 41

तस्माद‌ज्ञानसम्भूतं हृत्स्थं ज्ञानासिनात्मनः। छित्त्वैनं संशयं योगमातिष्ठोत्तिष्ठ भारत।। 42

The Yoga of Knowledge and Renunciation of Work

The Lord says:

I expounded this imperishable yoga to Vivasvan; Vivasvan communicated it to Manu, and Manu to Ikshvaku.

Thus handed down in succession, the royal sages learnt it, with long lapse of time it dwindled away in this world, O Parantapa. (1, 2)

We are doing things every moment, but it is God who has placed us on his wheel and is moving it like a potter, producing ever new shapes. "This yoga was known from the beginning of time, but has perished in this age. People have forgotten the art of working without attachment and aversion. Were it not so," Shri Krishna said, "I would not have had to be a witness to this battle."

The same ancient yoga have I expounded to thee today; for thou art My devotee and My friend; and this is the supreme mystery. (3)

The highest truth may be imparted only to a *bhakta*, for such a person will serve the world's good.

Shri Krishna says, this yoga was known in ancient times, I taught it to Vivasvan, he taught it to Manu, and Manu taught it to Ikshavaku. At this Arjuna wonders. You and I, he says, live in the present age, and you say you taught this to people in former times; how can that be?

Arjuna asks:

Later was Thy birth, my Lord, earlier that of Vivasvan. How then am I to understand that Thou didst expound it in the beginning? (4)

The Lord says:

Many births have we passed through; O Arjuna, both thou and I; I know them all, thou knowest them not, O Parantapa. (5)

When we sing about the succession of births for human beings through 84,00,000 living forms, we refer to our having had countless lives before the present one, and we state our inference that death is only a change from an old house into a new one. But it is only a person who remembers his previous lives that can say this with certainty. Shri Krishna states categorically that, being a yogi, he remembered his previous existences but that Arjuna could not remember his. He could say this we cannot.

Though unborn and inexhaustible in My essence, though Lord of all beings, yet assuming control over My nature, I come into being by My mysterious power. (6)

The Hindu belief in avatars may present a difficulty to some of us. Avatar means descent. Our descent means God's descent too, for He is present in every creature and in every object. All this is His *maya.* All concrete things—our body, the material objects, all these—exist at definite points in space and time, but the atman was not born in time, it pervades all space and exists through all time. We do not know it by direct experience. If we wish to understand the principle known as God, either with the help of reason or through faith, we should first know the atman. What is it? So long as we live in ignorance, it is more distant than even the sky, but in our awakened state we cannot say that it is removed from us by even so much as an inch. It is that through which we came into being and through which we exist if you believe that you are that, then "I" and "you" are identical—but only a person devoid of egotism can assert that. "I" and "you" are identical in the sense in which the ring and chain are in the final analysis but gold. Name and form are only for a moment; while things have them, they are no more real than a mirage. That into which things merge when they cease to have name and form is ever the same.

And so Krishna says: "Though I was never born in time, though I am the Lord of all creatures, I incarnate Myself and am born as a human being."

This is the essential nature of the atman. If we realize this truth, we would always act in conformity with that nature; we then act, though born as human beings, as if we were never born. If the atman in each of us is identical with the atman in everyone else, one atman born in a body means all of then born, and all others born means that one born too. This is a difficult idea to grasp. "This is *maya,*" says Shri Krishna "and through it I incarnate Myself in this world time and again."

We can follow reason only up to a point. What, then, does avatar mean? It is not as if God comes down from above. It would be right to say, if we can say it without egotism, that each one of us is an avatar. The atman in every body is as potent as the atman in any other, though outwardly we see differences. In our awakened state all are one, though in our ignorant state we may seem separate existences. In real truth there are not several, there is only one.

If we constantly reflect over this essence named the atman we shall regard no one as an enemy to be killed and shall have nothing to get angry about. We shall then see that anyone who hits us hits himself too.

When Krishna says that He incarnates Himself as a human being, he only uses the idiom of common speech. God never incarnates Himself as an atman and is never born as a human being. He is ever the same. When, from our human point of view, we see special excellence in some individual, we look upon him as an avatar. In God's language there is no such word as avatar; it exists only in the language of human beings.

Arjuna asked Shri Krishna how He could have expounded this yoga to other people of olden times, to which Shri Krishna replied that they had many previous existences, which He remembered but Arjuna could not. He added that, though He was not subject to birth and change, though He was the Lord who dwelt in the hearts of all creatures, He submitted to the action of *prakriti,* which was His creation, and through the power of his *maya* came down to live on the earth.

He then proceeds to explain in what circumstances God incarnates Himself as a human being.

> *For whenever Right declines and Wrong prevails, then O Bharata, I come to birth. (7)*

In these lines Shri Krishna held out an assurance to the entire world. If God remained inactive when dharma was eclipsed, man would be helpless. In this *Kaliyuga,* all human efforts produce results contrary to what was intended. **Hindus and Muslims, for instance, continue to fight among themselves. Can anyone prevent this? I was passionately eager to do such penance that they should never fight. But all my efforts failed.** Does that mean that this fighting will go on for ever? Assuredly not. Will God let human beings overindulge their senses with impunity? He tells us that He will tolerate our self-indulgence within limits, for He knows that we would weary of it. I will tolerate, He says, a little fighting and will not incarnate on the earth just because of that. But when men recognize no limits in fighting, demolish temples and kill people indiscriminately, that would mean eclipse of dharma. That would be wickedness in the name of dharma, it would mean the spread of *adharma* and disorder.

Do not, God says to comfort men, give way to despair when such things happen. "It is good," He says, "that you feel helpless at such a time, for by making you feel so I humble your pride." We remember what Surdas says: "I have tried my strength in one way and another, till I am weary and can do no more; you must save me now;" that is how man thinks in his pride, that he will do this, and he will do that, but God humbles his pride. Man, however, has this promise from the Lord. He need not despair and feel that, if he fails in some task, it will not be done. Let him have faith that God will have it done. So the Lord has said in these lines that, whenever necessary, He comes down to live on the earth, and sets everything right. If He did not do that, He would not enjoy our worship and reverence. What dishonour can there ever be for a man who lives as God's slave? It is the slave's master who will be judged from the manner in which the slave lives. Is it, therefore, ever likely that God will let dharma be eclipsed? **If *adharma* prevails, God will forfeit our reverence and worship. He has, therefore, no choice but to incarnate Himself as a human being.**

To save the righteous, to destroy the wicked, and to reestablish Right I am born from age to age. (8)

Shri Krishna has told us that we do nothing, nor does He. Who, then, destroys the wicked, and how are they destroyed? It is God's inviolable law that karma never fails to produce its effect. We can say that a human being may be able to counteract the effects of karma, and yet assert that karma never fails to produce its effect. The point is not that a person may not have to suffer the fruits of his actions, but that, if he cultivates non-attachment, even while in fact suffering the fruits of action, he would not inwardly feel that he suffered them. But suffer them he must. No karma is ever forgiven. It is, therefore, the wickedness of the wicked which destroys them. When, in this world, one human being kills another, the former is only an instrument. Arjuna was a bowman of prowess and a brave warrior. When he killed his enemies, it was not his strength which prevailed against Duryodhana. The latter was destroyed by his own sins. Hence the saying, "The pot of sin is bound to break one day." If it was true that God comes down from above and destroys the wicked, He would be as much under the sway of ignorance as we are. But that is not what happens. If we have faith and understand God's law, we would be sure that the wicked would be destroyed through their own sins.

Destruction of the wicked does not mean their physical destruction. Physically, both the wicked and the virtuous perish. It may be that a *bhakta* will pass away in the prime of his youth, and a wicked person will live up to the age of 76; shall we say that this was an instance of God's injustice? Kesar Bhagat was bitten by a serpent yesterday and died; should we, therefore, believe that he was a wicked man? In fact he was a good man; he was, though a mere labourer, a *bhakta* and a man of upright character. We would be punished with degradation if we believed that a man must have been wicked because he died early.

Yes, it is true in one sense that the good do not die, for we sing their glory ever afterwards. Everyone sings the glory of Rama, but no one of Ravana. If we think of him still, it is in order that we may keep ourselves free from his sins, run away from them. On the contrary, if we sing the virtues of a man and assimilate them, let them sink into our very soul, they are bound to become stronger in us day by day. Virtues never die. If we see the contrary in the world, that is but God's *maya*. It is true that virtues are cultivated with effort, and that vices require no such effort; but ultimately vices perish and virtues prosper. The appearance to the contrary is the effect of *maya*. If that were not so, what is said here about "destruction of the wicked" would not be true.

Shri Krishna does not mean here physical destruction of the wicked, while the *vasana* with which a man died exists. He cannot but be born again. It is stated, it is true, that a good man will not be born again, but only if he rises above the plane of *gunas*. There is, beyond the *gunas* of good and evil, a state which is characterized by no *guna*. It is not an undesirable state, but a desirable one. It is the state of *moksha*, a state which endures for ever. But the assurance which God holds out here is not that goodness never perishes, but that evil most certainly does. When evil seems to prevail in the world, He, the witness within, manifests Himself and shows that in truth it does not, shows it by the example of His own life. When evil spreads in the world, some persons, inspired by God, feel in their hearts that it is not enough for them to be a little good, that they must do *tapascharya* and be exceptionally good, so good that people would look upon them as perfect manifestation of the Divine in man. That is how Shri Krishna came to be worshipped as the fullest avatar. God has in these verses assured man that, whenever dharma is eclipsed and the reign of *adharma* spreads, He comes into the world to protect the good, to destroy the wicked and restore the rule of dharma. This means that dharma is never destroyed. Shri Krishna did not say that while the wicked are destroyed, the good are not. He himself passed away, and that too meeting an untimely death.

If we take a total view, we shall see that it is not wickedness but goodness which rules the world. The wicked can prevail only when they number crores, but goodness will rule when embodied to perfection even in one person. Non-violence has been described as so powerful that all forces of violence subside in its presence. Under its influence, even beasts forget their nature. Even one good person can change the world. Such a one enjoys an empire over people's hearts; we do not, because we follow goodness only as best we may. The type of good man I have mentioned has but to send a message, and people will do what he wants them to do, such is the power of goodness, Where wickedness prevails, there is disorder in every field of life: but where goodness rules, order prevails and people are happy. They are happy not in the sense that their material needs are satisfied but in the sense that they lead virtuous and contended lives. As for material possessions, some men have crores of rupees and yet lead a distracted life; that is no sign of being happy.

This verse, then means that when *adharma* spreads, some men undertake *tapascharya* and, through their *tapascharya*, generate goodness in the world, Even the wicked bow in reference before goodness. Its power is felt by beasts too. This can happen even in the present age. Anyone who has completely shed hatred and ill will, who has succeeded in making his life a perfect embodiment of truth, can command everything in life. He does not have to ask that anything be done. He has only to wish and the wish will be fulfilled.

God does not have to be born and to die, to incarnate Himself on earth as a human being. It is but His *maya* that we see in the world. That *maya* is described here and we are reassured that wickedness prevails only for a while but goodness endures for ever. We should, therefore, cultivate goodness in ourselves and see that we do nothing whereby we may become wicked.

God destroys evil and restores goodness by inspiring man's heart with noble ideals. On the balance goodness must prevail in the world, otherwise the world would perish. We see that a family in which evil increases is ruined, like, for instance, the Yadava race, which perished. It had taken to evil ways. Though a man like Krishna dwelt among them, the Yadavas took to immorality and, drinking, fought among themselves and were killed. Even a strong and self-willed man whom no one dares attack will sooner or later fall at someone's hands; this is so true that no member of the Yadava race survived. When there is so much evil in the world that on the balance there is more of it than good, that their sum is a minus quantity, the destruction of the world is certain. The body endures only so long as there is vitality in it; in the same way, the world would perish if at any time there should be less of goodness and more of evil in it. That is why the Lord said that He appeared in the world in every age.

He who knows the secret of this My divine birth and action is not born again, after leaving the body; he comes to Me, O Arjuna. (9)

Is there any reason why such a person should not merge into God? He would see that his body was perishable, and that it was not worthwhile to waste his energy on it. Was it not better, he would ask himself, to strive to realize the immortal atman? The atman is confined in the cage of this body, held in the prison of the body like a criminal. All of us have committed a crime, so to say, and are, therefore, imprisoned in the body; witness, for instance, Tulsidas and Surdas saying in their poems that there was no greater sinner in the world than they. We sin from the moment we are born, and that is why we are born again and again. Being confined in the cage of this body, we cannot soar as high as we wish. But we can do so if we reflect over the mystery of God's incarnations and actions in the world of men. If we realize the truth about the atman which is a lion, we shall become lions. How can we realize that truth? To explain that, Shri Krishna says:

> *Freed from passion, fear and wrath, filled full with Me, relying on Me, and refined by the fiery ordeal of knowledge, many have become one with Me. (10)*

Those who know the mystery of God's incarnations and actions become free from attachments, from fear and anger," says Shri Krishna. "They become absorbed in Me. (If you open their hearts, you will find the image of Rama inside.) They live in complete surrender to Me. Purified by knowledge and *tapascharya* they have become as I am, have lost themselves in Me." Shri Krishna has explained here how we may know that a person has understood the mystery of God's incarnations and actions.

> *In whatever way men resort to Me, even so do I render to them,*
> *In every way, O Partha, the path men follow is Mine. (11)*

In other words, people reap as they sow. As the quality of your *bhakti,* so is its reward. If there is any motive behind your *bhakti,* if you seek anything through it, you will get what the quality of your *bhakti* entitles you to. You will get not what you wish to get, but what you deserve to get. We may wish to become God, but that does not mean that we shall become God. We shall get only that which we have earned by our manner of life. We shall get what we deserve. If you walk a distance of four miles, you will get only what is at the end of it. If you eat the herb *kariatu* to have a purge, it does not mean that the effect will follow. *Kariatu* will at the most cure a mild fever. If you swallow castor oil and then wish that you should get no motion, you cannot have it so. This is the meaning of the line: In whatever way men resort to Me, even so do I render to them.

Shri Krishna then says: *mama vartmanuvartante manushyah Partha sarvashah.*

"Everyone follows a path which leads to Me:" This verse has a history behind it. When Tilak Maharaj was alive, he had cited this verse in the course of a discussion about violence and non-violence. I had argued that we should bear with a person who might have slapped us. In reply, he cited this verse to prove that the *Gita* upheld the principle of "tit for tat". That is, we should act towards a person as he acts towards us. I cling to the reply which I gave to him then. I had argued that this verse could not be used in support of his contention. We should not act towards a person as he acts towards us. If he is bad to us, we may not therefore be bad to him.

This verse merely lays down God's law. Shri Krishna says that He will worship a person as the latter worships Him. That means, we reap as we sow. One cannot do evil to others and expect good for oneself. Man has no right to return two slaps for one. But a principle quite the opposite of this prevails in the world, and as education spreads the position becomes worse. Uncivilized people may return two slaps for one, may fight back when attacked, and among them the relation of father and son may not be always sweet. If, however, a father behaves as a civilized man, he would use wisdom and endure the son's misconduct in patience, and so teach him to behave with humility. If the son is good, then he would suffer his parents weaknesses in patience, and that is the better way of the two. We prefer the second to the first. Besides, we read in the preceding verse about the type of man who can realize God. It says that those serene persons who are *vitaragabhayakrodhah,* that is, who are free from all attachment, fear and anger, realize God. The present verse cannot contradict that one, but completes its meaning. The previous verse says that a person who yields to attachment and anger will of realize God. If one yields to anger, one will reap the fruit of anger. We are thus taught not to yield to anger but to banish attachment, fear and anger from us.

In the second line, therefore, the Lord says that men are governed by His law. He means that law, the law of karma, which rules the world. We can truly say that God is law. God created His law and left the world to its governance, reserving to Himself no right to interfere with its operation. He then told men to decide for themselves whether they would or would not continue to be born in the world, as though making the position clear to them in advance so that they might not blame Him afterwards.

If we worship God, He would be pleased; but it does not mean that, if we do not worship Him, He would be displeased and would change His law. The law is immutable. Ishvar is not a ruler though literally the word means "a ruler". But, then, since God does nothing, he suffers nothing either. He neither acts nor suffers the consequences of action. He stands apart, detached. We have given free rein to our imagination and employed all manner of epithets to describe God, and we quarrel about Him needlessly. Take the instance of the Jain and the Vedanta philosophies. According to the latter, all things are pervaded by God, whereas the former holds that no such being as God exists. We adopt a third attitude,—one which is the right one for laymen to adopt—namely, that God both exists and does not exist. God is not a ruler; He is all-pervasive, He is life, He is unconditioned and devoid of form. His rule consists in the rule of His law. No one has questioned the existence of His law. Not a single school of philosophy has done so. That law is of course a living law. If we equate it with God, recognize that it is God, people will then have no reason for quarrelling. That is the implication of this verse.

The principle of "You will reap as you sow" is part of even man-made law. Anyone who steals is punished. Even a thief has to submit to the law. He is not a rebel. The person who defies a law with deliberate intention to do so is an outlaw, but the murderer who is punished for his crime is not an outlaw. We become outlaws when we commit civil disobedience, for our disobedience is deliberate. Those who commit civil disobedience, and do so deliberately, are also outlaws, but the person who steals in abject helplessness is still ruled by the country's law. In the same way, man too is ruled by God's law, whether he submits to it willingly or not. That immutable truth is stated in this verse:

> *Those who desire their actions to bear fruit worship the gods here; for in this world of men the fruit of actions is quickly obtainable. (12)*

Every desire bears its proper fruit. So long as any desire is left in us, we cannot escape the round of birth and death. If we strive for yogic powers, our effort will certainly be rewarded, though not necessarily in the manner described in books on Yoga. Chanting a *mantra* is not necessarily rewarded in exactly the same way as described in the Shastras. Men try to discover God's laws, they conclude that certain actions will have certain results. If they get hold of the truth, may be there will be some efficacy in the *mantras* which they employ; but, then, even self-seeking and insincere men use this method. Or, it may be that the ceremonies accompanying the chanting of the *mantra* were not correctly performed; if so, the hoped-for result would not follow. I do not know anything about *mantras* for counteracting the effects of snake-bite, but there may be something in these claims. Some persons assert that we still know very little about the laws underlying the efficacy of such *mantras*. **In this age they are discovering the laws of the visible world, but the number of such laws is infinite. Shall we ever succeed in discovering them all? Similarly, there are laws governing the invisible world too. In future, the laws of that world—the powers of the mind—may also be discovered. *Mantras* originated in the discovery of such laws. But, like the hypotheses about the visible world,** the principles behind **particular *mantras* may or may not be true and,** according as they **are true or not, the *mantras* may succeed or fail.**

The author of the *Gita* knew this and, therefore, advised us to take no interest at all in these things. If we go after them, we may perhaps have our desires fulfilled, and so he said that people who hanker after worldly success worship various gods. But that, he said, will profit them little in the end. It will not increase the sum of happiness in the world. If, however, we decide to work in a spirit of disinterested service, we would not concern ourselves with *mantras*, nor shall we be required to study innumerable Shastras. Just one little Shastra will suffice, the practice of *bhakti*—Ramanama. We shall not even have to study the whole of the *Gita*, it will suffice if we understand its substance. We should find out and take the place appointed for us in this world-machine created by God. A man who has no desires, how well his work shines! We suffer because of our innumerable desires. People do not keep to their places of duty and that creates disorder and confusion in the world. That man who, instead of being absorbed in his work, is always discontented has not found his right place in the world-machine. If even in a family every member is discontented, the family would be disrupted. In similar circumstances there could be chaos in a country's government, too.

If everyone working in this world-machine seeks a reward for his work and, therefore, constantly changes the spheres of his work, there will be no order anywhere; the condition of such a person is like that of one who wastes himself in pleasures and then runs about in search of tonics and pills. With our minds full of carvings, we run after things in the world. While our attachment to the ego remains, we shall never taste the sweet ambrosia of Óelf-knowledge. The *Gita,* therefore, tells us that if, giving up attachment to the ego, we attend to the best of our ability to the task which has fallen to our lot, an emperor's work and that of one who cleans lavatories will be esteemed of equal worth in God's court. There, King Janaka and the man who cleaned lavatories in his palace have an equally honoured place. Suppose, however, that a present-day ruler and Janaka's Bhangi were to present themselves in God's court at the same time, in all likelihood, the Bhangi would be given an exalted place and the ruler would be left out. In God's court a man with a crown is not esteemed as of greater worth than one who has nothing on his head. The latter will be regarded worthy of a crown while a man with a jewelled crown will receive no attention. Hence the *Gita* says that he who works without attachment to the ego works best and becomes qualified for *moksha.*

> *The order of the four varnas was created by Me according to the different gunas and karma of each; yet know that though, therefore, author, thereof, being changeless I am not the author. (13)*

"I have," Shri Krishna says, "created four *varnas* on the basis of character and work." These are Brahmin, Kshatriya, Vaisya and Sudra. What should be the character of a Brahmin? What is distinctive of him? He is a Brahmin who knows *Brahman,* who lives most in the consciousness of God. And a Brahmin's work in life is to teach and help people to realize God. Besides this particular gift, he will also have the qualities of character which mark the other *varnas.* The Kshatriya's special dharma is protection of society. He should, above all, be a brave man. The Vaisya occupies himself with commerce. That is his special dharma. If he did not follow it, perhaps the world would not go on as it does. The Sudra's special dharma is service. If he combines with his service the spirit of *yajna* or the motive of public good, he will win the reward of his life. There is here no question of higher and lower. If we regard the person who cleans lavatories as lower and another who reads the *Gita* as higher, that will be the end of us. The majority in the world are engaged in the work of service. If a man combines the spirit of *yajna* with such work, he will be a *mumukshu.* A Sudra is expected to have humility, but humility does not mean abjectness. He serves no one except God.

Anyone for whom action is a necessity is subject to continual change. God is spotless and without form. He has no need to sleep or eat and drink. He does not move, and yet it is He who does everything. The weather expert will tell us that the storm was produced by changes in atmospheric pressure, but as he looks back for antecedent causes, he will reach a point beyond which he will not be able to go. God is an expert law-maker, for He is the author of all laws, though, being perfect, He is under no necessity to act or do anything. He never violates His law. God is present in everything that exists and therefore, He and His law are one. He is spirit. That is, His law is spirit, it is God Himself. He is, and also is not, the doer of things. Since the universe displays some order in its running, we may assume that God is the author of that order. But the Lord has told us here that He is its author and yet is not its author—that is His mystery beyond human understanding.

> *"Actions do hot affect Me, nor am I concerned with the fruits thereof." (14)*

"Fruits of action do not cling to me, for I have no desire for them," says Shri Krishna. Once a machine is set in motion, every part in it works automatically. When we have learnt to function in this manner, like a machine, we shall have gained the true end of human effort. We shall then be fit for direct realization of God.

God works like a machine. He is His law. He is the author of law and He it is who administers it. What perfect order this represents! There is never a question of His suspending His law or of deciding to uphold it. The machine has been going on from eternity. God's law exists and has been in operation since the time that He came into being, if we can say such a thing about Him. We indeed conceive such a necessity for Him. He never suffers the effects of karma, for He has no wish to be fulfilled through any karma. Every part in a machine goes on working ceaselessly; it is the man behind the machine who operates it. In regard to God, we also imagine that He is Himself the machine and its operator. Can anyone say of a machine that it suffers the effects of karma or has any wish to be fulfilled through karma? A machine simply goes on working. If, in the same manner, we become totally immersed in our work; so that we are one with our work, we lose ourselves in that work. But, then, we should first ascertain our duty.

The man of lust loses himself in his lust, so much so that he becomes the very embodiment of lust. Even simple contact with such a person is dangerous. We should not lose ourselves in our passions in that manner. Our duty is to strive for self-realization and we should lose ourselves in that aim. Such a person can never be disturbed by evil desire and, at last, he becomes one with God. If we lose ourselves in God, become machines, make ourselves as clay in God's hands, is it any wonder that we may become one with Him? We should lose ourselves in God so completely that we do not remain separate from Him at all. This verse explains how we can do so. It is to explain this that the Lord says here that karma has no effect on him, for he desires nothing through karma.

> *"Anyone who knows this truth about Me is never bound by karma." (14)*

How can he be? He who knows God's law will work but will desire nothing through work. Why do we feel the strain of work? Because, as we work, we remain attached to the "I" within us; were it not so, we would never feel impatient or worried. We should be so absorbed in our work that we do not even notice the time when we should stop it. We should thus work on like machines. I once saw a beautiful painting in a Roman Catholic Church, the work of a gifted painter. It is the time of prayer. Women have been working in the fields, pickaxes in hand. As one of them was about to dig with her pickaxe, the bell tolled for prayer and the pick-axe fell from her hand, she bent her body as though kneeling for prayer and started praying. The poet—for the painter is a poet—had imagined the woman as working like a machine. For these women work was worship. There is a saying in Latin which means that bodily labour is a form of worship. Anyone who believes that it is so will automatically kneel down at prayer time. A person who has resolved that he will always get up at four will roll up his bed as the clock strikes four. If such a person misses praying at prayer time, he will feel weary and oppressed and will not be able to concentrate on any work.

A person who works with such devotion, how can he suffer the effects of karma? That is, he never feels the strain of work. He is ever fresh. There are so many who cannot be happy unless they are working. They never feel the need to stop work for a moment and stretch themselves for rest. If any visitors interrupt them in their work, they feel miserable. Such persons never feel the effects of karma.

The man of lust loses himself in his lust, but he wearies of his indulgence because he seeks pleasure from it. Anyone who seeks pleasure is bound to weary of it sooner or later. If a person indulges his palate, he cannot but fall ill; he is bound to suffer from some disease. But what disease can he suffer from who never indulges his palate, who does not eat for enjoyment? One should do the task on hand without expecting pleasure from doing it, do it merely as one's duty. He who approaches his work in this spirit, who desires nothing through it, will not have to suffer the effects of karma. God does not suffer the effects of karma though He controls this vast machine.

The signs which indicate that we suffer such effects are the need we feel for food and water and the wearing out of our bodies. God is ever awake. We are awake for some time and then sleep, we eat and feel hungry. But God, though He is ever awake, does not have to make an effort to keep Himself awake. He does not sleep and does not eat. Though He acts, He does nothing. Behind every act of ours, there is a trace of egotism and attachment to the "I",—an action of the will. We will to act, we have to do so, before we do anything. God keeps awake for ever without a moment's interruption. We cannot do so. If, however, we keep such a state before us as our ideal, we can do the best work. That is why Shri Krishna said: yoga is skill in action. That is, the man who is firmly established in yoga always does better work than one who is restless and impatient in his work.

> *Knowing this did men of old, desirous of Freedom, perform action; do thou, then just as they did—the men of old in days gone by. (15)*

The seekers of *moksha* in old days knew this truth and worked in such a spirit. To realize God means to work like God, with single-minded devotion and ceaseless vigilance. Though living in the human body, we should imitate God as much as we can. "Our forefathers did this. You too." Shri Krishna tells Arjuna, "should act in the same manner." How is it that Arjuna thought about dharma when he was required to kill his relations? Shri Krishna, therefore, rebuked him and said that he should not think on those lines, for in old times people worked without thinking of any reward for work. If one works in that spirit, one is not bound by the effects of karma. "Think how I act," says Shri Krishna. "I create society with its four classes, but I am not bound by the effects of karma, for I remain unattached." "You too," He tells Arjuna, "should act in that manner."

Students should study with the same devotion as the *brahmacharis* of old days. They bore themselves in such a manner that, though mere boys, they seemed to be grown-up, mature men. I speak of more than forty years ago. I distinctly remember that, at our place, in the absence of the priest his young son read the *Bhagavata,* and he read it very well indeed; so good was the education he had received at home. He must have been barely fifteen. Those whom we describe as *brahmacharis* today must behave as the *brahmacharis* of old did. You should sit upright, like a pole. Practise prayers for a whole month, and then you will discover that you are making some progress. What is the meaning of your feeling restless as you sit here? What is the good if you feel that, when you leave this place, you will get back into bed?

"Do your work and leave the responsibility to me," says Shri Krishna. "What is it you can do? Everything is done by me. Left to yourself, you will remain slumbering. On your own, you do only evil. You cannot say that I incline you to remain slumbering or to do evil. I inspire you to do only good. It is Satan who inclines you to remain slumbering, to abuse people, to behave disrespectfully to others and to cheat people in the name of spinning."

> *'What is action? What inaction?'—here even the wise are perplexed. I will then expound to thee that action knowing which thou shalt be saved from evil. (16)*

"I will explain to you what right karma is and, having understood it, you will save yourself from evil, from the round of birth and death."

Our eyes are closed with bandages, like those over the eyes of the bullock in the oil-press. These bandages are not eternal, but we let them stay because we have grown used to them as natural, as fear is natural to us. There was a lion cub who, having always lived among goats, would tremble with fear like a goat. Then a real lion happened to meet him, and he held a mirror before him. The cub roared, and escaped from the company of the goats. This cub had not been forced to put a bandage over its eyes, the bandage had just grown of itself. In the same way, everyone of us has the bandage of ignorance grown over the eyes, and we do not know that it is not our dharma to live in evil, to submit to the round of birth and death. Our dharma is to rise ever higher until at last we can rise no more. We can have no rest till we have reached the goal. There will be eternal peace when we have reached it, that is, the peace of moksha.

If you are on the top of the Himalayas, you are certain to fall from there, that top itself will crumble one day. It will crumble because it is ever changing. There is no changing in the state of *moksha* and no failing from there. *Moksha* means destruction of the shackles of birth and death, getting out of that round, it means deliverance from evil. If we meet a worthy guru, and he loosens the bandage of ignorance over our eyes and holds before us the mirror of knowledge, we would know what we are, would know whether we deserve to go from birth to birth or are fit for something else. In truth we deserve better than to follow this round, we belong to a higher station. We shall become fit for that station when the darkness of ignorance has vanished. The Lord told Arjuna that He would show the way by following which he could save himself from evil, that his actions till then were only a means of binding him. Shri Krishna wished to help Arjuna to deliver himself from that bondage, but what could He have taught him if the latter had not questioned Him eagerly, had not shown that he thirsted for knowledge if he had not told Him: "I am like one sunk in ignorance; I do not know what my duty is; I have faith in you; show me what my dharma is?"

For it is need to know the meaning of action, of forbidden action, as also of inaction. Impenetrable is the secret of action. (17)

One should know what karma is, what *vikarma*—that is, forbidden karma—is, what *akarma*—that is, ceasing from karma—is. The truth about karma is a deep mystery.

Who sees inaction in action and action in inaction, he is enlightened among men, he is a yogi, he has done all he need do. (18)

The aim of this verse is to show that one who does karma may still not be doing anything. I have already in a previous discourse mentioned my own example and told you that if I worked with attachment to my ego there were occasions when I would become mad. But things go on and leave me unaffected because I do everything merely as my duty. Even if every boy here were to leave me, I would not shed one tear. I would, on the contrary, dance with joy like Narasinh Mehta and sing "Happy am I that the net is no more". If we work in such a disinterested spirit, we can follow the example of the Lord who said that though He had created society with its four classes, He was not their creator. That is so because of the principle that one may do karma and still not have done it.

We are caught in the motion of the wheel of this world. Our duty is to work ceaselessly as a part of this machine. We should spend every minute of our waking life in doing work which has fallen to our lot, and do it as if we are impatient over it and yet not be so, be calm in fact. The bullock that keeps the water-wheel in motion goes round and round, but no bucket falls from its place. If it were not a bucket but our heart in that place, it might even fall off; the bucket, however, does not fall off, it remains in its place, calm. We should be filled with such calm. On the other hand, if our heart is agitated, we may rest from work but shall not have ceased from action, we would still be working. The bonds tighten round such a person and there is but misery in store for him. If he believes that those who let themselves be entangled in the affairs of life weave bonds of karma round them and that he himself is free, he will be under a delusion, for every thought is a form of karma. That is why the Lord has said that the truth about karma is a deep mystery. Those who do karma through their thoughts load themselves with burdens so heavy that they will never be able to throw them off. On the other hand, the man who becomes absorbed in work, does it as duty, and, if he finds that he cannot do a particular thing, leaves it alone,—such a person weaves no bond of karma round him.

One day, I rebuked some boys. On that, someone told me that there was harshness in my voice and asked me if it was not a sign of anger in me. I said that I was not God. I only strive for perfection, but I am not fit to be anyone's guru. I am full of desires, and so, when I am excited, my voice is naturally raised. If I had succeeded in banishing every desire from me, I would be able to do as much work as I am doing now, but my voice would ever be the same. I aspire to reach such a state. It is true that sometimes my voice is raised and there is a little flash of anger in my eyes.

This is the state Arjuna had in mind when he asked the Lord how a person is overcome with evil desire against his Will, I am still swayed by desire and anger. I say this to illustrate the truth that we cease from karma in the measure that we do karma without any thought of its fruit. If I run away from a task in despair, if I get upset or raise my voice because someone does not listen to me, I weave the bonds of karma round me. Having undertaken a duty, having agreed to look after some children entrusted to me and sharing the responsibility of bringing them up, how can I now run away from the task? If I retire to the heights of the Himalayas and live there in peace, I would be indulging my body in idle comfort and weave round myself the bonds of karma. I must, therefore, remain in the midst of these responsibilities, and win *moksha* through them. If I become free from anger and shake off ignorance, if I become more vigilant and alert, I would be doing no karma even when occupied in some karma. This illustration explains both the ideas, of a person doing no karma even when occupied in karma and of another who, though he believes that he is doing no karma, is in fact weaving the bonds of karma round himself.

Everyone should apply this illustration to himself, forgetting all about me as an individual. I have mentioned my own example merely in order to explain that we are all imperfect. I say, not merely out of modesty or as a matter of form, but with detachment, that I am imperfect. This is not my modesty, but the simple truth. When I am completely free from the sway of desire and anger, you will always see me calm, more so than you see me today. I am striving to be free from these. I feel that one day I shall attain such a state of calm.

In this age, we do not have the means with which to measure ourselves. The *Gita* was composed to help as. It says that we should work like machines and pour out life in our work.

We should think further about the first line of the verse beginning with *karmanyakarma*. We saw in a previous verse that no human being ceases from karma altogether even for a moment. That means that the very process of living is a form of karma. Eating, speaking, thinking, sleeping, all these are forms of karma someone said that, when he retired to that place to seek peace, he had tried to stop even thinking, for thinking, too, is a .orm of karma. Thus, no one can escape doing karma. Still the *Gita* distinguishes between karma and *akarma*, between the yogi and ordinary human beings, between night and day, and explains that the involuntary processes in the body are not karma; that is, even though we do such kàrma, we weave no bond round us through it. I have an aim in this discussion of the *Gita*, and that is that children should understand some of the ideas and act accordingly, and, therefore, the discussion is certainly a form of karma for me.

If I had accepted the work of teaching and if explaining the *Gita* came naturally to me, then this very work would perhaps deserve to be described as *akarma*. Even so, the idea of *akarma* is like the Euclidean definition of a straight line, and the work of explaining the *Gita* would be *akarma* only in a relative sense. Karma becomes relatively *akarma* when it is undertaken for the service of others, for the sake of our higher good. We may be said to eat and breathe with that aim only if we have voluntarily and deliberately dedicated our body to the service of Shri Krishna. He who lives with the knowledge that his body is not his, that God makes it dance as He wills, may be said to have realized God. All karma done in that spirit is *akarma*. Anything else, though seeming *akarma*, is in truth karma. A yogi may have ceased riding fancy's horses, and still his *samadhi* may be a form of karma for him if he has sought it for better health.

It some persons suffering from consumption learn to enter into such *samadhi;* it is plain that their aim in doing so is to cure themselves of their disease. Their karma in this case is not inspired by the motive of higher good. Only that karma is so inspired in which our aim is realiaation of God and nothing else, when this aim, too, is pursued with spontaneous naturalness. The person who is inspired by it is not in the least conscious of it. In all that he does, there is only the yearning for realizing God and no other thought. Such a person loses the very consciousness of his body, as the *gopis* did. Even those who are possessed by lust lose the consciousness of their bodies, but they go to hell because they have given themselves up to the pursuit of lust and do not yearn to see God. When such a person, after he has had enough of pleasure, experiences the joy of devotion to God, he realizes that this latter joy is far superior to the pleasure he got by giving himself up to lust, that by losing himself in the pleasure of lust he grew weaker, whereas by losing himself in the joy of God he was filled with strength. After this experience, he is no more negligent in work but learns to be proficient in it. He who does everything for the sake of the higher good and dedicates all his work to God has ceased from karma. Just as the judge dispenses justice and the hangman hangs the condemned man in the name of the king, so if we feel that in this empire of the universe we are God's slaves and are prompted by Him to do what we do, all our actions will be for our higher good.

> *He whose every undertaking is free from desire and selfish purpose, and he who has burnt all his actions in the fire of knowledge—such a one the wise call a pandita. (19)*

That person whose undertakings are never inspired by selfish desire or personal aims but are altogether spontaneous, whose karmas have been burnt up by the fire of knowledge—everything that exists and will cease has life in it, which means that a piece of stone has life in it, but, though it does no karma it has no knowledge either—such a person will not be like a stone in regard to karma but, on the contrary, may do all manner, of karma and will still have his karma burnt up by the fire of knowledge. For instance, this earth created by God is in unceasing motion and yet seems at rest; it seems so though it is spinning with a speed which would make us giddy if we could see it. When typing on a typewriter has become mechanical work with the typist, the finger will alight on the right letter even when he is not looking at the keyboard; he who is able to work in such spontaneous manner and is fully alert, like the typist, in everything he does, may be described as the Buddha.

We may be doing much work, but without any consciousness that we are working. We wish to know the atman dwelling in this human body—wish to know it directly so that its knowledge may become a part of our being as it was with Sudama. An experienced carpenter will make a board effortlessly, whereas one with only a theoretical knowledge of the craft will not be able to make one. He who has learnt to work effortlessly in this manner goes on working mechanically and still remains detached. The verse beginning with *yasya sarve samarambhah* describes the character of such a person. We do not have to make any effort for winking the eye; all our actions should become spontaneous like this. Anyone who has acquired control over his thoughts to this degree will never have an evil thought; such a person will move in the world as if he was no more than a corpse. He will seem so to us because he has no desire and no aim, is not subject to attachments and aversions; he is a man who has ceased from karma.

This work of explaining the *Gita* which I am doing is prompted by a personal motive, the wish to see that the boys understand it.

He who has renounced attachment to the fruit of action, who is ever content, and free from all dependence,—he, though immerised in action, yet acts not. (20)

He who has given up desire for the fruits of karma, who is ever contented, not more so at one time and less at another time, who is always satisfied with what he has—such a person may be ever deeply engrossed in work but in truth he does nothing. As Narasinh Mehta has said, an ascetic and a perfect woman do not know the pleasure of earthly love; if any such person were to come and see us plying the charkha all the hours of the day, he would think that we had become mad, that we were so occupied with work that we paid no attention to performing daily worship. But according to the *Gita,* we can say that we were doing no work, for we had no selfish aim in our work and did it simply as our dharma, did it merely because of our faith in the value of spinning: With scepticism all round us, to go on spinning with the faith that it would bring swaraj indicates the state of unvarying inner content in which we live. This is true, of course, of only those people who attribute all this power to the charkha and devote themselves whole-heartedly to it.

Expecting naught, holding his mind and body in check, putting away every possession, and going through action only in the body, he incurs no stain. (21)

He alone does not feel the body to be a burden who hopes for nothing, whose mind is ever steady and who has completely given up the desire for possessions. How does this become possible? The body, too, is a kind of property which we possess. We should so use it that we would not mind its perishing today rather than tomorrow. If we cultivate such an attitude, we would not feel the body to be a burden. Ladah Maharaj had given up all concern with this particular form of property, the body, and kept repeating the name Siva all the hours of the day; anyone who works in that spirit, with the sole aim of giving the body its here and not for the sake of pleasures, may be doing karma all the time and still he stores up no sins.

That person who is described as doing *shariram* karma does not have to suffer the fruits of karma. This does not mean that his karma bears no fruit, but only that he seeks none. In other words, he does not attribute the karma to his atman. For instance, I listen to the *Gita* being read out. I should do so with humility, for listening to it is my duty; the fruit of listening to it will follow of itself, whether we think of it or not, in the same way that a seed which has been sown grows by itself into a tree. This seed has no ego. We are animals to the extent that we have some needs in common with them, but in certain respects we are different from them. The consciousness that we do things should disappear from us. A person who writes his diary everyday does not think about how such his hand worked during the day; in that way all our work should be done mechanically.

Even an action which one took to be most virtuous karma may turn out to be sin. Supposing one is born a prince through the virtue of meritorious work, how does it profit one? What good is there in being born a prince? To be born poor and to be born a prince, these are two extremes of the same state. We say that we should try to make do with less sleep, and that may seem contrary to the teaching of the verse we are discussing. But we make the effort in order that by and by sleeping less may become natural to us, just as we try to rise above *rajas* and *tamas* by engaging ourselves in *sattvik* activity.

Shariram karma means karma for keeping the body alive. Observance of *brahmacharya* and other rules has become difficult for us because we pamper the body too much. We have made difficult what should be quite natural to us. It is not natural for human beings to violate *brahmacharya*. We seek pleasures because we live as if the body and the atman were identical. If, instead, we look upon the body as only a material object and think merely of keeping it alive somehow, we would not run after pleasures. How can we be ever disturbed by evil desires if we look upon our body as the temple of the atman? Should anyone maintain himself merely by doing half an hour's writing everyday? No. Anyone who does so is a thief. The mind works for the atman, and so does the body, but we ought to undertake physical labour to maintain the body. Even the work of teaching cannot serve as a means for this purpose. Only agriculture or similar work can count as work for the sake of the body.

> *Content with whatever chance may bring, rid of the pairs of opposites, free from ill will, even-minded in success and failure, he is not bound though he acts. (22)*

He who is satisfied with that he gets in the ordinary course of things, who has risen above the pairs of opposites, such as happiness and suffering, has no ill will in him and bears an equal mind towards success and failure, is indifferent towards them or is not affected by them—such a person does not dance with joy on getting something which is welcome to him and does not start lamenting his lot when disagreeable things happen—he may do karma and still be not doing it, that is, will not be bound by the effects of his karma.

Of the free soul who has shed all attachment, whose mind is firmly grounded in knowledge, who acts only for sacrifice, all karma is extinguished. (23)

That person who works without attachment is free, that is, he is not bound by the effects of karma. He whose mind has become steady through knowledge and who always works in the spirit of *yajna* has all his karmas burnt up in the fire of knowledge.

It would be far better that we die than that we eat merely to serve ourselves. That is, if we cultivate a state of mind such that we eat and drink in order that we may serve God, serve the atman, that is, eat and drink in the spirit of *yajna,* then we shall have ceased from karma.

If we recite certain verses thousands of times over and over again and with faith, they acquire great power for us. A Muslim should not tire of reciting *kalamas* and a Hindu should not tire of reciting the *gayatri* or of repeating Ramanama or the *dwadash mantra.*

I have discussed these verses at great length with Vinobaji, too, but I am not sure of their meaning. The *Gita* was composed after the time of the Vedas, and the different sects have tried so to interpret its teaching that it may support their own tenets. It is too much to believe that the *Gita* condemned Vedic rituals. I have, therefore, tried again and again to get a meaning which would not conflict with the Vedic practices. Not that this was necessary for myself. My task is to find in them a meaning that would satisfy you. The teacher of the *Gita* did not lay down that those who came after him should always read in it only the meaning which he himself had in mind. Now, it says that every karma done in the spirit of *yajna* leaves no effects behind it. Any action done without reference to one's own interest is a form of *yajna.* The next verse follows as a consequence from this, and also explains the manner of doing such *yajna.*

The offering of sacrifice is Brahman; the oblation is Brahman; it is offered by Brahman in the fire that is Brahman; thus he whose mind is fixed on acts dedicated to Brahman must needs pass on to Brahman. (24)

That which is thrown into the *yajna* is *Brahman* and so is the oblation (*arpan* has been interpreted to mean all the materials used for the purpose of the *yajna*). If that oblation is thrown by *Brahman* into the fire which is also *Brahman*, it is bound to act as *Brahman*. Anyone who relates all his karmas to *Brahman* will merge into the latter. How can a person who sees God in every aspect of a *yajna* have to suffer the fruits of karma? He becomes both the ladle used in the *yajna* and the oblation poured out by its means. He looks upon god as a potter and offers himself as clay to Him and lets Him make from it any pot He pleases. The verse thus explains how there may be *akarma* in karma.

Shri Krishna now explains the different types of *yajna:*

Some yogis perform sacrifice in the form of worship of the gods, others offer sacrifice of sacrifice itself in the fire that is Brahman. (25)

I have been told by Vinoba that there is support in the Vedas for the view that a person who has attained to knowledge of the *Brahman* need not worry about performing *yajna*. One who has made his life itself a long *yajna*, why should he undertake any other *yajna?*

A woman who is nearly blind has come among us. She has a fine voice and sings *Raghupati Raghav Raja Ram*. She is a Tamilian. She has come here with her husband's permission. She appears intelligent. We should feel that anyone who serves her performs a *yajna*. Such service serves our higher good. But to a person who performs a *yajna* by means of a *yajna*, that is, who has made his whole life a *yajna*, doing a *yajna* comes most naturally. Such a person is ever engaged in doing *yajna* with ceaseless vigilance. He identifies himself with all creatures in their suffering. The meaning here is not that he gives up doing *yajna*. Rather, it becomes his very nature to engage himself in *yajna*, just as it is natural for God to dwell in the heart of the basest of human beings. Some persons make a sacrificial offering of sense organs, hearing and others, into the fire of self-control; that is, they stop hearing with their ears, speaking with their tongues, savouring food and drink with the palate and seeing with their eyes. Others make a sacrificial offering of sound and other objects of sense into the fire of the sense-organs. Here the process is reversed. Since we cannot stop our ears altogether, we should hear only what is good. Since we cannot keep our eyes shut for ever, we should use them only to see the glory of God everywhere. This is what is meant by saying that some persons sacrifice the objects of sense into the fire of the organs of sense.

When Kishorelal was living apart from others in a cottage, he tried to cultivate self-control. He was disturbed by the noise of passing trains while reading the *Jnaneshvari*. I made the suggestion to him that he should block his ears with pieces of rubber. But he got used to the situation and declined to use any such pieces.

But what about children? The only course for them in such circumstances is to take measures to stop the functioning of the organ in question, for the state of inward concentration is not easy for them to cultivate. That is how we should act in regard to sound and other objects of sense.

Proceeding, Shri Krishna says:

> *Others again sacrifice all the activities of the senses and of the vital energy in the yogic fire of self-control kindled by knowledge.* (27)

Others stop the functioning of all sense organs, step even the movement of *prana*, that is, breathing, make themselves motionless and enter into *samadhi*, become firmly established in the atman and, lighting this yoga with the fire of knowledge, make a sacrificial offering of all the organs into it.

If a person cannot control his mind by any other means, he may adopt this way. Or one may get angry with oneself and stop the functioning of all one's organs. Some persons become angry with themselves because they do not succeed in their efforts to observe *brahmacharya*. Those who sail to the North Pole sacrifice money in millions over and over again, without getting disheartened. The man who tries to observe *brahmacharya* but fails in his efforts becomes desperate and undertakes an indefinite fast, resolving in his mind that he will not let any organ of the body function because, so long as even one of them is functioning, his mind revels in evil thoughts; he, therefore, decides that it is best to stop all organs from functioning. This is lighting up the fire of the yoga of control of the atman. This is no mere *samadhi* of the body, it is *samadhi* illumined by knowledge. A man striving for success in *brahma-charya* suffers pain as a woman in labour does. If a person cannot bear obstruction to his efforts to cultivate self-control, we see that he gets upset. This is why I often say that such a person is like a milch cow and that we should bear his kicks.

> *Some sacrifice with material gifts; with austerities; with yoga; some with the acquiring and some with the imparting of knowledge. All these are sacrifices of stern vows and serious endeavour. (28)*

There are people in this world who perform the *yajna* of money (who let their wealth be shared by others). Some others perform *tapas* and imprison the monkey which is our mind. Some others, still, practise yoga or devote themselves regularly to holy studies, to the study of the Vedas. Some perform the *yajna* of the pursuit of knowledge. They do not read, but devote themselves to reflection and meditation. Ascetics who put themselves under strict vows perform a *yajna* in that manner.

> *Others absorbed in the practices of the control of the vital energy sacrifice the outward in the inward and the inward in the outward, or check the flow of both the inward and the outward vital airs. (29)*

Some throw *pranavayu* as sacrifice into *apanarvayu,* while others hold the latter in the former. Some others still hold both. All these are practitioners of *pranayama.*

> *"Yet others, abstemious in food, sacrifice one form of vital energy in another. All these know what sacrifice is and purge themselves of all impurities by sacrifice." (30)*

> *Those who partake of the residue of sacrifice—called amrita (ambrosia)—attain to everlasting Brahman. Even this world is not a non-sacrificer; how then the next, O Kurusattama? (31)*

To strive and conquer desire is also a form of *yajna.* The *Gita* teaches us to look upon all activities for *paramartha* as forms of *yajna. Paropakar* means working for others; but the idea that we work for others is only an illusion we always work for ourselves. We shall attain deliverance only if we work exclusively for our higher self. All activities for *paramartha,* therefore, aim at one's own good.

Coming back to the verse, those who consume what remains after the *yajna* is over, that is, those who utilize for themselves only the time which remains after they have completed the *yajna,* enjoy *amrita* and attain to the timeless *Brahman.* The person who has done no work during the day but, like a heifer idling in mud, has spent his time in bed, steals the sleep which he enjoys at night. The man who does no *yajna* can win nothing in this world; what then can he win in the other world? He is lost in both.

The verse which we have been discussing has a wide meaning. It means that we should eat only after all others have had their food. So long as the embodied soul lives in this world, it has no choice but to have relations with others. To become disinterested in the body, therefore, means that one should devote oneself exclusively to the service of others so that one may attain the *Brahman* beyond time. We should be as impatient to attain it as a lost sheep is to get back to its fold. Those who, on the contrary, live only for themselves prosper neither in this world nor in the next. Therefore, Shri Krishna tells Arjuna: stop thinking of some people being and others not being your relations. If you may kill all people, you should kill these too.

> *Even so various sacrifices have been described in the Vedas; know them all to proceed from action; knowing this thou shalt be released. (32)*

One meaning given to this verse is that there are these different types of *yajna* in the sight of the *Brahman.* This interpretation omits any reference to the Vedas, for the *Gita* has actually denounced them. And, moreover, the verses in question are found nowhere in the Vedas. Ordinarily, of course, the verse should mean this: "The Vedas describe these different types of *yajna.* You should know that all of them exist through karma; only so can you win *moksha.*" After explaining the meanings of karma and *akarma,* the Lord makes it clear in this verse that it is simply impossible for anyone to live without doing karma. That of course does not mean that a state of *akarma* is impossible. Every karma done for the good of the atman, though it appears to be karma is in reality *akarma.* If we can renounce the fruits of karma, that is, work only for others, then we may work like horses. On the other hand, when working for ourselves, we should be like a piece of inert matter, have no interest in the work at all. This is a state of the heart, an attitude of mind. Anyone who cultivates that attitude towards everything he does, sleeping, eating, drinking or cleaning the lavatory, will attain to *moksha.*

The words *evam bahuvidhuh* in this verse mean that the different types of *yajna* are enumerated only as illustrations. Others can also be included if they satisfy the *Gita's* definition of *yajna.*

> *Knowledge-sacrifice is better, O Parantapa, than material sacrifice, for all action which does not bind finds its consummation in Knowledge (jnana). (33)*

The person who performs the *yajna* of knowledge makes a greater sacrifice than another who performs the *yajn a* of money, for the *yajna* of knowledge includes everything, money and all other things. Knowledge covers everything which exists in the world, without reference to the distinction between living and non-living. If we understand the terms *dravya* and *jnana* in a wide sense, a *yajna* of knowledge includes *yajna* of every kind of *dravya.* Anyone who imparts the highest knowledge to us, convinces us to the very depth of our being that the body is not the atman, performs a very great *yajna* indeed.

> *The masters of knowledge who have seen the Truth will impart to thee this Knowledge: learn it through humble homage and service and by repeated questioning. (34)*

"You can obtain this knowledge," Shri Krishna tells Arjuna, "by bowing before a guru in utmost humility,—by prostrating yourself before him, fuel in hand,—by serving him and by frequent questioning, by harassing him with questions, and in no other way. The enlightened ones who have seen the truth will impart this knowledge to you."

> *When thou hast gained this knowledge, O Pandava, thou shalt not again fall into such error, by virtue of it thou shalt see all beings without exception in thyself and thus in Me. (35)*

"When you have received that knowledge," proceeds Shri Krishna, "your understanding will never again be clouded by the darkness of ignorance and you will make no distinction like that between kinsmen and others, you will learn to regard all beings with an equal eye so that you will see them all as existing in you and in Me; in other words, for you everyone will be a kinsman. The entire universe is filled by Me, and, therefore, you will see Me in all objects. When the 'I' in you has melted away, then it "will be *jale Vishu, sthale Vishnu Parvatamastake* for you." Once we have realized that this whole "Universe exists in God, how can there be any problem of violence and non-violence for us? We would feel even thieves and tigers to be ourselves. Till we feel in that way, we may be sure that we have not attained to a state of knowledge at all.

Can we claim that we have the knowledge described in the verse which we have been discussing? Suppose that we learn in one day to recite it; do we then become seers of truth? Do we become so when we teach that verse to others? Of course not. We cannot have this knowledge merely by talking about it. We understand with our reason that the universe is the same as ourselves, but we can only imagine what that means. We cannot grasp the idea or feel its truth. The moment we leave this place, we shall treat all others as different from us. Only that person in whom this idea has sunk from the intellect to the heart—even an intellectual nincompoop can have a heart which is an ocean of compassion—can feel its truth in direct experience. Shri Krishna says to Arjuna, "When I say that men of knowledge will impart this knowledge to you, I do not mean that they will convince your reason; I mean that they will awaken in you the faith that it is so. You will then realize that it is because of your reason that you see things as separate from one another, that in truth they are one." God, ourselves and all objects in the universe are in essence one Reality. Even God vanishes and we have only *neti, neti*. When a person has realized this, his ignorance will have completely vanished.

Even though thou be the most sinful of sinners, that shalt cross the ocean of sin by the boat of knowledge. (36)

"Even if you are the most wicked of sinners," says Shri Krishna, "you will cross the sea of darkness and ignorance with the ship of knowledge"—crossing the Swayambhu-Raman sea of *moha*, the vast sea which no one can cross, according to Jain scriptures.

Hunger cannot be satisfied by the knowledge that there is food in the vessel, or even when that food is swallowed down into the stomach; it is only when it is digested in the stomach and converted into blood that we may say that our hunger is satisfied.

As a blazing fire turns its fuel to ashes, O Arjuna, even so the fire of Knowledge turns all actions to ashes. (37)

First, knowledge was compared to a ship, and now it is compared to fire. It burns up the bonds of karma.

For me, the *Gita* is the ship, not because it is a learned work but because I have liked it, it has appealed to me in my old age, or because some verse in it has been a great support to me, put it any way you like.

Man does not live by bread alone, whereas the lower creatures need only food to live. Anna Kingsford used to say that men seemed like tigers and snakes. Certainly, the lower creatures are as brethren to us. We all come from the same source. But they need only food to live, whereas man lives by performing *yajna.* Everyone performs *yajna* in one way or another. The spinning wheel is one type of *yajna.* Prayers, too, are a *yajna* for us. They represent a mode of spiritual cleansing. Till we have performed that *yajna,* we should feel uneasy inside us. Only those who attend to these readings of the *Gita* in that spirit, not others, may be said to be really interested in it. If we were not thus interested in these readings, we would engage a teacher more learned than even Vinoba and with his help, study the *Gita* in order to learn Sanskrit or be honoured as pundits in society Instead, we join these prayers in order that they may sustain us in our life.

Man's need for prayer is as great as his need for bread. A bad man will use his ears to hear evil of others and see sinful things, but the good man says that, had he a thousand eyes and ears, he would use them to contemplate the vision of God for ever and to hear devotional songs, and employ his five thousand tongues to sing His praises. It is only after I have prayed here everyday that I feel the bliss of having tasted the *amrita* of knowledge. For that man who wishes to be a real human being, *dal* and *roti* are not his food. They count little to him. His real food is prayer. On Sundays, I need to lie in bed till late in the morning, and in vain would Ba try to get me out of it. She used to spoil my mornings, which was not right. Many women do this sort of thing. They should not. Actually I had an excuse for what I did, for in those days I did not pray as I do now. Even so, I tell you of my mistake.

> *There is nothing in this world so purifying as Knowledge. He who is perfected by yoga finds it in himself in the fulness of time. (38)*

We see nothing in this world as holy as this knowledge. The purest *yajna,* therefore, is the *yajna* of knowledge. He who has become fit for *moksha* through the practice of yoga comes to this knowledge in the course of time by his own effort. That knowledge is realization of the self. As soon as this realization is attained, all the burden of this body and of karma will melt away.

> *It is the man of faith who gains knowledge—the man who is intent on it and who has mastery over his senses; having gained knowledge, he comes ere long to the supreme peace. (39)*

Anyone who has unshakable faith will win deliverance with the help of Ramanama only. Parents purposely give their children the names of the Lord. That also may save them. That person who is for ever devoted to the Lord, who is self-controlled and who can fall into sleep any time he chooses, who has perfect control over every sense, attains this knowledge and soon wins peace—*moksha* through it.

We do a sum in mathematics with the help of our reasoning faculty. It does not matter whether or not we have faith in mathematics. But, for spiritual knowledge, faith is essential. Does a child have to train his intellect in order to love its mother or father? An illiterate mother loves her child with her heart. We may have a love relationship of any kind with God. The poet has presented to us only a few aspects of Divine love. A person who had no conception of the vast sea may be given some idea of it by telling him of rivers and streams.

> *But the man of doubt, without knowledge and without faith, is lost; for him who is given to doubt there is neither this world nor that beyond, nor happiness. (40)*

That person who does not value knowledge, who lacks faith, that is, who is a sceptic, will perish. He prospers neither in this world nor in the other.

> *He who has renounced all action by means of yoga, who has severed all doubt by means of knowledge—him self-possessed, no actions bind, O Dhananjaya. ((41)*

"Therefore," Shri Krishna says, "the doubt in your heart, born of ignorance, destroy it with the sword of knowledge and take up yoga—karmayoga—and get ready."

5

कर्मसंन्यासयोग

अर्जुन उवाच

संन्यासं कर्मणां कृष्ण पुनर्योगं च शंससि। यच्छ्रेय एतयोरेकं तन्मे ब्रूहि सुनिश्चितम्।। 1

श्रीभगवानुवाच

संन्यासः कर्मयोगश्च निःश्रेयसकरावुभौ। तयोस्तु कर्मसंन्यासात्कर्मयोगो विशिष्यते।। 2
ज्ञेयः स नित्यसंन्यासी यो न द्वेष्टि न काङ्क्षति। निर्द्वन्द्वो हि महाबाहो सुखं बन्धात्प्रमुच्यते।। 3
साङ्ख्ययोगौ पृथग्बालाः प्रवदन्ति न पण्डिताः। एकमप्यास्थितः सम्यगुभयोर्विन्दते फलम्।। 4
यत्साङ्ख्यैः प्राप्यते स्थानं तद्योगैरपि गम्यते। एक साङ्ख्यं च योगं च यः पश्यति स पश्यति।। 5
संन्यासस्तु महाबाहो दुःखमाप्तुमयोगतः। योगयुक्तो मुनिर्ब्रह्म नचिरेणाधिगच्छति।। 6
योगयुक्तो विशुद्धात्मा विजितात्मा जितेन्द्रियः। सर्वभूतात्मभूतात्मा कुर्वन्नपि न लिप्यते।। 7
नैव किञ्चित्करोमीति युक्तो मन्येत तत्त्ववित्। पश्यञ्शृण्वन्स्पृशञ्जिघ्रन्नश्नन्गच्छन्स्वपञ्श्वसन्।। 8
प्रलपन्विसृजन्गृह्णन्नुन्मिषन्निमिषन्नपि। इन्द्रियाणीन्द्रियार्थेषु वर्तन्त इति धारयन्।। 9
ब्रह्मण्याधाय कर्माणि सङ्गं त्यक्त्वा करोति यः। लिप्यते न स पापेन पद्मपत्रमिवाम्भसा।। 10
कायेन मनसा बुद्ध्या केवलैरिन्द्रियैरपि। योगिनः कर्म कुर्वन्ति सङ्गं त्यक्त्वाऽऽत्मशुद्धये।। 11
युक्तः कर्मफलं त्यक्त्वा शान्तिमाप्नोति नैष्ठिकीम्। अयुक्तः कामकारेण फले सक्तो निबध्यते।। 12
सर्वकर्माणि मनसा संन्यस्यास्ते सुखं वशी। नवद्वारे पुरे देही नैव कुर्वन्न कारयन्।। 13
न कर्तृत्वं न कर्माणि लोकस्य सृजति प्रभुः। न कर्मफलसंयोगं स्वभावस्तु प्रवर्तते।। 14

नादत्ते कस्यचित्पापं न चैव सुकृतं विभुः। अज्ञानेनावृतं ज्ञानं तेन मुह्यन्ति जन्तवः।। 15

ज्ञानेन तु तदज्ञानं येषां नाशितमात्मनः। तेषामादित्यवज्ज्ञानं प्रकाशयति तत्परम्।। 16

तद्बुद्धयस्तदात्मानस्तन्निष्ठास्तत्परायणाः। गच्छन्त्यपुनरावृत्तिं ज्ञाननिर्धूतकल्मषाः।। 17

विद्याविनयसम्पन्ने ब्राह्मणे गवि हस्तिनि। शुनि चैव श्वपाके च पण्डिताः समदर्शिनः।। 18

इहैव तैर्जितः सर्गो येषां साम्ये स्थितं मनः। निर्दोषं हि समं ब्रह्म तस्माद् ब्रह्मणि ते स्थिताः।। 19

न प्रहृष्येत्प्रियं प्राप्य नोद्विजेत्प्राप्य चाप्रियम्। स्थिरबुद्धिरसम्मूढो ब्रह्मविद् ब्रह्मणि स्थितः।। 20

बाह्यस्पर्शेष्वसक्तात्मा विन्दत्यात्मनि यत्सुखम्। स ब्रह्मयोगयुक्तात्मा सुखमक्षय्यमश्नुते।। 21

ये हि संस्पर्शजा भोगा दुःखयोनय एव ते। आद्यन्तवन्तः कौन्तेय न तेषु रमते बुधः।। 22

शक्नोतीहैव यः सोढुं प्राक् शरीरविमोक्षणात्। कामक्रोधोद्भवं वेगं स युक्तः स सुखी नरः।। 23

योऽन्तःसुखोऽन्तरारामस्तथान्तर्ज्योतिरेव यः। स योगी ब्रह्मनिर्वाणं ब्रह्मभूतोऽधिगच्छति।। 24

लभन्ते ब्रह्मनिर्वाणमृषयः क्षीणकल्मषाः। छिन्नद्वैधा यतात्मानः सर्वभूतहिते रताः।। 25

कामक्रोधवियुक्तानां यतीनां यतचेतसाम्। अभितो ब्रह्मनिर्वाणं वर्तते विदितात्मनाम्।। 26

स्पर्शान् कृत्वा बहिर्बाह्यांश्चक्षुश्चैवान्तरे भ्रुवोः। प्राणापानौ समौ कृत्वा नासाभ्यन्तरचारिणौ।। 27

यतेन्द्रियमनोबुद्धिर्मुनिर्मोक्षपरायणः। विगतेच्छाभयक्रोधो यः सदा मुक्त एव सः।। 28

भोक्तारं यज्ञतपसां सर्वलोकमहेश्वरम्। सुहृदं सर्वभूतानां ज्ञात्वा मां शान्तिमृच्छति।। 29

-.-

The Yoga of Renunciation of Work

Arjuna says:

Thou laudest renunciation of actions, O Krishna, whilst at the same time thou laudest performance of action; tell me for a certainty which is the better. (1)

Shri Vyasa uses the figure of Arjuna to make it clear that he wrote the *Mahabharata* only as a *yajna* and that those who read it for their spiritual good would also be performing a *yajna*.

When can we say that a person who is eating is, nevertheless, not eating? Can we say that because, while eating, he absentmindedly puts a morsel into his nostril? Anyone who thinks about play while he is eating is merely inattentive; we cannot say that he is disinterested in eating. But a person may be eating with proper attention and yet we may say of him that he is, nevertheless, not eating. Of whom can we say this? Of one who eats as though he was performing a *yajna*, who offers up his action of eating to Shri Krishna, who eats with the feeling that he does so in obedience to the Lord's command. Or, such a person may also tell himself that it is not he, but his body, that is eating—the atman does not eat, or drink or sleep; he will then eat to serve others, to serve the lame, the crippled and the afflicted.

That will be service of God, for God who dwells in the afflicted is also like them. That person's karma of eating will be in truth *akarma*, and will not bind him. If we aspire to be good, we must ceaselessly work to serve others, serve them in a perfectly disinterested spirit. We should not serve anyone with the hope that he, too, will serve us one day, but we may serve him because the Lord dwells in him and we serve that Lord. If we hear anyone crying in distress for help, we should immediately run to him and help him. We should help the Lord crying in distress. After doing what was needed, we should feel that it was all a dream. Would the Lord ever cry in distress? In this way, all our acts of service will seem to us as dreams.

Those who offer delicacies to the Lord before partaking of them, do they really perform an act of dedication to Shri Krishna? No, they don't. They themselves eat those delicacies. They do not eat them in the spirit of *yajna*. If a person offers the best part of such dainties to others to eat and himself eats only the indifferent items which remain behind, we may describe him as *yajnashishtamritabhuj*.

The Lord answers:

> *Renunciatian and performance of action both lead to salvation; but of the two, karmayoga (performance) is better than sannyasa (renunciation). (2)*

When Shri Krishna said *nehabhikramanashosti*, He assured us that no effort undertaken to follow dharma is ever wasted. Man cannot completely refrain from karma, and therefore, it is easy for everyone to follow karmayoga. Renunciation of karma, on the other hand, is a difficult matter, for it requires knowledge, whereas karmayoga can be followed even by an ordinary person. To retire into a cave in the Himalayas and sit there for ever doing nothing—it is extremely difficult to succeed in such an effort. It is a hard task to cultivate such stillness that one would not be tempted by anything even in one's thoughts. The Lord, therefore, tells us that karmayoga is a better path, since the other one is beset with obstacles and is likely to encourage hypocrisy, while the karmayogi runs no such risk.

> *Him one should know as ever renouncing who has no dislikes and likes; for he who is free from the pairs of opposites is easily released from bondage. (3)*

Why should a karmayogi be looked upon as superior to a sannyasi? A karmayogi is necessarily a sannyasi. But a karmayogi of what type? One who has no ill will, who desires nothing and is ever devoted to his duty, who is not affected by the pairs of opposites, easily becomes free from the binding effects of karma.

> *It is the ignorant who speak of sankhya and yoga as different, not so those who have knowledge. He who is rightly established even in one wins to the fruit of both. (3)*

Sankhya here means sannyasa and yoga means karmayoga. Men of little understanding think them to be distinct from each other, but not so the wise. In truth, they are two sides of the same coin. Anyone who becomes established in either reaps the fruit of success in the other too.

A thing at rest and another in intense motion seem alike. The earth, for instance. Rest and motion are a pair of opposites. But he who remains unaffected by such opposites reaps the fruit of both.

The goal that the sankhyas attain is also reached by the yogis.
He sees truly who sees both sankhya and yoga as one. (5)

The state which is attained through sankhya, that is, through renunciation of karma, is attained by the karmayogi too. He alone has true knowledge who understands that sankhya and karmayoga are the same thing. That is, if we consider the essence of the two, we shall find no difference between them at all. Hence work done in the spirit of *yajna,* done without egotism for our higher good and for the service of others, has a place in both.

Karma means work which circumstances make it necessary for us to undertake, not that which we do of our own choice. We should feel that we need not even pray for *praninamarti mashnam* or wish to work ceaselessly with that aim. When the 'I' in a person has vanished and he has merged into God, he feels no need to pray for anything. He will do only such work as circumstances make necessary for him. If he has no inclination of his own, only the purest type of work will come to him, and he will do it with the feeling that Narayana does everything.

When Harishchandra got ready to put the knife to his wife's throat, was it really Harishchandra who was acting? It was the Lord who prompted him to act as he did, and Harishchandra only carried out His order. The unhappy man, he had made himself a mere servant. Having made ourselves servants of the Lord, it is not for us to choose what we shall do and what we shall not. We should do any work which comes to us and at the same time leave the burden of such work to Narayana to shoulder.

But renunciation, O Mahabahu, is hard to attain except by yoga, the ascetic equipped with yoga attains Brahman ere long. (6)

For him who has not learnt to offer all his actions to Shri Krishna, sannyasa is extremely difficult to practise. The truth is that sannyasa is impossible to practise except through karmayoga. Really speaking, therefore, sannyasa is karamyog and nothing else. He who has become free from attachments and aversions, who has shed the 'I' in him, has become a true sannyasi.

> *The yogi who has cleansed himself, has gained mastery over his mind and all his senses, who has become one with the* atman *in all creation, although he acts he remains unaffected. (7)*

He who is established in yoga soon attains the *Brahman*. Anyone who successfully follows karmayoga becomes established in yoga. He who has become pure, he whose evil impulses have all been burnt away and become reduced to a burnt thread in which only the twists of the original material are visible, will act mechanically in everything he does. That of course does not mean that he pays no attention to what he is doing; it only means that he has no egotistic feeling that he himself is doing anything, through the thread which he draws out will be as straight as that drawn by a machine. An unthinking person works mechanically and the Lord's servant, too, does merely what he is asked to do. But he does not work for payment and, therefore, his work shines out, whereas the hired labourer's work does not shine out as he works for money.

No supervisor is required to keep watch over a Lord's servant at work. Outwardly, he seems dull, but inwardly he ever lives in the *Brahman*. He will have all the virtues of a machine and none of its defects. Besides, the man who lives in the atman, who has subdued the demons in him and mastered the senses; who sees himself in all creatures and all creatures in himself, will make no distinction between relations and others. He will ever live as a servant of all, and will partake only of what remains after others have had their share. Of such a person it can be said, *kurvannapi na lipyate,* that he works, but is not bound by the effects of karma.

> *The yogi who has seen the Truth knows that it is not he that acts whilst seeing, hearing, touching, smelling, eating, walking, sleeping or breathing.*

Talking, letting go, holding fast, opening or closing the eyes—in the conviction that it is the senses that are moving in their respective spheres. (8, 9)

These two verses are a commentary on the preceding verse. The man who knows the Truth acts as if he himself did nothing. Whether seeing or hearing, smelling, eating, walking, laying down to sleep, breathing, speaking, parting with or accepting anything, winking—in all these he will feel that it is his senses which are functioning according to their nature. Such a person acts but does not do anything. A yogi can take up this attitude, and so can a rogue, as also a devotee of the Lord. He who has consecrated his heart to the Lord will feel no desire to do anything for himself. Even when he retires to sleep, he will say that it is his body which will fall into sleep. The functions of the body are not evil in themselves. We make them so. If the body works without interference by us, it will emit nothing but fragrance. We can thus take it as a mathematical truth that our work will tend to evil in proportion as we are conscious of the 'I' in us and it will tend to good in proportion as we shed that 'I'.

If we keep loudly reciting the two verses which we have been discussing, we do not become yogis thereby. We should cultivate such a state that we wholly cease to be conscious of the 'I' in us. Only that person can apply these verses to himself who is always completely absorbed in the task on hand, whose every action is dedicated to Shri Krishna and who seeks no benefit for himself from anything he does. If he uses his ears, if is to hear praise of God. If he uses his eyes, if is to have *darshan* of the Lord. Nor does he ever suffer. Whenever anything happens which might cause him pain, he would think that the pain was not felt by him. 'If', he would tell himself, I forget the 'I' in me when suffering this pain and think of Rama, no one would be able to know that I had been stung by a scorpion.' He would feel that it had stung his body and that there was a red spot on it, that is all. He works mechanically, and still everything he does shines out. His actions grow ever more beautiful. He never tires of work, never feel upset and confused.

He who dedicates his actions to Brahman and performs them without attachment is not smeared by sin, as the lotus leaf by water. (10)

Shri Krishna says this to guard against anyone making unworthy use of the preceding two verses. Such a person remains untouched by sin, as the lotus leaf remains untouched by water. The term "sin" is used here in a wide sense, and covers both sin and virtue. Such a person does not have to suffer the consequences of either sinful or virtuous action. He goes on working, but remains unaffected by work. Leaves of other plants get wet and decay, but the lotus is not moistened by water.

Only with the body, mind and intellect and also with the senses do the yogis perform action without attachment for the sake of self-purification. (11)

The yogis work, but only with their bodies, with their minds or their intellectual faculties or their senses, and feel that they themselves are not working since they work without attachment and with the aim of self-purification. To work with this aim means to dedicate one's work to the *Brahman.*

We worked for self-purification in 1921, but afterwards strayed from that path and so found ourselves in difficulties.

He who works for self-purification goes on working with machines in a disinterested spirit.

A man of yoga obtains everlasting peace by abandoning the fruit of action: the man ignorant of yoga, selfishly attached to fruit, remains bound. (12)

Renouncing the fruits of karma, the yogi wins the peace which is the reward of faith and devotion, the peace which brings *moksha,—the* peace enjoyed by the man established in *Brahman.* That is not the peace of a stone or the peace which the unthinking man enjoys, or that which the man of lust absorbed in the pursuit of lust enjoys for a while; it is the peace of the man established in *Brahman,* the bliss which belongs to the atman.

The man who is not established in yoga stays in the grip of desire. He who works under the sway of ignorance must be a man attached, that is, one who is bound through attachment to fruits of work or with the snake-like coil of expectation and sense-cravings. When a snake is provoked, it can coil round us and crush us to death, but at the most it breaks our bones. To Mirabai, however, the snake in front of her seemed Shaligram dancing. At the worst it would have harmed her physically, but the snake which bites the man of lust destroys his very soul.

We should understand the meaning of the words of the *Gita* not merely to satisfy our curiosity but with the aim of putting its teaching into practice. In my case, the constant reading of the *Gita* has filled my life with prayer. We should leave alone what we cannot put into practice. It is a misuse of our intellectual energy and a waste of time to go on reading what we cannot put into practice. I have to say this because of a complaint Shri Vinoba has made. As the students do not go to bed early, they find it difficult to rise early and their health suffers. The students complain that the teachers, too, do not retire early but keep awake talking till midnight. This does not accord well with the spirit in which we have been reading the *Gita*. We should be *sarvabhutatmabhutatma* or *atmavat sarvabhuteshu*. For the sake of our neighbour, we should desist from making noise or, if we talk, **talk in low whispers, as thieves do.** I, too, should retire early in the evening. What does the phrase *brahmanyadhaya karmam* mean? God does not arouse him who does not wish to wake up. That means that we should adjust ourselves to the weakest limbs in society; or eliminate them, destroy and burn or bury them. If we are not ready for this, we should not exert ourselves to reform or raise any class of people.

> *Renouncing with the mind all actions, the dweller in the body,*
> *who is master of himself, rests happily in his city of nine gates,*
> *neither doing nor getting anything done. (13)*

The self-controlled man, that is, the man established in the atman, mentally renounces all karma and lives in peace. To renounce all karma mentally means to make the mind indifferent to them, to withdraw it into an attitude of detachment towards work and feel that we are not doing what we are engaged in, that it is God who impels us to do it. Surely we do not feel, as we breathe, that we are breathing. We have mentally renounced that karma. It becomes necessary to breathe with a conscious effort of mind only when natural breathing is obstructed. At all other times, it goes on mechanically. The atman dwells, ever at rest, in this body with nine doors, doing nothing and causing nothing to be done. Though it may be working or acting to make others work, it will not be doing so if it has mentally renounced karma.

This life is a play proceeding before us. If we devote ourselves to our work without taking interest in the play or letting our mind be distracted by it, would be *karmasannyasis*. Suppose that a prisoner is asked to attend and witness another being whipped. He attends without any interest. His eyes see what is happening, but his mind may not be attentive. I would see a thing to which I become a witness by chance, but I would leave the place without stopping even a moment longer.

We recognize relationships, that this is a son and that is a brother, regard it as our duty to see that the bonds endure, and act accordingly—in all this we are involved with our mind. There is no mental renunciation of karma.

> *The Lord creates neither agency nor action for the world, neither does He connect action with its fruit. It is nature that is at work. (14)*

The Lord says: "Ultimately I am the Creator of all beings. That means that, when you see I see, and when you do not see I, too, do not see." That is (His) nature. This is a truth which speech fails.

We may assert, from different points of view, that God is the Doer, and also that He is not.

If you withdraw interest from the functioning of your senses they will never feel any strain and you will not feel exhausted. Of course, some exhaustion you will always feel, since complete annihilation of the 'I' sense is impossible. We have already discussed the idea that we should speak not of "self-realization" but of "self-purification". Self-purification is to be achieved through the body. We act through the atman to the degree that we have to act through the body. In truth, however, the atman does nothing, nor does it cause anything to be done.

When God the Artist painted this human eye, He so made it that the atman should shine through it. He certainly could not have intended it to cast lustful glances. The function of the eye is to ensure the safety of the body and to see God. What are the thoughts which come to your mind when you look upon the image of Hanuman? Of *brahmacharya, bhakti* and service. And of strength, for he was Ramachandra's servant and Ramachandra always gives his servants the strength they need. In this way the moment we look at anyone's eyes we should be able to see the atman behind.

The Lord does not take upon Himself anyone's vice or virtue; it is ignorance that veils knowledge and deludes all creatures. (15)

Man's real nature is to serve others and to work for self-purification, and so we should not cherish the 'I' in us. This is why it is said here that God does not take upon Himself anyone's sin.

But to them whose ignorance is destroyed by the knowledge of atman, *this their knowledge, like the sun, reveals the Supreme. (16)*

When a man's ignorance, which envelops the knowledge in him, has been destroyed by that knowledge, this light of God is revealed to him. God is the witness of all that occurs. The idea that we should live in obedience to Him, act only as prompted by Him—that is knowledge. We can experience its truth directly only when all the twists in the heart have straightened out and the atman alone shines there forever.

When the night in one's mind has turned to dawn, one comes in the presence of God.

Those whose intellect is suffused with That, whose self has become one with That, who abide in That, and whose end and aim is That, wipe out their sins with knowledge, and go whence there is no return. (17)

He whose intellect has become fixed on the Lord, who has merged in Him, who is exclusively devoted to Him and whoever lives absorbed in Him, who has dedicated his all to the Lord and trusts to Him alone, such a person, attains deliverance; the sins of such a one are washed away by knowledge.

The men of Self-realization look with an equal eye on a Brahmin possessed of learning and humility, a cow, an elephant, a dog and even a dogeater. (18)

Pundits, that is, men of knowledge, see all things with an equal eye. They have the same regard for a Brahmin rich in learning and gentleness, for a cow, an elephant, a dog or a *Chandal.* They feel that the atman in each of these is identical with the atman in themselves. The only difference is that in some the atman is enveloped by layers upon layers of ignorance, and in others these layers have fallen off. What was said earlier, that the yogi sees himself in others, means the same thing as this. Ganga water in separate vessels is Ganga water after all.

In this very body they have conquered the round of birth and death, whose mind is anchored in sameness; for perfect Brahman is same to all, therefore in Brahman they rest. (19)

They have conquered the world on this very earth, in this very life, who are equal in mind to all human beings, who have no taint of impurity in them, who abide in God and live ever devoted to Him.

When can we say of a person that he is *samadarshi?* Can we say so of that man who would give equal quantities to an elephant and an ant? Indeed no. We can say it of him who gives to each according to his or her need. A mother will give nothing to her child who is ill and will give another who is well as much as he can eat. A person who is filled with the spirit of non-violence, with compassion, will so act that the world will say of him that he behaved towards all as if they were himself, did justice to all; that he gave water to him who needed water and milk to him who needed milk.

No one can be like God, absolutely free from impurity and equal towards all. One can, therefore, become *samadarshi* only by losing oneself in Him.

Let us describe some instances of equal regard for all. One is that of the elephant and the ant. Second, if an enemy and a friend arrive at his place together, both hungry, the *samadarshi* will offer food first to the enemy. He would feel that to be justice. He would be afraid lest there be some hatred for the enemy lurking in his heart, and he would satisfy him first. The friend, too, would appreciate his motive.

A pundit does not mean one who is merely learned, but one who is both learned and wise. If anyone warns him that feeding an enemy would be like giving milk to a snake, he would cite in reply this verse from the *Gita* and say that he was a man of faith, that his father was a lover of the *Gita* and so was he, that they had never come to harm by following its teaching. 'Why should I, therefore, not continue to do so? he would ask.

One role of swadeshi is that in serving people we should give priority to those who live near us. There is also an opposite rule, that we should serve first those who are distant from us and then those who are near us. Near in the first rule means physically near, and distant in the second rule means distant from us mentally. Both may mean the same thing. An enemy may be physically near and distant mentally; we should, despite his being distant, serve him first.

The reason behind this rule of swadeshi is that we cannot reach all human beings in this world. If you ignore your neighbour and seek to serve someone living far away, that would be pride on your part.

We display good manners, culture and learning in serving first those who are mentally distant from us.

Those who follow this rule in their conduct have won the battle of this life. They hold enemy and friend in equal regard. The enemy is the elephant and the friend is the ant of our illustration. We should make ourselves like that with which we wish to be one. If we wish to lose ourselves in *Brahman*, we must become *Samadarshi* as *Brahman* is.

> *He whose understanding is secure, who is undeluded, who knows Brahman and who rests in Brahman, will neither be glad to get what is pleasant, nor sad to get what is unpleasant.* (20)
>
> *He who has detached himself from contacts without finds bliss in* atman; *having achieved union with Brahman he enjoys eternal bliss.* (21)

The person, who has become liberated into unity with *Brahman* and who is not attached to the objects of his outgoing senses, experiences true happiness in his atman. One can have peace only by remaining unattached. It is impossible to prevent the impact of sense-impressions; that is why Shri Krishna speaks of the need to become unattached. If we constantly meditate on the holy feet of Rama, the impact *of* external impressions will have no effect on us. The atman that is united in yoga with *Brahman*, that is, which has attained to the state of *samadhi* in which it merges into *Brahman* and abides in it for ever, such an atman enjoys undying bliss.

> *For the joys derived from sense-contacts are nothing but mines of misery; they have beginning and end, O Kaunteya; the wise man does not revel therein.*
>
> *The man who is able even here on earth, ere he is released from the body, to hold out against the flood-tide of lust and wrath—he is a yogi, he is happy.* (22, 23)

Shri Krishna is repeating here what he has already explained in Chapter II.

He who finds happiness only within, rest only within, light only within,—that yogi, having become one with Nature, attains to oneness with Brahman. (24)

The yogi who finds his happiness and his peace within him, who does not need external objects to make him happy, who is ever self-absorbed and is inspired by the light which shines within him, such a yogi has merged into *Brahman* and attains nirvana in it.

We should read the *Gita* in order that its poetry may be revealed to us. There are two types of nirvana. One is destruction of one's body, after which, however, the necessity of being born again and again remains as ever. The other nirvana is *brahmanirvana,* which is a state of void. But the void is in regard to the external world; within it is all bliss of illumination.

They win oneness with Brahman—the seers whose sins are wiped out, whose doubts are resolved, who have mastered themselves, and who are engrossed in the welfare of all beings. (25)

Rishis who are sinless and pure attain *to brahmanirvana.* Rishis of what description? Those whose doubts have vanished, who hold their atman a prisoner have control over it and who rejoice in the good of all creatures.

Such a rishi can bear ill will to no one. He is ever ready to serve the welfare of even the most wicked. He serves the whole world. A person can become the very embodiment of selfless service only if Rama dwells in his heart. Anyone who is earnestly concerned for the good of another cannot bear any real suffering on the part of the latter. We have heard of fathers who get cholera if their sons are infected by it, though of course their concern was only for their sons. A father may not be happy with his son, and still he cannot bear when the latter suffers. A rishi like this would be moved to profuse tears by the suffering of others, and he would strive ceaselessly to end it.

Sarvabhutahite ratah: We have an instance of this in the story of Yudhishthira and his dog. We should not merely cure the fever of a member of our family, but try to discover the cause of the fever from which the whole world is suffering and remove that cause. All beings in the world are sunk in ignorance.

Do you know anything about the atman? Perhaps a little. Well, a *rotla* is unbaked before it is baked. The cause of disease is not in the stomach, it is indulgence of the palate, and the cause of that, again, is the mind.

> *Rid of lust and wrath, masters of themselves, the ascetics who have realized* atman *find oneness with Brahman everywhere around them. (26)*

Those yogis who are free from desire and anger, whose minds have become steady and who are ever absorbed in their *sadhana*, who have realized the self, are always and in all circumstances in a state of *brahmanirvana.*

> *That ascetic is ever free—who, having shut out the outward sense contacts, sits with his gaze fixed between the brows, outward and inward breathing in the nostrils made equal; his senses, mind, and reason held in check; rid of longing, fear and wrath; and intent on Freedom. (27, 28)*

Outward action is a symbol of inner action. It is not enough that breathing is regular and the eyes are focused on a point between the brows; these actions should be symbols of inner state.

The first verse here runs on into the second one.

> *Knowing Me as the Acceptor of sacrifice and austerity, the great Lord of all the worlds, the Friend of all creation, the yogi attains to peace. (29)*

Since God is the Friend of all creatures, why need such a person fear Him? Since He accepts all service and all our karmas, they can never be fruitless. In dedicating everything to Him, we necessarily act without thought of self. And we are convinced in the heart of our hearts that nothing that we do will remain fruitless.

6

आत्मसंयमयोग

श्रीभगवानुवाच

अनाश्रितः कर्मफलं कार्यं कर्म करोति यः। स संन्यासी च योगी च न निरग्निर्न चाक्रियः।। 1

यं संन्यासमिति प्राहुर्योगं तं विद्धि पाण्डव। न ह्यसंन्यस्तसङ्कल्पो योगी भवति कश्चन।। 2

आरुरुक्षोर्मुनेर्योगं कर्म कारणमुच्यते। योगारूढस्य तस्यैव शमः कारणमुच्यते।। 3

यदा हि नेन्द्रियार्थेषु न कर्मस्वनुषज्जते। सर्वसङ्कल्पसंन्यासी योगारूढस्तदोच्यते।। 4

उद्धरेदात्मनाऽऽत्मानं नात्मानमवसादयेत्। आत्मैव ह्यात्मनो बन्धुरात्मैव रिपुरात्मनः।। 5

बन्धुरात्माऽऽत्मनस्तस्य येनात्मैवात्मना जितः। अनात्मनस्तु शत्रुत्वे वर्तेतात्मैव शत्रुवत्।। 6

जितात्मनः प्रशान्तस्य परमात्मा समाहितः। शीतोष्णसुखदुःखेषु तथा मानापमानयोः।। 7

ज्ञानविज्ञानतृप्तात्मा कूटस्थो विजितेन्द्रिय ः। युक्त इत्युच्यते योगी समलोष्टाश्मकाञ्चनः।। 8

सुहृन्मित्रार्युदासीनमध्यस्थद्वेष्यबन्धुषु। साधुष्वपि च पापेषु समबुद्धिर्विशिष्यते।। 9

योगी युञ्जीत सततमात्मानं रहसि स्थितः। एकाकी यतचित्तात्मा निराशीरपरिग्रहः।। 10

शुचौ देशे प्रतिष्ठाप्य स्थिरमासनमात्मनः। नात्युच्छ्रितं नातिनीचं चैलाजिनकुशोत्तरम्।। 11

तत्रैकाग्रं मनः कृत्वा यतचित्तेन्द्रियक्रियः। उपविश्यासने युञ्ज्याद् योगनात्मविशुद्धये।। 12

समं कायशिरोग्रीवं धारयन्नचलं स्थिरः। सम्प्रेक्ष्य नासिकाग्रं स्वं दिशश्चानवलोकयन्।। 13

प्रशान्तात्मा विगतभीर्ब्रह्मचारिव्रते स्थिरः। मनः संयम्य मच्चित्तो युक्त आसीत मत्परः।। 14

युञ्जन्नेवं सदाऽऽत्मानं योगी नियतमानसः। शान्तिं निर्वाणपरमां मत्संस्थामधिगच्छति।। 15

नात्यश्नतस्तु योगोऽस्ति न चैकान्तमनश्नतः। न चातिस्वप्नशीलस्य जाग्रतो नैव चार्जुन।। 16

युक्ताहारविहारस्य युक्तचेष्टस्य कर्मसु। युक्तस्वप्नावबोधस्य योगो भवति दुःखहा।। 17

यदा विनियतं चित्तमात्मन्येवावतिष्ठते। निःस्पृहः सर्वकामेभ्यो युक्त इतयुच्यते तदा।। 18

यथा दीपो निवातस्थो नेङ्गते सोपमा स्मृता। योगिनो यतचित्तस्य युञ्जतो योगमात्मनः।। 19

यत्रोपरमते चित्तं निरुद्धं योगसेवया। यत्र चैवाऽऽत्मनाऽऽत्मानं पश्यन्नात्मनि तुष्यति।। 20

सुखमात्यन्तिकं यत्तत् बुद्धिग्राह्यमतीन्द्रियम्। वेत्ति यत्र न चैवायं स्थितश्चलति तत्त्वतः।। 21

यं लब्ध्वा चापरं लाभं मन्यते नाधिकं ततः। यस्मिन् स्थितो न दुःखेन गुरुणापि विचाल्यते।। 22

तं विद्याद् दुःखसंयोगवियोगं योगसञ्ज्ञितम्। स निश्चयेन योक्तव्यो योगो निर्विण्णचेतसा।। 23

सङ्कल्पप्रभवान् कामांस्त्यक्त्वा सर्वानशेषतः। मनसैवेन्द्रियग्रामं विनियम्य समन्ततः।। 24

शनैःशनैरुपरमेद् बुद्ध्या धृतिगृहीतया। आत्मसंस्थं मनः कृत्वा न किञ्चिदपि चिन्तयेत्।। 25

यतो यतो निश्चरति मनश्चञ्चलमस्थिरम्। ततस्ततो नियम्यैतदात्मन्येव वशं नयेत्।। 26

प्रशान्तमनसं ह्येनं योगिनं सुखमुत्तमम्। उपैति शान्तरजसं ब्रह्मभूत कल्मषम्।। 27

युञ्जन्नेवं सदाऽऽत्मानं योगी विगतकल्मषः। सुखेन ब्रह्मसंस्पर्शमत्यन्तं सुखमश्नुते।। 28

सर्वभूतस्थमात्मानं सर्वभूतानि चात्मनि। ईक्षते योगयुक्तात्मा सर्वत्र समदर्शनः।। 29

यो मां पश्यति सर्वत्र सर्वं च मयि पश्यति। तस्याहं न प्रणश्यामि स च मे न प्रणश्यति।। 30

सर्वभूतस्थितं यो मां भजत्येकत्वमास्थितः। सर्वथा वर्तमानोऽपि स योगी मयि वर्तते।। 31

आत्मौपम्येन सर्वत्र समं पश्यति योऽर्जुन। सुखं वा यदि वा दुःखं स योगी परमो मतः।। 32

अर्जुन उवाच

योऽयं योगस्त्वया प्रोक्तः साम्येन मधुसूदन। एतस्याहं न पश्यामि चञ्चलत्वास्थितिं स्थिराम्।। 33

चञ्चलं हि मनः कृष्ण प्रमाथि बलवद्दृढम्। तस्याहं निग्रहं मन्ये वायोरिव सुदुष्करम्।। 34

श्रीभगवानुवाच

असंशयं महाबाहो मनो दुर्निग्रहं चलम्। अभ्यासेन तु कौन्तेय वैराग्येण च गृह्यते।। 35

असंयतात्मना योगो दुष्प्राप इति मे मतिः। वश्यात्मना तु यतता शक्योऽवाप्तुमुपायतः।। 36

अजुर्नउवाच

अयतिः श्रद्धायोपेतो योगाच्चलितमानसः। अप्राप्य योगसंसिद्धिं कां गतिं कृष्ण गच्छति।। 37

कच्चिन्नोभयविभ्रष्टश्छिन्नाभ्रमिव नश्यति। अप्रतिष्ठो महाबाहो विमूढो ब्रह्मणः पथि।। 38

एतन्मे संशयं कृष्ण छेत्तुमर्हस्यशेषतः। त्वदन्यः संशयस्यास्य छेत्ता नह्युपपद्यते।। 39

श्री भगवानुवाच

पार्थ नैवेह नामुत्र विनाशस्तस्य विद्यते। न हि कल्याणकृत्कश्चिद् दुर्गतिं तात गच्छति।। 40

प्राप्य पुण्यकृतॉंल्लोकानुषित्वा शाश्वतीः समाः। शुचीनां श्रीमतां गेहे योगभ्रष्टोऽभिजायते।। 41

अथवा योगिनामेव कुले भवति धीमताम्। एतद्धि दुर्लभतरं लोके जन्म यदीदृशम्।। 42

तत्र तं बुद्धिसंयोगं लभते पौर्वदेहिकम्। यतते च ततो भूयः संसिद्धौ कुरुनन्दन।। 43

पूर्वाभ्यासेन तेनैव ह्रियते ह्यवशोऽपि सः। जिज्ञासुरपि योगस्य शब्दब्रह्मातिवर्तते।। 44

प्रयत्नाद्यतमानस्तु योगी संशुद्धकिल्बिषः। अनेकजन्मसंसिद्धस्ततो याति परां गतिम्।। 45

तपस्विभ्योऽधिको योगी ज्ञानिभ्योऽपि मतोऽधिकः। कर्मिभ्यश्चाधिको योगी तस्माद्योगी भवार्जुन।। 46

योगिनामपि सर्वेषां मद्गतेनान्तरात्मना। श्रद्धावान् भजते यो मां स मे युक्ततमो मतः।। 47

-.-

THE YOGA OF SELF CONTROL

The last Chapter raised the question, "Of sannyasa and karmayoga, which is superior?" Shri Krishna has tried to answer the question, but the problem is not one which can be easily solved. The personal God and the impersonal *Brahman*, both are real; and likewise he who rests in absolute peace and he who is ceaselessly occupied in work, both are right, for the sannyasi is in fact working and the other one who is always working rests in absolute peace. One person may feel that there is nothing he need to do, that he is already in the presence of God; such a person can cease from work. He who has free access to the king's court, what more need he do? When the subjects themselves know the king's will and carry it out, what work need the king do? It would surprise the subjects only if he came forward to work.

But Arjuna does not say yet that he has understood the point, and so Shri Krishna takes up the same argument again in Chapter VI.

The Lord says:

He who performs all obligatory action, without depending on the fruit thereof, is a sannyasi and a yogi—not the man who neglects the sacrificial fire nor he who neglects action. (1)

He who deposits all his works in God's treasury, and goes on doing his duty without looking for reward—for, as we know, God is the enjoyer of *yajna* and *tapas* — is both a sannyasi and a yogi. But that person who never lights the fire for *yajna*—originally it was an act of public service to keep a fire burning in the home for performing a *yajna*—or never works, is neither a sannyasi nor a yogi. Such a person would in fact be a prince of idlers.

What is called sannyasa, know thou to be yoga, O Pandava; for none can become a yogi who has not renounced selfish purpose. (2)

Shri Krishna says: "Know that yoga is the same thing that the learned describe as sannyasa. For you, it is not sannyasa to run away from the battle; sannyasa for you lies in fighting—it is. I that enjoy a *yajna*—for the person who has not renounced personal motives for action can never be a yogi. Sannyasa is not something which can be demonstrated outwardly; it is a matter of the spirit within. The restless play of desires and fancies should cease; only then can one be a sannyasi."

For the man who seeks to scale the heights of yoga, action is said to be the means; for the same man, when he has scaled those heights, repose is said to be the means. (3)

For the muni who aspires to master yoga, the only means is work for yoga has been defined as skill in action. If a person lets himself be beaten for a long time on the anvil of work, some day he may be shaped into a yogi. For him who has established himself in yoga, who has attained to a state of spiritual equipoise, whose mind has become steadfast, for such a person the right means of continuing in this state is *shama,* that is, resting in peace.

The argument here is the same that we have already discussed, I have to try and explain my meaning in different ways. To succeed in my effort, I have to see that my meaning sinks into you, so that you understand it as clearly as I do. This effort is a kind of yoga and will be rewarded with success. When you learn to understand my meaning through a mere gesture, then the right means for us will be silence. A factory is filled with noise the whole day, but, when the time for closing it arrives, complete peace reigns in it. That machine required is the means of work in order to be a yogi; afterwards, peace became the means. That is how a well-ordered machine acts. Such peace is not the peace of the grave or the peace of lethargy or inertness; it is the peace of conscious life, the peace of the sea.

When a man is not attached either to the objects of sense or to actions and sheds all selfish purpose, then he is said to have scaled the heights of yoga. (14)

When a person remains unattached to objects of the senses or to work, but uses his senses and works in a detached spirit, such a person, then, who has renounced all personal motives for work, is said to have established himself in yoga.

By one's Self should one raise oneself, and not allow oneself to fall; for Atman *(self) alone is the friend of self and Self alone is self's foe. (5)*

You can win *moksha* only by your own effort. Today, we simply act as enemies of our atman. The atman is self-effulgent, and so it must win its freedom by its own effort. Who can light the divine sun? He rises into freedom as soon as it is dawn. He comes, established in yoga, and sinks into peace in the evening. But does the sun really sink into peace? Shall I have sunk into peace even when I die?

In our ordinary language we say that God grants freedom to the atman, for we do not know how to express the idea in any other way. But can the atman ever merge in God except through its own power? It has all the attributes of God, and that is why it can merge in Him. As the atman is self-effulgent, so is God. A thing cannot merge in something else with unlike attributes. We are advised to take care and see that our atman does not destroy itself, for it is in the power of the atman to do so, though, of course, it cannot annihilate itself completely because it is imperishable. The man who says "I am an atheist" contradicts himself in that very statement. We cannot add a single moment to the life of this universe, and so also we can never succeed in destroying the atman.

> *His Self alone is friend who has conquered himself by his Self; but to him who has not conquered himself and is thus inimical to himself, even his Self behaves as foe. (6)*

While we live, there are two sides in us: the demoniac and the divine, the God-like and the Satanic. So long as this strife goes on, it is our duty to fight Satan and protect ourselves. In the war between gods and demons, it is the former who always win in the end. When the world is no more, God will laugh and ask where Satan was. The atman of the atheist acts as his enemy. The truth is that the atman of each of us does so, thanks to the evil of *kaliyuga*.

> *Of him who has conquered himself and who rests in perfect calm the Self is completely composed, in cold and heat, in pleasure and pain, in honour and dishonour. (7)*

That person who has overcome the lower self in him and who is ever unperturbed, in heat or cold, pleasure or pain, honour or dishonour—any praise or censure given to us is like a stream which flows away towards God and disappears—the *Param*atman in such a person becomes *samahita*. Even in him who is the very image of unquiet, who is filled, not with violence, but with non-violence, who is not truthful but untruth—even in such a one the Supreme Self abides in perfect equipoise.

We can say that the atman dwells in perfect equipoise when what is outside of us is a reflection of what is within. It will not do if the body is erect but the mind is not so. **Today our minds are not erect. The dog has four legs, and we have two and yet our minds behave like those of four-legged creatures.**

> *The yogi who is filled with the contentment of wisdom and discriminative knowledge, who is firm as a rock, who has mastered his senses, and to whom a clod of earth, a stone and gold are the same, is possessed of yoga.* (8)

Jnana here means listening to readings from the Shastras, meditating over them, studying them, and *vijnana* means realizing the atman in direct experience. *Jnana* is understanding through reason, and *vijnana* is that knowledge which sinks through reason into experience. *Jnana* is knowledge obtained from the Shastras, whereas *vijnana* is knowledge which is part of one's experience. Non-violence will have become direct experience for us in this sense when our whole life comes to be permeated with the spirit of compassion, when non-violence manifests itself in us in its true essence. That boy who comes to feel compassion as his own experience will to that extent have purified himself, or attained knowledge of the self.

He whose atman is filled to perfect contentment with such *jnana* and *vijnana*, who dwells firmly like *kuta*—he is a *kutastha*, that is, who endures blows as the anvil does without ever breaking into pieces, remains unshaken in the midst of even extreme suffering—who has subdued his senses completely, such a one may be described as a yogi who has attained freedom. He has become united with God, has become inwardly purified. To such a yogi, clay, stone and gold, all are equal. All three come from earth. Earth which has hardened is stone. Gold, silver, diamonds, sapphire, all these are transformations of earth. But they are all without any worth—everyone of them is but dust. If we shed greed, we would look upon all these articles with the same eye.

> *He excels who regards alike the boon companion, the friend, the enemy, the stranger, the mediator, the alien and the ally, as also the saint and the sinner. (9)*

He who has the same regard for friend and foe, for one who deserves to be hated and one who is a kinsman, for the sadhu and the sinner, as he would have for clay and gold, he may be said to have won the battle of this life. The same law applies to the world of the living which applies to the world of inert matter. As clay and gold are ultimately the same substance, so the sadhu and the sinner are ultimately one.

The sadhu and the sinner are forms of the same reality. They are both manifestations of the atman. The layer of uncleanliness has disappeared from over the sadhu's atman and is becoming ever thicker over the sinner's. We shall have risen above this ordinary level only when we learn to have equal regard for either. Tulsidas has shown by his example how we can do that.

Let the yogi constantly apply his thought to atman *remaining alone in a secluded place, his mind and body in control, rid of desires and possessions. (10)*

A yogi should constantly live in solitude and be in union with the atman. To live in solitude means to withdraw the mind from the outside world. He who lives by himself and seeks to control his mind should shed all desires and, having renounced all possessions, yoke the atman to the *Param*atman in contemplation. Renunciation of possessions includes renunciation of the desire for possessions too. He who practises *japa* in solitude in the hope of winning a kingdom is no yogi. A man who possesses a few lakhs of rupees may be less acquisitive than another who daily gives away money in charity and sacrifices wealth but is constantly thinking of money.

Rahasi means in a quiet place free from noise and *ekaki* means living by oneself. One can live in solitude and by oneself even in the midst of a bazaar.

Even so, one must have physical solitude. One can go to a cremation ground and, thinking on the perishable body, experience the feeling of solitude. *Yatachittatma* means one who is free from physical or mental restlessness. **A man can make do with a mere *langoti*, which even a flying kite may bring him. Can anyone, however, do without some possessions for the comfort of the body? We should supply the body its minimum needs and not seek to multiply them.** If we go on multiplying bodily needs, we shall ever be going from birth to death and from death to birth. So long as the turban is there, we may use it but we should not buy another to replace it; likewise, we may look after the body, but only to supply its minimum needs. We shall not then have to be born and to die again and again. Atman*am unjita* means yoking the atman to the *Paramatman,* fixing it on the *Param*atman.

> *Fixing for himself, in a pure spot, a firm seat, neither too high nor yet too low, covered with kusha grass, thereon a deerskin and thereon a cloth. (11)*

One should place a seat in a holy spot—*desha* may mean even "country", for it was supposed that Bharat was *karmabhumi*—a country in which people engage themselves in *karma* with ceaseless vigilance is a *karmabhumi*—whereas one is born in other countries to enjoy the fruits of one's actions (though India is no longer such a country today)—one should place a firm seat, neither too high nor to low. One should spread out *kusha* grass and *ajin,* and then cover the spot with a piece of cloth. *Ajin* means deerskin. This is mentioned because in those days deer used to be hunted. A yogi devotes himself to his practice for quite a long time. He should, therefore, protect himself carefully lest he should feel cold and his limbs become cramped. He should place himself on such a seat and remain there motionless.

> *Sitting on that seat, with mind concentrated, the functions of thought and sense in control, he should set himself to the practice of yoga for the sake of self-purification. (12)*

I gave a wrong meaning to the phrase *yatachittendriya.* To control the activity of the *chitta* and the senses means to restrain such activity. *Yogah chittavrittinirodhah.* If the waves are continually rising, we describe the sea as stormy. There is no essential difference between the sea and the waves in it. All souls are like waves in water, that is, they are but different forms of that water. We need not ask why we should let waves rise in ourselves. **Human beings conceive God as a kind of doll and respectable people even make gold images of Him.** All this goes on. The rising of a wave means being born, and the wave subsiding means death. Telling himself this, a man may become steady in mind and let the wave of desire subside in it. Patanjali tells us that if we restrain the waves from rising, we shall know whether the master of the *chitta* is desire or whether it is God. Expanding the phrase *chittavriti,* Shri Krishna spoke of *chitta* and *indriyas* in this verse.

Keeping himself steady, holding the trunk, the neck and the head in a straight line and motionless, fixing his eye on the tip of his nose, and looking not around.

Tranquil in spirit, free from fear, steadfast in the vow of brahmacharya, holding his mind in control, the yogi should sit, with his thoughts on Me, absorbed in Me. (13, 14)

These four verses describe processes of yoga. I remember to have read in jail that they would take not less than six months to learn. **These processes are physical actions, and we cannot be certain that everyone will profit from them. The body and the mind, however, are so difficult to control that in our country people attach special importance to these processes. When such ideas are given importance in theory, all kinds of experiments are undertaken, as for instance, climbing Dhavalgiri as a holy effort.**

Two Italian boys had decided to tour round the whole earth walking. They were just young boys. They were happy with what they had undertaken. When I asked them what they hoped to learn from their tour, one of them got very angry. They would acquire a venturesome spirit, from which they themselves would profit, but in other ways they would have simply thrown away their lives. **The same is true about *pranayama* and other processes which have been mentioned. There is no fraud behind them, and no intention to impose on people; they are a means of fixing our mind on God.** If I resolve to observe silence even when in the midst of a bazaar, why should I let my mind be distracted by the noise around me? Similarly, while attending these prayers, too, we are at once in the midst of society and in solitude.

The yogi, who ever thus, with mind controlled, unites himself to atman, *wins the peace which culminates in Nirvana, the peace that is in Me. (15)*

We may attain the peace which follows our merging in *Brahman* if we are good children of God.

Yoga is not for him who eats too much, nor for him who fast too much, neither for him who sleeps too much, nor yet for him who is too wakeful. (16)

Yoga is not meant for the person who eats too much. He will not succeed in his efforts for spiritual discipline. Nor will the person who eats nothing, who takes a vow of total abstinence from God, succeed in his yoga. Similarly, the man who sleeps or keeps awake too long also will not succeed.

It should be borne in mind that this is said in continuation of the preceding four verses. It is true that anyone who eats or sleeps too much can achieve nothing. Some persons live merely on the physical level; they can achieve nothing worthwhile. But the converse requires a little thinking about. He who has undertaken spiritual discipline but cannot bear hunger will be in the same mental condition as the starving millions in the country. He will not be able to provide his *chitta* the nourishment it needs and so he will not succeed in filling his thoughts on God. And the same is true about keeping awake.

There is no fear that anyone here intends to abstain from food or to keep awake too long in this manner. This verse refers to a person who imposes such discipline on himself for progress in yoga. But a person who, however hard he tries, cannot acquire control over his senses, whose eyes are always open to cast lustful glances and whose other senses, too, crave indulgence—let such a person certainly undertake long fasts, even if his body should perish in consequence. He should do nothing for outward show. We look upon truth as the chain which binds us all together here. Any of us here who fasts will not deceive himself. He may fast if he feels that he cannot curb his cravings in any other way. An idea has come to prevail nowadays that in this world one must satisfy one's desires. Hence my advice to you that you should not spare yourself any harshness in striving for self-purification. If a person loves to boast about secretly gratifying his eye, ear or palate, it would do him much good to take any number of vows to curb the body and cultivate vigilance. If we wish to, we can certainly control the senses. But we do not wish to do so, and then look for excuses. The *Gita* advises such persons not to eat or sleep too much.

The four verses we have discussed describe a method which serves as a kind of help like that with which a child may learn to walk. They advise one to follow the golden mean. Having adopted such a method, one's effort should be to do or to die. **If people sacrifice so much to discover the North Pole, will it be**

too much if we lay down our lives in the effort to discover the North Pole of the atman?

Shri Krishna advised moderation in the beginning, the avoiding of excess in all matters. It is only by and by that one can judge what constitutes excess. He said, therefore, that in the beginning one should proceed slowly.

A time may come, however, when we shall not feel as excess what may seem to be so to an ordinary person. When a person is distracted by innumerable evil impulses and feels himself helpless to curb them, he may employ satyagraha against his body and against God. We should scrupulously practise non-violence towards others, but we would come to grief if we adopt it in dealing with our body. Against our body we must employ non-cooperation. That is, we must begin by non-cooperating with the evil impulses in our heart. We must tell the body that we have been paying it hire in the form of food for working as our watchman, but that we have decided to stop paying it from today because it is not doing its duty properly. We may pay rent only for a home which serves to protect us, of which the roof does not leak and the walls are not dilapidated. Why pay for a house which is rotten inside? The other one with a leaking roof and dilapidated walls can be repaired, but what can we do with a house the air in which has become poisoned? Thus, if the body does not fulfil the conditions of our leasing it, we have a right to go on an indefinite fast.

> *To him who is disciplined in food and recreation, in effort in all activities, and in sleep and waking, yoga (discipline) becomes a relief from all ills. (17)*

The man who avoids excess, what does he gain? He who is regular in food, rest and so on, who acts with due moderation in everything, who is moderate even in his sleep, will find that his practice of yoga ends all his suffering.

> *When one's thought, completely controlled, rests steadily only on* atman, *when one is free from longing for all objects of desire, then one is called a yogi. (18)*

When the mind has come under our complete control, when it is easily restrained by us, when it is fixed constantly on the atman, that is, acts in everything in obedience to the atman, when it has become completely disinterested, that is, become free from all desires, then the person may be said to be established in yoga.

> *As a taper in a windless spot flickers not, even so is a yogi, with his thought controlled, seeking to unite himself with* atman. *(19)*

The condition of the yogi who is regularly practising yoga and who has acquired control over his mind is like that of a lamp in a windless place, which does not flicker. If we are unsteady in mind, the storm of the cravings of the senses blows out the atman as a breeze blows out the lamp. As the letter gets its food from air, so the atman gets the food it needs through the senses and the mind. The lamp gets its food from air which is motionless; likewise the atman gets nourishing food from the mind if we keep the air of its impulses still.

> *Where thought curbed by the practice of yoga completely ceases, where a man sits content within himself,* atman *having seen* atman. *(20)*

When the impulses in a person's mind have subsided and the mind is filled with peace, when through the practice of yoga the mind has come under one's control and its impulses have subsided, when the person sees the atman through the atman, that is, when his mind has become absorbed in the atman and he lives for ever content in the atman—such a person has become a yogi.

Watt discovered that if we collect steam and let it escape through a pipe, it will draw a load of any weight. Similarly, those boys who restrain ail their outgoing impulses and concentrate them in one direction will be able to carry any weight on their shoulders. How much, then, would we benefit if we restrain all these impulses and let them subside and be transformed into devotion to God.

> *Where he experiences that endless bliss beyond the senses which can be grasped by reason alone; wherein established he swerves not from the Truth. (21)*

When compared with the highest bliss—the bliss which abides for ever—the pleasures of the senses are but momentary. That bliss cannot be felt though the senses, it can be experienced only by the intellect. If a person has perceived with his intellect the reality which God is, if he has understood with it his duty and then yoked himself to the chariot of God, if, shaking off lethargy, he has entered his name in God's office for duty—such a person will never be shaken from his purpose.

A person whose mind has become fixed in this manner does not cease even for a moment to be conscious of the reality which is God. He is a yogi.

Where he holds no other gain greater than that which he has gained; and where, securely seated, he is not shaken by any calamity however great. (22)

Having attained this state, the person does not even dream that he can gain anything better still. Such a condition is possible only if one thinks about nothing but Ramanama even in one's dreams, if one has worked the whole day in a disinterested spirit of service. If we have not spent the night in sound sleep, if we have had a bad dream, we may understand that our mind is still full of greed, attachment, etc. He whose mind does not sleep at all during any hour of the day is firmly established in yoga, he is single-minded in his devotion.

I once saw in Pretoria jail a Negro who had a mind so strong, like a demon's, that he never shrank back, no matter how much he was flogged. The yogi's mind, however, becomes like a god's; his skin glows and the mind never wavers. If the mind of a person who dwells in solitude is wandering in all directions, though physically alone, he lives amidst a crowd.

That state should be known as yoga (union with the Supreme), the disunion from all union with pain. This yoga must one practise with firm resolve and unwearying zeal. (23)

What has been described as yoga means complete absence of suffering. The state beyond happiness and suffering cannot be described in words. We speak of it as peace. When we are in that state, we are said to be in yoga. We should establish ourselves in such yoga with a determined mind, without getting tired of the effort.

Anyone who depends for his happiness on external circumstances makes it plain that in fact he does not want to be happy. In the end such a person becomes unhappy. But he who feels neither happiness nor misery—we should throw both into the river—if we become glad on getting something which is to our liking and feel miserable when we get something which we do not like, either state of mind is bad—he who rises above both happiness and misery has achieved yoga. Yoga means absence of suffering, never feeling miserable. If anyone abuses us, we should lay the abuse at God's feet. Likewise, if anyone praises us, the praise too we should lay at His feet. This is the meaning of non-possessive-ness. He is a yogi who cultivates such a state of mind and feels himself as light as a flower.

Shaking oneself completely free from longings born of selfish purpose, reining in the whole host of senses, from all sides, with the mind itself.

With reason held securely by the will, he should gradually attain calm and with the mind established in atman *think of nothing.* (24, 25)

Such a person is a yogi; that is, he escapes from the dualities of happiness and suffering.

Wherever the fickle and unsteady mind wanders, thence should it be ruined in and brought under the sole sway of atman. *(26)*

Proceeding, Shri Krishna explains in different words the idea of the preceding verses. He has asked Arjuna to fix the mind on the atman. What more can He say? But He tries to explain the idea still more clearly.

One should withdraw the mind from any object or thought to which it wanders, hold it in check and bring it under the control of the atman.

The speed of air can be measured by a meteorologist and that of electricity by a scientist. But no machine has yet been invented to measure the speed of the mind. It is unsteady and restless. We should withdraw it from every direction in which it flies and fix it in the right place, that is, in the atman.

For, supreme bliss comes to this yogi, who, with mind becalmed, with passions stilled, has become one with Brahman, is purged of all stain. (27)

Such a yogi, whose mind has become stilled, whose *rajasik* impulses, whose egotism and pride, have all completely subsided, and who has become merged in *Brahman*—such a yogi will experience the supreme bliss.

The yogi, cleansed of all stain, unites himself ever thus to atman, *easily enjoys the endless bliss of contact with Brahman. (28)*

The yogi who has thus learnt to yoke his atman constantly (to God), who has been purified of his sins, who has felt the contact of *Brahman,* enjoys everlasting bliss.

The man equipped with yoga, looks on all with an impartial eye, seeing atman *in all beings and all beings in* atman. *(29)*

He who is established in yoga, who looks upon all with an equal eye, sees himself in all other creatures and all other creatures in himself such a yogi with an equal eye for all can enjoy the bliss of merging in *Brahman.*

The verse which we took up is an important one. The yogi is not one who sits down to practise breathing exercises; he is one who looks upon all with an equal eye, sees other creatures in himself. Such a one attains *moksha.* To look upon all with an equal eye means to act towards others as we would towards ourselves. That idea is explained still further in the following verse:

He who sees Me everywhere and everything in Me, never vanishes from Me nor I from him. (30)

He who sees Me everywhere and sees all creatures and objects in Me, I am never absent from such a person. He is always dear to Me, he is never far from Me—as Hanuman was never far from Ramachandra.

It is not easy to see all creatures in ourselves. The key with which to achieve this is given in the next verse, and that is, that one should see others in oneself by seeing them and oneself in God. As ice becomes what it is from water, so we have all come from the same water and shall turn again into that water. The hailstone which realizes that it is water in substance will feel itself as water. God and God's *maya* are one; what distinction, then, can there be between a Brahmin, a *Chandal* and a Sudra? That is why the sage Bharadwaja asked Rama whether the latter had killed Ravana or only his own *maya.* Rama is never absent from us and we are never far from Rama.

The yogi who, anchored in unity, worships Me abiding in all beings, lives and moves in Me, no matter how he live and move. (31)

"The yogi," says Shri Krishna, "who worships Me the dweller in all creatures, who, after merging in *Brahman,* feels that he is *Brahman* and that the world exists in *Brahman* and who worships Me with that feeling, such a yogi, though ever engaged in outward activities, lives in Me."

As they say, "walking with unsteady steps on the earth but fixing the mind on the sky," so a person who has his eyes always fixed on the sky of his heart dwells in God every moment, whether walking or eating or drinking, or in any condition whatever. There are impostors who claim that, though they may indulge in immoral pleasures, they are still yogis. They tell us that, being victims of *maya,* we may hold that some things are permitted and others forbidden, but that they themselves are bound by no rules. If we ask them to exchange their gold for our stone, they will not agree. They will answer that they are learned men and the gold had better be with them. But about the actions of a person who has banished all evil from his heart, the world will say—he himself will not claim it—that though doing karma he dwells in God.

He who, by likening himself with others, senses pleasure and pain equally for all as for himself, is deemed to be the highest yogi, O Arjuna. (32)

He who acts towards others as if they were himself will meet their needs as if they were his own, will do to others what he would to himself, will learn to look upon himself and the world as one. He is a true yogi who is happy when others are happy and suffers when others suffer.

Only that person who has reduced himself to a cipher, has completely shed his egotism, can claim to be so. He alone may be said to be such a person who has dedicated his all to God. But this is a difficult state to achieve, and so Arjuna puts a question.

Arjuna asks:

I do not see, O Madhusudana, how this yoga, based on the equal-mindedness that Thou hast expounded to me, can steadily endure, because of fickleness of the mind. (33)

When we are travelling in a train, we cannot see clearly the things outside. That is how it is.

For fickle is the mind, O Krishna, unruly, overpowering and stubborn; to curb it is, I think, as hard as to curb the wind. (34)

Arjuna says: "O Krishna, the mind is fickle, it unsteadies the heart, it is strong, and obstinate in its fickleness. We can see this truth if we can curb it, but it is as difficult to curb it as it is to curb air."

The Lord says:

Undoubtedly, O Mahabahu, the mind is fickle and hard to curb; yet, O Kaunteya, it can be held in check by constant practice and dispassion.

Without self-restraint, yoga, I hold, is difficult to attain; but the self governed soul can attain it by proper means, if he strives for it. (35, 36)

We may have studied the *Gita* with great care and attention, but we can achieve nothing if we lack strength of heart. We should strive for self-purification in respect of all our attachments. We should overcome ignorant attachments and carry out self-purification. Arjuna has become a bridge between Shri Krishna and the world. Possessing such knowledge and after having enjoyed the privilege of Shri Krishna's company for so long a time, he should have no question to ask. It is for the benefit of the world that he puts all the questions.

Arjuna asks:

If one, possessed of faith, but slack of effort, because of his mind straying from yoga, reach not perfection in yoga, what end does he come to, O Krishna? (37)

He who does not persevere in his effort to be a yogi, who does not strive hard enough, who has faith but whose mind has wandered away from yoga—he may have retired into a secluded spot in a forest but his thoughts dwell in the world without—what becomes of such a person who has failed to reach the goal of his yoga? Does he rise or does he fall?

Without a foothold, and floundering in the path to Brahman, fallen from both, is he indeed not lost, O Mahabahu, like a dissipated cloud? (38)

A person may have read a number of books and been struggling for some spiritual progress. But afterwards he thinks and tells himself: "No, I feel inclined to retire into solitude and put my head in God's lap and offer satyagraha to him." One, however, who has let his mind wander in all sorts of ways and has become full of doubts perishes like a scattered cloud. He becomes like a jug without a bottom. Because he has strayed from the path towards *Brahman* which he has been following, does such a person perish?

This my doubt, O Krishna, do Thou dispel utterly; for there is to be found none other than Thou to banish this doubt. (39)

Shri Krishna answers this question with a solemn assurance. The Lord says:

Neither in this world, nor in the next, can there be ruin for him, O Partha; no welldoer, oh loved one, meets with a sad end. (40)

Shri Krishna says: "No, Arjuna, such a person is destroyed neither in this world nor in the other, for a weak yogi who strives half-heartedly is certainly not destroyed. No one who strives for good ever comes to harm." In these words, Shri Krishna assured the whole world that He would always welcome those who sought Him as persons engaged in a good effort, no matter with what energy they pursued their aim. Every action bears fruit and in particular no effort for realizing God is ever wasted. A person making such an effort never falls, but always rises. If he has faith, what does it matter if he cannot strive with determination? Whatever his achievement, he will be counted as a soldier in God's army.

Fallen from yoga, a man attains the world of righteous souls, and having dwelt there for numberless years is then born in a house of pure and gentle blood. (41)

Such a person rises, after his death, to the world which men of good deeds attain and, after dwelling in it for a long time, is born in a family of men who are holy and possess *shri*—that is, men who enjoy God's grace, not necessarily possess riches—for it is difficult for one born in a rich family to practise yoga or chant Ramanama. **Is Vishnu, with whom dwells Lakshmi, believed to be the Lord of Lakshmi because He owns a mint? No. Lakshmi means *bhakti*.**' The sage Agastya may be described as a man who enjoyed *shri*, for he had obtained from Shiva the boon of *bhakti*. Shri Krishna ate a dish of green leaves offered by Vidura. It is in the family of such a person that one who has fallen from the path of yoga, a weak yogi who nonetheless has faith, is born.

Or he may even be born into a family of yogis, through such birth as this is as too rare in this world. (42)

Or he is born in the family of a wise yogi. Born in such a family, he learns to have an equal mind in all things right from his childhood. *Bhakti* is a daily practice in the family of such a yogi. We may say that Sudhanva and Narad were so fortunately born.

There, O Kurunandana, he recovers the intellectual stage he had reached in his previous birth, and thence he stretches forward again towards perfection. (43)

He acquires in this family the state of equal-mindedness which I explained to you. He acquires in this life the state which he had failed to acquire in his previous life, whether or not he remembers his effort in that life.

In Italy, there is an eight-year-old boy who plays on the Sitar as if he was born with the skill. Similarly, if a boy of eight can look upon all with equal regard, we shall conclude that that is the effect of his mode of life in a previous birth. He will then strive further in the same direction and ultimately reach his goal.

By virtue of that previous practice he is borne on, whether he will sit or not; even he with a desire to know yoga passes beyond the Vedic ritual. (44)

Because of his experience in the previous life, such a person is spontaneously drawn towards God. He who is a yogi and yearns for knowledge crosses the *shabdabrahman,* that is, goes beyond the endless forms of karma and rituals enjoined in the Vedas, not beyond the karma which we undertake with a view to service or in a disinterested spirit, but beyond the karma prompted by personal motive and activities undertaken for the sake of various personal gains.

But the yogi who perseveres in his striving, cleansed of sin, perfected through many births, reaches the highest state. (45)

Persevering in his effort, such a yogi destroys the effects of his sins and, succeeding in his aim after many lives, attains *moksha.*

The capital of self-purification acquired in this life will never be wasted.

The yogi is deemed higher than the man of austerities; he is deemed also higher than the man of knowledge; higher is he than the man engrossed in ritual; therefore be thou a yogi, O Arjuna! (46)

Shri Krishna says: "I ask you to be a yogi, for the yogi is superior to the person who performs *tapascharya,* and he is considered superior even to the man who is a *jnani.* Here *jnani* does not signify a person who is merely learned in Shastras or is wise in practical affairs. The yogi is superior also to one who spends all his time in rituals and similar pursuits. You should, therefore, be a yogi."

And among all yogis, he who worships Me with faith, his inmost self all rapt in Me, is deemed by Me to be the best yogi. (47)

Among all classes of yogis; the best of course is the one who has faith in God. As the rays of the moon are the only thing which will make the *chataka* bird happy, so nothing is as effective as constant repetition of the Lord's name for ending man's threefold suffering in this world.

A Swami from Pushkar Raj once came to visit me. He asked me: "Why have you taken up the spinning-wheel now in your old age?" In a region in which water is scarce, anyone who digs with a shovel—digs for water so that he may serve others—is repeating Ramanama though he may not be literally doing so, and reaps the fruit of repeating it. **There are many in the world for whom food is the only *Brahman.* It is dharma to undertake physical labour and make such a starving person labour too, till he can get food.** That sannyasi put his question to me, but he did not know that I was practising *akarma* through karma.

In this sixth Chapter, Shri Krishna has explained how one may cultivate the spirit of sacrifice through work; he has explained the means of learning self-control. As the method, however, is difficult to practise—though it is not essential that everyone should follow it—, the question is raised whether a person who fails in such an effort does not get the worst of both the worlds. Replying, Shri Krishna says: "No; nothing done with a spiritual motive is lost."

❑❑❑

7

ज्ञानविज्ञानयोग

श्रीभगवानुवाच

मय्यासक्तमनाः पार्थ योगं युञ्जन्मदाश्रयः। असंशयं समग्रं मां यथा ज्ञास्यसि तच्छृणु।। 1

ज्ञानं तेऽहं सविज्ञानमिदं वक्ष्याम्यशेषतः। यज्ज्ञात्वा नेह भूयोऽन्यज्ज्ञातव्यमवशिष्यते।। 2

मनुष्याणां सहस्रेषु कश्चिद्यतति सिद्धये। यततामपि सिद्धानां कश्चिन्मां वेत्ति तत्त्वतः।। 3

भूमिरापोऽनलो वायुः खं मनो बुद्धिरेव च। अहंकार इतीयं मे भिन्ना प्रकृतिरष्टधा।। 4

अपरेयमितस्त्वन्यां प्रकृतिं विद्धि मे पराम्। जीवभूतां महाबाहो ययेदं धार्यते जगत्।। 5

एतद्योनीनि भूतानि सर्वाणीत्युपधारय। अहं कृत्स्नस्य जगतः प्रभवः प्रलयस्तथा।। 6

मत्तः परतरं नान्यत्किञ्चिदस्ति धनञ्जय। मयि सर्वमिदं प्रोतं सूत्रे मणिगणा इव।। 7

रसोऽहमप्सु कौन्तेय प्रभास्मि शशिसूर्ययोः। प्रणवः सर्ववेदेषु शब्दः खे पौरुषं नृषु।। 8

पुण्यो गन्धः पृथिव्यां च तेजश्चास्मि विभावसौ। जीवनं सर्वभूतेषु तपश्चास्मि तपस्विषु।। 9

बीजं मां सर्वभूतानां विद्धि पार्थ सनातनम्। बुद्धिर्बुद्धिमतामस्मि तेजस्तेजस्विनामहम्।। 10

बलं बलवतां चाहं कामरागविवर्जितम्। धर्माऽविरुद्धो भूतेषु कामोऽस्मि भरतर्षभ।। 11

ये चैव सात्त्विका भावा राजसास्तामसाश्च ये। मत्त एवेति तान् विद्धि न त्वहं तेषु ते मयि।।12

त्रिभिर्गुणमयैर्भावैरेभिः सर्वमिदं जगत्। मोहितं नाभिजानाति मामेभ्यः परमव्ययम्।। 13

दैवी ह्येषा गुणमयी मम माया दुरत्यया। मामेव ये प्रपद्यन्ते मायामेतां तरन्ति ते।। 14

न मां दुष्कृतिनो मूढाः प्रपद्यन्ते नराधमाः। माययापहृतज्ञाना आसुरं भावमाश्रिताः।। 15

चतुर्विधा भजन्ते मां जनाः सुकृतिनोऽर्जुन। आर्तो जिज्ञासुरर्थार्थी ज्ञानी च भरतर्षभ।। 16

तेषां ज्ञानी नित्ययुक्त एकभक्तिर्विशिष्यते। प्रियो हि ज्ञानिनोऽत्यर्थमहं स च मम प्रियः।। 17

उदाराः सर्व एवैते ज्ञानी त्वात्मैव मे मतम्। आस्थितः स हि युक्तात्मा मामेवानुत्तमां गतिम्।। 18

बहूनां जन्मनामन्ते ज्ञानवान् मां प्रपद्यते। वासुदेवः सर्वमिति स महात्मा सुदुर्लभः।। 19

कामैस्तैस्तैर्हृतज्ञानाः प्रपद्यन्तेऽन्यदेवताः। तं तं नियममास्थाय प्रकृत्या नियताः स्वया।। 20

यो यो यां यां तनु भक्तः श्रद्धयार्चितुमिच्छति। तस्य तस्याचलां श्रद्धां तामेव विदाम्यहम्।। 21

स तया श्रद्धया युक्तस्तस्याराधनमीहते। लभते च ततः कामान् मयैव विहितान् हितान्।। 22

अन्तवत्तु फलं तेषां तद्भवत्यल्पमेधसाम्। देवान् देवयजो यान्ति मद्भक्ता यान्ति मामपि।। 23

अव्यक्तं व्यक्तिमापन्नं मन्यन्ते मामबुद्धयः। परं भावमजानन्तो ममाव्ययमनुत्तमम्।। 24

नाहं प्रकाशः सर्वस्य योगमायासमावृतः। मूढोऽयं नाभिजानाति लोको मामजमव्ययम्।। 25

वेदाहं समतीतानि वर्तमानानि चार्जुन। भविष्याणि च भूतानि मां तु वेद न कश्चन।। 26

इच्छाद्वेषसमुत्थेन द्वन्द्वमोहेन भारत। सर्वभूतानि सम्मोहं सर्गे यान्ति परन्तप।। 27

येषां त्वन्तगतं पापं जनानां पुण्यकर्मणाम्। ते द्वन्द्वमोहनिर्मुक्ता भजन्ते मां दृढव्रताः।। 28

जरामरणमोक्षाय मामाश्रित्य यतन्ति ये। ते ब्रह्म तद्विदुः कृत्स्नमध्यात्मं कर्म चाखिलम्।। 29

साधिभूताधिदैवं मां साधियज्ञं च ये विदुः। प्रयाणकालेऽपि च मां ते विदुर्युक्तचेतसः।। 30

-.-

THE YOGA OF WISDOM AND KNOWLEDGE

The Lord says:

Hear, O Partha, how, with thy mind rivetted on Me, by practising yoga and making Me the sole refuge, thou shalt, without doubt, know Me fully.

I will declare to thee, in its entirety, this knowledge combined with discriminative knowledge, which when thou hast known there remains here nothing more to be known.

Among thousands of men hardly one strives after perfection; among those who strive hardly one knows Me in truth. (1-3)

That is, this knowledge is of supreme worth and not everyone can acquire it.

Earth, Water, Fire, Air, Ether, Mind, Reason and Ego—thus eightfold is my prakriti divided.

This is My lower aspect; but know thou My other aspect, the higher—which is Jiva (the Vital Essence) by which, O Mahabahu, this world is sustained. (4, 5)

Shri Krishna says to Arjuna. "There is also another *prakriti* of Mine which you may call *para prakriti*. It exists in living creatures, and is superior to the *prakriti* in inert matter; through it the entire universe exists."

We should regard an enemy as one with us. We should reflect how we wish someone who is afraid of us to behave towards us. Even if it is in his power to cut us to pieces, we want him to be fair to us. If we have imprisoned someone, we should not put him under greater restraint than necessary, though he may be our enemy. In any case, we cannot torture him to death. This is no more than the law of the world. Even obeying that law, though we fear snakes and do not wish to die, **we also want to complete the reading of the *Gita* and to acquire the highest knowledge, to serve a few people in the world and bring the spinning-movement to success, to work in the cause of cow-protection.** With this aim, we may wish to protect ourselves. I don't wish to suggest that you cruelly tortured the snake. But certainly you did not simply lift it and remove it elsewhere. This is a difficult matter. **We may catch a snake and remove it, but should do so gently. We should not inflict pain on it.** We should think on this matter not because Kishorelal wants us to do so, but because we want to put the teaching of the *Gita* into practice. We should certainly not beat up a snake for our pleasure. **We must not derive pleasure from tossing a kitten. This is ignorance and cruelty.** Even a child should think how he or she would feel if someone treated him or her in the same manner.

Why does the *Gita* counsel us to treat *Chandals* and *Bhangis* in the same manner as we do others?

We should actually feel towards them in the same manner. It is in vain that one reads the *Gita* if one does not try to live in such a spirit. We should not get pleasure in torturing snakes and other creatures like them. We catch a snake and hold it tight with sticks, but we may do this because we have no choice in the manner. Our attitude should be the same as when we take special care of the body and even pamper it, but feel how much better it would be if we did not do this. We should adopt a fixed attitude of mind, that in such matters we should do the minimum necessary and no more.

Do not tell yourselves that you will think about these matters when you have white hair on your heads. You must make the best use of your youth right now. As Lord Krishna said, among thousands only one person strives for self-realization, that is, for self-purification, and among the thousands who strive only a rare person comes to a right knowledge of Him. Hence we should strive hard and long. We should look upon ourselves as those exceptional persons among thousands. **We should try to become philosophers. We should aspire to be the rare individuals among those thousands, and hope that we shall succeed.**

> *Know that these two compose the source from which all beings spring; I am the origin and end of the entire universe. (6)*

Shri Krishna says: "The *apara prakriti,* the soul that lives in the visible world, and the *para prakriti,* the invisible world, believe these to be the cause of all creatures that live. For I am the source of the whole universe, and am that in which it subsides. That is, I am the cause of creation and destruction. Do not think, therefore, that you kill anyone."

> *There is nothing higher than I, O Dhananjaya; all this is strung on Me as a row of gems upon a thread. (7)*

"As the beads are held together by the string, so this universe is held by Me."

> *In water I am the savour, O Kaunteya; in the sun and the moon I am the light; the syllable AUM in all the Vedas; the sound in ether, and manliness in men.*
>
> *I am the sweet fragrance in earth; the brilliance in fire; the life in all beings; and the austerity in ascetics.*
>
> *Know Me, O Partha, to be the primeval seed of all beings; I am the reason of rational beings and the splendour of the splendid. (8-10)*
>
> *Of the strong, I am the strength, divorced from lust and passion; in beings I am desire undivorced from righteousness. (11)*

"I am the strength of the strong, but that strength which is used without selfish motive or attachment. Such was King Janaka's strength. I am the *kama* in creatures which is not contrary to dharma." "Kama not contrary to dharma" means the desire for *moksha,* or the desire to end the suffering of creatures.

If we desire to end the suffering of others, our suffering, too, will end. This is true in the ordinary sense of the words. **But in Sanskrit the desire to end the suffering of others is described as a *mahaswartha.* It means interest in the *moksha,* of all creatures.** Anyone who feels such a desire would be striving hard for his own *moksha.*

> *Know that all the manifestations of the three gunas, sattva, rajas, and tamas, proceed from none but Me; yet I am not in them; they are in Me. (12)*

We say that we should offer up everything to God, even evil. The two, good and evil, are inseparable, and so we should offer up both. If we wish to give up sin, we should give up virtue too. There is possessiveness in clinging even to virtue.

We say of the physical Rama that he both had and did not have a body. He had contradictory attributes, he was personal God and impersonal *Brahman,* he had attributes and was beyond attributes. For the evil, God is evil. He is in truth the very image of compassion, but He cannot violate His law and so we say that He destroys evil.

> *Befogged by these manifestations of the three gunas, the entire world fails to recognize Me, the imperishable, as transcending them. (13)*

Truly speaking, even those who are ruled by *sattvik* impulses may be said to be under their power because of their ignorance.

> *For this My divine delusive mystery made up of the three gunas is hard to pierce; but those who make Me their sole refuge pierce the veil. (14)*

It is said in the *Bhagavat* that in *kaliyuga* anyone who constantly repeats *Om Namo Bhagavate Vasudevaya* will cross this sea of becoming and reach the other shore. This is true of Ramanana, too.

> *The deluded evildoers, lowest of men, do not seek refuge in Me; for, by reason of this delusive mystery, they are bereft of knowledge and given to devilish ways. (15)*

> *Four types if welldoers are devoted to Me, O Arjuna; they are, 0 Bharatarshabha, the afficted, the spiritual seeker, the material seeker, and the enlightened. (16)*

My worshippers whose actions are ever the holiest fall into four classes, says Shri Krishna. They are: (1) those in distress, (2) those who yearn for *jnana* or seek *moksha,* (3) those who worship Me for worldly benefits, and (4) the *jnanis* who worship God as His servants and seek nothing from Him. They tell God that it was simply their duty as His subjects, to worship Him, and that it made no difference *to* them whether or not He rewarded them.

> *Of these the enlightened, ever attached to Me in single-minded devotion, is the best; for to the enlightened I am exceedingly dear and he is dear to Me. (17)*

Among them all, the *jnani,* who always lives in union with Me, yoked with Me, calls upon Me *"tunhi, tunhi"* and lives as a *bhakta,* keeps repeating My name as if he was reciting a *kalama* from the Koran, is the best.

Mirabai was a great devotee of the Lord, but she belonged to the class of *jnanis.* "I am," Shri Krishna says, "very dear to such *jnanis* and they to Me. We are thus like the lover and the beloved."

> *All these are estimable indeed, but the enlightened I hold to be My very self; for he, the true yogi, is stayed on Me alone, the supreme goal. (18)*

All these four classes are noble people, though maybe some of them believe in *mantras* and worship God through them. Is it not better that, instead of spending their time in sin, they should worship God?

Is not a man who begs before the king's palace better than another who enters it to rob? The self-respect of a suffering man is fully preserved only if he approaches the king and no one else for help. There are people in the world who, when they suffer, seek succour not from God but from others. The Lord, therefore, is certainly pleased when people go to Him. "All these are certainly worthy men," says Shri Krishna, "but of them all the *jnani* is My very soul, Myself as it were. He who has yoked himself to Me has risen to the highest state."

> *At the end of many births the enlightened man finds refuge in Me; rare indeed is this great soul to whom Vasudeva is all. (19)*

After many lives, the *jnani* seeks refuge in Me. "After many lives" means after a long and hard struggle. Such a person is always saying, not with his tongue merely but with his very heart, that this whole universe is a manifestation of Vasudeva. A mahatma of that greatness is very rare.

> *Men, bereft of knowledge by reason of various longings, seek refuge in other gods, pinning their faith on diverse rites, guided by their own nature. (20)*

Selfish men whose minds are clouded by all kinds of worldly desires and who seek the help of witch-doctors worship lower deities. Some, for instance, vow to make a gift of so much rice or so many coconuts to the Mother-goddess at Khodiar; they obey their nature and worship her in that manner.

> *Whatever form one desires to worship in faith and devotion, in that very form I make that faith of his secure. (21)*

If they think that they of their own accord worship the gods whom they do, they are ignorant. They do not get their faith from those deities. What help can a mere courtier give to one who has direct access to the king? For instance, Sudama went straight to Shri Krishna, and then the courtiers' attitude towards him changed. Such a person need not worship any other deity.

> *Possessed, of that faith he seeks to propitiate that one, and obtains there through his longings, dispensed in truth by none but Me. (22)*

If there were many independent deities who could act on their own, there would be no God.

> *But limited is the fruit that falls to those shortsighted ones; those who worship the gods go to the gods, those who worship Me come unto Me. (23)*

Shortsighted worshippers of gods reap perishable fruits. Only one type of person wins deliverance. Those who worship the lower gods rise so far as the world of those gods. Those who worship Me come direct to Me.

> *Not knowing My transcendent, imperishable, supreme character the undiscerning think Me who am unmanifest to have become mani-fest. (24)*

"These persons of little intelligence do not know My unmanifest state," says Shri Krishna. "They mistake the manifest universe for the invisible reality behind. They do not know the best part of Me at all (the part beyond the manifest), do not know Me as the changeless, supreme Purushottama." If, for instance, we worship the Sun, who gives light and heat, we divide the divine power of God into several aspects and worship one of them. Instead, we should try to know the highest, the invisible state of God. This visible universe is ever taking new shades. The gods change their forms but God is ever the same.

Our intellect has not the power to tear up the veil from before the *atman* and set it free. One who has felt the desire to do this has no little intellectual power. So long as we have not reflected deeply over these matters, we imagine beings with as many as ten heads. Then someone may wake up and ask whether the *atman* can ever have heads. He would then remember his study of the *Gita*, remember the verses in the Second Chapter and realize that the *atman* was unmanifest and could not be pierced or wetted. "Unthinking men," Shri Krishna says, "wish to measure Me with their little yardsticks, they make an image of Me and act as if it was Myself."

Veiled by the delusive mystery created by My unique power, I am not manifest to all; this bewildered world does not recognize Me, birthless and changeless. (25)

"I do not vouchsafe light to all. Everyone cannot know Me, for I am veiled by the *maya* of My yoga." If God had not created such *maya*, we could not have existed in this visible universe. But, then, **one may ask, why did God create this universe at all? To ask this question is like a clock asking why its maker made it. A creature must have complete faith in its creator.** "The unthinking man enveloped in *maya*," says Shri Krishna, "does not know Me, the Unborn and the Immutable.

"I am not luminous to all, that is, everyone cannot see Me. Human beings are blinded by My light. Such is the power of My *maya* that people can truthfully say that at this moment some lives are being born and some are dying." But we should understand that these transformations are not real. Who can know that Reality which is veiled behind objects with name and form? If someone told us that in his country rivers get frozen and that human beings and vehicles pass over them, we would not easily understand his statement, this idea of Reality veiled behind these objects with name and form is similar to that. It is true, nonetheless. The Lord says that this is due to the power of His *yogamaya* that, His real essence is the Unmanifest.

I know, O Arjuna, all creatures past, present and to be; but no one knows Me.

All creatures in this universe are bewildered, O Parantapa, by virtue of the delusion of the pairs of opposites sprung from likes and dislikes, O Bharata.

But those virtuous men whose sin has come to an end, freed from the delusion of the pairs of opposites, worship Me in steadfast faith.

Those who endeavour for freedom from age and death by taking refuge in Me, know in full that Brahman, adhyatma and all karma.

Those who know Me, including Adhibhuta, Adhidaiva, Adhiyajna, possessed of evenmindedness, they know Me even at the time of passing away. (26-30)

Those who think of Me, even at the moment of death, as *adhibhuta, adhidaiva* and *adhiyajna,* are men who have become steady. They who know Me as the Lord of all creatures, of the gods and of *yajnas,* that is, as the Creator and Preserver of the whole universe, and know that this world of flux has no effect on Me whatever, are men united to Me in yoga.

❑❑❑

8

अक्षरब्रह्मयोग

अर्जुन उवाच

किं तद्ब्रह्म किमध्यात्मं किं कर्म पुरुषोत्तम। अधिभूतं च किं प्रोक्तमधिदैवं किमुच्यते।। 1

अधियज्ञः कथं कोऽत्र देहेऽस्मिन् मधुसूदन। प्रयाणकाले च कथं ज्ञेयोऽसि नियतात्मभिः।। 2

श्रीभगवानुवाच

अक्षरं ब्रह्म परमं स्वभावोऽध्यात्ममुच्यते। भूतभावोद्भवकरो विसर्गः कर्मसञ्ज्ञितः।। 3

अधिभूतं क्षरो भावः पुरुषश्चाधिदैवतम्। अधियज्ञोऽहमेवात्र देहे देहभृतां वर।। 4

अन्तकाले च मामेव स्मरन् मुक्त्वा कलेवरम्। यः प्रयाति स मद्भावं याति नास्त्यत्र संशय।। 5

यं यं वापि स्मरन् भावं त्यजत्यन्ते कलेवरम्। तं तमेवैति कौन्तेय सदा तद्भावभावितः।। 6

तस्मात्सर्वेषु कालेषु मामनुस्मर युद्धय च। मय्यर्पितमनोबुद्धिर्मामेवैष्यस्यसंशयम्।। 7

अभ्यासयोगयुक्तेन चेतसा नान्यगामिना। परमं पुरुषं दिव्यं याति पार्थानुचिन्तयन्।। 8

कविं पुराणमनुशासितार-मणोरणीयांसमनुस्मरेद्यः।
सर्वस्य धातारमचिन्त्यरूपमादित्यवर्णं तमसः परस्तात्।। 9

प्रयाणकाले मनसाऽचलेन भक्त्या युक्तो योगबलेन चैव।
भ्रुवोर्मध्ये प्राणमावेश्य सम्यक् स तं परं पुरुषमुपैति दिव्यम्।। 10

यदक्षरं वेदविदो वदन्ति विशन्ति यद्यतयो वीतरागाः।
यदिच्छन्तो ब्रह्मचर्यं चरन्ति तत्ते पदं सङ्ग्रहेण प्रवक्ष्ये।। 11

सर्वद्वाराणि संयम्य मनो हृदि निरुध्य च। मूर्ध्न्याधायात्मनः प्राणमास्थितो योगधारणाम्।। 12
ओमित्येकाक्षरं ब्रह्म व्याहरन् मामनुस्मरन्। यः प्रयाति त्यजन् देहं स याति परमां गतिम्।। 13
अनन्यचेताः सततं यो मां स्मरति नित्यशः। तस्याहं सुलभः पार्थ नित्ययुक्तस्य योगिनः।। 14
मामुपेत्य पुनर्जन्म दुःखालयमशाश्वतम्। नाप्नुवन्ति महात्मानः संसिद्धिं परमां गताः।। 15
आब्रह्मभुवनाल्लोकाः पुनरावर्तिनोऽर्जुन। मामुपेत्य तु कौन्तेय पुनर्जन्म न विद्यते।। 16
सहस्त्रयुगपर्यन्तमहर्यद्ब्रह्मणो विदुः। रात्रिं युगसहस्त्रान्तां तेऽहोरात्रविदो जनाः।। 17
अव्यक्ताद् व्यक्तयः सर्वाः प्रभवन्त्यहरागमे। रात्र्यागमे प्रलीयन्ते तत्रैवाव्यक्तसञ्ज्ञके।। 18
भूतग्रामः स एवायं भूत्वा भूत्वा प्रलीयते। रात्र्यागमेऽवशः पार्थ प्रभवत्यहरागमे।। 19
परस्तस्मात्तु भावोऽन्योऽव्यक्तोऽव्यक्तात्सनातनः। यः स सर्वेषु भूतेषु नश्यत्सु न विनश्यति।। 20
अव्यक्तोऽक्षर इत्युक्तस्तमाहुः परमां गतिम्। यं प्राप्य न निवर्तन्ते तद्धाम परमं मम।। 21
पुरुषः स परः पार्थ भक्त्या लभ्यस्त्वनन्यया। यस्यान्तःस्थानि भूतानि येन सर्वमिदं ततम्।। 22
यत्र काले त्वनावृत्तिमावृत्तिं चैव योगिनः। प्रयाता यान्ति तं कालं वक्ष्यामि भरतर्षभ।। 23
अग्निर्ज्योतिरहः शुक्लः षण्मासा उत्तरायणम्। तत्र प्रयाता गच्छन्ति ब्रह्म ब्रह्मविदो जनाः।। 24
धूमो रात्रिस्तथा कृष्णः षण्मासा दक्षिणायनम्। तत्रस चान्द्रमसं ज्योतिर्योगी प्राप्य निवर्तते।। 25
शुक्लकृष्णे गती ह्येते जगतः शाश्वते मते। एकया यात्यनावृत्तिमन्ययाऽऽवर्तते पुनः।। 26
नैते सृती पार्थ जानन् योगी मुह्यति कश्चन। तस्मात्सर्वेषु कालेषु योगयुक्तो भवार्जुन।। 27

वेदेषु यज्ञेषु तपःसु चैव दानेषु यत्पुण्यफलं प्रदिष्टम्।
अत्येति तत्सर्वमिदं विदित्वा योगी परं स्थानमुपैति चाद्यम्।। 28

The Imperishable Supreme

In Chapter VII, Shri Krishna fulfilled his promise, explained both *jnana* and *vijnana* and assured Arjuna that once he had understood these he would never be touched by evil.

The *apara prakriti,* the world of visible objects, can be perceived with the senses and known through the intellect, but the *para prakriti* can be apprehended only when we go beyond the senses, the intellect and the ego. If we wish to know God's transcendent essence, we should in some measure be what He is. We, too, have the two essences, *apara* and *para,* in us, of which we should subdue the *apara* and acquire better knowledge of the *para.*

The main question raised in Chapter I was, how can one kill one's kinsmen? The answer to this extended to seven Chapters. And now begins the eighth. Shri Krishna is making all this effort with the aim of removing the confusion of thought and the ignorance which had unsettled Arjuna's mind. He has been brought to the point of distinction between the *apara* and the *para prakriti.*

Arjuna asks Shri Krishna:

> *What is the Brahman? What is Adhyatma? What karma, O Purushottama? What is called Adhibhuta? And what Adhidaiva? And who here in this body is Adhiyajna and how? And how at the time of death art Thou to be known by the self-controlled? (1, 2)*

"You have told me about *Brahman, adhyatma,* karma, *adhibhuta* and so on. But what do these terms mean? And what is *adhiyajna?* What is meant by saying that he whose mind is yoked to the Lord can know all this at the moment of death?"

Shri Krishna answers Arjuna's question.

> *The Supreme, the Imperishable is Brahman; its manifestation is Adhyatma; the creative process whereby all beings are created is called karma. (3)*

That which never perishes and is the ultimate Reality is *Brahman.* Our nature is *adhyatma.*

The Lord of us all is the power which creates this *adhyatma.* Creating all beings and keeping them in existence if an act of renunciation and is known as karma.

We cannot have personal relation with all beings in the world, but can have spiritual relation with them.

Anyone who feels no desire to do good to others harms not only himself but the other, too. If a woman expecting a baby does not protect it, she may die and the baby, too, may die. To protect it is her karma, which is a form of renunciation. If such a woman is not regular in eating, if she thinks evil thoughts and eats unwholesome food, both she and the baby would be harmed. We are continually harming ourselves in this manner. Some of us may be inclined to ask how the world is concerned if we harm ourselves. But in harming ourselves, we harm both ourselves and the world.

Karma here certainly does not mean an act of creation. Vyasa's writing of the *Gita* and *Mahabharata* was a great *visarga,* an act of renunciation. It is impossible that the jewel of a work like the *Gita* would signify by the term karma, the merely physical act of creation.

> *Adhibhuta is My perishable form; Adhidaivata is the individual self in that form; and O best among the embodied, Adhiyajna am I in this body, purified by sacrifice. (3, 4)*

That is, Shri Krishna says that He is the Lord of *yajnas* and grants their fruit. The modes of being which belong to the living creatures in the world are perishable modes.

There is a saying in Latin which means that the way to Hell is paved with good intentions. Good intentions by themselves do not succeed, but the person doomed to Hell believes that they do, without his having to strive to realize them. We cannot give all that we wish to, but we can receive everything we would. However much I try, if you do not receive what I give, what can I do? If all of you make a serious effort, you can stop wasting others' time. If you but try to get up at four, you will most certainly not fail. What does it matter even if the effort breaks us? *Moksha* is for those who strive till they break.

Shri Krishna is the Lord of *yajna*, and we worship Him because though in human form, He worked all His life. He was awake every moment, awake even when the Pandavas slept. The latter's eyes were always fixed on Him. He did not wish to harm the Kauravas or help the Pandavas; His only aim was to see that right prevailed. He spent his body working ceaselessly all His life, but it retained its light till the last. The word *prayatna* is just an ordinary word, but the thing itself is such that the moment you resolve on it you will begin to reap the fruit. Krishna had resolved that the Pandavas should win and, therefore, their victory was certain. He was the very embodiment of disinterested service, and wished to harm none. When Parashuram was lying with his head in Karna's lap, the latter was bitten by some deadly creature and was bleeding profusely, but he did not move an inch. Surely, he too was a human being, like any of us. We should, similarly, make good resolutions and strive to realize them, offering up the fruit of our effort to Shri Krishna.

By describing Arjuna as the best among beings endowed with a body, Shri Krishna suggests that he need not fear anyone at all.

> *And he who, at the last hour remembering Me only, departs leaving the body, enters into Me; of that there is no doubt.*
>
> *Or whatever form a man continually contemplates, that same he remembers in the hour of death, and to that very form he goes, O Kaunteya. (5, 6)*

Hence they say, you will reap as you sow.

We should let no impurity enter our thoughts. Parents give us the human form, sometimes a form like their own. The subtle changes which take place within us become visible through our eyes. If we get a disease, we should believe that we ourselves are the cause of it. A person whose mind is so strong that he influences his surroundings, instead of being influenced by them, gets no disease. It is for our good, therefore, to believe that our illness is the result of our sins. If we have been repeating Ramanama from the depth of our heart, how can even a dream, if it is evil, leap over that protecting wall and enter our mind? If any does, we may believe that we have been uttering Ramanama only with our lips.

If we have any fear whatever in our heart, that too is a form of evil and we suffer from many serious diseases because of it. Hence, as we free ourselves more and more from evil impulses and desires, we become less and less subject to disease. Even persons whose ears and noses and all other limbs had been infected are known to have recovered. The body possesses a natural power of recovery. Recovery brought about with the help of herbs lasts for some time only; and the man who has overcome his evil desires and cultivated devotion to God will refuse to be cured with the help of herbs and say that, when the evil in him has disappeared, he wili be all right. If as a result of this attitude, he dies, he will welcome death.

Anyone who thinks wicked thoughts will find that in oneday his body has become ugly. Once a person charged with murder came to me. I merely looked at him and told him that he was trying to deceive me. He left at once.

Thinking is a form of karma. Thoughts have such power that sometimes their effects are more terrible than those of actions. If someone finds a pistol placed in his hand by another person and is forced to fire it, he cannot be said to have committed violence because the had acted under force. But he who harbours violence in his thoughts and, keeping himself in the background, incites others to do violence, is guilty of terrible violence. Besides, there are also enemies within which prompt us to commit violence. Despite our effort to think the best thoughts and act upon them, we are driven to commit sin. It is the desire and anger in us which are responsible for this. All the same, our effort at self-control and good thoughts help us. If the God of death himself puts a pistol in a person's hands and forces him to commit violence, such violence will not harm him. He will ever have the name of Narayana on his lips and, when he dies, his end will be good. Ordinarily we do not see this happen, for our thoughts are those of miserable wretches. They ought ever toflow in a self-controlled stream. A person whose thoughts are of this kind repeats the name of Narayana while engaged in any work. His actions are not his, they are prompted by the Lord within.

Shri Krishna has packed in these two verses the essence of all philosophy: man will reap as he thinks.

Therefore at all times remember Me and fight on; thy mimd and reason thus on Me fixed thou shalt surely come to me.

With thought steadied by constant practice, and wandering nowhere, he who meditates on the Supreme Celestial Being, O Partha, goes to Him. (7, 8)

No one should believe that it will suffice if he does this at the moment of death. He who has been striving in this direction from his childhood will win the battle and the other will lose. We boarded a ship at Delagoa Bay to see Gokhale off. The latter was playing billiards. I had not joined him. He thought I did not like his playing that game and asked me: "Do you think I enjoy playing this?" "No," I said, "you are trying to prove the ability of our countrymen." In this way, even his playing was dedicated to Lord Krishna. I of course knew it. **I am sure in my mind that my effort to learn dancing was also not prompted by the love of dancing. At that time, my only thought was to acquire all the accomplishments which make a gentleman.**

The point is that everything we do should be dedicated to Shri Krishna. We can so dedicate only the work which comes to us unsought, not that which we undertake of our own choice. Though the inmates of the Ashram attend to different tasks, dedicating them to Shri Krishna, in reality all of them are doing the same work if there is complete harmony in their thoughts. If that is not so, and only one person is earnest about spinning and others let their minds wander, then they cannot be said to join the former in spinning.

Who, so, at the time of death, with unwavering mind, with devotion, and fixing the breath rightly between the brows by the power of yoga, medi tates on the Sage, the Ancient, the Ruler, subtler than the subtest, the Supporter of all, the Inconceivable, glorious as the sun beyond the darkness—he goes to that Supreme Celestial Being. (9, 10)

He who knows all attains to that supreme, divine Purusha. At the moment of departing, that is, when dying, one should think on that Purusha Who is beginningless, Who rules the world and Who is in essence finer than the finest we can conceive.

In the sixth century B.C., there ruled in Lydia a king named Croesus. He had immense wealth. The Greek saint and lawgiver, Solon, once went to see him. Croesus asked him whether anyone could be happier than he himself was. Solon's reply was that only after a man has died can we say whether he had been happy.

This same Croesus was afterwards attacked and defeated by King Cyrus of Persia. He was sentenced to be hanged. As he was being taken to the gallows, he shouted Solon's name thrice. On being asked by Cyrus why he did that, he repeated Solon's reply to his question. Cyrus freed him and kept him as his adviser. When the King died, he left his son in the care of Croesus. In much the same way, it is only after a man's death that we can say whether he has passed into a higher world.

Proceeding, Shri Krishna describes that supreme Purusha, Who is the Creator of everything that exists, Whose essence cannot be comprehended by our minds, Whom only the yogis see in their contemplation, Who has the glory of the sun shines like the sun, with the light of timeless consciousness, and who is beyond the darkness of ignorance. Our reason cannot conceive how infinitely small and how infinitely vast He is. He who, when leaving this world, thinks with a fixed mind on this Purusha,—only his mind is fixed who has yoked himself to the Lord in *bhakti* and who possesses the strength acquired by long *sadhana*—thinks of Him with *bhakti* and with the power of his yoga, who refuses any treatment or medicine to save his life—keeps his mouth shut,—who knows that he is leaving for a world where there is no darkness and no suffering or happiness and who focuses his *prana* on the point midway between his brows and meditates,—such a person attains to the realm of the Supreme, the Divine Purusha described in this verse.

> *That which the knowers of the Vedas call the Imperishable (or that word which the knowers of the Vedas repeat), wherein the ascetics freed from passion enter and desiring which they practise brahmacharya, that Goal (or Word) I will declare to thee in bnef.*
>
> *Closing all the gates, locking up the mind in the hridaya, fixing his breath within the head, rapt in yogic meditation.*
>
> *Who so departs leaving the body uttering AUM—Brahman in one syllable—repeatedly thinking on Me, he reaches the highest state. (11-13)*

While in the previous verse—Shri Krishna referred to other states of mind, here He speaks only of meditation on the Lord.

> *That yogi easily wins to Me, O Partha, who, ever attached to Me, constantly remembers Me with undivided mind.*

Great souls, having come to Me, reach the highest perfection; they come not again to birth, unlasting and (withal) an abode of misery. (14, 15)

Why is it misery to be born over and over again?

A student: One may not be born a human being—in every life.

But what does it matter if one is born a monkey. We may enjoy our life dancing and jumping about all the time.

Another Student. Can one be sure that, after one dies, in the next life, one will be born a Brahmin?

Should we not welcome that state in which there is no death? Are there any who like dying? Those who do, die again and again. He who does not want death gives up his attachment to bodily life, closes all the bodily doors without much thinking. If he forgets the body mortifies it every moment, he will not have to die. It is because there is death for everyone who is born that life is a cause of suffering. The birds are ever happy, but then they have no knowledge and are not free. Would you like it if someone changed all the boys into birds? That state in which there is no death and no birth, no disease, no attachment and no aversion, that supreme state is known as *moksha.*

Even big mountains, sun and moon and stars, all things are transient. If our lives were as long as one crore years, perhaps we would not feel the transience of our existence. We are not conscious of the transience of the sun, but science tells us that it is not eternal. Both from a profound and from a superficial view, it is transient. Ramanama alone is imperishable. Life and dealh are both transitory states; not only are they so, they are the cause of all suffering.

Why? It is not because the *Gita* says so that we should regard them as the cause of suffering; we should feel in our own lives that they are so. The best way of ensuring that after death we pass to a higher world is to feel every moment that **life in this world is from its very nature full of suffering, so that we give up attachment to it and free ourselves from the dualities of love and hatred.**

We can understand even with our reason that life in this world is full of suffering. If we but think, we shall realize that the very process of birth of all creatures is something repulsive. This is what is meant by saying "I am sin", "I have my source in sin". This existence being enveloped in *maya,* we take pleasure every moment in what should repel us. We have no sense through which we can feel in all ita intensity this pain (which the process of birth means). Even our state after birth is, from the beginning to the end, one long imprisonment. We love fondling a child, because it smiles with pleasure. But, then, prisoners also laugh. **We take pleasure in this slavery because it is a part of our existence but in truth it is a state in which we cannot rest in peace even for a moment.**

Look at the physical frame of this body. It excretes dirt through countless pores, such dirt as we cannot bear touching. If only we reflect, we shall find nothing to attract us in this body. But, then, even this prison is a house through which we can win our freedom. If we come to regard it in that light, we shall make the minimum necessary use of it. The way to freedom, of course, does not lie in committing suicide. Anyone who kills himself will certainly be born again. He will yearn all the more to return to life. **The ideal of self-control had its origin in the knowledge of the manner in which life comes into existence and of other facts of our physical life.** This body is not to be pampered, but to be mortified and subjugated. If it sees that it does not get what it craves, it will on its own leave us in terror.

If Shri Krishna says, people realize the misery of this existence, the state to which He will raise them will be a little better than their present one. That supreme state is not to be conceived as one in which the higher bliss which we experience in this life will also vanish. On the contrary, we shall have it thousandfold in that other state. With this thought constantly in one's mind, one should get absorbed in the duties of this life, forget oneself altogether in them. One should see oneself in the whole world and the world in oneself, and act towards others accordingly. **The ideal of non-violence also had its origin in this realization that, when human life as such is full of suffering, we should cause suffering to none.**

From the world of Brahma down, all the worlds are subject to return, O Arjuna; but on coming to Me there is no rebirth. (16)

All the worlds, including the world of Brahma, will return to their source. The sun, the moon, Brahma, Vishnu, all will perish. "But," Shri Krishna says, "once a human beings comes to Me, he never perishes."

There is great poetry in this verse. This little drop contains knowledge as vast as the sea, and the more that knowlege becomes part of our experience the more we discover its poetry. In such a verse, the poet soarns on the wings of his imagination, released from the bondage of the body and the senses. His imagination works on what he has heard with his ears and seen with his eyes and, going beyond the certainties of reason, he says that all that is known through the sense is a product of the human mind; that is, he imagines that since we ourselves perish, this whole universe will perish, too. All that the human mind can imagine or conceive is perishable, is subject to ceaseless change. He who has dedicated himself to truth will not be prepared to forsake it merely because the world does not agree with him, as if his truth depended on the world and he was acting in a play. Shri Krishna, therefore, the Prince of Yogis that He is, says here that we believe there is happiness in the world of Brahma but that there is no happiness even there.

He asks Arjuna to go to the world beyond all these worlds, the world in which He Himself dwells. This is simply beyond Our imagination. But what is beyond our imagination does exist, nevertheless. If a person dies striving to reach that world, there is no rebirth for him.

Those men indeed know what is Day and what is Night, who know that Brahma's day lasts a thousand yugas and that his night too is a thousand yugas long. (17)

A day and a night of ours are made up of 24 hours. They say that anyone who focuses his eyes on the tip of his nose and meditates will find bliss, but it is necessary to go beyond this. In order to become a *jnani* one must learn to look deep into things. Anyone who practises this method but goes beyond it will study his self and draw far-reaching conclusions, will realize that things are not what they seem. We do not, thus, require a *Gita* to tell us that Brahma must have a day different in length from ours; we can see this ourselves if we use our brains. It seems to us an absolute certainty that the Sun will always be there. He will be a *jnani* who understands the nature of time from a study of one object existing in time. Such a person will take into account all the factors, which ordinary men and women fail to do. The latter would generally reason that, since no one practises control of the senses, it is impossible to practise and ought not to be attempted;

if we reason thus, we shall invite ruin upon ourselves. This is fallacious reasoning.

If we want to know what is a day and what a night, we should have a standard of measurement. How can we measure infinite time? A day as long as a thousand *yugas* and a night of equal length! We should know that there is a day and night of such length in order that we may learn patience, and that, if the result af our effort takes time to show itself, we may not give way to despair. We may have faith in the spinning-wheel, but what progress can we expect from devoted work of only four or five years? We may see no tangible result in our own life-time. Nonetheless, we should have faith and go on working. Having devoted ourselves to this work, we should not give way to despair, nor be proud of ourselves. Let us remember that a thousand *yugas* make one day, and out of a thousand Parvatis one succeeds. There were a great many Parvatis and Shambhus who failed, before one Parvati and one Shambhu succeeded. We should know that this is how the power of *tapas* works.

> *At the coming of Day all the Manifest spring forth from the Unmanifest, and at the coming of Night they are dissolved into that same Unmanifest. (18)*

When Brahma's day begins, the Unmanifest becomes manifest. All these creatures, which had vanished into nothingness, come to life again. When his night begins, the whole creation vanishes, that is, merges into the Unmanifest. In this way, all creation appears and vanishes, and does so endlessly. We have no reason to believe that the universe is fixed and motionless; in fact it is revolving, with a speed a thousand times greater than that of a spindle. The Earth will return into nothingness, will perish, but there will certainly be some who will survive that final destruction.

> *This same multitude of creatures come to birth, O Partha, again and again; they are dissolved at the coming of Night, whether they will or not; and at the break of Day they are reborn. (19)*

When the night comes, whether we wish it or not, the universe returns into nothingness, and when the day comes a new creation appears.

How long shall we remain caught in this endless cycle? To reassure us on this, Shri Krishna says:

But higher than that Unmanifert is another Unmanifest Being, everlasting, which perisheth not when all creatures perish. (20)

There is another Unmanifest Reality beyond this Unmanifest and it is immutable; it is the immutable Reality immanent in all perishable creatures. Everything which exists will perish, but the ground of all this existence is imperishable. Thus, we go a good deal further than the tip of our nose.

This Unmanifest, named the Imperishable, is declared to be the highest goal. For those who reach it there is no return. That is My highest abode. (21)

Shri Krishna says: "You can come to Me by patient striving and living in this world only as a witness. Have faith and devoting yourself to duty, work out the welfare of your soul." The substance of all this is that the supreme *Brahman"* never perishes, everything else does.

The form in which the timeless essence which is God manifests itself is known as His incarnation. We can know that essence in every creature. The principle of oneness does not mean that all of us should become beasts; it means, on the contrary, that God is present in the heart of even the most wicked of creatures, and that the latter awakes to His presence when the time comes. Ramachandra's picture as a child is a product of the poet's imagination, but we may believe it as true, knowing that higher consciousness is present even at that age. If a little child is a *jnani* and still behaves as we know children do, we should say: "The *Brahman* sports before the *Brahman*. Such a child would be a visible form of the *Brahman;* in the same sense that Parivati was the embodiment of *tapascharya* and Krishna of yoga, of the *Brahman*.

This Supreme Being, O Partka, may be won by undivided devotion; in It all beings dwell, by It all is pervaded. (22)

"That supreme state, to be attained in yogic contemplation is beyond my reach": so sang Raychandbhai.

Now I will tell thee, Bharatarshabha, the conditions which determine the exemption from return, as also the return, of yogis after they pass away hence. (23)

"I shall now describe that state"—the word may also mean time— "after reaching which, or that path after treading which, there is no returning."

Fire, Light, Day, the Bright Fortnight, the six months of the Northern Solstice—through these departing men knowing Brahman go to Brahman. (24)

It is often said that this and the next verse do not fit into the teaching of the *Gita,* but we will treat them as if they did.

The *Gita* did not drop down from heaven, nor is it as if every word that Krishna said to Arjuna was written down. Vyasa has given what the Lord said to a seeker and, in doing so, he would include even things which he himself did not understand from his own experience. It may have been a general belief in those times which made people particular that they did important things at particular hours of the day only, or welcomed death during a certain part of the day. The favourites of a king can approach him only at a fixed hour, and no one else can go to him at that time. Similarly, **it may have been the prevalent belief in those days that only people who died in an auspicious hour would reach God; this, of course, did not mean that those who died in some other hour had not aspired and striven in their lives to reach God after death.**

Those who die when there is fire and light, on any day in the bright half of one of the six months following the winter solstice, will reach the *Brahman.* This statement may be intended to have either a literal or an allegorical meaning. If the latter, it means that anyone who has attained a state like the bright half of the month, a state of knowledge as bright as light, will not return to this world after death. On the other hand:

Smoke, Night, the Dark Fortnight, the six months of the Southern Solstice—therethrough the yogi attains to the lunar light and thence returns. (25)

Such a person lives in heaven and, when the merit earned by his virtuous deeds is exhausted, he returns to the earth.

We may, therefore, take either of the two meanings. Anyone who has not attained to full illumination will have to return to this earth; in other words, he who spends his life in disinterested work and prays daily to the Lord with love and devotion will not have to return, for he will have cut as under the bonds of karma. Anyone who departs after a life of disinterested *bhakti* will not have to return.

Some persons treat these two verses as interpolated; we cannot do so, for the copies of the *Gita* which we use contain them. If the meaning of any verse contradicts the very meaning of the *Gita,* we may reject that verse, otherwise we should try to reconcile it with the rest of the teaching. *Kala* in these verses means state, condition. We do not know whether, in the age when the *Gita* was composed, the North and the South Poles were discovered. For those who live in the region of the North Pole, the day and the night are as long as our six months. The period following the winter solstice is a time of light and signifies a waking state, whereas the period following the summer solstice signifies a state of ignorance. We have compared the latter state with the state full of desire and the former with that which is free from desire.

The Lord, Shri Krishna, now proceeds:

> *These two paths—bright and dark—are deemed to be the eternal paths of the world; by the one a man goes to return not, by the other he returns again. (26)*

These two paths, the bright and the dark, that which leads to a state from which there is no returning and the other which leads to a state which is impermanent, have existed from the beginning of time. The bright state is that of the illumination of knowledge and the dark state is that of ignorance. Dying in one state, a person never returns; dying in other, he is bound to return.

> *The yogi knowing these two paths falls not into delusion, O Partha; therefore, at all times, O Arjuna, remain steadfast in yoga. (27)*

The yogi who knows the distincticon between these two paths never succumbs to darkness. He realizes that disinterested *bhakti* is the best form of *bhakti.* If we have faith in the Lord and *bhakti* for Him, why should we forever be begging things from Him? Anyone who is filled with faith and love will feel that there is nothing for him to beg. He will have offered everything to the Lord, placed himself at His mercy. He may say: "All that is mine is yours." Such single-minded *bhakti* is *uttarayana,* it is light, and so on. What, again, is the significance of Krishna's advice to remain yoked to Him at all times? It means that one should cling to knowledge and single-minded devotion. The gods are immortal, but only compared to human beings. They, too, will perish in time. "Therefore," says Shri Krishna, "instead of going to the gods who will perish, if you come to Me, then alone will you get knowledge and in no other way." Arjuna should, Shri Krishna says, keep the knot in his heart, the little grains of dust which cover the knowledge within, so thoroughly cleaned that at the moment of death he will spontaneously have the right thoughts.

> *Whatever fruit of good deeds is laid down as accruing from (a study of) the Vedas, from sacrifices, austerities, and acts of charity—all that the yogi transcends, on knowing this, and reaches the Supreme and Primal Abode. (28)*

We saw in the verse beginning with *yavanartha udapane* that he who has acquired this light and knowledge is in the condition of one who has secured that beyond which nothing else remains to be obtained.

❑❑❑

9

राजविद्याराजगुह्ययोग

श्रीभगवानुवाच

इदं तु ते गुह्यतमं प्रवक्ष्याम्यनसूयवे। ज्ञानं विज्ञानसहितं यज्ज्ञात्वा मोक्ष्यसेऽशुभात्।। 1
राजविद्या राजगुह्यं पवित्रमिदमुत्तमम्। प्रत्यक्षावगमं धर्म्यं सुसुखं कर्तुमव्ययम्।। 2
अश्रद्दधानाः पुरुषा धर्मस्यास्य परन्तप। अप्राप्य मां निवर्तन्ते मृत्युसंसारवर्त्मनि।। 3
मया ततमिदं सर्वं जगदव्यक्तमूर्तिना। मत्स्थानि सर्वभूतानि न चाहं तेष्ववस्थितः।। 4
न च मत्स्थानि भूतानि पश्य मे योगमैश्वरम्। भूतभृन्न च भूतस्थो ममात्मा भूतभावनः।। 5
यथाऽऽकाशस्थितो नित्यं वायुः सर्वत्रगो महान्। तथा सर्वाणि भूतानि मत्स्थानीत्युपधारय।। 6
सर्वभूतानि कौन्तेय प्रकृतिं यान्ति मामिकाम्। कल्पक्षये पुनस्तानि कल्पादौ विसृजाम्यहम्।। 7
प्रकृतिं स्वामवष्टभ्य विसृजामि पुनः पुनः। भूतग्राममिमं कृत्स्नमवशं प्रकृतेर्वशात्।। 8
न च मां तानि कर्माणि निबध्नन्ति धनञ्जय। उदासीनवदासीनमसक्तं तेषु कर्मसु।। 9
मयाऽध्यक्षेण प्रकृतिः सूयते सचराचरम्। हेतुनाऽनेन कौन्तेय जगद्विपरिवर्तते।। 10
अवजानन्ति मां मूढा मानुषीं तनुमाश्रितम्। परं भावमजानन्तो मम भूतमहेश्वरम्।। 11
मोघाशा मोघकर्माणो मोघज्ञाना विचेतसः। राक्षसीमासुरीं चैव प्रकृतिं मोहिनीं श्रिताः।। 12
महात्मानस्तु मां पार्थ दैवीं प्रकृतिमाश्रिताः। भजन्त्यनन्यमनसो ज्ञात्वा भूतादिमव्ययम्।। 13
सततं कीर्तयन्तो मां यतन्तश्च दृढव्रताः। नमस्यन्तश्च मां भक्त्या नित्ययुक्ता उपासते।। 14
ज्ञानयज्ञेन चाऽप्यन्ये यजन्तो मामुपासते। एकत्वेन पृथक्त्वेन बहुधा विश्वतोमुखम्।। 15

अहं क्रतुरहं यज्ञः स्वधाऽहमहमौषधम्। मन्त्रोऽहमहमेवाज्यमहमग्निरहं हुतम्।। 16

पिताहमस्य जगतो माता धाता पितामहः। वेद्यं पवित्रमोङ्कार ऋक् साम यजुरेव च।। 17

गमिर्भर्ता प्रभुः साक्षी निवासः शरणं सुहृत्। प्रभवः प्रलयः स्थानं निधानं बीजमव्ययम्।। 18

तपाम्यहमहं वर्षं निगृह्णाम्युत्सृजामि च। अमृतं चैव मृत्युश्च सदसच्चाहमर्जुन।। 19

त्रैविद्या मां सोमपाः पूतपापा यज्ञैरिष्ट्वा स्वर्गतिं प्रार्थयन्ते।

ते पुण्यमासाद्य सुरेन्द्रलोकमश्नन्ति दिव्यान्दिवि देवभोगान्।। 20

ते तं भुक्त्वा स्वर्गलोकं विशालं क्षीणे पुण्ये मर्त्यलोकं विशन्ति।

एवं त्रयीधर्ममनुप्रपन्ना गतागतं कामकामा लभन्ते।। 21

अनन्याश्चिन्तयन्तो मां ये जनाः पर्युपासते। तेषां नित्याभियुक्तानां योगक्षेमं वहाम्यहम्।। 22

येऽप्यन्यदेवताभक्ता यजन्ते श्रद्धयान्विताः। तेऽपि मामेव कौन्तेय यजन्त्यविधिपूर्वकम्।। 23

अहं हि सर्वयज्ञानां भोक्ता च प्रभुरेव च। न तु मामभिजानन्ति तत्त्वेनातश्च्यवन्ति ते।। 24

यान्ति देवव्रता देवान् पितृन् यान्ति पितृव्रताः। भूतानि यान्ति भूतेज्या यान्ति मद्याजिनोऽपि माम्।। 25

पत्रं पुष्पं फलं तोयं यो मे भक्त्या प्रयच्छति। तदहं भक्त्युपहृतमश्नामि प्रयतात्मनः।। 26

यत्करोषि यदश्नासि यज्जुहोषि ददासि यत्। यत्तपस्यसि कौन्तेय तत्कुरुष्व मदर्पणम्।। 27

शुभाशुभफलैरेवं मोक्ष्यसे कर्मबन्धनैः। संन्यासयोगयुक्तात्मा विमुक्तो मामुपैष्यसि।। 28

समोऽहं सर्वभूतेषु न मे द्वेष्योऽस्ति न प्रियः। ये भजन्ति तु मां भक्त्या मयि ते तेषु चाप्यहम्।। 29

अपि चेत्सुदुराचारो भजते मामनन्यभाक्। साधुरेव स मन्तव्यः सम्यग्व्यवसितो हि सः।। 30

क्षिप्रं भवति धर्मात्मा शश्वच्छान्तिं निगच्छति। कौन्तेय प्रतिजानीहि न मे भक्तः प्रणश्यति।। 31

मां हि पार्थ व्यपाश्रित्य येऽपि स्युः पापयोनयः। स्त्रियो वैश्यास्तथा शूद्रास्तेऽपि यान्ति परां गतिम्।। 32

किं पुनर्ब्राह्मणाः पुण्या भक्ता राजर्षयस्तथा। अनित्यमसुखं लोकमिमं प्राप्य भजस्व माम्।। 33

मन्मना भव मद्भक्तो मद्याजी मां नमस्कुरु। मामेवैष्यसि युक्त्वैवमात्मानं मत्परायणः।। 34

-.-

The Most Secret and Sovereign Yoga of Knowledge

The Lord says:

I will now declare to thee, who art uncensorious, this mysterious knowledge, together with discriminative knowledge, knowing which thou shalt be released from ill.

This is the king of sciences, the king of mysteries, pure and sovereign, capable of direct comprehension, the essence of dharma, easy to practise, changeless. (1, 2)

There was a man who, whenever he got very angry, sat down to do sums in algebra; anyone else who tried to do this, when he ought to be repeating Ramanama, would find the effort a burdensome task. **If someone is dying and cries for help, it would be unfeeling arrogance to tell him that you were busy doing sums in algebra, for it would be a moment when the Shastras could well be thrown into the sea.** Doing a sum in algebra is not in itself a duty, but the aim behind it maybe a duty. Through it, I may know who and where I am. Doing a sum is not by itself a duty, the first duty is service. For instance, eating is never a duty in itself. He is a true man who leaves the dinner table and runs to do an act of service.

The knowledge of this duty is *rajavidya*. It is the king of all secrets, it is sacred and the highest knowledge, it is dharma and worthy to be followed in action, and easy to follow besides; once acquired, it is never destroyed. "I will impart that knowledge to you," says Shri Krishna.

Men who have no faith in this doctrine, O Parantapa, far from coming to Me, return repeatedly to the path of this world of death.

By Me, unmanifest in form, this whole world is pervaded; all beings are in Me, I am not in them. (3, 4)

So long as our eyes of knowledge have not opened, we have no choice but to see with the eyes of faith.

And yet those beings are not in Me. That indeed is My unique power as Lord! Sustainer of all beings, I am not in them; My Self brings them into existence.

As the mighty wind, moving everywhere, is ever contained in ether, even so know that all beings are contained in Me. (5, 6)

Air fills space, but space is not identical with air. We can say that air fills space. Though space is empty, we can say that it is filled with air. And yet space is not air. The air which fills space is still not in it, so God who dwells in all creatures is still not in them. In one sense, He is not in them, for we can see other things with our eyes but not Him.

He who has faith and he who lacks it, both are sincere in their beliefs. God exists for him who has faith, but does not exist for him who lacks it.

A Shastri will be able to explain the point of these two verses.

The Ganga water does, and yet does not, contain dirt. Similarly, even the most wicked of beings exists in God. The cruellest of men, even a *Chandal*, exists in Him, and yet does not. God is above good and bad. **Vyasa puts these contradictory statements together, for our reason knows its limitation in trying to describe the truth. It is enough if we understand that God pervades the entire universe.**

Innumerable ways of falling are open to a man, he need not make any effort for the purpose; it is for rising that one has to strive. We may revere and always keep in a proper place a holy book which we believe helps us on the path of good; but anyone who goes no further than showing it outward reverence will find such reverence a means of bondage. There should, therefore, be discrimination even in reverence; only so will that reverence help us to advance. Outward reverence for a holy book is not all. We should go further than that. We should try to follow the teaching of the book in our life. God is omnipotent and we are His creatures. When, however, we, who are mere ants in His sight try to eat Him up, He uses a part of His infinite power. He is so near that we feel we can touch Him this very moment, and yet we never do, so far away He is. As space and air exist one in the other, so do God and the universe. He who has faith certainly exists in God; he who lacks it does not. God does not force Himself on anyone, but He does not close the door, either, against anyone, who aspires to be united to Him—such is His nature.

All beings, O Kaunteya, merge into my prakriti, at the end of a kalpa, and I send them forth again when a kalpa begins. (7)

The holy books speak of such rise and disappearance of the worlds.

The individual soul, of course, passes through birth and death. But the universe, too, comes into existence and disappears. If the soul, therefore, wishes to know its essence, it will have to transcend the universe. We know for certain that this lamp will one day be destroyed, and yet it is the only thing we can use; it is essential, therefore, that we take care to keep it clean. This Ashram has buildings, which are its body, so to say. They will be destoyed one day. But the Ashram's soul, which is its ideals, will never perish. To realize that imperishable essence, we may even need to put up buildings of brick and mortar. In this way, we must use our reason and discrimination and keep working. If we wish to live in this world, we must put to use even things which will perish, but only with the aim of realizing the imperishable essence beyond them.

Resorting to my prakriti, I send forth again and again this multitude of beings powerless under the sway of prakriti. (8)

But all this activity, O Dhananjaya, does not bind Me, seated as one indifferent, unattached to it. (9)

God acts according to His *prakriti*, and yet He does nothing since He is above even His *prakriti*.

If a king does sinful things, his subjects too suffer. But God, being omniscient, can do nothing without thought. Sin means only what is done without taking thought. How can a person who thinks before acting commit a sin? Likewise, how can one who is by nature inclined to sin act virtuously? If one does good spontaneously, in the same way that our eyes wink automatically, one will not have to suffer the fruits of such good actions. It is man's nature to do good, for all selves are one. That being so, the apparent separateness of each self has no significance. When this is realized, man's ego melts away. Man's essence, which is *atman*, is all-pervading, for he who has realized it will not see himself as different from others, but will see all in himself. For such a person, therefore, doing good becomes his nature. When he seems to be serving other creatures, he is doing so not out of kindness to them but is merely following his own nature. To us who are enveloped in *maya,* it may seem that he is practising virtue, but in truth it is not so; he is acting only according to his nature towards all creatures.

> *With me as Presiding Witness, prakriti gives birth to all that moves and does not move; and because of this, O Kaunteya, the wheel of the world keeps going.*
>
> *Not knowing My transcendent nature as the sovereign Lord of all beings, fools condemn Me incarnated as man. (10, 11)*

"Creatures sunk in darkness, dwelling in the human body, do not know Me," says Shri Krishna, "they disregard Me." Has not Tulsidas said that those who make a distinction between Rama and God are ignorant and know nothing? We project our ignorance on to God too. "They do not know My supreme state, do not know Me as the Lord of all creatures. Labouring under the illusion that I am a human being, they do not know My real essence."

> *Vain are the hopes, actions and knowledge of those witless ones who have resorted to the delusive nature of monsters and devils.*
>
> *But those great souls who resort to the divine nature, O Partha, know Me as the Imperishable Source of all beings and worship Me with an undivided mind. (12, 13)*

The mahatmas, who are ruled by their divine *prakriti,* like Vibhishana and others, worship Me with their minds illumined by knowledge and with single-minded devotion—Me who am the Creator of all beings.

> *Always declaring My glory, striving in steadfast faith; they do Me devout homage; ever attached to Me, they worship Me.*
>
> *Yet others, with knowledge-sacrifice, worship Me, who am to be seen everywhere, as one, as different or as many. (14, 15)*

Others worship Me by striving for knowledge. Some of them worship Me as the only One (that is, believing that all this is Vasudeva), some others worship My different manifestations and others still worship Me in everything which exists.

We may take *vishvatomukham* to go with *man,* and understand the line to mean that "they worship Me who am the same in all or dwell in all"; or we may interpret *ekatvena* to mean "with devotion" and *prithaktvena* to mean that "they look upon Me as the Lord and themselves as My devotees and worship Me in that spirit". Or, *ekatvena* may mean "Worshipping Me as Impersonal Absolute" and *prithakatvena* may mean "Worshipping Me as personal God". In any case, *vishvatomukham* taken as an independent, third term, yields no sense.

> *I am the sacrificial vow; I am the sacrifice; I the ancestral oblation; I the herb; I the sacred text; I the clarified butter; I the fire; I the burnt offering.*
>
> *Of this universe I am Father, Mother, Creator, Grandsire; I am what is to be known, the sacred syllable AUM; the Rig, the Sama and the Yajur.*
>
> *I am the Goal, the Sustainer, the Lord, the Witness, the Abode, the Refuge, the Friend; the Origin, the End, the Preservation, the Treasure-house, the Imperishable Seed. (16-18)*

I am *gati* which means *moksha*—the state which human beings strive to attain. I am the sustainer, the Lord, and the witness. I am the abode, and the shelter. I am *suhrid* which means a kind friend who serves me without expectation of reward.

> *I give heat; I hold back and pour forth rain; I am deathlessness and also death, O Arjuna; Being and not-Being as well. (19)*

I give heat, but in the form of the sun which gives happiness and the light of knowledge to all creatures. I draw the rains and release them. I am death and I am immortality; I am being and also non-being.

That is, every object and every state which we can think of in this universe are God. This means that God is not merely all that is good, He is also the evil. Nothing exists unless He wills it. It is not true that God is Lord of light and Satan of darkness. While we live in this body, we may believe in these dualities. We should engrave Tulsidasji's words in our hearts, that while we are enveloped in *maya,* all this, which is false, will seem as true. The nacre will appear as silver and the sun's rays will appear as the mirage. We shall continue to think in this way till a *jnani* opens our eyes and convinces us that the appearance of the rope as serpent, of the nacre as silver and of the sun's rays as mirage is but the work of our imagination.

We believe that God is both good and evil and, believing that, some of us ask what harm there is in following evil. But it is quite wrong if we argue thus. The point is not that we should act like scorpions or centipedes, but that we should have goodwill for them, without ourselves becoming poisonous like them. The Lord has here stated a profound truth which is beyond the capacity of our reason to comprehend. What He has stated cannot possibly be true in this world. We can only imagine that it must be true in some sense. Being and non-being, virtue and sin, immortality and death. these are contradictory things. They cannot be true for human beings, they can be so only for God. That third state in which contraries are reconciled is not a mere mixture of the two. Hydrogen and oxygen together yield water, but water does not display the separate properties of either; it has characteris,tics of it own. Similarly, we must not imagine that God has in Him the qualities of both virtue and sin, but should think that He has something else which is different from either. If we had both virtue and sin in us, there would be an explosion, but Siva swallows both. The existence of the two in God is a miracle, and He alone knows its mystery. We should make no attempt to cultivate such a state. If we try to combine the two in us, such an attempt to imitate God will simply destroy us.

Followers of the three Vedas, who drink the soma juice and are purged of sin, worship Me with sacrifice and pray for going to heaven; they reach the holy world of the gods and enjoy in heaven the divine joys of the gods. (20)

Those who perform the rituals enjoined in the three Vedas, who drink *somarasa* **(in the region of the North Pole *somarasa* was food and it would be a crime to refuse it to anyone, for if given to a dying man it saved life)**, who wash away their sins and worship the Lord by performing sacrifices, pray that they should go to heaven. They go to the sacred realm of Indra and there enjoy divine pleasures such as gods do.

They enjoy the vast world of heaven, and their merit spent, they enter the world of the mortals; thus those who, following the Vedic law, long for the fruit of their action earn but the round of birth and death.

As for those who worship Me, thinking on Me alone and nothing else, ever attached to Me, I bear the burden of getting them what they need. (21, 22)

Yoga means realization of God and *Kshema* means safeguarding of the means which help us to attain it.

Even those who, devoted to other gods, worship them in full faith, even they, O Kaunteya worship none but Me, though not according to the rule. (23)

The right method is to have no intermediary between oneself and God. "But," Shri Krishna says, "those who seek Me through the gatekee-pers that stand between, they too worship Me, for they worship these in order to reach Me."

For I am the Acceptor and the Director of all sacrifices; but not recognizing Me as I am, they go astray. (24)

"I am," says the Lord "the recipient and the Lord of all *yajnas.*" That is, he who does everything without thinking that he himself does it can say that not he but the Lord does everything. "Those, however, who do not know the truth and, therefore, do not know Me, return again to the world."

The sinful man, so long as he is conscious of his ego describes himself as the most wicked of men. Tulsidas says, on the one hand, that there could be none as lustful, lecherous, degraded and adulterous as he was and, on the other hand, attributes all his sins to God, for, since he had no ego in him, how could he have committed those sins? The river Ganga washes away all kinds of sins, but she receives no stain. Likewise, the timeless body in Rama is sinless. The physical Rama, of course, is subject to sin. If we pervert this idea and start committing sins and then say that sins cannot touch us, we shall be like the frog in the fable who tried to blow his body into the size of an ox and so burst. A *bhakta* will say: "I am a sinful man, but I am in your hands." Beyond this, our reason does not work. "Do not describe man as God; he is not God, but he is not different from the Iight of God."

Those who worship the gods go to the gods; those who worship the manes go to the manes; those who worship the spirits go to the spirits; but those who worship Me come to Me.

Any offering of leaf, flower, fruit, or water made to Me in devotion by an earnest soul, I lovingly accept. (25, 26)

The Lord did not accept the fruit sent by Duryodhana, for he had not sent it with love. His motive was to get his own aim served through Shri Krishna. He wanted the Lord's help on his own terms. He had not mastered the self. But Vidura, who was a man of simple heart, offered a plain dish of leafy greens and the Lord accepted it with love, for Vidura's *bhakti* was unrivalled and his heart was straightforward and clean. He felt no awe for the wealth of the mighty.

> *Whatever thou dost, whatever thou eatest, whatever thou offerest as sacrifice or gift, whatever austerity thou dost perform, O Kaunteya, dedicate all to Me.*
>
> *So doing thou shalt be released from the bondage of action yielding good and evil fruit; having accomplished both renunciation and performance, thou shalt be released from birth and death and come unto Me. (27, 28)*

"If you live thus, you will be free from the bonds of karma which are sometimes good sometimes evil in their fruit, for I shall be the recipient of all that you enjoy." He who has purified himself through sannyasa yoga—who dedicates to the Lord all that he does, who keeps on doing useful work right till the end of his life, but in a spirit of dedication to the Lord—such a one goes to Him after death.

> *I am the same to all beings; with Me there is none disfavoured, none favoured; but those who worship Me with devotion are in Me and I in them. (29)*

If we seek refuge in the Lord, He will give us all that we can wish. If we go to the Ganga, we can have the Ganga water, but we shall have only as much as fills our cupped palm if that is all we seek. The Lord provides a grain for the ant and a cartload for the elephant.

> *A sinner, howsoever great, if he turns to Me with undivided devotion, must indeed be counted a saint; for he has a settled resolve. (30)*

A man like Ajamila may have resolved to purify himself of the evil in him, and he may sit down in a firm posture for yoga; maybe his thoughts do not leave him, but he is none theless a sadhu who keeps repeating Om and is firm in his resolution. But another person who is not firm is his mind and not regular in practice, who follows no method in his work, may be a good man and still he does not deserve to be called a sadhu.

For soon he becomes righteous and wins everlasting peace; know for a certainty, O Kaunteya, that My bhakta never perishes. (31)

Such a person soon becomes a holy man, and attains inviolable peace of mind. We should not, therefore, regard even the most wicked of men as wicked. He can become good in this very life. Shri Krishna says: "Be certain, O Arjuna, that no *bhakta* of mine ever perishes."

This body perishes, but he dies after becoming a good man rather than a wicked one.

For finding refuge in Me, even those who though are born of the womb of sin, women, Vaisyas and Sudras too, reach the supreme goal. (32)

Anyone who surrenders himself or herself to Me,"assures the Lord, "whether man or woman, Vaisya or Sudra, or one born among wicked people— in a family of the most wicked *Chandals*— even then such a person will attain the supreme state."

The Lord has given a great assurance to the world in these verses. This is His reply to those learned in the Vedas. Such persons argue that those who have not studied the Vedas cannot realize God. It was believed in those days that women, Vaisyas and Sudras cannot attain *moksha.* In fact, Krishna tended cows as a boy in Nanda's family and did the work of a Sudra. The Vaisya's function was rearing cow and agriculture. But in course of time those who were engaged in agriculture came to be regarded as Sudras. **Shri Krishna says here that, even if Vaisyas and Sudras are not able to study the Vedas, they can certainly attain the blessed state. Anyone who, though ignorant of the Vedas, knows the *Brahman,* and has a pure heart is certain to attain this state.**

How much more then, the pure Brahmins and seer-kings who are my devotees? Do thou worship Me, therefore, since thou hast come to this fleeting and joyless world.

On Me fix thy mind, to Me bring thy devotion, to Me offer thy sacrifice, to Me make thy obeisance; thus having attached thyself to Me and made Me thy end and aim, to Me indeed shalt thou come. (33, 34)

"Forget yourself in Me," says Shri Krishna, "meditate constantly on Me, let your atman be in ceaseless communion with Me, and live with your heart ever united with Me; if you live thus, I shall draw you towards Me."

"You need only allow yourself to be drawn, and shall not resist. You may not draw Me, but I can draw you. You will be able to understand this riddle, no one else will."

This chapter has also been named *Rajavidya* and *Rajaguhyayoga.* Shri Krishna tells Arjuna that He has explained the highest knowledge and expounded the highest mystery—the meaning of yoga and *kshema.* The union of yoga is to be achieved with the Lord; one should not aspire to earn great riches or rise to a position of honour or win an empire in this world. All that is needed is fixed determination to realize God. What is the good of any pleasure we can get through the senses—the eyes, the nose, the ears and so on? We hould not be allured by it, for such pleasure is shortlived. There were emperors, but they have passed away. He whom we seek dwells in our hearts, and the holy temple in which He sits opens only by the means of prayer. The Lord explained this by saying *manmana bhava madbhakto madyaji* "I, am," He says, "the author and sustainer of all, I am the friend, I am the source, the cause of existence and of the final destruction I am all this. There is nothing else. I am all that there is. You are of no consequence. The other gods in the worlds in between will also perish, like you. I alone never perish. If you wish that you should not perish, you should come to My world. and that you can do by surrendering your whole mind to Me. Whether you are engaged in bathing or washing or any other like activities, if you are repeating my name the while and if you dedicate to Me all that you eat, if you worship Me as you give your body its hire, you will surely come to Me."

❑❑❑

10

विभूतियोग

श्रीभगवानुवाच

भूय एवं महाबाहो श्रृणु मे परमं वचः। यत्तेऽहं प्रीयमाणाय वक्ष्यामि हितकाम्यया।। 1

न मे विदुः सुरगणाः प्रभवं न महर्षयः। अहमादिर्हि देवानां महर्षीणां च सर्वशः।। 2

यो मामजमनादिं च वेत्ति लोकमहेश्वरम्। असम्मूढः स मर्त्येषु सर्वपापैः प्रमुच्यते।। 3

बुद्धिर्ज्ञानमसम्मोहः क्षमा सत्यं दमः शमः। सुखं दुःखं भवोऽभावो भयं चाभयमेव च।। 4

अहिंसा समता तुष्टिस्तपो दानं यशोऽयशः। भवन्ति भावा भूतानां मत्त एव पृथग्विधाः।। 5

महर्षयः सप्त पूर्वे चत्वारो मनवस्तथा। मद्भावा मानसा जाता येषां लोक इमाः प्रजाः।। 6

एतां विभूतिं योगं च मम यो वेत्ति तत्त्वतः। सोऽविकम्पेन योगेन युज्यते नात्र संशयः।। 7

अहं सर्वस्य प्रभवो मत्तः सर्वं प्रवर्तते। इति मत्वा भजन्ते मां बुधा भावसमन्विताः।। 8

मच्चित्ता मद्गतप्राणा बोधयन्तः परस्परम्। कथयन्तश्च मां नित्यं तुष्यन्ति च रमन्ति च।। 9

तेषां सततयुक्तानां भजतां प्रीतिपूर्वकम्। ददामि बुद्धियोगं तं येन मामुपयान्ति ते।। 10

तेषामेवानुकम्पार्थमहमज्ञानजं तमः। नाशयाम्यात्मभावस्थो ज्ञानदीपेन भास्वता।। 11

अर्जुन उवाच

परं ब्रह्म परं धाम पवित्रं परमं भवान्। पुरुषं शाश्वतं दिव्यमादिदेवमजं विभुम्।। 12

आहुस्त्वामृषयः सर्वे देवर्षिर्नारदस्तथा। असितो देवलो व्यासः स्वयं चैव ब्रवीषि मे।। 13

सर्वमेतदृतं मन्ये यन्मां वदसि केशव। न हि ते भगवन् व्यक्तिं विदुर्देवा न दानवाः।। 14

स्वयमेवात्मनाऽऽत्मानं वेत्थ त्वं पुरुषोत्तम। भूतभावन भूतेश देवदेव जगत्पते।। 15

वक्तुमर्हस्यशेषेण दिव्या ह्यात्मविभूतयः। याभिर्विभूतिभिर्लोकानिमांस्त्वं व्याप्य तिष्ठसि।। 16

कथं विद्यामहं योगिंस्त्वां सदा परिचिन्तयन्। केषु केषु च भावेषु चिन्त्योऽसि भगवन्मया।। 17

विस्तरेणात्मनो योगं विभूतिं च जनार्दन। भूयः कथय तृप्तिर्हि शृण्वतो नास्ति मेऽमृतम्।। 18

श्रीभगवानुवाच

हन्त ते कथयिष्यामि दिव्या ह्यात्मविभूतयः। प्राधान्यतः कुरुश्रेष्ठ नास्त्यन्तो विस्तरस्य मे।। 19

अहमात्मा गुडाकेश सर्वभूताशयस्थितः। अहमादिश्च मध्यं च भूतानामन्त एव च।। 20

आदित्यानामहं विष्णुर्ज्योतिषां रविरंशुमान्। मरीचिर्मरुतामस्मि नक्षत्राणामहं शशी।। 21

वेदानां सामवेदोऽस्मि देवानामस्मि वासवः। इन्द्रियाणां मनश्चास्मि भूतानामस्मि चेतना।। 22

रुद्राणां शङ्करश्चास्मि वित्तेशो यक्षरक्षसाम्। वसूनां पावकश्चास्मि मेरुः शिखरिणामहम्।। 23

पुरोधसां च मुख्यं मां विद्धि पार्थ बृहस्पतिम्। सेनानीनामहं स्कन्दः सरसामस्मि सागरः।। 24

महर्षीणां भृगुरहं गिरामस्म्येकमक्षरम्। यज्ञानां जपयज्ञोऽस्मि स्थावराणां हिमालयः।। 25

अश्वत्थः सर्ववृक्षाणां देवर्षीणां च नारदः। गन्धर्वाणां चित्ररथः सिद्धानां कपिलो मुनिः।। 26

उच्चैःश्रवसमश्वानां विद्धि माममृतोद्भवम्। एरावतं गजेन्द्राणां नराणां च नराधिपम्।। 27

आयुधानामहं वज्रं धेनूनामस्मि कामधुक्। प्रजनश्चास्मि कन्दर्पः सर्पाणानस्मि वासुकिः।। 28

अनन्तश्चास्मि नागानां वरुणो यादसामहम्। पितृणामर्यमा चास्मि यमः संयमतामहम्।। 29

प्रह्लादश्चास्मि दैत्यानां कालः कलयतामहम्। मृगाणां च मृगेन्द्रोऽहं वैनतेयश्च पक्षिणाम्।। 30

पवनः पवतामस्मि रामः शस्त्रभृतामहम्। झषाणां मकरश्चास्मि स्रोतसामस्मि जाह्नवी।। 31

सर्गाणामादिरन्तश्च मध्यं चैवाहमर्जुन। अध्यात्मविद्या विद्यानां वादः प्रवदतामहम्।। 32

अक्षराणामकारोऽस्मि द्वन्द्वः सामासिकस्य च। अहमेवाक्षयः कालो धाताऽहं विश्वतोमुखः।। 33

मृत्यु सर्वहरश्चाहमुद्भवश्च भविष्यताम्। कीर्तिः श्रीर्वाक्च नारीणां स्मृतिर्मेधा धृतिः क्षमा।। 34

बृहत्साम तथा साम्नां गायत्री छन्दसामहम्। मासानां मार्गशीर्षोऽहमृतूनां कुसुमाकरः।। 35

द्यूतं छलयतामस्मि तेजस्तेजस्विनामहम्। जयोऽस्मि व्यवसायोऽस्मि सत्त्वं सत्त्ववतामहम्।। 36

वृष्णीनां वासुदेवोऽस्मि पाण्डवानां धनञ्जयः। मुनीनामप्यहं व्यासः कवीनामुशना कविः।। 37

दण्डो दमयतामस्ति नीतिरस्मि जिगीषताम्। मानं चैवास्मि गुह्यानां ज्ञानं ज्ञानवतामहम्।। 38

यच्चापि सर्वभूतानां बीजं तदहमर्जुन। न तदस्ति विना यत्स्यान् मया भूतं चराचरम्।। 39

नान्तोऽस्मि मम दिव्यानां विभूतीनां परन्तप। एष तूद्देशतः प्रोक्तो विभूतेर्विस्तरो मया।। 40

यद्यद्विभूतिमत्सत्त्वं श्रीमदूर्जितमेव वा। तत्तदेवावगच्छ त्वं मम तेजोंऽशसम्भवम्।। 41

अथवा बहुनैतेन किं ज्ञानेन तवार्जुन। विष्टभ्याहमिदं कृत्स्नमेकांशेन स्थितो जगत्।। 42

'I AM EVERYTHING, AND THE BEST'

The Lord says:

Yet once more, O Mahabahu, hear My supreme word, which I will utter to thee, gratified one, for thy benefit.

Neither the gods nor the great seers know My origin; for I am, every way, the origin of them both.

He who knows Me, the great Lord of the worlds, as birthless and without beginning, he among mortals, undeluded, is released from sins. (1-3)

Those who know Me as the Unborn, the Beginningless and the Supreme Lord of all creatures do not sink into the darkness of ignorance. A person who has sunk in darkness knows the night as day and the day as night. Among all these creatures who are bound to perish, the *jnani* becomes free from all sins, for he will have no vestige of aversion and attachment, no trace of egotism; he will remain unaffected by the pairs of opposites, will ever be humble and believe that it is the Lord who provides for his living.

Discernment, knowledge, freedom from delusion, long suffering, truth, self-restraint, inward calm, pleasure, pain, birth, death, fear and fearlessness.

Non-violence, even-mindedness, contentment, austerity, beneficence, good and ill fame,—all these various attributes of creatures proceed verily from Me. (4, 5)

All the qualities mentioned in these two verses, intellect, knowledge, the absence of ignorant attachment, forgiveness, truthfulness, control of the senses, serenity, happiness and suffering, birth and death, fear and absence of fear, ahimsa, inward poise and contentment, *tapas,* making gifts, good name or evil reputation among men—these conditions exist in all creatures and I am the cause of each one of them.

The creator of all beings is also the cause of all the good and evil which we see in these beings.

The seven great seers, the ancient four, and the Manus too were born of Me and of My mind, and of them were born all the creatures in the world.

He who knows in truth this My immanence and My yoga becomes gifted with unshakable yoga; of this there is no doubt. (6, 7)

Everything which exists is created by the Lord. He who believes, not merely with his reason but with his heart, that no creature can live or act without His permission or except as He wills, yokes himself to Him in single-minded devotion, but he who forgets the Lord and believes in his pride that he rises by his own efforts labours under a delusion. There is no doubt at all that he who believes in God from the depth of his heart and obeys the Lord who dwells in him attains to a state of serenity which is never perturbed.

I am the source of all, all proceeds from Me; knowing this, the wise worship Me with hearts full of devotion.

With Me in their thoughts their whole soul devoted to Me, teaching one another, with Me ever on their lips, they live in contentment and joy.

To these, ever in tune with Me worshipping Me with affectionate devotion, I give the power of selfless action, whereby they come to Me. (8-10)

In this way knowledge comes spontaneously to a *bhakta*. He does not have to wade through big volumes. But he who believes that he will acquire knowledge first and cultivate *bhakti* afterwards will fail miserably in his aim. No one can acquire knowledge in that way. Such knowledge breeds, if anything, pride. But he who lovingly cultivates devotion for the Lord and constantly thinks on Him gets knowledge without any special effort to that end.

Out of very compassion for them, I who dwell in their hearts, destroy the darkness, born of ignorance, with the refulgent lamp of knowledge. (11)

Arjuna said:

Lord! Thou art the supreme Brahman, the supreme Abode, the supreme Purifier! Everlasting Celestial Being, the Primal God, Unborn; All-pervading.

Thus have all the seers-the divine seer Narada, Asita, Devala, Vyasa—declared Thee; and Thou Thyself dost tell me so.

All that Thou tellest me is true, I know, O Keshava, verily, Lord, neither the gods nor the demons know Thy manifestation. Thyself alone Thou knowest by Thyself, O Purushottama, O Source and Lord of all beings, God of gods, O Ruler of the universe! Indeed Thou oughtest to tell me of all Thy manifestations, without a remainder, whereby Thou dost pervade these worlds.

O Yogi! constantly meditating on Thee, how am I to know Thee? In what various aspects am I to think of Thee, O Lord?

Recount to me yet again, in full detail, Thy unique power and Thy immanence, O Janardana! For my ears cannot be sated with listening to Thy life-giving words. (12-18)

One who does engraving work everyday does not tire of it. He returns to it whenever he is free. Similarly, Arjuna, who loves repeating Shri Krishna's name in devotion, requests Him again and again to describe His powers till the latter can say no more.

The Lord says:

Yea, I will unfold to thee, O Kurushreshtha, My divine manifestation, —the chiefest only; for there is no limit to their extent.

I am the Atman, O Gudakesha, seated in the heart of every being; I am the beginning, the middle and the end of all beings.

Of the Adityas I am Vishnu; of luminaries, the radiant Sun; of Maruts I am Marichi; of constellations, the moon.

Of the Vedas I am the Sama Veda; of the gods, Indra; of the senses I am the mind; of beings I am the consciousness.

Of Rudras I am Shankara; of Yakshas and Rakshasas Kubera; of Vasus I am the Fire; of mountains Meru.

Of priests, O Partha, know Me to be the chief Brihaspati; of army captains I am Kartikeya; and of waters, the ocean.

Of the great seers I am Bhrigu; of words lam the one syllable

'AUM', of sacrifices I am the Japa sacrifice; of things immovable, the Himalayas.

Of all trees I am Ashvattha; of the divine seers, Narada; of the heavenly choir I am Chitraratha; of the perfected I am Kapila the ascetic.

Of horses, know Me to be Uchchaihshravas born with Amrita; of mighty elephants I am Airavata; of men, the monarch.

Of weapons I am Vajra; of cows, Kamadhenu; I am Kandarpa, the god of generation; of serpents I am Vasuki.

Of cobras I am Ananta; of water-dwellers I am Varuna; of the manes I am Aryaman; and of the chastisers, Yama.

Of demons I am Prahlada; of reckoners, the Time; of beasts I am the lion; and of birds, Garuda.

Of cleansing agents I am the Wind; of wielders of weapons Rama; of fishes I am the crocodile; of rivers, the Ganges.

Of creations I am the beginning, end and middle, O Arjuna; of sciences, the science of spiritual knowledge; of dehaters, the right argument.

Of letters, the letter A; of compounds I am the Dvandva; I am the imperishable Time; I am the creator to be seen everywhere.

All-seizing Death am I, as also the source of things to be; in feminine virtues I am Kirti (glory), Shri (beauty), Vak (speech), Smriti (memory), Medha (intelligence), Dhriti (constancy) and Kshama (forgiveness).

Of Saman hymns I am Brihat Saman; of metres, Gayatrii of months I am Margashirsha; of seasons, the spring. (19-35)

"I am *Brihat Saman* among *Saman* hymns and *Gayatri* among metres. Among the months, I am *Margashirsha.* (When in old times the Aryans lived in the region of the North Pole, this was regarded as the first month of the year and that is why it is mentioned here). Among the seasons I am Spring."

Of deceivers I am the dice-play; of the splendid, the splendour; I am victory, I am resolution, I am the goodness of the good. (36)

"I am the gaming of those who indulge in gambling." This is merely intended to point out that God exists not only in what is good in the world, but also in what is evil. Shri Krishna could also have said that He was the sin of the wicked. He could certainly have said that He was Ravana among the demons, for He let Ravana have his way and enjoy himself only as long as He chose. The author's intention is only to assert that God is omnipotent. God's creation contains both good and evil. By saying this, Shri Krishna gives us some freedom to choose between the two. To us who are confined in the prison of this body, he grants that freedom. He gives us the freedom to shake off our bonds. If a prisoner condemned to imprisonment for life is permitted a seemingly unimportant condition by fulfilling which he can be free, it will be a great thing for him, for he can secure his freedom through It. We are in the same condition, for the Lord has assured us that we can be what we wish to be.

I am the splendour of the splendid. I am victory, resolution and the goodness of the good.

> *Of Vrishnis I am Vasudeva; of Pandavas Dhananjaya; of ascetics I am Vyasa; and of seers, Ushanas.*
>
> *I am the rod of those that punish; the strategy of those seeking victory; of secret things I am silence, and the knowledge of those that know.*
>
> *Whatever is the seed of every being, O Arjuna, that am I; there is nothing, whether moving or fixed, that can be without Me.*
>
> *There is no end to my divine manifestations; what extent of them I have told thee now is only by way of illustration.*
>
> *Whatever is glorious, beautiful and mighty know thou that all such has issued from a fragment of My splendour.*
>
> *But why needst thou to learn this at great length, O Arjuna? With but a part of Myself I stand upholding this universe. (37-42)*

If we have an idea of the infinite powers of the Lord, we shall become humble. We will not then follow the example of Narad who once felt proud of the one power which he possessed. The Lord has said that even being proud is His privilege. The substance of all that He has said is that we should learn to be the humblest of the humble. Knowing that there is no limit to the power of God, we should submit to violence if anyone attacks us, without offering violence in return. If we attempt to resist him with violence, God will humble our pride, for there has been no demon, from Ravana downwards, whom the Lord has not destroyed.

❑❑❑

11

विश्वरूपदर्शनयोग

अर्जुन उवाच

मदनुग्रहाय परमं गुह्यमध्यात्मसञ्ज्ञितम्। यत्त्वयोक्तं वचस्तेन मोहोऽयं विगतो मम।। 1

भवाप्ययौ हि भूतानां श्रुतौ विस्तरशो मया। त्वतः कमलपत्राक्ष माहात्म्यमपि चाव्ययम्।। 2

एवमेतद्यथाऽऽत्थ त्वमात्मानं परमेश्वर। द्रष्टुमिच्छामि ते रूपमैश्वरं पुरुषोत्तम।। 3

मन्यसे यदि तच्छक्यं मया द्रष्टुमिति प्रभो। योगेश्वर ततो मे त्वं दर्शयात्मानमव्ययम्।। 4

श्रीभगवानुवाच

पश्य मे पार्थ रूपाणि शतशोऽथ सहस्रशः। नानाविधानि दिव्यानि नानावर्णाकृतीनि च।। 5

पश्यादित्यान् वसून् रुद्रानश्विनौ मरुतस्तथा। बहून्यदृष्टपूर्वाणि पश्याश्चर्याणि भारत।। 6

इहैकस्थं जगत्कृत्स्नं पश्याद्य सचराचरम्। मम देहे गुडाकेश यच्चान्यद् द्रष्टुमिच्छसि।। 7

न तु मां शक्यसे द्रष्टुमनेनैव स्वचक्षुषा। दिव्यं ददामि ते चक्षुः पश्य मे योगैश्वरम्।। 8

सञ्जय उवाच

एवमुक्त्वा ततो राजन् महायोगेश्वरो हरिः। दर्शयामास पार्थाय परमं रूपमैश्वरम्।। 9

अनेकवक्त्रनयनमनेकाद्भुतदर्शनम्। अनेकदिव्याभरणं दिव्यानेकोद्यतायुधम्।। 10

दिव्यमाल्याम्बरधरं दिव्यगन्धानुलेपनम्। सर्वाश्चर्यमयं देवमनन्तं विश्वतोमुखम्।। 11

दिवि सूर्यसहस्रस्य भवेद्युगपदुत्थिता। यदि भाः सदृशी सा स्याद्भासस्तस्य महात्मनः।। 12

तत्रैकस्थं जगत्कृत्स्नं प्रविभक्तमनेकधा। अपश्यद् देवदेवस्य शरीरे पाण्डवस्तदा।। 13

ततः स विस्मयाविष्टो हृष्टरोमा धनञ्जयः। प्रणम्य शिरसा देवं कृताञ्जलिरभाषत।। 14

अर्जुन उवाच

पश्यामि देवांस्तव देव देहे सर्वांस्तथा भूतविशेषसङ्घान्।

ब्रह्माणमीशं कमलासनस्थ-मृषींश्च सर्वानुरगांश्च दिव्यान।। 15

अनेकबाहूदरवक्त्रनेत्रं पश्यामि त्वां सर्वतोऽनन्तरूपम्।

नान्तं न मध्यं न पुनस्तवादिं पश्यामि विश्वेश्वर विश्वरूप।। 16

किरीटिनं गदिनं चक्रिणं च तेजोराशिं सर्वतो दीप्तिमन्तम्।

पश्यामि त्वां दुर्निरीक्ष्यं समन्ताद् दीप्तानलार्कद्युतिमप्रमेयम्।। 17

त्वमक्षरं परमं वेदितव्यं त्वमस्य विश्वस्य परं निधानम्।

त्वमव्ययः शाश्वतधर्मगोप्ता सनातनस्त्वं पुरुषो मतो मे।। 18

अनादिमध्यान्तमनन्तवीर्य-मनन्तबाहुं शशिसूर्यनेत्रम्।

पश्यामि त्वां दीप्तहुताशवक्त्रं स्वतेजसा विश्वमिदं तपन्तम्।। 19

द्यावापृथिव्योरिदमन्तरं हि व्याप्तं त्वयैकेन दिशश्च सर्वाः।

दृष्ट्वाऽद्भुतं रुपमुग्रं तवेदं लोकत्रयं प्रव्यथितं महात्मन्।। 20

अमी हि त्वां सुरसङ्घा विशन्ति केचिद्भीताः प्राञ्जलयो गृणन्ति।

स्वस्तीत्युक्त्वा महर्षिसिद्धसङ्घाः स्तुवन्ति त्वां स्तुतिभिः पुष्कलाभिः।। 21

रुद्रादित्या वसवो ये च साध्या विश्वेऽश्विनौ मरुतश्चोष्मपाश्च।

गन्धर्वयक्षासुरसिद्धसङ्घा वीक्षन्ते त्वां विस्मिताश्चैव सर्वे।। 22

रूपं महत्ते बहुवक्त्रनेत्रं महाबाहो बहुबाहूरुपादम्।

बहूदरं बहुदंष्ट्राकरालं दृष्ट्वा लोकाः प्रव्यथितास्तथाऽहम्।। 23

नभः स्पृशं दीप्तमनेकवर्णं व्यात्ताननं दीप्तविशालनेत्रम्।

दृष्ट्वा हि त्वां प्रव्यथितान्तरात्मा धृतिं न विन्दामि शमं च विष्णो।। 24

द्रंष्टाकरालानि च ते मुखानि दृष्ट्वैव कालानलसन्निभानि।

दिशो न जाने न लभे च शर्म प्रसीद देवेश जगन्निवास।। 25

अमी च त्वां धृतराष्ट्रस्य पुत्राः सर्वे सहैवावनिपालसङ्घैः।

भीष्मो द्रोणः सूतपुत्रस्तथासौ सहास्मदीयैरपि योधमुख्यैः।। 26

वक्त्राणि ते त्वरमाणा विशन्ति दंष्ट्राकरालानि भयानकानि।

केचिद्विलग्ना दशनान्तरेषु सन्दृश्यन्ते चूर्णितैरुत्तमाङ्गैः।। 27

यथा नदीनां बहवोऽम्बुवेगाः समुद्रमेवाभिमुखा द्रवन्ति।

तथा तवामी नरलोकवीरा विशन्ति वक्त्राण्यभिविज्वलन्ति।। 28

यथा प्रदीप्तं ज्वलनं पतङ्गा विशन्ति नाशाय समृद्धवेगाः।

तथैव नाशाय विशन्ति लोका-स्तवापि वक्त्राणि समृद्धवेगाः।। 29

लेलिह्यसे ग्रसमानः समन्ता-ल्लोकान् समग्रान् वदनैर्ज्वलद्भिः।

तेजोभिरापूर्य जगत्समग्रं भासस्तवोग्राः प्रतपन्ति विष्णो।। 30

आख्याहि मे को भवानुग्ररूपो नमोऽस्तु ते देववर प्रसीद।

विज्ञातुमिच्छामि भवन्तमाद्यं न हि प्रजानामि तव प्रवृत्तिम्।। 31

श्रीभगवानुवाच

कालोऽस्मि लोकक्षयकृत्प्रवृद्धो लोकान् समाहर्तुमिह प्रवृत्तः।

ऋतेऽपि त्वां न भविष्यन्ति सर्वे येऽवस्थिताः प्रत्यनीकेषु योधाः।। 32

तस्मात्त्वमुत्तिष्ठ यशो लभस्व जित्वा शत्रून् भुङ्क्ष्व राज्यं समृद्धम्।

मयैवैते निहताः पूर्वमेव निमित्तमात्रं भव सव्यसाचिन्।। 33

द्रोणं च भीष्मं च जयद्रथं च कर्णं तथाऽन्यानपि योधवीरान्।

मया हतांस्त्वं जहि मा व्यथिष्ठा युद्धयस्व जेताऽसि रणे सपत्नान्।। 34

एतच्छ्रुत्वा वचनं केशवस्य कृताञ्जलिर्वेपमानः किरीटी।

नमस्कृत्वा भूय एवाह कृष्णं सगद्गदं भीतभीतः प्रणम्य।। 35

अर्जुन उवाच

स्थाने हृषीकेश तव प्रकीर्त्या जगत्प्रहृष्यत्यनुरज्यते च।

रक्षांसि भीतानि दिशो द्रवन्ति सर्वे नमस्यन्ति च सिद्धसङ्घाः।। 36

कस्माच्च ते न नमेरन्महात्मन् गरीयसे ब्रह्मणोऽप्यादिकर्त्रे।

अनन्त देवेश जगन्निवास त्वमक्षरं सदसत्तत्परं यत्।। 37

त्वमादिदेवः पुरुषः पुराण-स्त्वमस्य विश्वस्य परं निधानम्।

वेत्ताऽसि वेद्यं च परं च धाम त्वया ततं विश्वमनन्तरूप।। 38

वायुर्यमोऽग्निर्वरुणः शशाङ्कः प्रजापतिस्त्वं प्रपितामहश्च।

नमो नमस्तेऽस्तु सहस्त्रकृत्वः पुनश्च भूयोऽपि नमो नमस्ते।। 39

नमः पुरस्तादश पृष्ठतस्ते नमोऽस्तु ते सर्वत एव सर्व।

अनन्तवीर्यामितविक्रमस्त्वं सर्वं समाप्नोषि ततोऽसि सर्वः।। 40

सखेति मत्वा प्रसभं यदुक्तं हे कृष्ण हे यादव हे सखेति

अजानता महिमानं तवेदं मया प्रमादात्प्रणयेन वापि।। 41

यच्चावहासार्थमसत्कृतोऽसि विहारशय्यासनभोजनेषु।

एकोऽथवाप्यच्युत तत्समक्षं तत् क्षामये त्वामहमप्रनेयम्।। 42

पितासि लोकस्य चराचरस्य त्वमस्य पूज्यश्च गुरुर्गरीयान्।

न त्वत्समोऽस्त्यभ्यधिकः कुतोऽन्यो लोकत्रयेऽप्यप्रतिमप्रभाव।। 43

तस्मात्प्रणम्य प्रणिधाय कायं प्रसादये त्वामहमीयमीड्यम्।

पितेव पुत्रस्य सखेव सख्युः प्रियः प्रियायार्हसि देव सोढुम्।। 44

अदृष्टपूर्व हृषितोऽस्मि दृष्ट्वा भयेन च प्रव्यथितं मनो मे।

तदेव मे दर्शय देवरूपं प्रसीद देवेश जगन्निवास।। 45

किरीटिनं गदिनं चक्रहस्त-मिच्छामि त्वां द्रष्टुमहं तथैव।

तेनैव रूपेण चतुर्भुजेन सहस्त्रबाहो भव विश्वमूर्ते।। 46

श्रीभगवानुवाच

मया प्रसन्नेन तवार्जुनेदं रुपं परं दर्शितमात्मयोगात्।

तेजोमयं विश्वमनन्तमाद्यं यन्मे त्वदन्येन न दृष्टपूर्वम्।। 47

न वेदयज्ञाध्ययनैर्न दानै-र्न च क्रियाभिर्न तपोभिरुग्रैः।

एवंरूपः शक्य अहं नृलोके द्रष्टुं त्वदन्येन कुरुप्रवीर।। 48

मा ते व्यथा मा च विमूढभावो दृष्ट्वा रूपं घोरमीदृङ्ममेदम्।
व्यपेतभीः प्रीतमनाः पुनस्त्वं तदेव मे रूपमिदं प्रपश्य।। 49

सञ्जय उवाच

इत्यर्जुनं वासुदेवस्तथोक्त्वा स्वकं रूपं दर्शयामास भूयः।
आश्वासयामास च भीतमेनं भूत्वा पुनः सौम्यवपुर्महात्मा।। 50

अर्जुन उवाच

दृष्ट्वेदं मानुषं रूपं तव सौम्यं जनार्दन। इदानीमस्मि संवृत्तः सचेताः प्रकृतिं गतः।। 51

श्रीभगवानुवाच

सुदुर्दर्शमिदं रूपं दृष्टवानसि यन्मम। देवा अप्यस्य रूपस्य नित्यं दर्शनकाङ्क्षिणः।। 52
नाहं वेदैर्न तपसा न दानेन न चेज्यया। शक्य एवंविधो द्रष्टुं दृष्टवानसि मां यथा।। 53
भक्त्या त्वनन्यया शक्य अहमेवंविधोऽर्जुन। ज्ञातुं द्रष्टुं च तत्त्वेन प्रवेष्टुं च परन्तप।। 54
मत्कर्मकृन्मत्परमो मद्भक्तः सङ्गवर्जितः। निर्वैरः सर्वभूतेषु यः स मामेति पाण्डव।। 55

'Behold My Cosmic form, Arjuna'

This is regarded as an important chapter. The *Gita* is a poem with a profound meaning, and the eleventh chapter is the most poetic of all. If we wish to learn true *bhakti,* we should know this chapter by heart. If we do so, we shall feel, when reciting it, that we are bathing in a sea of *bhakti.*

Arjuna says:

Out of Thy grace towards me, Thou hast told me the supreme mystery revealing the knowledge of the Supreme; it has banished my delusion.

Of the origin and destruction of beings I have heard from Thee in full detail, as also of Thy imperishable majesty, O Kamalapatraksha!

Thou art indeed just as Thou hast described Thyself. Parameshvara! I do crave to behold now that form of Thine as Ishvara. If, Lord, Thou thinkest it possible for me to bear the sight, reveal to me, O Yogeshvara, Thy imperishable form. (14)

The Lord replies:

Behold, O Partha, my forms divine in their hundreds and thousands, infinitely diverse infinitely various in colour and aspect.

Behold the Adityas, the Vasus, the Rudras, the two Ashwins, and the Maruts; behold, O Bharata, numerous marvels never revealed before.

Behold today, O Gudakesha, in my body, the whole universe moving, and unmoving all in one, and whatever else thou cravest to see. (5-7)

"See the *Adityas,*" Shri Krishna says, "the *Vasus,* the *Rudras,* the *Ashwins* and the *Maruts,* all together. See the entire world, animate and inanimate, all as one reality."

This cosmic form includes, good and evil, Hindus and Muslims, believers and atheists, all.

"You may also see," Shri Krishna adds, "anything else you wish to see."

But thou canst not see Me with these thine own eyes, I give thee the eye divine; behold My sovereign power! (8)

Sanjaya says:

With these words, O King, the great Lord of Yoga, Hari, then revealed to Partha His supreme form as Ishvara. (9)

The teaching of the *Gita* was not meant to be merely preserved in a book; it was meant to be translated into action. Mahadev and Punjab Bhai take notes of what I speak, but had we arranged recording on a gramophone plate, every word could have been taken down. Could we have said, then, that the gramophone machine had understood the *Gita?* It is an inanimate object. Similarly, what will this knowledge profit us if we merely take down notes and do not put the teaching into practice? We should, therefore, serve the people among whom we live, and help our elders in their domestic chores. Why should Ba find it necessary to send for Kusum to help her? Why should she request Ramachandra, who is a guest here just for a few days, to help her wash the kitchen? Why should she, who is at present under a vow of eating only once a day, not get some time for rest? If you give her no help, you are like the gramophone in our example.

With many mouths, and many eyes, many wondrous aspects, many divine ornaments and many brandished weapuns divine; Wearing divine garlands and vestments, anointed with divine perfumes, it was the form of God, all marvellous, infinite, seen everywhere.

Were the splendour of a thousand suns to shoot forth all at once in the sky that might perchance resemble the splendour of that Mighty One.

Then did Pandava see the whole universe in its manifold divisions gathered as one in the body of that God of gods. (10-13)

The whole universe, despite its manifold divisions, is gathered there in Him. Like a tree and its leaves. The tree is like the cosmic form of the Lord, the root and the leaves being one.

The root contains the whole world of the tree, and the leaves represent that world divided into many forms! Arjuna saw thus the cosmic form of the God of gods.

> *Then Dhananjaya, wonderstruck and thrilled in every fibre of his being, bowed low his head before the Lord, addressing Him thus with folded hands:*
>
> Arjuna says:
>
> *Within Thy form, O Lord, I see all the gods and the diverse multitudes of beings, the Lord Brahma on his lotus-throne and all the seers and the serpents divine.*
>
> *With many arms and bellies, mouths and eyes, I see Thy infinite form everywhere. Neither Thy end, nor middle, nor beginning do I see, O Lord of the Universe, Universal-formed! (14-16)*

On the one hand, Arjuna says that Shri Krishna has a definite form and, on the other, he says that He is formless. In other words, His form is so vast that in truth He is formless.

> *With crown and mace and disc, a mass effulgence, gleaming every-where I see Thee, so dazzling to the sight, bright with the splendour of the fiery sun blazing from all sides—incomprehensible. (17)*

You bear crown, mace and disc. You are a mass of radiance which glows at all places.

The sun gives some faint idea of the Lord's light, but it is no more than a dim point of light in comparison with the Lord's. Thou art as lustrous as fire and the sun. Thou art dazzling to the sight because of thy immeasurable effulgence.

> *Thou art the supreme Imperishable worthy to be known; Thou art the final resting-place of this universe; Thou art the changeless guardian of the Eternal Dharma; Thou art, I believe, the Everlasting Being. (18)*

Cannot we say that the rains yesterday were an aspect of this infinite cosmic form of God? He has placed the sun at such a great distance from us; what would have been our condition if it had been a little nearer? Can we, then, imagine Arjuna's condition with Shri Krishna standing near him, Krishna glowing with the light of a thousand suns?

Thou hast no beginning, middle nor end; infinite is Thy might; arms innumerable; for eyes, the sun and the moon; Thy mouth a blazing fire, overpowering the universe with Thy radiance. (19)

By Thee alone are filled the spaces between heaven and earth and all the quarters; at the sight of this Thy wondrous terrible form, the three worlds are sore oppressed, O Mahatman. (20)

This Sabarmati, too, is an aspect of the infinite power of God. If the warning received yesterday comes true and there is a heavy flood, we would simply shake with fear.

Here, too, the multitudes of gods are seen, to enter Thee; some awestruck praise Thee with folded arms; the hosts of great seers and siddhas, 'All Hail' on their lips, hymn Thee with songs of praise. (21)

One feels as though these verses were specially written for us.

We had information from the Collector that there would be a heavy flood in the Sabarmati. Naturally, I was agitated in my heart, not knowing what to do. But I reminded myself of the verses which I daily recite before the women: *"Govind, Dwarkavasin"* and so on. Krishna would be welcome if he flew to our help on His Garuda. Otherwise, if all these things were carried away in the flood, our honour would be saved. Let anyone who survives to witness the destruction live on faithful to our vows.

I had advised them to construct the loom-shed as far away as the road. "The weak will pretend to be good," as the saying goes, and so we have nothing to do but wait in patience. If the authorities of the Sabarmati jail invite us to take shelter in it, I will ask them if they have invited the people of Vadaj too. I will tell them that they should offer shelter to all others before they invite us.

You should eat, not to gratify your palate, but to keep yourselves alive to keep up your strength. As I sit here in peace, we heard the blowing of the mill whistles, and so I remarked, "No one can escape work." It is the same story: "We seek refuge with the Lord who is the ship that ferries us across this sea of creation." Shall we never be free from this affliction of work? When afflicted with other diseases, we may keep repeating the Lord's name, or the *dwadash mantra* or any other prayer which will bring us peace of mind. Which is greater storm, the inward storm in the heart or this outward storm of work? Is this latter storm more of an affliction than that our eyes and ears should disobey us and attend to things which they ought to shun? **Every inmate of the Ashram has wings. I should like even the women to have them. Anyone who wishes to leave is certainly free to do so, either by train or to the city on the other side.** As the headman of a village, this is all I can tell you. If you can think of anything better, please do.

The Rudras. Adityas, Vasus, Sadhyas all the gods, the twin Ashwins, Maruts, Manes, the hosts of Gandharvas, Yakshas, Asuras and Siddhas—all gaze on Thee in wonderment.

At the sight of Thy mighty form, O Mahabahu, many-mouthed, with eyes, arms, thighs and feet innumerable, with many vast bellies, terrible with many jaws, the worlds feel fearfully oppressed, and so do I.

For as I behold Thee touching the sky, glowing, numerous-hued with gaping mouths and wide resplendent eyes, I feel oppressed in my innermost being; no peace nor quiet I find, O Vishnu!

And as I see Thy mouths with fearful jaws, resembling the Fire of Doom, I lose all sense of direction, and find no relief. Be gracious, O Devesha, O Jagannivasa!

All the sons of Dhritarashtra, and with them the crowd of kings, Bhishma, Drona, and that Karna too, as also our chief warriors—

Are hastening into the fearful jaws of Thy terrible mouths. Some, indeed, caught between Thy teeth are seen, their heads being crushed to atoms.

As rivers in their numerous torrents rush headlong to the sea, even so the heroes of the world of men rush into Thy flaming mouths.

As moths, fast-flying, plunge into blazing fire straight to their doom, even so these rush headlong into Thy mouths, to their destruction.

Devouring all these from all sides, Thou lappest them with Thy flaming tongues; Thy fierce rays blaze forth, filling the whole universe with their lustre.

Tell me, Lord, who Thou art so dread of form! Hail to Thee, O Devavara! Be gracious! I desire to know Thee, Primal Lord; for I comprehend not what Thou dost. (22-31)

The Lord said:

Doom am I, full-ripe, dealing death to the worlds engaged in devouring mankind. Even without thy slaying them, not one of the warriors, ranged for battle against thee, shall survive.

Therefore, do thou arise, and win renown! Defeat thy foes and enjoy a thriving kingdom. By Me have these already been destroyed; be thou no more than an instrument, O Savyasachin. (32, 33)

"Savyasachin" means one who can use a bow with the left hand, that is, with either hand.

Drona, Bhishma, Jayadratha and Karna, as also the other warrior chiefs—already slain by Me—slay thou! Be not dismayed! Fight! Victory is thine over thy foes in the field.

Hearing this word of Keshava, crown-wearer Arjuna folded his hands, and trembling made obeisance. Bowing and all hesitant, in faltering accents he proceeded to address Krishna once more. Right proper it is, — Hrishikesha, that Thy praise should stir the world to gladness and tender emotion; the Rakshasas in fear fly to every quarter and all the hosts of Siddhas do reverent homage. (34-36)

And why should they not bow to you? You are the destroyer of the demons. The demons are our enemies, external and internal. What even if the river should swallow us and destroy us? How much more fearful is the flood inside us? Who will destroy the demons inside?

And so Arjuna said:

And why should they not bow down to Thee, O Mahatman? Thou art the First Creator, greater even than Brahma. O Ananta, O Devesha, O Jagannivasa, Thou art the Imperishable Being, not-Being, and That which transcends even these.

Thou art the Primal God, the Ancient Being; Thou art the final resting-place of this Universe; Thou art the Knower, the 'to-be-known', the supreme Abode; by Thee, O myriad-formed, is the Universe pervaded.

Thou art Vayu, Yama, Agni, Varuna, Shashanka, Prajapati and Prapitamaha! All hail to Thee, a thousand times all hail! Again and yet again all hail to Thee! (37-39)

There was once a woman in Madras who was a devotee of the Lord. She used to worship Him with her back towards the idol. A learned man rebuked her for doing so, but she cited this verse in reply, and the learned pundit was speechless. If all space is pervaded by God, when we find his eyes, ears and noses on all sides, why should we sit facing in a particular direction to worship Him?

All hail to Thee from before and behind! All hail to Thee from every side, O All; Thy prowess is infinite, Thy might is measureless! Thou holdest all; therefore Thou art all.

If ever in carelessness, thinking of Thee as comrade, I addressed Thee saying, 'O Krishna!', 'O Yadava!' not knowing Thy greatness in negligence or in affection,

If ever I have been rude to Thee in jest, whilst at play, at resttime, or at meals, whilst alone or in company, O Achyuta, forgive Thou my fault—I beg of Thee, O Incomprehensible one!

Thou art Father of this world, of the moving and the unmoving; Thou art its adored, its worthiest, Master; there is none equal to Thee; how then is any greater than Thee? Thy power is matchless in the three worlds.

Therefore, I prostrate myself before Thee, and beseech Thy grace, O Lord Adorable! As father with son, as comrade with comrade, so shouldst Thou bear, beloved Lord, with me, Thy loved one.

I am filled with joy to see what never was seen before, and yet my heart is oppressed with fear. Show me that original form of Thine, O Lord! Be gracious, Devesha, O Jagannivasa!

I crave to see Thee even as Thou wast, with crown, with mace, disc in hand; wear Thou, once more, that fourarmed form, O thousand-armed Vishvamurti! (40-46)

The Lord said:

It is to favour thee, O Arjuna, that I have revealed to thee, by My own unique power, this My Form Supreme, Resplendent, Universal, Infinite, Primal—which none save thee has ever seen. Not by the study of the Vedas, not by sacrifice, not by the study of other scriptures, not by gifts, nor yet by performance of rites or of fierce austerities can I, in such a form, be seen by anyone save thee in the world of men, O Kurupravira!

Be thou neither oppressed nor bewildered to look on this awful form of Mine. Banish thy fear, ease thy mind, and lo! behold Me once again as I was. (47-49)

Arjuna said:

Beholding again Thy benign human form I am come to myself and am once more in my normal state. (50)

The Lord said:

Very hard to behold is that Form of Mine which thou hast seen; even the gods always yearn to see it.

Not by the Vedas, not by penance, nor by gifts, nor yet by sacrifice, can any one behold Me in the Form that thou hast seen.

But by single-minded devotion, O Arjuna, I may in this Form be known and seen and truly entered into, O Parantapa! (51-54)

First we should know the Lord, then see Him and then merge into Him. We may tell Him: "You may eat me up, I will not resist if You do. I am Yours, and I want to be one with You. What harm can it do even if You eat me up?" Telling us that He can grind us into paste with his teeth and throw it out, He tells us that we can know Him through *bhakti.* We can pass His test only through faith. When we know that everything takes place through Him and that we live and die as He wills, how can we be affected by anything?

He alone comes to Me, O Pandava, who does My work, who has made Me his goal, who is My devotee, who has renounced attachment, who has ill will towards none. (55)

The Lord has given the whole substance of Chapter XI in this last verse. "He who works for Me is ever devoted to Me, who is attached to nothing and bears ill will to none—not even to a person who may have committed a heinous sin—but ever blesses him instead,—such a person comes to Me."

❑❑❑

12

भक्तियोग

अर्जुन उवाच

एवं सततयुक्ता ये भक्तास्त्वां पर्युपासते। ये चाप्यक्षरमव्यक्तं तेषां के योगवित्तमाः।। 1

श्रीभगवानुवाच

मय्यावेश्य मनो ये मां नित्ययुक्ता उपासते। श्रद्धया परयोपेतास्ते मे युक्ततमा मताः।। 2

ये त्वक्षरमनिर्देश्यमव्यक्तं पर्युपासते। सर्वत्रगमचिन्त्यं च कूटस्थमचलं ध्रुवम्।। 3

सन्नियम्येन्द्रियग्रामं सर्वत्र समबुद्धयः। ते प्राप्नुवन्ति मामेव सर्वभूतहिते रताः।। 4

क्लेशोऽधिकतरस्तेषामव्यक्तासक्तचेतसाम्। अव्यक्ता हि गतिर्दुःखं देहवद्भिरवाप्यते।। 5

ये तु सर्वाणि कर्माणि मयि संन्यस्य मत्पराः। अनन्येनैव योगेन मां ध्यायन्त उपासते।। 6

तेषामहं समुद्धर्ता मृत्युसंसारसागरात्। भवामि नचिरात्पार्थ मय्यावेशितचेतसाम्।। 7

मय्येव मन आधत्स्व मयि बुद्धिं निवेशय। निवसिष्यसि मय्येव अत ऊर्ध्वं न संशयः।। 8

अथ चित्तं समाधातुं न शक्नोषि मयि स्थिरम्। अभ्यासयोगेन ततो मामिच्छाप्तुं धनञ्जय।। 9

अभ्यासेऽप्यसमर्थोऽसि मत्कर्मपरमो भव। मदर्थमपि कर्माणि कुर्वन् सिद्धिमवाप्स्यसि।। 10

अथैतदप्यशक्तोऽसि कर्तुं मद्योगमाश्रितः। सर्वकर्मफलत्यागं ततः कुरु यतात्मवान्।। 11

श्रेयो हि ज्ञानमभ्यासाज्ज्ञानाद्ध्यानं विशिष्यते। ध्यानात्कर्मफलत्यागस्त्यागाच्छान्तिरनन्तरम्।। 12

अद्वेष्टा सर्वभूतानां मैत्रः करुण एव च। निर्ममो निरहङ्कारः समदुःखसुखः क्षमी।। 13

सन्तुष्टः सततं योगी यतात्मा दृढनिश्चयः। मय्यर्पितमनोबुद्धिर्यो मद्भक्तः स मे प्रियः।। 14

यस्मान्नोद्विजते लोको लोकान्नोद्विजते च यः। हर्षामर्षभयोद्वेगैर्मुक्तो यः स च मे प्रियः।। 15
अनपेक्षः शुचिर्दक्ष उदासीनो गतव्यथः। सर्वारम्भपरित्यागी यो मद्भक्तः स मे प्रियः।। 16
यो न हृष्यति न द्वेष्टि न शोचति न काङ्क्षति। शुभाशुभपरित्यागी भक्तिमान् यः स मे प्रियः।। 17
समः शत्रौ च मित्रे च तथा मानापमानयोः। शीतोष्णसुखदुःखेषु समः सङ्गविवर्जितः।। 18
तुल्यनिन्दास्तुतिर्मौनी सन्तुष्टो येन केनचित्। अनिकेतः स्थिरमतिर्भक्तिमान्मे प्रियो नरः।। 19
ये तु धर्म्यामृतमिदं यथोक्तं पर्युपासते। श्रद्दधाना मत्परमा भक्तास्तेऽतीव मे प्रियाः।। 20

The Yoga of Devotion and Contemplation

To love God means to be free from attachment to any work. We should of course do work, but without egotistic attachment to it, simply for the love of God. A lustful man forgets his love for parents and children when seeking gratification of his lust and abandons himself blindly to it. This also is a form of non-attachment. But the cause is a filthy one, whereas love for God is good. And now for the meaning of the verse with which we began.

Arjuna asks:

Of the devotees who thus worship Thee, incessantly attached, and those who worship the Imperishable, Unmanifest, which are the better yogis?

The Lord replies:

Those I regard as the best yogis who, riveting their minds on Me, ever attached, worship Me, with the highest faith.

But those who worship the Imperishable, the Indefinable, the Unmanifest, the Omnipresent, the Unthinkable, the Rock-seated, the Immovable; the Unchanging,

Keeping the whole host of senses in complete control, looking on all with an impartial eye, engrossed in the welfare of all beings—these come indeed to Me.

Greater is the travail of those whose mind is fixed on the Unmanifest; for it is hard for embodied mortals to gain the Unmanifest Goal. (2-5)

Those who have fixed their minds on the Unmanifest, that is, who worship the formless *Brahman*, experience greater difficulty in their effort, for it is extremely difficult for us, embodied souls, to know the unmanifest state.

It is very difficult to meditate on *Shunya.* The moment we attribute a single quality to God we cease to worship the Unmanifest. We must all, nevertheless, realize that beyond the Personal God there is a Formless Essence which are reason cannot comprehend. The consummation of *bhakti* has in the *bhakta* merging in God, so that ultimately nothing but One Formless God remains. Since, however, it is easier to reach this state through the worship of the Personal God, the Lord says that the other path of seeking the Formless Essence directly is difficult to follow.

> *But those who casting all their actions on Me, making Me their all in all, worship, Me with the meditation of undivided devotion,*
>
> *Of such, whose thoughts are centred on Me, O Partha, I become ere long the Deliverer from the ocean of this world of death. (6-7)*

The verse beginning with *kleshodhikatarastesham* has given me great light; for it says that devotion to the Unmanifest is difficult to cultivate and that it is a harder path to follow. The reason given is very significant. If one retires to a forest and meditates on God, one can certainly realize Him. Likewise, one who serves as an accountant or clerk or manager in a firm can also do that. Both may be in the same state of mind and can, therefore, reach the same goal.

If we are sincere in our devotion to the cause of the spinning-wheel movement, the country is bound to embrace it in course of time. This faith is an illustration of the path which human beings should adopt, this is the path of *bhakti,* of the worship of a Personal God, for the spinning wheel is visible to us and we see power in it. If, however, we worship the Spinning-wheel for itself, our worship will be like the worship of the Unmanifest *Brahman.* It will be so, that is, if we merely worship the spinning-wheel without spinning on it. In my view, however, even if a time comes when we decide to withdraw into complete silence, it will not mean that we have abandoned the spinning-wheel or forsaken our aspiration for the *Brahman.* If indeed we ever retire to some high peak on the Himalayas, it will not be because we shall have lost interest in the spinning-wheel or been disillusioned with the people. To retire with such a motive will be no way of worshipping the Unmanifest. Of course, we shall benefit in some way even if we do so. If a man decides out of disgust to observe *brahmacharya* or to give up immorality, he will certainly benefit. But his action will not have been prompted by true knowledge. Similarly, this idea of retirement is not meant for anyone who is disgusted with the spinning-wheel or with the people.

If a person, however, feels that there is an Essence beyond this universe of objects with name and form and that he must know it, and if he leaves this world and withdraws into solitude with that aim, that also is a legitimate path. But it is a difficult one even if one is sincere in one's aspiration to cultivate *bhakti* of the Unmanifest. The idea that the *Brahman* is real and that the visible universe is illusory is simply beyond the capacity of our reason to comprehend. How difficult it must be, then, to live according to it? It is only when our body is completely transformed into an armour that nothing will pierce it. The Shastras narrate the stories of Prahlad and Sudhanva. As these stories show, it is possible, even while one is physically alive, to live as if one had renounced one's body. It is extremely difficult for a man to cultivate such a state of mind and live for ever absorbed in the atman. All but one in a crore live in illusion and error. They will not break away from their ignorant attachment and will have to be born again in this world.

The path of karma is the easiest to follow. The path of reason can lead one into great error. The path along which we have the least danger of falling into error is the one described in the verse beginning with *nehabhikramanashosti*. Neither Christians nor Muslims, nor certainly Hindus have risen above the worship of the Personal God.

There is a book by Shibli in which he has discussed the question whether or not God has a body. Even a person who aspires to cultivate devotion exclusively for the Unmanifest worships some visible symbol. We can of course understand with our intellect the idea that the body is unconnected with the atman. To say that one can attain *moksha* while physically alive only means that, after death, one will not have to be born again. Has anyone ever been able to say what his state after death will be? **The spiritualists and Theosophists are not correct, in my view, about what they say concerning spirits, in the sense that no-one has been able to know and tell the whole truth.**

For this reason, Shri Krishna told Arjuna that it would be better for him to take no interest in the problem at all. "Silence is golden in this matter," he says. **"Don't you see, you dear**

simpleton, that I Myself have taken on a human body? And you ask Me, of all persons, whether worship of the Unmanifest is better, or that of the Personal God. You had better stop asking such questions and do as I tell you. Free yourself from all thoughts of violence and act towards all creatures with equal love and regard." If we understand this truth, we would escape many problems. We should not mind if, because we worship the Personal God, we are called idolaters and criticized for being so. And, therefore, proceeding Shri Krishna says:

> *On Me set thy mind, on Me rest thy conviction; thus without doubt shalt thou remain only in Me hereafter.*
>
> *It thou canst not set thy mind steadily on Me, then by the method of constant practice seek to win Me, O Dhananjaya. (8, 9)*

What is the difference between *abhyasa yoga* and meditating on God? I think the former means listening to readings from holy books, reflecting on them and letting the mind dwell on their teachings. It means associating ourselves with men who are engaged in doing these things and listening to prayer songs and group devotions, for every little offering we make, leaf, flower fruit, or water, ultimately reaches God.

> *If thou art also unequal to this method of constant practice, concentrate on service for Me, even thus serving Me thou shalt attain perfection.*
>
> *If thou art unable even to do this, then dedicating all to Me, with mind controlled, abandon the fruit of action. (10-11)*

"Do not," Shri Krishna says, "be impatient to reap the fruit of your efforts."

> *Better is knowledge than practice, better than knowledge is concentration, better than concentration is renunciation of the fruit of all action, from which directly issues peace. (12)*

Here *jnana* does not mean mere learning, but it means genuine experience of truth in however limited a measure. Meditation, which means concentration of the mind on God, is better than such *jnana,* but renunciation of the fruit of action is said to be better even than such meditation. Shri Krishna says this because a person practising meditation may possibly be deceiving himself. Moreover, *jnana* does not mean ultimate self-realization. *Jnana* and meditation are compared here in their restricted meanings and one is described as better than the other. Renunciation of the fruits of action is mentioned last, but in truth it should be the first step. One who practises it becomes free from attachment to the ego.

Shri Krishna then proceeds to describe the characteristics of a man of this type.

> *Who has ill will towards none, who is friendly and compassionate, who has shed all thought of 'mine' or 'I', who regards pain and pleasure alike, who is long-suffering. (13)*

Friendship can exist only between equals, but one should feel compassion towards all. We cannot throw a cricket bat at a dog to hit it. How would we feel if our parents or teachers did that to us? Even if we are obedient sons of our parents, how would we feel towards them if they threw a bat at us to hit us? We shall not discuss here what our duty towards a dog is. It is certain, however, that it is not right for us to hit one. Forgiveness lies in not being angry even with a dog which may have bitten us. Tit for tat is a wrong principle. It is certainly not based on forgiveness. What can we gain by being wicked with the wicked? The good of both lies only in our showing love and compassion even for such persons.

We should understand the difference between selflessness and freedom from egotism. The first means not making a distinction between ourselves and others. It describes a person who regards the entire world as his family. The second term describes a person who believes that it is not he who has done a particular thing, that it is God who has done it.

> *Who is ever content, gifted with yoga, self-restrained, of firm conviction, who has dedicated his mind and reason to Me— that devotee (bhakta) of Mine is dear to Me.*
>
> *Who gives no trouble to the world, to whom the world Causes no trouble, who is free from exultation, resentment, fear and vexation,—that man is dear to Me. (14-15)*

The meaning of this verse is already contained in the term *adweshta*.

> *Who expects naught, who is pure, resourceful, unconcerned untroubled, who, indulges in no undertakings,—that devotee of Mine is dear to Me. (16)*

The whole of Chapter XII describes the characteristics of a *bhakta.* If we compare the verses which describe a *sthitaprajna* with these, we shall find them similar.

On whom does a *bhakta* of God rely except on Him? *Shuchi* means a person who is pure both in body and mind. *Daksha* means a person who does everything which he undertakes, wholly in a spirit of dedication to God. *Udasin* means one who remains unaffected even if all his many plans come to nothing. One who is a *sarvarambhaparityagi* will not go in search of work, work will come seeking him. God Himself will appoint his work and call him to it. Such a person, knowing that God shoulders the burdens of us all, leaves everything to Him. A slave need not go looking for work.

> *Who rejoices not, neither frets nor grieves, who covets not, who abandons both good and ill—that devotee of Mine is dear to Me.*
>
> *Who is same to foe and friend, who regards alike respect and disrespect, cold and heat, pleasure and pain, who is free from attachment.*
>
> *Who weighs in equal scale blame and praise, who is silent, content with whatever his lot, who owns no home, who is of steady mind—that devotee of Mine is dear to Me. (17-19)*

"He does not get elated, though an emperor may bow to him," so sang Raychandbhai.

> *They who follow this essence of dharma, as I have told it, with faith, keeping Me as their goal,—those devotees are exceedingly dear to Me. (20)*

All of us have our appointed tasks, as Brahmins or Kshatriyas, Vaisyas or Sudras. Anyone who does his work without hope of reward and in a disinterested spirit is a *bhakta* of God. The second chapter contains verses describing a *sthitaprajna.* They describe the state of mind of a yogi living absorbed in a mystic world. This Chapter XII describes, in our ordinary language, the state of mind of a *bhakta.*

13

क्षेत्रक्षेत्रज्ञविभागयोग

श्रीभगवानुवाच

इदं शरीरं कौन्तेय क्षेत्रमित्यभिधीयते। एतद्यो वेत्ति तं प्राहुः क्षेत्रज्ञ इति तद्विदः।। 1

क्षेत्रज्ञं चापि मां विद्धि सर्वक्षेत्रेषु भारत। क्षेत्रक्षेत्रज्ञयोर्ज्ञानं यत्तज्ज्ञानं मतं मम।। 2

तत्क्षेत्रं यच्च यादृक् च यद्विकारि यतश्च यत्। स च यो यत्प्रभावश्च तत्समासेन मे श्रृणु।। 3

ऋषिभिर्बहुधा गीतं छन्दोभिर्विविधैः पृथक्। ब्रह्मसूत्रपदैश्चैव हेतुमद्भिर्विनिश्चितैः।। 4

महाभूतान्यहङ्कारो बुद्धिरव्यक्तमेव च। इन्द्रियाणि दशैकं च पञ्च चेन्द्रियगोचराः।। 5

इच्छा द्वेषः सुखं दुःखं सङ्घातश्चेतना धृतिः। एतत्क्षेत्रं समासेन सविकारमुदाहृतम्।। 6

अमानित्वमदम्भित्वमहिंसा क्षान्तिरार्जवम्। आचार्योपासनं शौचं स्थैर्यमात्मविनिग्रहः।। 7

इन्द्रियार्थेषु वैराग्यमनहङ्कार एव च। जन्ममृत्युजराव्याधिदुःखदोषानुदर्शनम्।। 8

असक्तिरनभिष्वङ्गः पुत्रदारगृहादिषु। नित्यं च समचित्तत्वमिष्टानिष्टोपपत्तिषु।। 9

मयि चानन्ययोगेन भक्तिरव्यभिचारिणी। विविक्तदेशसेवित्वमरतिर्जनसंसदि।। 10

अध्यात्मज्ञाननित्यत्वं तत्त्वज्ञानार्थदर्शनम्। एतज्ज्ञानमिति प्रोक्तमज्ञानं यदतोऽन्यथा।। 11

ज्ञेयं यत्तत्प्रवक्ष्यामि यज्ज्ञात्वाऽमृतमश्नुते। अनादिमत्परं ब्रह्म न सत्तन्नाऽसदुच्यते।। 12

सर्वतः पाणिपादं तत् सर्वतोऽक्षिशिरोमुखम्। सर्वतःश्रुतिमल्लोके सर्वमावृत्य तिष्ठति।। 13

सर्वेन्द्रियगुणाभासं सर्वेन्द्रियविवर्जितम्। असक्तं सर्वभृच्चैव निर्गुणं गुणभोक्तृ च।। 14

बहिरन्तश्च भूतानामचरं चरमेव च। सूक्ष्मत्वात्तदविज्ञेयं दूरस्थं चान्तिके च तत्।। 15

अविभक्तं च भूतेषु विभक्तमिव च स्थितम्। भूतभर्तृ च तज्ज्ञेयं ग्रसिष्णु प्रभविष्णु च।। 16
ज्योतिषामपि तज्ज्योतिस्तमसः परमुच्यते। ज्ञानं ज्ञेयं ज्ञानगम्यं हृदि सर्वस्य धिष्ठितम्।। 17
इति क्षेत्रं तथा ज्ञानं ज्ञेयं चोक्तं समासतः। मद्भक्त एतद्विज्ञाय मद्भावायोपपद्यते।। 18
प्रकृतिं पुरुषं चैव विद्ध्यनादी उभावपि। विकारांश्च गुणांश्चैव विद्धि प्रकृतिसम्भवान्।। 19
कार्यकारणकर्तृत्वे हेतुः प्रकृतिरुच्यते। पुरुषः सुखदुःखानां भोक्तृत्वे हेतुरुच्यते।। 20
पुरुषः प्रकृतिस्थो हि भुङ्क्ते प्रकृतिजान् गुणान्। कारणं गुणसङ्गोऽस्य सदसद्योनिजन्मसु।। 21
उपद्रष्टानुमन्ता च भर्ता भोक्ता महेश्वर। परमात्मेति चाप्युक्तो देहेऽस्मिन् पुरुषः परः। 22
य एवं वेत्ति पुरुषं प्रकृतिं च गुणैः सह। सर्वथा वर्तमानोऽपि न स भूयोऽभिजायते।। 23
ध्यानेनात्मनि पश्यन्ति केचिदात्मानमात्मना। अन्ये साङ्ख्येन योगेन कर्मयोगेन चापरे।। 24
अन्ये त्वेवमजानन्तः श्रुत्वान्येभ्य उपासते। तेऽपि चातितरन्त्येव मृत्युं श्रुतिपरायणाः।। 25
यावत्सञ्जायते किञ्चित् सत्त्वं स्थावरजङ्गमम्। क्षेत्रक्षेत्रज्ञसंयोगात् तद्विद्धि भरतर्षभ।। 26
समं सर्वेषु भूतेषु तिष्ठन्तं परमेश्वरम्। विनश्यत्स्वविनश्यन्तं यः पश्यति स पश्यति।। 27
समं पश्यन् हि सर्वत्र समवस्थितमीश्वरम्। न हिनस्त्यात्मनात्मानं ततो याति परां गतिम्।। 28
प्रकृत्यैव च कर्माणि क्रियमाणानि सर्वशः। यः पश्यति तथात्मानमकर्तारं स पश्यति।। 29
यदा भूतपृथग्भावमेकस्थमनुश्यति। तत एव च विस्तारं ब्रह्म सम्पद्यते तदा।। 30
अनादित्वान्निर्गुणत्वात् परमात्मायमव्ययः। शरीरस्थोऽपि कौन्तेय न करोति न लिप्यते।। 31
यथा सर्वगतं सौक्ष्म्यादाकाशं नोपलिप्यते। सर्वत्रावस्थितो देहे तथात्मा नोपलिप्यते।। 32
यथा प्रकाशयत्येकः कृत्स्नं लोकमिमं रविः। क्षेत्रं क्षेत्री तथा कृत्स्नं प्रकाशयति भारत।। 33
क्षेत्रक्षेत्रज्ञयोरेवमन्तरं ज्ञानचक्षुषा। भूतप्रकृतिमोक्षं च ये विदुर्यान्ति ते परम्।। 34

THE FIELD AND ITS KNOWER

From Chapter XIII begins a new subject. It discusses the body and its nature. The Lord says:

This body, O Kaunteya, is called the Field; he who knows it is called the knower of the Field by those who know. (1)

Pandavas and Kauravas, that is, divine and demoniacal impulses, were fighting in this body, and God was watching the fight from a distance. Please do not believe that this is the history of a battle which took place on a little field near Kurukshetra; the war is still going on. This is the verse we should keep in mind in order to understand the meaning of the phrase *dharmakshetra.*

And understand Me to be, O Bharata, the knower of the Field in all the Fields; and the knowledge of the Field and the knower of the Field, I hold, is true knowledge. (2)

Our bodily life will have been lived to some purpose if it is spent in thinking which of these two we should serve and which we should go to for refuge.

What that Field is, what its nature, what its modifications, and whence is what, as also who He is, and what His power— hear this briefly from Me.

This subject has been sung by seers distinctly and in various ways, in different hymns as also in aphoristic texts about Brahman well reasoned and unequivocal. (3, 4)

This theme has been expounded analytically by seers in manifold ways in various hymns. It has been discussed in the *Brahmasutras* with steps logically arranged and clearly explaining the connection between cause and effect; and every word has been weighed so that not a syllable could be altered.

The great elements, Individuation, Reason, the Unmanifest, the ten senses, and the one mind, and the five spheres of the senses;

Desire, dislike, pleasure, pain, association, consciousness, cohesion—this, in sum, is what is called the Field with its modifications. (5, 6)

The five *mahabhutas, ahamkar,* which sustains those *bhutas, buddhi,* the *avyakta (prakriti),* the ten senses, the mind and the objects of the five senses, so also desire, ill will, happiness, misery, association, consciousness, cohesion—this, in brief, is the Field with its modifications.

Sanghat means the power of the different elements in the body to cooperate with one another. *Dhriti* does not mean the abstract virtue of patience, but the property of the atoms in physical bodies to cohere. This property is made possible by *ahamkar,* which is latent in the unmanifest *prakriti.*

Freedom from pride and pretentiousness, non-violence, forgiveness, uprightness, service of the Master, purity, steadfastness, self restraint;

Aversion from sense-objects, absence of conceit, realization of the painfulness and evil of birth, death, age and disease;

Absence of attachment, refusal to be wrapped up in one's children, wife, home and family, even-mindedness whether good or ill befall;

Unwavering and all-exclusive devotion to Me, resort to secluded spots, distaste for the haunts of men;

Settled conviction of the nature of the atman, *perception of the goal of the knowledge of Truth,—*

All this is declared to be knowledge and the reverse of it is ignorance. (7-11)

Shauch means outer and inner purity. It can be achieved by repeating Ramanama. This purity can be properly preserved only if the heart is constantly kept clean by repeating Ramanama. Every morning, we should weep with tears streaming from our eyes and ask ourselves why we did not remember to start repeating Ramanama, and why we, of all people, had a bad dream.

Absence of interest in the objects of senses means the awareness that certain things ought to be treated as forbidden by us, that they ought to be unacceptable to us.

The attributes described include the realization of the evils of birth and death, of old age, disease and suffering. One who realizes this starts with the thought: "I am sin." Why is it, we should ask ourselves, that we are afflicted with all manner of diseases? We ought to learn to cultivate equanimity of mind towards everything which may happen, good and evil. What does living in solitude mean? Retiring into a cave to live there alone by oneself? Our effort will have been worthwhile only if we can feel solitude even in the midst of a huge crowd. To live in solitude means to sit in a spot meditating on one single thought.

I will now expound to thee that which is to be known and knowing which one enjoys immortality; it is the supreme Brahman which has no beginning, which is called neither Being nor non-Being. (12)

Why does Shri Krishna say this, when they say that the *Brahman* is *sachchidananda* and that it alone is real? What he means to say is that *Brahman* does not mean being, the contrary of non-being. When we use the word *sat* in connection with the *Brahman,* its meaning transcends the two opposites and it signifies neither being nor non-being. It is, so to say, a neutral term. God cannot be described as evil, nor as good. He is above either. The reality which is God is beyond the three categories of time.

Everywhere having hands and feet, everywhere having eyes, heads, mouths, everywhere having ears, It abides embracing everything in the universe.

Seeming to possess the functions of the senses, It is devoid of all the senses; It touches naught, upholds all; having no gunas, It experiences gunas.

Without all beings, yet within; immovable yet moving; so subtle that It cannot be perceived; so far and yet so near It is.

Undivided, It seems to subsist divided in all beings; this Brahman—That which is to be known is the Sustainer of all, yet It is their Devourer and Creator. (13, 16)

Though indivisible He seems to be there divided in all beings. He is worth knowing. He sustains all the creatures.

He is their Destroyer and yet the Creator of them all.

All contrary qualities are attributed to God because we cannot free our minds from dualities.

Light of all lights, It is said to be beyond darkness; It is knowledge, the object of knowledge, to be gained only by knowledge; It is seated in the hearts of all. (17)

He is the Superlight. He is beyond darkness, that is, He is self-effulgent.....

He is Himself Knowledge. He is also the object of Knowledge to be realized only by Knowledge.

Thus have I expounded in brief the Field, Knowledge and That which is to be known; My devotee, when he knows this is worthy to become one with Me.

Know that prakriti and purusha are both without beginning; know that all the modifications and gunas are born of prakriti. Prakriti is described as the cause in the creation of effects from causes; purusha is described as the cause of the experiencing of pleasure and plain. (18-20)

Karya, anything done under compulsion of desires, and *karan,* the *desires,—prakriti* is the cause of their creation. *Purusha* is the cause of the experience of happiness and misery.

God is described as having two aspects. Under one aspect we should know Him as *prakriti* and under the other as *purusha.* The world is ever changing, and is therefore *maya.* The *purusha* is not transient, for He is the witness.

For the purusha, residing in prakriti experiences the gunas born of prakriti; attachment to these gunas is the cause of his birth in good or evil wombs. (21)

It is enough if we look upon God as king and if all of us become His slaves, that is, disclaim any right over our bodies.

What is called in this body the Witness, the Assentor, the Sustainer, the Experiencer, the Great Lord and also the Supreme Atman, *is the Supreme Being. (22)*

The *purusha* dwelling in this body is *para,* that is, beyond *maya* but He witnesses and gives consent. He is the *bharta* who sustains everything, and also the Enjoyer. He is, moreover, the God of gods and is described as *Paramatman.*

Fire has the power of burning, but it can burn nothing without God's consent.

He who thus knows purusha and prakriti with its gunas, is not born again, no matter how he live and move. (23)

If anyone claims that he is a *bhakta* of God and that, therefore, the sins he may commit are committed by God, he is wrong. But it would be right if the world said of him that he was a man of God and that everything he did was done through him by God. If anyone asks us whether we have attained spiritual knowledge, our reply should be "Only God knows; I do not know." Our reason may be carried away by pride at any time and become evil, but the man who has attained to perfect knowledge will never be misguided by his reason. Our belief is that Rama and Krishna were incarnations of God. How can we be sure that King Rama was a hypocrite and his rule was not evil? How do we know that Krishna was not the most wicked of men? But we have no right to indulge in such doubts. Whomsoever we worship, we should look upon as *Purna Purushottam,* that is best. If we believe that the people of India have faith in God, we should worship Him accordingly.

This verse does not sanction self-indulgence, but points out the great value of *bhakti.* Every karma has the effect of binding the soul, but one can become free from the bonds of karma by dedicating all one's karmas to God. Thus, anyone who has become free from the egotistic idea of being the author of anything and who recognizes every moment of his life the authority of the Dweller within will never commit sin. It is in egotism that sin has its source. There is no sin where there is no consciousness of the "I". This verse explains how to act so that one may commit no sin.

Some through meditation behold the atman*by themselves in their own self; others by Sankhya Yoga, and others by Karma Yoga.*

Yet others, not knowing Him thus, worship Him having heard from others; they too pass beyond death, because of devoted adherence to what they heard. (24, 25)

If, having heard it explained that we shall be saved by dedicating all our work to God, we act in this spirit, then we can say that "he who... is not born again, no matter how he live and move" applies to us.

> *Wherever something is born, animate or inanimate, know, thou Bharatarshabha, that it issues from the union of the Field and the knower of the Field. (26)*

If we examine things separately, human beings, grains of dust, water, and so on, our conclusions about their origin will be different in each case. If, instead, we go to the very first cause, we shall no more think of objects having their distinctive forms and names. The Ravana who invests things with such charm that we willingly submit to its spell is far more dangerous than the other one of the story who killed people physically.

> *Who sees abiding in all beings the same Parameshvara, imperishable in the perishable, he sees indeed. (27)*

Though things are ever perishing, there is an indestructible element in everything which remains unaffected by any change, he alone sees who sees this.

> *When he sees the same Ishvara abiding everywhere alike, he does not hurt himself by himself and hence he attains the highest goal. (28)*

When he sees the same God abiding alike at all places he does not destroy the self by the self—believes that, with the destruction of his body, he himself does not perish—and consequently he achieves the highest status.

> *Who sees that it is prakriti that performs all actions and thus knows that* atman*performs them not, he sees indeed. (29)*

Who realizes that *prakriti* is the doer of all actions and sees that atman is not the doer—though all things take place through God's maya, the Supreme Purusha involved in the process is not their author—he alone who does so sees indeed.

> *When he sees the diversity of being as founded in unity and the whole expanse issuing therefrom, then he attains to Brahman. (30)*

The *Gita* is a work intended to be a guide in life and we should be able to find in it support for all our actions in practical life. Not all can understand Dr. Tribhuvandas's book; a vaid or a doctor can understand it more easily than laymen. We are in the same position as the latter in relation to the *Gita.*

> *This Imperishable Supreme Atman, O Kaunteya, though residing in the body acts not and is not stained, for He has no beginning and no gunas.*
>
> *As the all pervading ether, by reason of its subtlety, is not soiled, even so atman pervading every part of the body is not soiled.*
>
> *As the one Sun illumines the whole universe, even so the Master of the Field illumines the whole field.*
>
> *Those who, with the eyes of knowledge, thus perceive the distinction between the Field and the knower of the Field, and the secret of the release of beings from prakriti, they attain to Supreme. (31-34)*

Who knows the difference between the Field and the knower of the Field, and who knows how creatures may become free from the bonds of *prakriti* and *maya,* he realizes *moksha.*

In Chapter XIII Shri Krishna explained the nature of the Field, and the knower of the field, the means of understanding the nature of each, and the different characteristics of such characteristic of knowledge, is stated to be *amanitva.* Hence, knowledge. The very first, however great one's knowledge, if one is proud of that knowledge, one has read the *Gita* in vain. Where there is pride, there is no knowledge. A man who has knowledge is always free from pride and ostentation, is straightforward, serves his guru, is pure and steady, is a man of self-control and is free from egotism, and he does not suffer because of old age and disease. He is not attached to his son or wife or home, is filled with unswerving devotion for the Lord, lives in solitude, takes interest in spiritual studies and is devoted to the pursuit of philosophic truth.

14

गुणत्रयविभागयोग

श्रीभगवानुवाच

परं भूयः प्रवक्ष्यामि ज्ञानानां ज्ञानमुत्तमम्। यज्ज्ञात्वा मुनयः सर्वे परां सिद्धिमितो गताः।। 1

इदं ज्ञानमुपाश्रित्य मम साधर्म्यमागताः। सर्गेऽपि नोपजायन्ते प्रलये न व्यथन्ति च।। 2

मम योनिर्महद्ब्रह्म तस्मिन् गर्भं दधाम्यहम्। सम्भवः सर्वभूतानां ततो भवति भारत। 3

सर्वयोनिषु कौन्तेय मूर्तयः सम्भवन्ति याः।। तासां ब्रह्म महद्योनिरहं बीजप्रदः पिता।। 4

सत्त्वं रजस्तम इति गुणाः प्रकृतिसम्भवाः। निबध्नन्ति महाबाहो देहे देहिनमव्ययम्।। 5

तत्र सत्त्वं निर्मलत्वात् प्रकाशकमनामयम्। सुखसङ्गेन बध्नाति ज्ञानसङ्गेन चानघ।। 6

रजो रागात्मकं विद्धि तृष्णासङ्गसमुद्भवम्। तन्निबध्नाति कौन्तेय कर्मसङ्गेन देहिनम्।। 7

तमस्त्वज्ञानजं विद्धि मोहनं सर्वदेहिनाम्। प्रमादालस्यनिद्राभिस्तन्निबध्नाति भारत।। 8

सत्त्वं सुखे सञ्जयति रजः कर्मणि भारत। ज्ञानमावृत्य तु तमः प्रमादे सञ्जयत्युत।। 9

रजस्तमश्चाभिभूय सत्त्वं भवति भारत। रजः सत्त्वं तमश्चैव तमः सत्त्वं रजस्तथा।। 10

सर्वद्वारेषु देहेऽस्मिन् प्रकाश उपजायते। ज्ञानं यदा तदा विद्याद् विवृद्धं सत्त्वमित्युत।। 11

लोभः प्रवृत्तिरारम्भः कर्मणामशमः स्पृहा। रजस्येतानि जायन्ते विवृद्धे भरतर्षभ।। 12

अप्रकाशोऽप्रवृत्तिश्च प्रमादो मोह एव च। तमस्येतानि जायन्ते विवृद्धे कुरुनन्दन्।। 13

यदा सत्त्वे प्रवृद्धे तु प्रजयं याति देहभृत्। तदोत्तमविदां लोकानमलान् प्रतिपद्यते।। 14

रजसि प्रलयं गत्वा कर्मसङ्गिषु जायते। तथा प्रलीनस्तमसि मूढयोनिषु जायते।। 15

कर्मणः सुकृतस्याहुः सात्त्विकं निर्मलं फलम्। रजसस्तु फलं दुःखमज्ञानं तमसः फलम्।। 16

सत्त्वात्सञ्जायते ज्ञानं रजसो लोभ एव च। प्रमादमोहौ तमसो भवतोऽज्ञानमेव च।। 17

ऊर्ध्वं गच्छन्ति सत्त्वस्था मध्ये तिष्ठन्ति राजसाः। जघन्यगुणवृत्तिस्था अधो गच्छन्ति तामसाः।। 18

नान्यं गुणेभ्यः कर्तारं यदा द्रष्टानुपश्यति। गुणेभ्यश्च परं वेत्ति मद्भावं सोऽधिगच्छति।। 19

गुणानेतानतीत्य त्रीन् देही देहसमुद्भवान्। जन्ममृत्युजरादुःखैर्विमुक्तोऽमृतमश्नुते।। 20

अर्जुन उवाच

कैर्लिङ्गैस्त्रीन् गुणानेतानतीतो भवति प्रभो। किमाचारः कथं चैतांस्त्रीन् गुणानतिवर्तते।। 21

श्रीभगवानुवाच

प्रकाशं च प्रवृत्तिं च मोहमेव च पाण्डव। न द्वेष्टि सम्प्रवृत्तानि न निवृत्तानि काङ्क्षति।। 22

उदासीनवदासीनो गुणैर्यो न विचाल्यते। गुणा वर्तन्त इत्येव योऽवतिष्ठति नेङ्गते।। 23

समदुःखसुखः स्वस्थः समलोष्टाश्मकाञ्चनः। तुल्यप्रियाप्रियो धीरस्तुल्यनिन्दात्मसंस्तुतिः।। 24

मानापमानयोस्तुल्यस्तुल्यो मित्रारिपक्षयोः। सर्वारम्भपरित्यागी गुणातीतः स उच्यते।। 25

मां च योऽव्यभिचारेण भक्तियोगेन सेवते। स गुणान् समतीत्यैतान् ब्रह्मभूयाय कल्पते।। 26

ब्रह्मणो हि प्रतिष्ठाऽहममृतस्याव्ययस्य च। शाश्वतस्य च धर्मस्य सुखस्यैकान्तिकस्य च।। 27

The Three Basic Kinds

When we have a stomachache, we consult a book of home remedies and use the medicine suggested. The *Gita* is such a book of home remedies for us. We find in it medicines for our spiritual diseases. If we want to make the *Gita* our *Kamadhenu,* we should make it our only source as far as possible. We may consult any number of books in the world in support of what we derive from the *Gita,* but should be satisfied with its sole authority. For this, we should have single-minded devotion to it. Such devotion should become spontaneous in us.

In a certain place, people used secretly to catch fish from the village pond; The village committee decided that, since in any case people caught fish,—did so in secret and were then afraid of being discovered—they should be required to take out licences for catching fish and some revenue raised by that means. This led to a dispute between two parties and the dispute was brought to me for settlement. I was afraid to give a decision, for people are not content to leave it to others to exercise discrimination in religious matters and faith on their behalf. If we are guided by some other person's ideas about dharma, we would be lost when he was dead. It would have been much better if those village people had decided to consult the *Gita* or the Veda or the Koran, instead of asking me. We should look upon any of these works as the means of solving our spiritual problems. But I was told afterwards in reply to my suggestion that one could find support from a book for any idea.

The true meaning of *Kamadhuk,* however, is that it satisfies a pure wish only. If the *Gita* satisfies any wish, it would not be *Kamadhuk* but would be aunt Putana. When the authors of the Shastras said that Sudras and others should not read the Vedas and other sacred works, probably their reason was that the latter might interpret these works to justify their own wishes in particular matters. Anyone who approaches the Shastras without scrupulous regard for truth and non-violence will derive no benefit from them. It is possible to draw any number of evil ideas from the Bible, the Vedas, the Koran and other scriptures. I have come across persons who justified even murder on the authority of these works. The *Gita,* however, will serve as a safe guide to anyone who reads it with truth and non-violence as his guiding principles. Everyone should decide for himself with its help. The work will not be a *Kamadhenu* to any person who consults Kishorelal or me, and accepts our interpretation of it. Instead of borrowing faith from others, one should have one's own faith and come to decisions accordingly. If the intention is sincere and there is no desire for outward show, any error that the decision may contain will be forgiven. A person acting in this manner learns a lesson from his error and discovers the right path.

The Lord said:

> *Yet again will I expound the highest and the best of all knowledge, knowing which all the sages passed hence to the highest Perfection.*
>
> *By having recourse to this knowledge they became one with Me. They need not come to birth even at a creation, nor do they suffer at a dissolution.*
>
> *The great prakriti is for me the womb in which I deposit the germ; from it all beings come to birth, O Bharata. (1-3)*

Among the very first sentences in the Bible is; God said let there be light, and there was light; that is, let there be a universe, and a universe came into existence. A potter has to mould clay into a shape on his wheel and then put the thing into fire to bake; God does not have to act in that manner. He is a magician, He simply puts the seed in his imagination—which is *prakriti,* Lakshmi or Mother Goddess of the world—and the universe comes into existence.

> *Whatever forms take birth in the various species, the great prakriti is their Mother and I the seed-giving Father. (4)*

I am the *mahadyoni* of all the forms which take birth in the various species, as also the source of the seed—

> *Sattva, rajas and tamas are the gunas sprung from prakriti; it is they, O Mahabahu, that keep the imperishaole Dweller bound to the body.*

Of these sattva, being stainless, is light-giving and healing; it binds with the bond of happiness and the bond of knowledge, O sinless one. (5, 6)

Those persons whose food, recreation and thoughts are *sattvik* are healthy. A person who merely eats *sattvik* food but is not *sattvik* in his general way of living and in his thoughts should be looked upon as a diseased person.

Rajas, know thou, is of the nature of passion? The source of thirst and attachment; it keeps man bound with the bond of action. (7)

Know that *rajas* is associated with desire. This may mean either that it has its source in, or that it is the cause of, desire. It creates attachment for cravings. It keeps the embodied one i.e., living being bound with the bond of karma.

Tamas, know thou, is born of ignorance, of mortal man's delusion; it keeps him bound with heedlessness, sloth and slumber, O Bharata. (8)

Pramad means all kinds of unworthy wishes arising in us. *Alas* is *pramad* in a worse form still. *Nidra,* which is next, is the state of mind natural to those sunk in darkness. A man who is established in *samadhi* and is always awake feels no need to recline for rest or stretch his limbs for relaxation. A lethargic person would not get up even from a place which had caught fire. It is his slumber that is referred to as part of the meaning of *tamas.*

Sattva attaches man to happiness, rajas to action, and tamas, shrouding knowledge, attaches him to heedlessness. (9)

Sattva leads to happiness and the quality of *rajas* to karma. But this is not karma as it is defined in the *Gita;* it is the karma of him who is always doing something or other without pausing to think. *Tamas* covers up knowledge and leads to *pramad.*

Sattva prevails, O Bharata, having overcome rajas and tamas; rajas, when it has overpowered sattva and tamasi; likewise tamas reigns when sattva and rajas are crushed.

If a person overcomes *rajas* and *tamas,* he can create *sattva.* All the three exist in us. We should make a special effort to cultivate that which we want to strengthen. If we wish to strengthen *rajas,* we should subdue the other two and, if the quality of *tamas*, we should stop the activity of both *sattva* and *rajas*.

> *When the light—knowledge—shines forth from all the gates of this body, then it may be known that the sattva thrives.*
>
> *Greed, activity, assumption of undertakings, restlessness, craving—these are in evidence, when rajas flourishes, O Bharatarshabha.*
>
> *Ignorance, dullness, heedlessness and delusion—these are in evidence when tamas reigns, O Kurunandana,*
>
> *If the embodied one meets his end whilst sattva prevails, then he attains to the spotless worlds of the knowers of the Highest. (11-14)*

That is, he attains spiritual welfare. When he is nearing death, such a person refuses to take any medicine which may be offered, and says that he will have nothing but Ganga water. He who awaits death in peace in this manner is a *sattvik* man.

> *If he dies during the reign within him of rajas, he is born among men attached to action; and if he dies in tamas, he is born in a species not endowed with reason. (15)*

The world of beings of action means the human world. The dark world means the world of brutes.

> *The fruit of sattvik action is said to be stainless merit; that of rajas is pain and that of tamas ignorance.*
>
> *Of sattva, knowledge is born; of rajas, greed; of tamas, heedlessness, delusion and ignorance.*
>
> *Those abiding in sattva rise upwards, those in rajas stay mid way, those in tamas sink downwards.*
>
> *When the seer perceives no agent other than the gunas and knows Him who is above the gunas, he attains to My being. (16-19)*

When the atman dwelling as witness in this body sees none else, but knows only Him who is above the *gunas*, that person comes to Me.

> *When the embodied one transcends these three gunas which are born of his contact with the body, he is released from the pain of birth, death and age and attains moksha. (20)*

Arjuna asks:

What, O Lord, are the marks of him who has transcended the three gunas? How does he conduct himself? How does he transcend the three gunas? (21)

The Lord replies:

He, O Pandava, who does not disdain light, activity, and delusion when they come into being, nor desires them when they vanish. (22)

He who transcends the three *gunas*, does not suffer because of light or activity or darkness—that is, when any of them predominates over the others—and does not wish that it should prevail or subside.

This is one of the few difficult verses in the *Gita*. Should not one wish to have knowledge? In fact, in the *gayatri mantra* itself—in the best Vedic prayer—we pray to the shining Being to purify our intellect, to make it *sattvik*. We also pray: *tamaso ma jyotirgamaya*. We aspire to be lifted from the darkness of attachment to illumination, from darkness to light. What, then, should we make of the statement in this verse? If we, living in the Ashram, did not cherish the aspiration which we do, we would fail in our aims. We must teach every child to say this prayer the very first thing in the morning. We should pray, tears streaming from our eyes, to be saved from the army of Kauravas, the army of deep slumber.

What, then, does the *Gita* teach? That we should not mind even if the slumber becomes deeper, should not even wish to get out of it? Should we say, I have no wish, the three states are the same to me? If anyone feels thus, you may be sure he will be totally ruined. Either we should regard this verse as an interpolation, or as the very key to the meaning of the *Gita*. If you remember, in the beginning Arjuna does not ask whether or not it is proper to kill, but asks what good he could expect from killing his kinsmen. And so the Lord asks him: "What is this distinction you make between kinsmen and others? Your duty is to do the job of killing, irrespective of whether they are your kinsmen or others.

Similarly, Arjuna does not here ask Shri Krishna which of the three *gunas* is best. He knows that ultimately one must transcend all the three. We can know a person who possesses one of the three *gunas*. It is not difficult to distinguish among the three classes. But can we find anyone in this world who has risen above the *gunas* altogether? This verse gives the Lord's reply to that question. What other reply could He give? A person who has risen above the three *gunas* will not let himself be deceived by the threefold distinction of good, bad and indifferent, and we shall not see in him the effects of any of the three *gunas*, so rare will be his state of mind. But this is an important chapter.

Talking of a person who does not feel concerned whether light, activity or darkness prevails or subsides, we saw that we find no one of the sort in the world. We come across no person who does not wish to get rid of what we regard as evil—lethargy, inertia or excessive activity—or does not wish to acquire pure knowledge. On the contrary, we pray for such knowledge. The word *jijnasu* came into use because of our aspiration for knowledge, and we should pray that this aspiration may ever grow. This verse, therefore, should fill us with greater enthusiasm for doing our duty. Our aim is to strive to end the suffering of the entire world.

It is a general rule that we should not take any statement of a writer in isolation, but should consider it in its total context.

Now, then, for whom is this verse meant? Well, it is meant for one who has risen above the *gunas*. It enumerates the characteristics of such a person. This is what he would appear to us to be. We do not know how he in fact acts. We say, for instance, that the sun is a blazing fire; but scientists say that it is utterly black. An English poet has said that things are not what they seem. This is Sankara's theory of *maya*. It means that things do not appear as they are not what they seem to be, for everything is known to us through the medium of the waves in our minds.

Surely, the rainbow is not in truth what it seems to be. It is mere appearance. That is why it has been said that this world is like waves in water, or like a rainbow.

By what sign shall we, who live in the three-coloured world, recognize the man who has transcended the three *gunas?* He will not feel unhappy if the world mistakenly labels a man bad, or regards him as a man of knowledge or a lethargic man. What does it matter if the world thinks that we are mere agitators?

Thus, one who has risen above the three *gunas* will not seem to the world to be happy when one sees activity or unhappy when one sees lethargy. Such a person has come out of the duality of happiness and misery. He has risen above the pairs of opposites. A person like this should seem to us untouched, unconcerned, by anything. He should be absolutely free from egotism.

There is, thus, a state which is different even from the middle one. The *Gita* has stressed this point again and again. It teaches you just one thing, to shed the thought of "I" in such matters. **We say *neti, neti*. You think I am such a person. In truth, I am "yes" and you are "no".** A person who has risen above the three *gunas* should appear to the world to be a cipher, a mere stone. That is, he should have got rid of his "I". The world has looked upon Rama as God incarnate, for it could not do otherwise. Shankara asked Parvati how she could suppose that Rama felt miserable because of separation from Sita. He was, he said, pained to see that she had attributed ignorance to Rama, who had shed his egotism and worked like a cipher.

Everyday we are born anew. *Ayurved* tells us that every seven years the whole body of a person changes into a new one, but that we are not aware of the change because it takes place slowly. The body does not change all of a sudden at the end of the seventh year, as if by magic, but the old body gradually wears out and is replaced by a new one. Thus, creation and destruction follow upon the heels of each other. There is no point of space so completely empty that you can put anything there without displacing something else, that is, you cannot create without destroying. Even the mind becomes either stronger or weaker day by day. Everything in the world is in a state of flux. Nothing is fixed. Only God is both fixed and changing.

A person who has risen above the three *gunas* is one who has become a cipher. But when can one be in such a state? In his poem beginning with the words *apurva avasar,* Shri Rajchandra sings: "When the body has become as the burnt rope". That should be our condition. When a rope is burnt, only its form remains, and none of its other properties survive. Such a rope may be said to have risen above the three *gunas,* for it no longer has the property in virtue of which it can be used for connecting or binding things or drawing water from a well. A person who has risen above the three *gunas* is like such a rope. As a rope may produce on us the illusion of a snake, so we may think of such a person as being like inert stone or having no interest in any activity but he does not care. It is our dharma to be like such burnt rope.

The only way of rising to this state beyond the three *gunas* is to cultivate the *sattvik* quality, for in order to rise to that state one is required to cultivate the virtues of fearlessness, humility, sincerity, and so on. So long as we live in the body, there is some evil, some violence. The most, therefore, that we can do is to be *sattvik* in the highest degree possible.

The state beyond the three *gunas* can only be imagined. It does not seem possible to maintain it in action. In concrete action, our state must be *sattvik* in the highest degree. We cannot say even of a seemingly perfect man that he has risen beyond the three *gunas*. We can only say that he seems to be like one who has so risen. Someone has said in English that, outwardly, we shall find no difference between a sinner and a man of virtue, but that the greater a sinner the more virtuous he can be. He ever thinks of his sinful life and gives up his vices one by one. To such a sinner, even a beautiful temptress like Rambha is but a wooden or stone figure. In this way, he becomes pure in no time.

If we wish to attain *moksha* any time, to rise above the three *gunas*, we should cultivate in us the *sattvik* qualities. That is why we pray: *tamaso ma jyotirgamaya*. So long as a person feels that he serves others, he is selfish. If he believes that he has risen above the three *gunas*, he is a great hypocrite. If we really serve others, people will certainly know that. How can we ourselves know it? It is said in the Bible: "Let not thy left hand know what thy right hand does." That is the mark of a person being *sattvik*. The characteristics of such a person are almost similar to those of one who has risen above the three *gunas*, though, of course, the latter is undoubtedly on a higher level than the former since he knows neither what his right and nor what his left hand does.

He, who, seated as one indifferent, is not shaken by the gunas and stays still and moves not, knowing it is the gunas playing their parts;

He who holds pleasure and pain alike, who is sedate, who regards earth, stone and gold as all the same, who is wise and weighs in equal scale things pleasant and unpleasant, who is even-minded in praise and blame;

Who holds alike respect, and disrespect, who is the same to friend and foe, who indulges is no undertaking—that man is called gunatita. (23-25)

A person who has risen above the three *gunas* know what it is to be in that state but cannot describe it. If anyone can describe his state, he is not a person who has so risen, for he is still conscious of his "I".

He who serves Me with an unwavering and exclusive bhaktiyoga transcends these gunas and is worthy to become one with Brahman.

For I am the very image of Brahman, changeless and deathless, as also of everlasting dharma and perfect bliss. (26-27)

A person who struggles ceaselessly and hard to overcome his shortcomings may not perhaps succeed, in this birth, in overcoming them all, but, in the end he will surely benefit. Today the world will censure him for his shortcomings; if, however, he bears all that in patience, and strives ever harder, he is sure ultimately to get peace of mind. Peace lies in the very fact of struggling. It is a source of great reassurance. Hence, we should strive to cultivate *sattvik* qualities.

❑❑❑

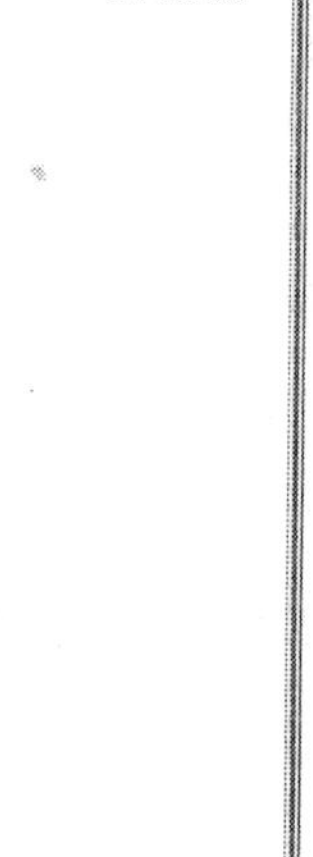

15

पुरुषोत्तमयोग

श्रीभगवानुवाच

ऊर्ध्वमूलमधः शाखमश्वत्थं प्राहुरव्ययम्। छन्दांसि यस्य पर्णानि यस्तं वेद स वेदवित्।। 1

अधश्चोर्ध्वं प्रसृतास्तस्य शाखा गुणप्रवृद्धा विषयप्रवालाः।

अधश्च मूलान्यनुसन्ततानि कर्मानुबन्धीनि मनुष्यलोके।। 2

न रूपमस्येह तथोपलभ्यते नान्तो न चादिर्न च सम्प्रतिष्ठा।

अश्वत्थमेनं सुविरूढमूल-मसङ्गशस्त्रेण दृढेन छित्त्वा।। 3

ततः पदं तत्परिमार्गितव्यं यस्मिन् गता न निवर्तन्ति भूयः।

तमेव चाद्यं पुरुषं प्रपद्ये यतः प्रवृत्तिः प्रसृता पुराणी।। 4

निर्मानमोहा जितसङ्गदोषा अध्यात्मनित्या विनिवृत्तकामाः।

द्वन्द्वैर्विमुक्ताः सुखदुःखसञ्ज्ञै-र्गच्छन्त्यमूढाः पदमव्ययं तत्।। 5

न तद्भासयते सूर्यो न शशाङ्को न पावकः। यद्गत्वा न निवर्तन्ते तद्धाम परमं मम।। 6

ममैवांशो जीवलोके जीवभूतः सनातनः। मनःषष्ठानीन्द्रियाणि प्रकृतिस्थानि कर्षति।। 7

शरीरं यदवाप्नोति यच्चाप्युत्क्रामतीश्वरः। गृहीत्वैतानि संयाति वायुर्गन्धानिवाशयात्।। 8

श्रोत्रं चक्षुः स्पर्शनं च रसनं घ्राणमेव च। अधिष्ठाय मनश्चायं विषयानुपसेवते।। 9

उत्क्रामन्तं स्थितं वापि भुञ्जानं वा गुणान्वितम्। विमूढा नानुपश्यन्ति पश्यन्ति ज्ञानचक्षुषः।। 10

यतन्तो योगिनश्चैनं पश्यन्त्यात्मन्यवस्थितम्। यतन्तोऽप्यकृतात्मानो नैनं पश्यन्त्यचेतसः।। 11

यदादित्यगतं तेजो जगद्भासयतेऽखिलम्। यच्चन्द्रमसि यच्चाग्नौ तत्तेजो विद्धि मामकम्।। 12

गामाविश्य च भूतानि धारयाम्यहमोजसा। पुष्णामि चौषधीः सर्वाः सोमो भूत्वा रसात्मकः।। 13

अहं वैश्वानरो भूत्वा प्राणिनां देहमाश्रितः। प्राणापानसमायुक्तः पचाम्यन्नं चतुर्विधम्।। 14

सर्वस्य चाहं हृदि सन्निविष्टो मत्तः स्मृतिर्ज्ञानमपाहनं च।

वेदैश्च सर्वैरहमेव वेद्यो वेदान्तकृद्वेदविदेव चाहम्।। 15

द्वाविमौ पुरुषौ लोके क्षरश्चाक्षर एव च। क्षरः सर्वाणि भूतानि कूटस्थोऽक्षर उच्यते।। 16

उत्तमः पुरुषस्त्वन्यः परमात्मेत्युदाहृतः। यो लोकत्रयमाविश्य बिभर्त्यव्यय ईश्वरः।। 17

यस्मात् क्षरमतीतोऽहमक्षरादपि चोत्तमः। अतोऽस्मि लोके वेदे च प्रथितः पुरूषोत्तमः।। 18

यो मामेवमसम्मूढो जानाति पुरुषोत्तमम्। स सर्वविद्भजति मां सर्वभावेन भारत।। 19

इति गुह्यतमं शास्त्रमिदमुक्तं मयानघ। एतद्बुद्ध्वा बुद्धिमान्स्यात् कृतकृत्यश्च भारत।। 20

-.-

The Supreme Person

The Lord said:

With its root above and branches below, the ashvattha tree, they say, is imperishable; it has Vedic hymns for leaves; he who knows it knows the Vedas. (1)

Shvah means "tomorrow", *Ashvattha,* therefore, means this transient world which will not last beyond tomorrow. It is changing every moment. That is why it is *ashvattha.* He is a man of spiritual knowledge who knows the real nature of this world and also knows dharma.

Above and below its branches spread, blossoming because of the gunas, having for their shoots the sense-objects; deep down in the world of men are ramified its roots, in the shape of the consequences of action. (2)

In the first verse, Shri Krishna shows the means of going beyond this world. In this verse, he has described the world from another point of view, that of the ignorant man.

Its form as such is not here perceived, neither is its end, nor beginning, nor basis. Let men first hew down this deep-rooted Ashvattha with the sure weapon of detachment:

Let him pray to win to that haven from which there is no return and seek to find refuge in the Primal Being from whom has emanated this ancient world of action. (2, 3)

We shall remain apart from this world, while working in it, when we no longer look upon it as God's sport but, regarding it as the sphere in which people run after enjoyments, cut it off at the root with the weapon of non-cooperation. In no other way is it possible to cut it off at the roots, for it is without beginning and without end. That is why Shri Krishna has advised non-cooperation.

To that imperishable haven those enlightened souls go—who are without pride and delusion, who have triumphed over the taints of attachment, who are ever in tune with the Supreme, whose passions have died, who are exempt from the pairs of opposites, such as pleasure and pain. (6)

They who crave to win that haven are indifferent to honour or insult. They are absolutely free from delusion. They have scored triumph over the taints of attachment. Those who are always *atmarthi* that is, who are aware every moment that they are not their physical bodies but are the atman, whose cravings for objects of senses have subsided who look not fear-struck but serene at the moment of death, are the enlightened souls that go to that imperishable haven.

On every leaf of the banyan tree are inscribed the Vedas, which means that Ramanama is inscribed on its every leaf. The world is a holy gift made by God out of His grace; the tree of the world grows from the navel of Brahma. But there is another world with its root below, whose leaves are the various objects of sense-pleasure; that world is the world of desire.

*Adhy*atman*ityah* means those whose thoughts dwell with love on Rama, who repeat His name and do His work.

Neither the sun, nor the moon, nor fire illumine it; men who arrive there return not—that is My supreme abode. (5)

Its light is not borrowed from the sun or the moon or the fire, for it shines with its own light, men who reach it return not—that is my supreme abode.

A part indeed of Myself which has been the eternal Jiva in this world of life attracts the mind and the five senses from their place in prakriti. (6)

"Every hair on the body chants the Vedas," so sang Tulsidas.

When the Master of the body acquires a body and discards it, He carries these with Him wherever He goes, even as the wind carries scents from flower-beds.

Having settled Himself in the senses—ear, eye, touch, taste, and smell—as well as the mind, through them He frequents their objects.

The deluded perceive Him not as He leaves or settles in a body or enjoys sense-objects in association with the gunas; it is only those endowed with the eye of knowledge that see Him. (7-9)

We see only the world, but do not see God who is immanent in it.

Yogis who strive to see Him seated in themselves: the witless ones who have not cleansed themselves see Him not, even though they strive. (10)

The first thing necessary, therefore!, is the observance of the rules of *yama-niyama.*

One who has not observed them is apt to give wrong meanings to the verses of the *Gita.* Such a person would tell himself that, since the objects of senses are created by God, we should accept and enjoy them. They alone, who have become purified, who have suffered in the furnace of *tapas,* will read the right meanings.

The l'ght in the sun which illumines the whole universe and which is in the moon and in the fire—that light, know thou, is mine. (11)

There is a story in an Upanishad which tells how some gods took the form of *yakshas* and went to test *Agni, vayu,* etc., but were worsted.

It is I who penetrating the earth, uphold all beings with my strength, and becoming the moon—the essence of all sap—nourish all herbs. (12)

Pervading the earth, I uphold all beings with my strength, and becoming the moon, the producer of all sap, nourish all herbs, food-crops and all else that grows in the fields.

It is I who, becoming the Vaishvanara Fire and entering the bodies of all that breathe, assimilate the kinds of food with the help of the outward and the inward breaths. (13)

Vaishvanara means the heat which digests food. The four types of food are what is sucked, what is licked, what is drunk and what is eaten.

And I am seated in the hearts of all; from Me proceed memory, knowledge and the dispelling of doubt; it is I who am to be known in all the Vedas, I, the author of Vedanta and the knower of the Vedas.

There are two Beings in the world: kshara (perishable) and akshara (imperishable). Kshara embraces all creatures and their permanent basis is akshara. (14-15)

In this world there are two beings—*akshara* and *kshara*. *Kshara* means all beings which are subject to death, which have a name and form. The immutable reality behind them, the power of which sustains all, is *akshara*.

The Supreme being is surely another—called Paramatman who as the Imperishable Ishvara pervades and supports the three worlds. (16)

Because I transcend the kshara and am also higher than the akshara, I am known in the world and in the Vedas as Purushottama the Highest Being. (17)

Because I transcend *kshara*, that is, the world of name and form and am also higher than *akshara*, the world and the Vedas know Me as the highest among all beings.

He who, undeluded, knows Me Purushottama, knows all, he worships Me with all his heart, O Bharata. (18)

He is above all opposites. Once we have risen above this world, which is but *maya*, need we think of God as its author?

Thus I have revealed to thee, sinless one, this most mysterious Shastra; he who understands this, O Bharata, is a man of understanding; he has fulfilled his life's mission. (19)

I have disclosed to thee this most secret, the best even of the best, Shastra; he who understands this becomes a man of understanding, fulfils his life's mission and also becomes free from his debt.

16

दैवासुरसंपद्विभागयोग

श्रीभगवानुवाच

अभयं सत्त्वसंशुद्धिर्ज्ञानयोगव्यवस्थितिः। दानं दमश्च यज्ञश्च स्वाध्यायस्तप आर्जवम्।। 1

अहिंसा सत्यमक्रोधस्त्यागः शान्तिरपैशुनम्। दया भूतेष्वलोलुप्त्वं मार्दवं ह्रीरचापलम्।। 2

तेजः क्षमा धृतिः शौचमद्रोहो नातिमानिता। भवन्ति सम्पदं दैवीमभिजातस्य भारत।। 3

दम्भो दर्पोऽभिमानश्च क्रोधः पारुष्यमेव च। अज्ञानं चाभिजातस्य पार्थ सम्पदमासुरीम्।। 4

दैवी सम्पद्विमोक्षाय निबन्धायासुरी मता। मा शुचः सम्पदं दैवीमभिजातोऽसि पाण्डव।। 5

द्वौ भूतसर्गौ लोकेऽस्मिन् दैव आसुर एव च। दैवो विस्तरशः प्रोक्त आसुरं पार्थ मे श्रृणु।।6

प्रवृत्तिं च निवृत्तिं च जना न विदुरासुराः। न शौचं नापि चाचारो न सत्यं तेषु विद्यते।। 7

असत्यमप्रतिष्ठं ते जगदाहुरनीश्वरम्। अपरस्परसम्भूतं किमन्यत्कामहैतुकम्।। 8

एतां दृष्टिमवष्टभ्य नष्टात्मानोऽल्पबुद्धयः। प्रभवन्त्युग्रकर्माणः क्षयाय जगतोऽहिताः।। 9

काममाश्रित्य दुष्पूरं दम्भमानमदान्विताः। मोहाद्गृहीत्वाऽसद्ग्राहान् प्रवर्तन्तेऽशुचिव्रताः।। 10

चिन्तामपरिमेयां च प्रलयान्तामुपाश्रिता। कामोपभोगपरमा एतावदिति निश्चिताः।। 11

आशापाशशतैर्बद्धाः कामक्रोधपरायणाः। ईहन्ते कामभोगार्थमन्यायेनार्थसञ्चयान्।। 12

इदमद्य मया लब्धमिमं प्राप्स्ये मनोरथम्। इदमस्तीदमपि मे भविष्यति पुनर्धनम्।। 13

असौ मया हतः शत्रुर्हनिष्ये चापरानपि। ईश्वरोऽहमहं भोगी सिद्धोऽहं बलवान् सुखी।। 14

आढ्योऽभिजनवानस्मि कोऽन्योऽस्ति सदृशो मया। यक्ष्ये दास्यामि मोदिष्य इत्यज्ञानविमोहिताः।। 15
अनेकचित्तविभ्रान्ता मोहजालसमावृताः। प्रसक्ताः कामभोगेषु पतन्ति नरकेऽशुचौ।। 16
आत्मसम्भाविताः स्तब्धा धनमानमदान्विताः। यजन्ते नामयज्ञैस्ते दम्भेनाविधिपूर्वकम्।। 17
अहङ्कारं बलं दर्पं कामं क्रोधं च संश्रिताः। मामात्मपरदेहेषु प्रद्विषन्तोऽभ्यसूयकाः ।। 18
तानहं द्विषतः क्रूरान् संसारेषु नराधमान्। क्षिपाम्यजस्रमशुभानासुरीष्वेव योनिषु।। 19
आसुरीं योनिमापन्ना मूढा जन्मनि जन्मनि। मामप्राप्यैव कौन्तेय ततो यान्त्यधमां गतिम्।। 20
त्रिविधं नरकस्येदं द्वारं नाशनमात्मनः। कामः क्रोधस्तथा लोभस्तस्मादेतत्त्रयं त्यजेत्।। 21
एतैर्विमुक्तः कौन्तेय तमोद्वारैस्त्रिभिर्नरः। आचरत्यात्मनः श्रेयस्ततो याति परां गतिम्।। 22
यः शास्त्रविधिमुत्सृज्य वर्तते कामकारतः। न स सिद्धिमवाप्नोति न सुखं न परां गतिम्।। 23
तस्माच्छास्त्रं प्रमाणं ते कार्याकार्यव्यवस्थितौ। ज्ञात्वा शास्त्रविधानोक्तं कर्म कर्तुमिहार्हसि।। 24

-.-

The Godlike and the Demoniac

The Lord said:

Fearlessness, purity of heart, steadfastness in jnana and yoga knowledge and action, beneficence, self-restraint, sacrifice, spiritual study, austerity and uprightness;

Non-violence, truth, slowness to wrath, the spirit of dedication, serenity, aversion to slander, tenderness to all that lives, freedom from greed, gentleness, modesty; freedom from levity;

Spiritedness, forgiveness, fortitude, purity, freedom from ill will and arrogance-these are to be found in one born with the divine heritage, O Bharata. (1-3)

Sattvasanshuddhi means purity of the self or inner puriy. *Jnanyogavyasthiti* means certainty of knowledge; *jnanavyavasthiti* means unceasing direct experience, and *yogavyavasthiti* means constant awareness of God, sense of identity with Him. Ahimsa also embraces violence deliberately committed out of compassion (When Dr. Nangi was to perform an operation, he used to fast on the day previous, so that no emotional disturbances in him, like anger, etc., might affect the patient.) A teacher who punishes his pupils without anger will have tears streaming from his eyes as he canes him. Consider Yudhishthira's forbearance—when, in King Virata's court, the king struck him, he did not let the drops of blood fall from his nostrils on the ground. Forbearance means returning good for evil, so profound is its significance.

Pretentiousness, arrogance, self-conceit, wrath, coarseness, ignorance—these are to be found in one born with the devilish heritage. (4)

Dambha means pretending to possess what one does not. *Darpa* means boasting about something which one possesses in only a small measure. *Abhiman* means being proud of a quality which one possesses. Narad showed pride when he had vanquished Kamadeva, and he fell because of his pride. *Parushya* means harshness.

> *The divine heritage makes for Freedom, the devilish for bondage. Grieve not O Partha; thou art born with a divine heritage.*
>
> *There are two orders of created beings in the world—the divine and the devilish; the divine order has been described in detail, hear from Me now of the devilish, O Partha.*
>
> *Men of the devil do not know what they may do and what they may not; neither purity, nor right conduct, nor truth is to be found in them. (5-7)*

Those who lack purity and truthfulness and whose conduct is not moral are diseased men and women. There can be no disease unless there is mental evil or bodily error. A person whose atman is awake every moment of his life constantly prays that his body be filled with light. How did Ladha Maharaj overcome his leukoderma? Every time he applied the *bel* leaves on the affected parts, he prayed that light should enter his body. We can prevent unhealthy emotions from disturbing our body only if we daily pray for the flow of light into it. I would ask every person who suffered from a disease if he was free from attachments and aversions. Outwardly we may be clean and our conduct may be moral, but, in the absence of truthfulness, it is all as hollow as a drum. We gather here to cultivate that truthfulness.

> *'Without truth, without basis, without God is the universe,' they say: 'born of the union after sexes, prompted by naught but lust.'*
>
> *Holding this view, these depraved souls, of feeble understanding and of fierce deeds, come forth as enemies of the world to destroy it.*
>
> *Given to insatiable lust, possessed by pretentiousness, arrogance and conceit, they seize wicked purpose in their delusion, and go about pledged to unclean deeds.*
>
> *Given to boundless cares that end only with their death, making indulgence or lust their sole goal, convinced that that is all.*

Caught in a myriad snares of hope, slaves to lust and wrath, they seek unlawfully to amass wealth for the satisfaction of their appetites. (8-12)

How can desire and anger overcome him who is protected by willing submission to holy authority?

Anger consumes many times more energy than does joy. It is because people spend more energy than they can afford that injustice and tyranny prevail in the world.

Anger involves expenditure of energy by thirteen muscles, whereas laughter by only ten. Enjoyment of sense-pleasure leads to death. *Brahmacharya* leads to immortality. Once Raychandbhai was suffering from headache. I asked him to which theatre he had been to see a play. He replied that he had been witnessing a play at night, lying at home, and said that he did not wish to consume his energy in trying to cure his headache. It was good, he told me, that I saw him as he was. He was, he said, less powerful than God's law.

Sexual indulgence necessarily leads to death. If people gave themselves up to it, God's rule in the world would end, and Satan's prevail.

This have I gained today; this aspiration shall I now attain; this wealth is mine; this likewise shall be mine hereafter.

This enemy I have already slain, others also I shall slay; lord of all am I; enjoyment is mine, perfection is mine, strength is mine, happiness is mine.

Wealthy am I, and high-born. What other is like unto me? I shall perform a sacrifice! I shall give alms! I shall be merry! Thus think they, by ignorance deluded. (13-15)

Living in this way, man gambles away the *ratnachintamani* of his body. Even Yudhishthira had gambled, and lost Draupadi too in the throw. We can, however, say that he had less of anger and desire in him than Duryodhana. We ourselves are full of that mixture. We must strive our best to raise ourselves to a higher level.

And tossed about by diverse fancies, caught in the net of delusion, stuck deep in the indulgence of appetites into foul hell they fall.

Wise in their own conceit, stubborn, full of the intoxication of pelf and pride, they offer nominal sacrifices for show, contrary to the rule. (16-17)

Yajna is only a pretext, their real aim is to serve their own interests.

Given to pride, force, arrogance, lust and wrath they are deriders indeed, scorning Me in their own and others' bodies.

These cruel scorners, lowest of mankind and vile, I hurl down again into devilish wombs.

Doomed to devilish wombs, these deluded ones, far from ever coming to Me, sink lower and lower in birth after birth.

Threefold is this gate of hell, leading man to perdition,— Lust, Wrath and Greed; these three, therefore, should be shunned. (18-20)

One who keeps himself free from these does not devote himself to the pursuit of worldly happiness, but follows the path of spiritual welfare.

The man who escapes these three gates of Darkness, O Kaunteya, works out his welfare and thence reaches the highest state.

He who forsakes the rule of Shastra and does but the bidding of his selfish desires, gains neither perfection, nor happiness, nor the highest state.

Therefore let Shastra be thy authority for determining what ought to be done and what ought not to be done; ascertain thou the rule of the Shastra and do thy task here accordingly. (21-24)

In this context, we should say that we would obey our conscience. But then, even Ravana would say that he obeyed his conscience. He alone can use this plea whose mind has become purified by knowledge acquired from Shastras. So the question is, what is Shastra? The Vedas, the work of history, the *Puranas,* all these are Shastras. They, however, contain contradictory statements. Shastra comes from the root *shas.* Someone has argued that the *Gita* teaches the principle of "tit for tat", and quotes Shaikh Sadi in his support, who said that he who was good to the bad would be bad to the good. But Shastra is subject to the principles of truth and non-violence. Shastra rules, and does not aim at spreading anarchy.

Whenever we have a social problem to discuss, we should think of authorities and consult them; as, for instance, in connection with the problem of dogs which is unnecessarily agitating me. If, however, our foundations are not strong, consulting a Shastra will avail us nothing. If the foundations strong, it should be our principle that we will cling to truth at any cost. We shall have read Shastras to some purpose if we are determined that, even if Yudhishthira told a lie, our ideal shall be truth.

If by Shastra we mean a book, the Bible, the Koran and other books have been before mankind for so many hundreds of years, but no one has come to the end of these problems. The intention in this verse is to tell us not to look upon ourselves as an authority, that is, not to be guided by our wishes and feelings. So long as one's intellect has not become vigilant and the heart is not filled exclusively with Ramanama, one should be ruled by the authority of the Shastras. Here Shri Krishna refers to the struggle in us between divine and demoniac impulses. So long as we are in that condition, we should be guided by the authority of the Shastras. That Shastra means *shishtachara,* that is, we should follow the example of those forefathers of ours who were holy and fearless.

The ideal of conduct among shepherds may be stealing sheep, and among meateaters eating meat. A boy once wanted to discuss with me whether or not we can eat meat, but his mother did not let me discuss the subject with him. She was right. She thought that nothing could be brought about by force. If the boy became a vegetarian, she thought, there would be a quarrel in the family. One must certainly fear *shishtachara.* It may be disregarded only if it requires one to violate truth, etc. Where the tradition of guru and disciple has disappeared, men will follow their own wishes. The *Gita* has advised us: *tadviddhi pranipanena,* but it is not so easy to find a guru. If we keep on the search for a guru, we shall always have some wholesome fear in our heart. With the thought of a guru constantly in our mind, it will remain pure. The *Gita* tells us that, if the divine impulse has quickened in us, we should be humble. One should think "I know nothing. I want to ask God, or a guru, but how may I see either?'

We should, therefore, pray. He who prays with faith in God will one day be saved. He who talks as if *Brahman* was in him will not be saved. The literal meaning of the verse is that we should be guided by the authority of the Shastras. The derived meaning is that we should be guided by *shishtachara.* To be *shishta* means that, in the absence of a guru, we should be humble, and to be humble means to worship our personal God. That is, we should look upon ourselves as insignificant creatures, like bugs and, fleas, and worship God. If you are humble, you will be saved. If you are humble and sincere, the veils before your eyes will be lifted one after another.

Chapter XVII begins with the idea explained in this verse.

❑❑❑

17

श्रद्धात्रयविभागयोग

अर्जुन उवाच

ये शास्त्रविधिमुत्सृज्य यजन्ते श्रद्धयान्विताः। तेषां निष्ठा तु का कृष्ण सत्त्वमाहो रजस्तमः।। 1

त्रिविधा भवति श्रद्धा देहिनां सा स्वभावजा। सात्त्विकी राजसी चैव तामसी चेति तां श्रृणु।।2

सत्त्वानुरूपा सर्वस्य श्रद्धा भवति भारत। श्रद्धामयोऽयं पुरुषो यो यच्छ्रद्धः स एव सः।। 3

यजन्ते सात्त्विका देवान्यक्षरक्षांसि राजसाः। प्रेतान् भूतगणांश्चान्ये यजन्ते तामसा जनाः।। 4

अशास्त्रविहितं घोरं तप्यन्ते ये तपो जनाः। दम्भाहङ्कारसंयुक्ताः कामरागबलान्विताः।। 5

कर्षयन्तः शरीरस्थं भूतग्राममचेतसः। मां चैवान्तःशरीरस्थं तान्विद्ध्यासुरनिश्चयान्।। 6

आहारस्त्वपि सर्वस्य त्रिविधो भवति प्रियः। यज्ञस्तपस्तथा दानं तेषां भेदमिमं श्रृणु।। 7

आयुःसत्त्वबलारोग्यसुखप्रीतिविवर्धनाः। रस्याः स्निग्धाः स्थिरा हृद्या आहाराः सात्त्विकप्रियः।।8

कट्वम्ललवणात्युष्णतीक्ष्णरूक्षविदाहिनः। आहारा राजसस्येष्टा दुःखशोकामयप्रदाः।। 9

यातयामं गतरसं पूति पर्युषितं च यत्। उच्छिष्टमपि चामेध्यं भोजनं तामसप्रियम्।। 10

अफलाकाङ्क्षिभिर्यज्ञो विधिदृष्टो य इज्यते। यष्टव्यमेवेति मनः समाधाय स सात्त्विकः।। 11

अभिसन्धाय तु फलं दम्भार्थमपि चैव यत्। इज्यते भरतश्रेष्ठ तं यज्ञं विद्धि राजसम्।। 12

विधिहीनमसृष्टान्नं मन्त्रहीनमदक्षिणम्। श्रद्धाविरहितं यज्ञं तामसं परिचक्षते।। 13

देवद्विजगुरुप्राज्ञपूजनं शौचमार्जवम्। ब्रह्मचर्यमहिंसा च शारीरं तप उच्यते।। 14

अनुद्वेगकरं वाक्यं सत्यं प्रियहितं च यत्। स्वाध्यायाभ्यसनं चैव वाङ्मयं तप उच्यते।। 15

मनःप्रसादः सौम्यत्वं मौनमात्मविनिग्रहः। भावसंशुद्धिरित्येतत्तपो मानसमुच्यते।। 16

श्रद्धया परया तप्तं तपस्तत्त्रिविधं नरैः। अफलाकाङ्क्षिभिर्युक्तैः सात्त्विकं परिचक्षते।। 17

सत्कारमानपूजार्थं तपो दम्भेन चैव यत्। क्रियते तदिह प्रोक्तं राजसं चलमध्रुवम्।। 18

मूढग्राहेणात्मनो यत्पीडया क्रियते तपः। परस्योत्सादनार्थं वा तत्तामसमुदाहृतम्।। 19

दातव्यमिति यद्दानं दीयतेऽनुपकारिणे। देशे काले च पात्रे च तद्दानं सात्त्विकं स्मृतम्।। 20

यत्तु प्रत्युपकारार्थं फलमुद्दिश्य वा पुनः। दीयते च परिक्लिष्टं तद्दानं राजसं स्मृतम्।। 21

अदेशकाले यद्दानमपात्रेभ्यश्च दीयते। असत्कृतमवज्ञातं तत्तामसमुदाहृतम्।। 22

ॐ तत्सदिति निर्देशो ब्रह्मणस्त्रिविधः स्मृतः। ब्राह्मणास्तेन वेदाश्च यज्ञाश्च विहिताः पुरा।। 23

तस्मादोमित्युदाहृत्य यज्ञदानतपःक्रियाः। प्रवर्तन्ते विधानोक्ताः सततं ब्रह्मवादिनाम्।। 24

तदित्यनभिसन्धाय फलं यज्ञतपःक्रिया। दानक्रियाश्च विविधाः क्रियन्ते मोक्षकाङ्क्षिभिः।। 25

सद्भावे साधुभावे च सदित्येतत्प्रयुज्यते। प्रशस्ते कर्मणि तथा सच्छब्दः पार्थ युज्यते।। 26

यज्ञे तपसि दाने च स्थितिः सदिति चोच्यते। कर्म चैव तदर्थीयं सदित्येवाभिधीयते।। 27

अश्रद्धया हुतं दत्तं तपस्तप्तं कृतं च यत्। असदित्युच्यते पार्थ न च तत्प्रेत्य नो इह।। 28

The Three Kinds of Faith, Food, Sacrifices, etc.

Arjuna said:

What, then, O Krishna, is the position of those who forsake the rule of Shastra and yet worship with faith? Do they act from sattva or rajas or tamas? (1)

By disregarding the manner enjoined in the Shastras means by disregarding the *shishtachara,* or without the guidance of a guru, and with faith means with some little humility. Shri Krishna's reply to this is indirect. No to accept Shastra as an authority and to have faith are inconsistent with each other. Faith consists in accepting the authority of Shastra.

Shri Krishna replies:

Threefold is the faith of men, an expression of their nature in each case; it is sattvik, rajas or tamas. Hear thou of it. (2)

Arjuna and Shri Krishna are friends, but the former does not understand that. Shri Krishna is playing with him. It is certainly not Arjuna's intention to corner Shri Krishna in argument. But the latter thinks that He might play with Arjuna a little. The Lord need not bother Himself why Arjuna put this question. He assumes that a person may disregard the manner enjoined in the Shastras, and then ask what kind of faith such a person has. Is it *sattvik* or *rajasik* or *tamasik?*

The faith of every man is in accord with his innate character, man is made up of faith; whatever his object of faith, even so is he. (3)

Faith can be enlightened. Everyone needs faith, provided one is not misguided by it. If anyone clings to a straw, he will certainly fall, but he will not fall who clings to the branch of a tree. Mrs Besant has said that a person needs steps till he has climbed to the top. Shastra is such a step. Once a person has climbed to the top, he needs neither steps nor banis- ters. The top appears so perfectly flat to him that he pays no attention to what is below.

Sattvik persons worship the gods, rajasik ones the Yakshas and Rakshasas; and others—men of tamas—worship manes and spirits.

Those men who, wedded to pretentiousness and arrogance, possessed by the violence of lust and passion, practise fierce austerity not ordained by Shastra,

They, whilst they torture the several elements that make up their bodies, torture Me too dwelling in them; know them of unholy resolves. (4-6)

Those who do not even abide by the rules enjoined by Shastras but in their pride follow their self-chosen way fall into such a state.

If you put truth in one scale of the measure and *tapas*, Shastras and similar things in the other scale, the former will weigh heavier. That Shastra which seeks to suppress truth is of little use. Those who follow such a Shastra are men of demoniac inclination. If truth is timeless, so is untruth; and, likewise, if light is timeless, so is darkness too. We should embrace what is timeless only if it is combined with truth.

If a Shastra is not supported by truth and non-violence, it may even be the means of our fall. As they say, we should swim in our father's well, not drown ourselves in it. Father in this context means *shishtachara.* It is said that one cannot get knowledge without a guru. The moment you have found one, you know what the *shishtachara* is. But these are such hard times that one does not easily find a guru. If we are doing God's work, it is bound to be in harmony with *shishtachara.* That is why we are enjoined to keep repeating tho Lord's name while doing any work. This verse explains in what spirit we should do this. Our faith must not be in ghosts and spirits or in demons. We ought to pray only to a beneficent deity.

Of three kinds again is the food that is dear to each; so also are sacrifice, austerity, and charity. Hear how they differ.

Victuals that add to one's years, vitality strength, health, happiness and appetite; are savoury, rich, substantial and inviting, are dear to the sattvik.

Victuals that are bitter, sour, salty, overhot, spicy, dry, burning, and causing pain, bitterness and disease, are dear to the rajas. Food which has become cold, insipid, putrid, stale, discorded and unfit for sacrifice, is dear to the tamas. (7-10)

If we cling to this classification, we shall not come to the right conclusion. Shri Krishna has first explained the qualities of the *sattvik* man and then his taste, etc. *Laddu*-lovers have included *laddus* in *sattvik* food. They do not help one to safeguard one's *brahmacharya.* In interpreting the meaning of *rasa,* too, we should use discrimination. There must have been a reason in that age for making such a classification, for there must have been persons even then who would eat a handful of chillies at a time. In the present age, there is no need for eating *snigdh* foods. If here we start eating ghee, our food would be, not *sattvik* or *rajasik,* but such as a demon would love. The inclusion of bitter, sour and saltish foods is quite correct. Then the verse mentions food which has been left over. Stilton cheese (a food containing countless germs) is of this class. *Daliya* and *mamara* do not belong to this class.

That sacrifice is sattvik which is willingly offered as a duty without desire for fruit and according to the rule.

But when sacrifice is offered with an eye to fruit and for vain glory, know, O Bharatashreshtha, that it is rajas.

Sacrifice which is contrary to the rule, which produces no food, which lacks the sacred text, which involves no giving up and which is devoid of faith is said to be tamas. (11-13)

A *yajna* without *dakshina* means one in which no gifts are made to the poor.

Homage to the gods, to Brahmins, to gurus and to wise men; cleanliness, uprightness, brahmacharya and non-violence—these constitute austerity (tapas) of the body.

That is *tapas* in which one goes through physical discomfort or harship.

Words that cause no hurt, that are true, loving and helpful, and spiritual study constitute austerity of speech.

Serenity, benignity, silence, self-restraint, and purity of the spirit—these constitute austerity of the mind.

This threefold austerity practised in perfect faith by men not desirous of fruit, disciplined, is said to be sattvik.

Austerity which is practised with an eye to gain praise, honour and homage and, for ostentation is said to be rajas; It is fleeting and unstable.

Austerity which is practised from any foolish o bsession, either to torture oneself or to procure another's ruin is called tamas. (15-19)

A person who fasts for a hundred days or keeps standing on one foot performs not *sattvik* but *tamasik tapas.*

Charity, given as a matter of duty, without expectation of any return, at the right place and time, and to the right person is said to be sattvik. (20)

It may not in all circumstamces be right to give what it is right to give in certain circumstamces. This is also true about recipients. It is but right to give: food to one who has lost the us of this limbs altogether. But suppose there is a blind man who is suffering from fever and comes begging. He would be an unworthy object of our charity if we gave him food. If we give him a blanket and he sells it, then also will our gift have been made to an unworthy person. In one place, it may be right to give food, in another something else, and in still another a third thing. The principle is the same in all cases, but its application will vary according to place, time and person. The same is true about *yajnas.*

Charity, which is given either in the hope of receiving in return, or with a view to winning merit, or grudgingly, is declared to be rajas.

Charity given at the wrong place and time, and to an undeserving recipient, disrespectfully and with contempt, is declared to be tamas.

AUM TAT SAT has been declared to be the threefold name of Brahman and by that name were created of old the Brahmanas, the Vedas and sacrifices.

Therefore, with AUM ever on their lips, all the rites of sacrifice, charity and austerity, proceed always according to the rule, by Brahmavadins. (21-24)

Those who seek knowledge of the *Brahman* dedicate all their *yajnas*, gifts and *tapas* to Shri Krishna. They do everything in the name of Hari, in the name of *Aum.*

With utterance of TAT and without desire for fruit are the several rites of sacrifice, austerity and charity performed by those seeking Freedom.

SAT is employed in the sense of 'real' and 'good'; O Partha, Sat is also applied to beautiful deeds.

Constancy in sacrifice, austerity and charity, is called SAT; and all work for these purposes is also SAT. (25-27)

Aum comes first in all these actions. *Sat* signifies the process of their performance. If we wish that we should be steady in our *yajnas* and gifts, then *Aum* signifies the commencement and *sat* signifies the process. *Sat* signifies process and also stands for Hari, *Brahma satyam jaganmithya* has been stated in this sense.

Whatever is done, O Partha, by way of sacrifice, charity or austerity or any other work, is called Asat if done without faith. It counts for naught hereafter as here. (28)

Aum tat sat means that all exists is *Aum*, that our "I" is unreal, that God alone is and nothing else is real, that we are all running after things in vain.

We should even eat our food in a *sattvik* spirit. There are persons who eat as an act of worship. We should resolve that we wish to live as ciphers in this world. The world may kick us from one place to another as if we were a ball, but we will not let ourselves be so kicked. We will use our knowledge, our bodies, our strength and money, all for the service of others, and that too with the desire to earn a good name for ourselves. Thus, *Aum tat sat* is a vow of humility. It teaches us to realize our utter insignificance, to be completely free from egotism. **If the Imam Sahib would recite it, here is a *kalama* for him.**

The threefold classification of gifts, faith, *tapas*, etc., given in Chapter XVII is only an illustration. We can make as many categories as we like. The intention was to show that the reign of the three *gunas* prevails throughout the universe. A cooking or other utensil is an inert object, but it contains air inside; likewise everything is pervaded by the spirit. Existing apart from the three *gunas* is God. We have to merge in Him. Even if we cultivate the *sattvik* qualities to their highest perfection in us, something of *rajasik* and *tamasik* will remain. But, without worrying ourselves about this, we should continue to strive and cultivate finer and finer *sattvik* qualities in us, for the impulses which agitate us the least and consume the least amount of our energy are *sattvik* impulses. Though Janaka was as good as a disembodied soul even while he lived is a body, the difference between him and us is only one of degree. It is true, of course, that for one like him there was no returning to this life after he was dead.

❑❑❑

18

मोक्षसंन्यासयोग

अर्जुन उवाच

संन्यासस्य महाबाहो तत्त्वमिच्छामि वेदितुम्। त्यागस्य च हृषीकेश पृथक्केशिनिषूदन।। 1

श्रीभगवानुवाच

काम्यानां कर्मणां न्यासं संन्यासं कवयो विदुः। सर्वकर्मफलत्यागं प्राहुस्त्यागं विचक्षणाः।। 2

त्याज्यं दोषवदित्येके कर्म प्राहुर्मनीषिणः। यज्ञदानतपःकर्म न त्याज्यमिति चापरे।। 3

निश्चयं शृणु मे तत्र त्यागे भरतसत्तम। त्यागो हि पुरुषव्याघ्र त्रिविधः सम्प्रकीर्तितः।। 4

यज्ञदानतपःकर्म न त्याज्यं कार्यमेव तत्। यज्ञो दानं तपश्चैव पावनानि मनीषिणाम्।। 5

एतान्यपि तु कर्माणि सङ्गं त्यक्त्वा फलानि च। कर्तव्यानीति मे पार्थ निश्चितं मतमुत्तमम्।। 6

नियतस्य तु संन्यासः कर्मणो नोपपद्यते। मोहात्तस्य परित्यागस्तामसः परिकीर्तितः।। 7

दुःखमित्येव यत्कर्म कायक्लेशभयात्त्यजेत्। स कृत्वा राजसं त्यागं नैव त्यागफलं लभेत्।। 8

कार्यमित्येव यत्कर्म नियतं क्रियतेऽर्जुन। सङ्गं त्यक्त्वा फलं चैव स त्यागः सात्त्विको मतः।। 9

न द्वेष्ट्यकुशलं कर्म कुशले नानुषज्जते। त्यागी सत्त्वसमाविष्टो मेधावी छिन्नसंशयः।। 10

न हि देहभृता शक्यं त्यक्तुं कर्माण्यशेषतः। यस्तु कर्मफलत्यागी स त्यागीत्यभिधीयते।। 11

अनिष्टमिष्टं मिश्रं च त्रिविधं कर्मणः फलम्। भवत्यत्यागिनां प्रेत्य न तु संन्यासिनां क्वचित्।। 12

पञ्चैतानि महाबाहो कारणानि निबोध मे। साङ्ख्ये कृतान्ते प्रोक्तानि सिद्धये सर्वकर्मणाम्।। 13

अधिष्ठानं तथा कर्ता करणं च पृथग्विधम्। विविधाश्च पृथक्चेष्टा दैवं चैवात्र पञ्चमम्।। 14

शरीरवाङ्मनोभिर्यत्कर्म प्रारभते नरः। न्याय्यं वा विपरीतं वा पञ्चैते तस्य हेतवः।। 15
तत्रैवं सति कर्तारमात्मानं केवलं तु यः। पश्यत्यकृतबुद्धित्वान्न स पश्यति दुर्मतिः।। 16
यस्य नाहङ्कृतो भावो बुद्धिर्यस्य न लिप्यते। हत्वापि स इमाँल्लोकान्न हन्ति न निबध्यते।। 17
ज्ञानं ज्ञेयं परिज्ञाता त्रिविधा कर्मचोदना। करणं कर्म कर्तेति त्रिविधः कर्मसङ्ग्रहः।। 18
ज्ञानं कर्म च कर्ता च त्रिधैव गुणभेदतः। प्रोच्यते गुणसङ्ख्याने यथावच्छृणु तान्यपि।। 19
सर्वभूतेषु येनैकं भावमव्ययमीक्षते। अविभक्तं विभक्तेषु तज्ज्ञानं विद्धि सात्त्विकम्।। 20
पृथक्त्वेन तु यज्ज्ञानं नानाभावान् पृथग्विधान्। वेत्ति सर्वेषु भूतेषु तज्ज्ञानं विद्धि राजसम्।। 21
यत्तु कृत्स्नवदेकस्मिन् कार्ये सक्तमहैतुकम्। अतत्त्वार्थवदल्पं च तत्तामसमुदाहृतम्।। 22
नियतं सङ्गरहितमरागद्वेषतः कृतम्। अफलप्रेप्सुना कर्म यत्तत्सात्त्विकमुच्यते।। 23
यत्तु कामेप्सुना कर्म साहङ्कारेण वा पुनः। क्रियते बहुलायासं तद्राजसमुदाहृतम्।। 24
अनुबन्धं क्षयं हिंसामनवेक्ष्य च पौरुषम्। मोहादारभ्यते कर्म यत्तत्तामसमुच्यते।। 25
मुक्तसङ्गोऽनहंवादी धृत्युत्साहसमन्वितः। सिद्ध्यसिद्ध्योर्निर्विकारः कर्ता सात्त्विक उच्यते।। 26
रागी कर्मफलप्रेप्सुर्लुब्धो हिंसात्मकोऽशुचिः। हर्षशोकान्वितः कर्ता राजसः परिकीर्तितः।। 27
अयुक्तः प्राकृतः स्तब्धः शठो नैकृतिकोऽलसः। विषादी दीर्घसूत्री च कर्ता तामस उच्यते।। 28
बुद्धेर्भेदं धृतेश्चैव गुणतस्त्रिविधं शृणु। प्रोच्यमानमशेषेण पृथक्त्वेन धनञ्जय।। 29
प्रवृत्तिं च निवृत्तिं च कार्याकार्ये भयाभये। बन्धं मोक्षं च या वेत्ति बुद्धिः सा पार्थ सात्त्विकी।। 30
यया धर्ममधर्मं च कार्यं चाकार्यमेव च। अयथावत्प्रजानाति बुद्धिः सा पार्थ राजसी।। 31
अधर्मं धर्ममिति या मन्यते तमसावृता। सर्वार्थान् विपरीतांश्च बुद्धिः सा पार्थ तामसी।। 32
धृत्या यया धारयते मनःप्राणेन्द्रियक्रियाः। योगेनाव्यभिचारिण्या धृतिः सा पार्थ सात्त्विकी।। 33
यया तु धर्मकामार्थान् धृत्या धारयतेऽर्जुन। प्रसङ्गेन फलाकाङ्क्षी धृतिः सा पार्थ राजसी।। 34
यया स्वप्नं भयं शोकं विषादं मदमेव च। न विमुञ्चति दुर्मेधा धृतिः सा पार्थ तामसी।। 35
सुखं त्विदानीं त्रिविधं शृणु मे भरतर्षभ। अभ्यासाद्रमते यत्र दुःखान्तं च निगच्छति।। 36
यत्तदग्रे विषमिव परिणामेऽमृतोपमम्। तत्सुखं सात्त्विकं प्रोक्तमात्मबुद्धिप्रसादजम्।। 37
विषयेन्द्रियसंयोगाद् यत्तदग्रेऽमृतोपमम्। परिणामे विषमिव तत्सुखं राजसं स्मृतम्।। 38

यदग्रे चानुबन्धे च सुखं मोहनमात्मनः। निद्रालस्यप्रमादोत्थं तत्तामसमुदाहृतम्।। 39

न तदस्ति पृथिव्यां वा दिवि देवेषु वा पुनः। सत्त्वं प्रकृतिजैर्मुक्तं यदेभिः स्यात्त्रिभिर्गुणैः।। 40

ब्राह्मणक्षत्रियविशां शूद्राणां च परन्तप। कर्माणि प्रविभक्तानि स्वभावप्रभवैर्गुणैः।। 41

शमो दमस्तपः शौचं क्षान्तिरार्जवमेव च। ज्ञानं विज्ञानमास्तिक्यं ब्रह्मकर्म स्वभावजम्।। 42

शौर्यं तेजो धृतिर्दाक्ष्यं युद्धे चाप्यपलायनम्। दानमीश्वरभावश्च क्षात्रं कर्म स्वभावजम्।। 43

कृषिगौरक्ष्यवाणिज्यं वैश्यकर्म स्वभावजम्। परिचर्यात्मकं कर्म शूद्रस्यापि स्वभावजम्।। 44

स्वे स्वे कर्मण्यभिरतः संसिद्धिं लभते नरः। स्वकर्मनिरतः सिद्धिं यथा विन्दति तच्छृणु।। 45

यतः प्रवृत्तिर्भूतानां येन सर्वमिदं ततम्। स्वकर्मणा तमभ्यर्च्य सिद्धिं विन्दति मानवः।। 46

श्रेयान् स्वधर्मो विगुणः परधर्मात्स्वनुष्ठितात्। स्वभावनियतं कर्म कुर्वन्नाप्नोति किल्बिषम्।। 47

सहजं कर्म कौन्तेय सदोषमपि न त्यजेत्। सर्वारम्भा हि दोषेण धूमेनाग्निरिवावृताः।। 48

असक्तबुद्धिः सर्वत्र जितात्मा विगतस्पृहः। नैष्कर्म्यसिद्धिं परमां संन्यासेनाधिगच्छति।। 49

सिद्धिं प्राप्तो यथा ब्रह्म तथाप्नोति निबोध मे। समासेनैव कौन्तेय निष्ठा ज्ञानस्य या परा।। 50

बुद्ध्या विशुद्धया युक्तो धृत्यात्मानं नियम्य च। शब्दादीन्विषयांस्त्यक्त्वा रागद्वेषौ व्युदस्य च।। 51

विविक्तसेवी लघ्वाशी यतवाक्कायमानसः। ध्यानयोगपरो नित्यं वैराग्यं समुपाश्रितः।। 52

अहङ्कारं बलं दर्पं कामं क्रोधं परिग्रहम्। विमुच्य निर्ममः शान्तो ब्रह्मभूयाय कल्पते।। 53

ब्रह्मभूतः प्रसन्नात्मा न शोचति न काङ्क्षति। समः सर्वेषु भूतेषु मद्भक्तिं लभते पराम्।। 54

भक्त्या मामभिजानाति यावान्यश्चास्मि तत्त्वतः। ततो मां तत्त्वतो ज्ञात्वा विशते तदनन्तरम्।। 55

सर्वकर्माण्यपि सदा कुर्वाणो मद्व्यपाश्रयः। मत्प्रसादादवाप्नोति शाश्वतं पदमव्ययम्।। 56

चेतसा सर्वकर्माणि मयि संन्यस्त मत्परः। बुद्धियोगमुपाश्रित्य मच्चित्तः सततं भव।। 57

मच्चित्तः सर्वदुर्गाणि मत्प्रसादात्तरिष्यसि। अथ चेत्त्वमहङ्कारान्न श्रोष्यसि विनङ्क्ष्यसि।। 58

यदहङ्कारमाश्रित्य न योत्स्य इति मन्यसे।। मिथ्यैष व्यवसायस्ते प्रकृतिस्त्वां नियोक्ष्यति।। 59

स्वभावजेन कौन्तेय निबद्धः स्वेन कर्मणा। कर्तुं नेच्छसि यन्मोहात् करिष्यस्यवशोऽपि तत्।। 60

ईश्वरः सर्वभूतानां हृद्देशेऽर्जुन तिष्ठति। भ्रामयन् सर्वभूतानि यन्त्रारूढानि मायया।। 61

तमेव शरणं गच्छ सर्वभावेन भारत। तत्प्रसादात्परां शान्तिं स्थानं प्राप्स्यसि शाश्वतम्।। 62

इति ते ज्ञानमाख्यातं गुह्याद्गुह्यतरं मया। विमृश्यैतदशेषेण यथेच्छसि तथा कुरु।। 63

सर्वगुह्यतमं भूयः शृणु मे परमं वचः। इष्टोऽसि मे दृढमिति ततो वक्ष्यामि ते हितम्।। 64

मन्मना भव मद्भक्तो मद्याजी मां नमस्कुरु। मामेवैष्यसि सत्यं ते प्रतिजाने प्रियोऽसि मे।। 65

सर्वधर्मान् परित्यज्य मामेकं शरणं व्रज। अहं त्वा सर्वपापेभ्यो मोक्षयिष्यामि मा शुचः।। 66

इदं ते नातपस्काय नाभक्ताय कदाचन। च चाशुश्रूषवे वाच्यं न च मां योऽभ्यसूयति।। 67

य इदं परमं गुह्यं मद्भक्तेष्वभिधास्यति। भक्तिं मयि परां कृत्वा मामेवैष्यत्यसंशयः।। 68

न च तस्मान्मनुष्येषु कश्चिन्मे प्रियकृत्तमः। भविता न च मे तस्मादन्यः प्रियतरो भुवि।। 69

अध्येष्यते च य इमं धर्म्यं संवादमावयोः। ज्ञानयज्ञेन तेनाहमिष्टः स्यामिति मे मतिः।। 70

श्रद्धावाननसूयश्च शृणुयादपि यो नरः। सोऽपि मुक्तः शुभाँल्लोकान्प्राप्नुयात्पुण्यकर्मणाम्।। 71

कच्चिदेतच्छ्रुतं पार्थ त्वयैकाग्रेण चेतसा। कच्चिदज्ञानसम्मोहः प्रणष्टस्ते धनञ्जय।। 72

अर्जुन उवाच

नष्टो मोहः स्मृतिर्लब्धा त्वत्प्रसादान्मयाच्युत। स्थितोऽस्मि गतसन्देहः करिष्ये वचनं तव।। 73

सञ्जय उवाच

इत्यहं वासुदेवस्य पार्थस्य च महात्मनः। संवादमिममश्रौषमद्भुतं रोमहर्षणम्।। 74

व्यासप्रसादाच्छ्रुतवानेतद्गुह्यमहं परम्। योगं योगेश्वरात्कृष्णात् साक्षात्कथयतः स्वयम्।। 75

राजन् संस्मृत्य संस्मृत्य संवादमिममद्भुतम। केशवार्जुनयोः पुण्यं हृष्यामि च मुहुर्मुहुः।। 76

तच्च संस्मृत्य संस्मृत्य रूपमत्यद्भुतं हरेः। विस्मयो मे महान्राजन् हृष्यामि च पुनः पुनः।। 77

यत्र योगेश्वरः कृष्णो यत्र पार्थो धनुर्धरः। तत्र श्रीर्विजयो भूतिर्ध्रुवा नीतिर्मतिर्मम।। 78

-.-

THE YOGA OF RELEASE BY RENUNCIATION

In Chapter XVIII Arjuna requests Shri Krishna to explain to him the distinction between sannyasa and *tyaga*. He says:

> *Mahabahu! I would fain learn severally the secret of sannyasa and of tyaga, O Hrishikesha, O Keshinishudana. (1)*

The Lord replies:

> *Renunciation of actions springing from selfish desire is described as sannyasa by the seers: abandonment of the fruit of all action is called tyaga by the wise. (2)*

There is no real distinction between the two. *Kamya* karma seems to mean all karma—though I am not sure that I am right. Total renunciation of karma is not possible. The renunciation of all karma, then, is *sannyasa*, and *tyaga* means renunciation of fruits of karma.

But, according to Vinoba, there are karmas undertaken with definite motives. But every karma has some motive behind it. That we may be unattached to it is a different matter, but the motive is bound to be served. The existence of the body itself means karma. That we live in the body, we can live unconcerned with it.

> *Some thoughtful persons say: "All action should be abandoned as an evil"; others say: "Action for sacrifice, charity and austerity should not be relinquished."*
>
> *Hear my decision in this matter of tyaga, O Bharatasattama; for tyaga, too, O mightiest of men, has been described to be of three kinds.*
>
> *Action for sacrifice, charity and austerity may not be abandoned; it must needs be performed. Sacrifice, charity and austerity are purifiers of the wise.*

But even these actions should be performed abandoning all attachment and fruit; such, O Partha, is my best and considered opinion.

It is not right to renounce one's allotted task; its abandonment, from delusion, is said to be tamas.

He who abandons action, deeming it painful and for fear of straining his limbs, he will never gain the fruit of abandonment for his abandonment is rajas.

But when an allotted task is performed from a sense of duty and with abandonment of attachments and fruit, O Arjuna, that abandonment is deemed to be sattvik.

Neither does he disdain unpleasant action, nor does he cling to pleasant action—this wise man full of sattva, who practises abandonment, and who has shaken off all doubts.

For the embodied one cannot completely abandon action; but he who abandons the fruit of action is named a tyagi. (3-11)

When we have resolved to renounce the fruits of all karmas, we will engage ourselves only in karma which is in the nature of a duty for us. By the sannyasa mentioned in the first verse, the poet meant renunciation of all karmas. The central idea of Chapter XVII was that one should work without selfish motives. The state of mind in which such motives will have disappeared most is the *sattvik* state. Total renunciation of karma is impossible while we live in the body and the atman's connection with the body will remain right till the moment of death.

What a person who has fallen into a state of *samadhi* can do is to stop the movements of the heart so that the heartbeat will not be perceived even with a stethoscope. The practitioners of yoga tell us that the soul can leave the body at will and fly away for a while. But to what purpose? We can certainly reduce the pulse-rate at will. The truth is that if a yogi really wishes that his soul should leave his body, his faculty of speech and his mind, it will certainly do so. I have no doubt that, if we do not will that the body should endure, it will certainly fall. But our desire to give up the body is never intense, for we feel even a pin-prick. A person like Ramdas Swami can even dwell in another's body and feel his suffering, but he cannot be conscious of the bodies of all, except in imagination. All that we can do therefore, is to shun karmas which have any trace of egotism in them.

Harishchandra's actions belonged to the category of *tyaga.* He was equally ready, when duty required him, to perform apparently evil as well as good actions.

> *To those who do not practise abandonment accrues, when they pass away, the fruit of action which is of three kinds; disagreeable, agreeable, mixed; but never to the sannyasis.*
>
> *Learn, from me, O Mahabahu, the five factors mentioned in the sankhya doctrine, for the accomplishment of all action; The field, the doer, the various means, the several different operations, fifth and the last, the Unseen.* (12-14)

When Fate was no longer favourable, Arjuna was robbed though he still had with him the same bow and arrows which he always had.

> *Whatever action, right or wrong, a man undertakes to do with the body, speech or mind, these are the five factors thereof.*
>
> *This being so, he who, by reason of unenlightened intellect, sees the unconditioned* atman *as the agent—such a man is dense and unseeing.*
>
> *He who is free from all sense of 'I', whose motive is untainted, slays not nor is bound, even though he slay these worlds.* (15-17)

If I put a pebble in somerne's hand and incite him to fling it at someone else would the sin be on his head or mine? Arjuna dragged Krishna all the way from Dwarka to Hastinapur and was now saying that he did not wish to fight. Was that right? Shri Krishna tells Arjuna: "I ask you to fight." What harm need Arjuna fear, then? The sword in Harishchandra's hand was not his, nor was it Kashiraja's. Harishchandra could have resorted to satyagraha, but should he have done that simply because the person in question was Taramati? When one's self-interest is involved, one should do an unpleasant thing irrespective of whether in itself it ought to be done. If, however, no self-interest had been involved, if it was not that the woman was his queen, if Harishchandra had been repelled by the deed itself, so much so that his hand would have refused to obey him, he could have resorted to satyagraha.

If read superficially, this verse is likely to mislead the reader. We shall not find anywhere in the world a perfect example of such a person; as in geometry we require imaginary, ideal figures, so in practical affairs, too, we require ideal instances when discussing ethical issues. This verse, therefore, can be construed thus only: "We may say for the sake of argument that he whose sense of 'I' has melted away altogether and one where reason is tainted with no trace of evil whatever, can kill the entire world; but one who is completely free from the egotistic sense of 'I' has no body, and one whose reason is absolutely pure is simultaneously conscious of time in all its categories, past, present and future, and there is only one such being, God, Who does nothing though doing everything and Who is non-violent though He kills." Man therefore has only one course open to him, that of not killing and of following the *shishtachara*—of following the Shastra.

Knowledge, the object of knowledge, and the knower compose the threefold urge to action; the means, the action and the doer compose the threefold sum of action. (18)

For instance, the idea that we must get swaraj is knowledge, and the person who deserves it is the knower. But this is not enough to bring us swaraj. There should be corresponding work for swaraj—the means of winning it. We can think out similar instances of any class of activities.

Knowledge, action, and the doer are of three kinds according to their different gunas; hear thou these, just as they have been described in the science of the gunas.

Know that knowledge whereby one sees in all beings immutable entity—a unity in diversity—to be sattvik. (19-20)

Things in this world seem distinct from one another, but in reality they are not so. If the jaundice in our eyes disappear, we would see all things as one, undivided reality.

That knowledge which perceives separately in all beings several entities of diverse kinds, know thou to be raja; that knowledge is rajasik which perceives separately in all beings different entities of various kinds. (21)

It is through the *rajas* spirit that we make these three classes: I, mine and others. Attachments and aversions arise from this. The *sattvik* state has no room for attachments and aversions.

And knowledge which, without reason, clings to one single thing, as though it were everything, which misses the true essence and is superficial is tamas. (22)

Tamas jnana is that in virture of which a person does everything with attachment, without seeing any purpose what he does and believing that it is without significance and of no consequence.

In *tamas* knowledge, all kinds of notions are mixed up and it is believed that there is no such Being as God.

That action is called sattvik which, being one's allotted task, is performed without attachment, without like or dislike, and without a desire for fruit.

That action which is prompted by the desire for fruit or by the thought of ' I', and which involves much dissipation or energy is called rajas. (23, 24)

A *sattvik* person does not go seeking work. A *rajasik* person is engaged one day in inventing an aeroplane and is busy the next in discovering how to reach India from England in five hours. Such a person sets apart half an hour out of twenty-four to deceive his atman, and devotes the remaining twenty-three and a half to his body.

Is the charkha work *rajasik,* or is it *sattvik* too? This can be decided only by reference to the spirit in which it is done. If a person plies the charkha merely for the sake of money his work is *rajasik,* but it will be *sattvik* if he does so for the good of the world, in the spirit of a *yajna.*

That action which is blindly undertaken without any regard to capacity and consequences, involving loss and hurt, is called tamas. (25)

In *tamas,* a person plunges into work without thinking of the consequences. One who works without desiring the fruit of his work knows what that fruit will be, but does not yearn for it.

That doer is called sattvik who has shed all attachment, all thought of 'I', who is filled with firmness and zeal, and who seeks neither success nor failure. (26)

Free from the sense of "I" means one who works merely as an instrument. To say that he should have no attachment does not mean that he should be indifferent; on the contrary, such a person should be more active than others. The relation of God's devotee to God is, in one sense, that of the lover and beloved, though in reality the two are different from each other as north is from south. The devotee remains unattached to sense-pleasures, where the lustful lover and beloved lose their vitality day by day.

Do the British officials who come out to India lack anything in endurance and energy? They seem to be yogis, but they are not free from attachment. They believe in ends, and will adopt any means, fair or foul, for their sake. But one who is free from attachment is concerned with nothing but work and displays unfailing determination and energy. He displays determination and energy even in plying the charkha. A person who works in this spirit is a *sattvik* doer.

> *That doer is said to be rajas who is passionate, desirous of the fruit of action, greedy, violent, unclean, and moved by joy and sorrow.*
>
> *The doer is called tamas who is undisciplined, vulgar, stubborn, knavish, spiteful, indolent, woebegone and dilatory.*
>
> *Hear now, O Dhananjaya, detailed fully and severally, the threefold division of understanding and will, according to their gunas.*
>
> *That understanding, O Partha, is sattvik which knows action from inaction, what ought to be done from what ought not to be done, fear from fearlessness and bondage from release.*
>
> *That understanding, O Partha, is rajas which decides erroneously between right and wrong, between what ought to be done and what ought not to be done.*
>
> *That understanding, O Partha, is tamas which, shrouded in darkness, thinks wrong to be right and mistakes everything for its reverse.*
>
> *That will, O Partha, is sattvik which maintains an unbroken harmony between the activities of the mind, the vital energies and the senses. (27-33)*

If a person clings to the decision he has made without being exercised about the consequences, does not change it from day to day, then we may say that he possesses a will that is unswerving. "By yoga" means in a spirit of dedication to God.

That will, O Partha, is rajas which clings, with attachment, to righteousness, desire and wealth, desirous of fruit in each case. (34)

The first signifies dedication to God and the second attachment. Because of that attachment, one pursues dharma, *artha, kama.* The decision of such a person may be faulty.

That will, O Partha, is tamas, whereby insensate man does not abandon sleep, fear, grief, despair and self-conceit. (35)

Everything we do involves grief and ignorance, and, at any rate, disappointment and fear.

Hear now from Me, O Bharatashabha, the three kinds of pleasure. Pleasure which is enjoyed only by repeated practice, and which puts an end to pain.

Which, in its inception, is as poison, but in the end as nectar born of the serene realization of the true nature of atman—the pleasure is said to be sattvik. (36-37)

One must do *tapascharya* for such happiness. It involves renunciation and, therefore, means hardship in the beginning. Everything in which one must sacrifice sleep and give up lethargy, for instance, study and learning and teaching, is a kind of *tapascharya.* But the reward is knowledge of the self. The bliss of knowing the atman is of the same character as the atman. The happiness of the body comes wholly from the satisfaction of desires, and because it depends on the satisfaction of desires it is transient. It is as transient as the life of a butterfly or a flash of lightning. The other happiness abides for ever. The happiness which springs from the serenity resulting from knowledge of the atman is like *amrita.*

That pleasure is called rajas which, arising from the contact of the senses with their objects, is at first as nectar but in the end like poison. (38)

Suppose we have been to a play or some such show. We enjoy witnessing it, but afterwards suffer for loss of sleep also on account of the effect of the play on our mind.

That pleasure is called tamas which, arising from sleep and sloth and heedlessness, stupefies the soul both at first and in the end.

There is no being, either on earth or in heaven among the gods, that can be free from these three gunas born of prakriti. (39, 40)

We should, therefore, strive to become free from these.

The duties of Brahmins, Kshatriyas, Vaisyas and Sudras are distributed according to their innate qualifications, O Parantapa.

Serenity, self-restraint, austerity, purity, forgiveness, uprightness, knowledge and discriminative knowledge, faith in God are the Brahmin's natural duties. (41-42)

Serenity, self-restraint, *tapas* to keep body, speech and mind under control by hard discipline, purity, forgiveness—to wish well, from the heart, even to a person who may have hit us with a stone, straightforwardness—to have no impurity in one's eyes, to behave decently,—knowledge and knowledge based on experience—not bookish, dry knowledge—, faith in God—these are the natural duties of the Brahmin.

A person may have the qualities enumerated above, but may not believe in God, may be lacking in faith and devotion; if so, those very qualities will prove harmful. For instance, in Europe they train the body for prize competitions and wrestling matches. These persons, too, are required to exercise discipline over the body, but that is done without devotion to God and helps them in no way. Hence belief in and devotion to God should be among the most important characteristics of a Brahmin.

Valour, spiritedness, constancy, resourcefulness, not fleeing from battle, generosity, and the capacity to rule are the natural duties of a Kshatriya. (43)

A Brahmin, too, should have these qualities. For instance, Vashishtha and other sages had them. Likewise, a Kshatriya should have the qualities of a Brahmin; for example, Yudhishthira, Ramachandra, etc., were Kshatriyas but possessed the virtues of Brahmins. Bharata was the very ideal of what a Brahmin should be. In this way every individual should display, in varying measure, the qualities associated with all the castes, and a person will belong to the caste whose virtues he possesses in a predominant measure. These will determine his natural karmas.

Tilling the soil, protection of the cow and commerce are the natural functions of a Vaisya, while service is the natural duty of a Sudra.

Each man, by complete absorption in the performance of his duty, wins perfection. Hear now how he wins such perfection by devotion to that duty.

By offering the worship of his duty to Him who is the moving spirit of all beings, and by Whom all this if pervaded, man wins perfection. (44-46)

Anyone who worships the atman—the *Brahman*—God that exists pervading the universe like its warp and woof,—reaches the goal; true success crowns him alone who sees prayer or worship in the karma which has fallen to his lot as his duty, who has made service and every karma of his a form of prayer.

Better one's own duty, though uninviting, than another's which may be more easily performed; doing duty which accords with one's nature, one incurs no sin.

One should not abandon, O Kaunteya, that duty to which one is born, imperfect though it be; for all action, in its inception, is enveloped in imperfection, as fire in smoke. (47, 48)

This does not apply to actions like stealing; it applies only to actions which have been described in the preceding verses as the natural karmas of the four castes. Even if one sees some evil in such karmas—as, for instance, Arjuna's shrinking from fighting because of his weakness of attachment—it is best to do them, for every karma, every beginning, is tainted with some evil.

He who has weaned himself from attachments of all kinds, who is master of himself, who is dead to desire, attains through renunciation the supreme perfection of freedom from action. (49)

Here by sannyasa is meant, not renunciation of all karmas but only the renunciation of the fruit of all karmas and it is such renunciation alone which can be successfully practised.

Learn now from Me, in brief, O Kaunteya, how he who has gained this perfection, attains to Brahman, the supreme consummation of knowledge.

Equipped with purified understanding, restraining the self with firm will, abandoning sound and other objects of the senses, putting aside likes and dislikes.

Living in solitude, spare in diet, restrained in speech, body and mind, ever absorbed in Dhyanayoga, anchored in dispassion,

Without pride, violence, arrogance, lust, wrath, possession, having shed all sense of 'mine' and at peace with himself, he is fit to become one with Brahman. (50-53)

Ahankar, bala and *darpa* include one another, but it would not be like the *Gita* to use only one term. Its manner is to say the same thing over and over again in different ways.

Laghvashi: I observe the vow of taking not more than five articles in my daily food, but, even if I keep it literally, I shall not have succeeded in keeping it well. Haridas mentioned dates and gave some good ones as gift. He watched my mood and offered me one to eat. I relished it, and immediately became conscious of a lapse. Even as it is, I told myself, you eat more than others do. I ate the date and it stuck in my throat. This is what should happen if we treat the body as something out of which we must take work.

In this verse, we are asked to purify the intellect and to be *laghvashi*. To be *laghvashi* does not mean merely to be moderate in eating, but to be satisfied with one article when we feel we can make do with two. It is as though this misfortune befell me because we would be discussing the word *laghvashi*. A person may have taken a vow that he would live exclusively on milk, and then consume fifteen pounds a day, or convert it into *mava* and eat it. Why is it that such a person won't add water to milk and drink it? A barrister friend in England used to read for sixteen hours a day. He used to add water to his soup. Real hunger will prompt one to eat things that taste like *amirita*.

One with Brahman and at peace with himself, grieves not, nor desires; holding all beings alike, he achieves supreme devotion to Me.

By devotion he realizes in truth how great I am, Who I am; and having known Me in reality he enters into Me.

Even whilst always performing actions, he who makes Me his, refuge wins, by My grace, the eternal and imperishable haven.

Casting, with thy mind, all actions on Me, make Me thy goal, and resorting to the yoga of even-mindedness, fix thy thought ever on Me.

Fixing thus thy thought on Me, thou shalt surmount all obstacles by My grace; but if possessed by the sense of 'I' thou listen not, thou shalt perish.

If obsessed by the sense of 'I', thou thinkest, "I will not fight", vain is thy obsession, thy nature will compel thee.

What thou will not do, O Kaunteya, because of thy delusion, thou shalt do, even against thy will, bound as thou art by the duty to which thou art born. (54-60)

"Hence," says Shri Krishna, "dedicate everything to me and, free from attachments and aversions and ever devoted to me do the task which has fallen to your lot; so acting, you will remain untouched by sin."

God, O Arjuna, dwells in the heart of every being and to His delusive mystery whirls them all, as though set on a machine. (61)

We are sitting on this ball of earth, which does not stop from rotating or revolving even for a moment. It keeps rotating and revolving all the twenty-four hours. The stars and the sun do the same. Thus, nothing in the world is motionless. But things do not move through their own power; it is God's power which keeps everything in motion. Just as we keep a machine in motion only as long as we choose and it has no power of its own to move, so also does God keep us in motion as He wills. We should not, therefore, be proud that we have done something. We should shed our egotism, become as a machine in God's hand and carry out His will, look upon Him as our all and obey His plan.

In Him alone seek thy refuge with all thy heart, O Bharata. By His grace shalt thou win to the eternal haven of supreme peace.

Thus have I expounded to thee the most mysterious of all knowledge; ponder over it fully, then act as thou wilt.

Hear again My supreme word, the most mysterious of all; dearly beloved thou art of Me, hence I desire to declare thy welfare.

On Me fix thy mind, to Me bring thy devotion, to Me offer thy sacrifice, to Me make thy obeisance; to Me indeed shalt thou come—solemn in My promise to thee, thou art dear to Me.

Abandon all duties and come to Me, the only refuge. I will release thee from all sins, grieve not! (62-66)

This verse is the essence of all Shastras and of the *Gita*. Shri Krishna tells Arjuna: "You should give up all arguing and take refuge in Me. That will be wholly for your supreme good. Only the service of the atman will advance a person's welfare."

Utter this never to him who knows no austerity, has no devotion, nor any desire to listen, not yet to him who scoffs at Me.

He who will propound this supreme mystery to My devotees, shall, by that act of highest devotion to Me, surely come to Me. (67, 68)

All knowledge is preserved only when imparted to a person who is worthy of it, and not when imparted to one who is unworthy of it.

Nor among men is there any who renders dearer service to Me than he; nor shall there be on earth any more beloved by Me than he.

And who so shall study this sacred discourse of ours shall worship Me with the sacrifice of knowledge. That is My belief. (69, 70)

That is, he who studies this intelligently will become free. Merely reciting the verses mechanically and without understanding their meaning will certainly not bring freedom.

And the man of faith who, scorning not, will but listen to it,— even he shall be released and will go to the happy worlds of men of virtuous deeds.

Has thou heard this, O Partha, with a concentrated mind? Has thy delusion, born of ignorance, been destroyed, O Dhananjaya? (71-72)

Arjuna said:

Thanks to Thy grace, O Achyuta, my delusion is destroyed, my understanding has returned, I stand secure, my doubts all dispelled; I will do Thy bidding. (73)

Arjuna's memory, which had become clouded, has become clear. He has understood what his nature and his duty are, and his doubt has gone.

Sanjaya said:

> *Thus did I hear this marvellous and thrilling discourse between Vasudeva and the great-souled Partha.*
>
> *It was by Vyasa's favour that I listened to this supreme and mysterious Yoga as expounded by the lips of the Master of Yoga, Krishna Himself*
>
> *O King, as often as I recall that marvellous and purifying discourse between Keshava and Arjuna, I am filled with recurring rapture. (74-76)*

If we do not feel a new interest in this every time we read it, the fault must lie with us, it cannot be that of the author of the *Gita.*

> *And as often as I recall that marvellous form of Hari, my wonder knows no bounds and I rejoice again and again.*
>
> *Wheresoever Krishna, the Master of Yoga, is, and wheresoever is Partha the Bowman, there rest assured are Fortune, Victory, Prosperity and Eternal Right. (77, 78)*

To Shri Krishna has been attached the epithet *Yogeshwar* and to Arjuna *Dhanurdhara;* this means that there are fortune, victory and eternal right only where there is perfect knowledge joined with light and power. He who has knowledge should have the fullest strength to use it; there should be perfection of knowledge and it should be fully translated into action.

• •

We have taken this to be an imaginary conversation. The author of the *Mahabharata* has given us a wonderful work; he has displayed in it his perfect knowledge. He had entered into Krishna's heart, *Dhanurdhara* means a person devoted to duty. Is there anyone who has attained to absolute knowledge? For that person, however, who has the strength of spirit to act upon what seems certain knowledge to him, there is no such thing as defeat; he may even have prosperity, and more than that he does not wish. If he goes on acting in that spirit, even his errors will be corrected in course of time. We know that we should always speak the truth, but manage to tell only half the truth; but he who has pure knowledge and the necessary energy to act upon it, that is, has taken up bow and arrow, will never depart from the path of morality.

This is a work which persons belonging to all faiths can read. It does not favour any sectarian point of view. It teaches nothing but pure ethics.

❑❑❑

THE ESSENCE OF THE GITA

The conclusion of our study of the *Gita* is that we should pray and read holy books, and know our duty and do it. If any book can help, it is this. Really, however, what help can a book or a commentary on it give? In the end, we achieve only as much as it is our good fortune to do. Our only right is to *purushartha*. We can only strive and work. All human beings, and animals too, struggle. The only differenc e is that we believe that behind our struggle there is an intelligent purpose What is the purpose, however? Merely to keep alive this body, or to know that which has taken on this body? To raise it or advance it, if that is possible.

For the first object we work in any case, whether we wish or no. Our body itself is so made that it makes us work for it, even if we are unwilling. For instance, while the baby is still in the mother's womb, its organs do function in one way or another. Though unconsciously, it does breathe. That also is a kind of effort. But it is not *purushartha*. Only effort aimed at the welfare of the atman can be described as *purushartha*. It has been described as the supreme *purushartha*. All else is futile expenditure of energy. For such *purushartha*, one of the means is reading the Shastras and reflecting and meditating on them. In order that our study may be really useful, it is necessary to repeat our recitation over and over again with attention to pronunciation, rhythm, etc. It is necessary to create an atmosphere of holiness round the *Gita*. If we are completely indifferent to it, then of course there is no question of attending to grammar, pronunciation, etc.

The truth about ourselves is that we strive for supreme *purushartha* and know how to seek the means for it. We should honour and revere the *Gita*. It will certainly protect us. It is a deity of the mind. If so, we should read it daily as a part of our prayer.

What lesson shall we draw from all this? I will place before you only one idea. The *Gita* does give central importance to karma, nor to *jnana* nor to *bhakti*. It gives importance to all these. Oxygen is a very useful ingredient of air, but we cannot have only oxygen, other gases are equally necessary. Similarly, every element which the *Gita* includes is essential. Karma, *jnana* and *bhakti*, all three are essential, and each in its place is of central importance. Without *bhakti* human effort by itself will not succeed, and, without *jnana*, *bhakti* will not bear fruit. Hence we see at places *bhakti* or *jnana* treated as a means which helps us in doing the right karma.

We can, however, do without any of the three elements, thanks to something else which has been explained. We cannot easily understand *jnana* and can understand *bhakti*, but we can understand karma more easily than either. Decorating the image, repeating Ramanama, all this is karma. Activity of every kind is karma. Karma means body. When any thought takes on a body, assumes form, it becomes karma. Body is a visible thing. To the degree that we can see the body, we can see karma. We cannot, therefore, live without karma, and that is why, we can say, the *Gita* has stressed karma. However, *bhakti* and *jnana*, too, are essential. Let us suppose that we have boarded the ship; who is to give it motion now? Who will start it? We feel happy at the sight of the ship and board it, with faith that it will move. Similarly, karma is indeed necessary, but shall reach the goal only when an intelligent engineer starts and drives the ship. The idea of renouncing karma is a futile one. Even a sannyasi cannot live without karma. This argument, however, comes in later.

The *Gita's* karma is not karma done under compulsion; it must be prompted by some little measure at any rate of knowledge.

The karma which the *Gita* advocates is done of one's own free will, and it is such karma as one cannot live without at all. So long as the body is connected with the soul, it has motion and acts. But karma also means violence. Hence complete freedom from karma, which means from the body, is *moksha*. We should seek an existence that dispenses with this body and is beyond this world full of violence. In this world which is all karma, we should strive to cultivate a state of *akarma*. The *Gita* has shown how we can do this.

Chapter III deserves special attention. This chapter dwells on the necessity of *yajna*. *Yajna* means work for the benefit of others. Afterwards, it is explained that every karma is tainted with evil, as it involves some measure of violence. However, violence committed for the sake of *yajna* is not violence. *Yajna* here does not mean that *yajna* in which they kill animals. There was a time when such *yajnas* were regarded as true *yajnas,* but now most people believe that they are not so.

Since, however, every karma involves violence, I have divided violence into two categories. There is violence when the intention is to give pain, otherwise it is only an act of killing. Breathing involves killing, which is unavoidable violence and is, therefore, forgiven. Without such unavoidable violence, we cannot keep alive the body for its sacred pilgrimage. It is a principle of homeopathy that the patient should take in the smallest possible quantity the very substance which has caused the disease. Similarly, if we wish to become non-violent in this violent world, we shall advance as we gradually become more and more non-violent. On the other hand, trying to overcome violence with violence leads to evil consequence. *Akarma* means reducing karma and the degree of violence involved in each karma. One who does that will not go seeking work to do. Such a person will ultimately reach a state in which his thought itself will be action. We cannot pursue even *bhakti* or *jnana* without some measure of karma—we shall see how this is so.

Since every karma involves violence, our ideal is to escape all karma, which means to win deliverance from this life. This does not mean that the world in which we live should vanish or be destroyed; it means that one should voluntarily renounce activity and sit at home quietly, that is, live in *Vaikunth,* knowing that this world of name and form is transient and that it is unprofitable to take pleasure in it. This, however, is not possible. We cannot, through force of will, have this world vanish from before us, or bring about the *moksha* of all people in it.

Everyone, then, should seek his *mokslha;* but how? By committing suicide? One who kills himself will not escape the body. It is opposing the law of nature to seek escape in this manner. It is with the mind that we have to renounce the body. If every karma involves violence and evil, we can mentally renounce karma. Does it mean that, after renouncing karma in that manner, one can do any karma one chooses? No. At present we mentally draw to ourselves innumerable things. When we have mentally renounced all karmas, a great many of them will fall off on their own. Such a person will then use to his benefit, as much as he can, the world from which all air will have escaped. "Only the outward form surviving, as of the burnt rope"; however, the burnt rope will also occupy a little space. Even if it is reduced to dust particles and they fly away into air, they will certainly occupy some space somewhere!

It is our belief that if the outward form vanishes and the dust particles, too, vanish, then everything will have vanished. Like the sea, God neither increases nor decreases. The dust particles, obeying their nature, will have merged in Him. When we have renounced karma mentally, all attachment to it will have ceased. Such a person will not even think what his duty is. He will be working only as directed by others. It is not he who will be doing the unavoidable, residual karma; God will be doing that. I am not responsible even for my breathing, I am doing it under force, not willingly. A person who acts in such manner is non-violent then this while living in the body. Hence, as we saw in Chapter III, karma done in the spirit of *yajna,* that is, for the benefit of others, does not bind. To do karma for the benefit of others means to enlist ourselves as soldiers in God's army, to dedicate to Him our all, body, mind, wealth, intellect.

I read a book by a Protestant named Wallace. He saw that their activity of converting others to Christianity did no good. He decided to mix with our people. He fell in love with the religions of India, but he could not forget Jesus. He then embraced the Roman Catholic Church, and felt that he was nothing as an individual, that the Church was all. He made an image, Parthiveshwar Chintamani, and resolved to surrender himself to it. As for the line of guru and disciple (to which he should belong), he looked upon society as a whole as his guru. This idea has appealed to me. If the Pope is immoral, there is bound to be corruption in society, but any person who has decided that he will do nothing on his own but do only what the Pope asks him to do, will only benefit himself. A Protestant would say that one should obey one's conscience, but this Wallace kept his conscience out and surrendered himself to the Pope. His giving up concern for his conscience was a great idea.

He has narrated a story. A Hindu once advised him that repeating Ramanama was good and a Muslim advised the name Khuda. He repeated the names Rama and Khuda by turn. He once saw that another person uttering Ramanama was floating on water. Thereupon, he started saying Khuda-Rama and began to sink. God then told him: "My friend, I am both Khuda and Rama." This man, Wallace, thus wanted to cultivate single-minded devotion. His worshipping another person wholeheartedly was itself worship of his conscience. Everything becomes easy only when one surrenders oneself to God and lives as a cipher. A person who does so will have renounced all karma.

Suppose a woman regularly goes to the temple and that the other women who go there find the images immoral. This woman, however, will be saved. The man who taught the *mantra* of Ramanama could not float, but the other one who learnt it and used it with faith did. Similarly, this woman who goes to the temple sees no immoral figure in the image, she sees only God. She would swim across and be saved; the others would be drowned. In the same way, anyone who mentally renounces all karma will be doing even the unavoidable, residual karma unwillingly and, therefore, will not be responsible for them. If he eats, he does so unwillingly; he breathes, too, unwillingly. How smooth everything becomes as soon as we mentally renounce all karma!

A person can be free from karma only when he gives up his body altogether. Even the wish to live in the body must be renounced. If it is not, one will have to pass through many more lives. The wish to live in this body is what is termed *dehadhyasa.* That is the sea of existence. While we remain in it, we shall ever be tossed about by the waves. In the course of time, then, we may perceive the deep truth that what we call happiness is not happiness but only an illusion of happiness, that misery is not misery but only an illusion of it. If a person mentally renounces karma, he becomes free from the sense of "I" and "Mine". He, therefore, resolves to work only in the spirit of *yajna* and for the benefit of others.

Work done in such spirit is ahimsa, but only when two conditions are fulfilled by it. One is that there should be no element of selfishness in our motive, and the second is that there should be no self-interest of ours in it, that on the contrary it should be for the good and for the benefit of the world. If these two conditions are fulfilled then even the most dreadful-seeming act may be regarded as an act of ahimsa. We attribute ahimsa to an act, but we can do that only if the act is for the service of others. If a person can truthfully claim that he eats and performs other like acts in a disinterested spirit he is free from attachments. The wish to live in the body remains so long as I cling to it. We cannot hold a string in a disinterested spirit; holding it is an act of will. If a person has withdrawn his mind from the body as much as is humanly possible, he wins freedom from bondage to the body.

What I am discussing is the question of violence and non-violence, of living in the body and being free from bondage to it. If this bodily life has no sense, use the body for the services of others, for a life of prayer to God. Those who advised us thus were not ignorant men, they spoke from experience. It is we who did not understand them. It is extremely difficult to give up our clinging to the body. Someone may well ask how we can explain this idea to a child. My reply is that it is only in young age that this idea is easily understood; one cannot understand it after one has lost one's teeth. A historian has said that there is no difference in outlook between youth and old age. Youth has desire and the capacity to satisfy it; in old age, the capacity is wanting and so the desire becomes stronger. If we do not follow the example of Menavati, who explained to Gopichand the futility of attachment to bodily life, we shall invite misery upon ourselves.

I go a step further and say that an old man is far more thoughtless than a young man. A prince is always surrounded by *hakims* and consuming *yakutis* but he is ever talking Vedanta. Thus, boys and old men are the same in this regard. Anyone who imbibes something, however little that may be, from these verses—from the whole work, commencing with *Aum*—can attain complete peace. For him there will be only work undertaken for the service of others; the innumerable other karmas will have fallen away. If, while we live in this body, we keep it yoked to work like a bullock to the cart, it will run after fewer things to do and with very much less intensity. We shall, then, seem to be doing nothing, but in fact we shall be working with energy which it is impossible to describe. We should seek out one activity or karma from among the countless in the world, or rather one activity or karma should come seeking us. Anyone who wants to serve will find objects of service anywhere. At the end of all discussion, Shri Krishna asked Arjuna in Chapter XVIII: "Surrender yourself to Me, do this very thing, but in obedience to My command. Dedicate your all to Me and go on with it."

Right at the end of the work, Vyasa wondered what he had been making Krishna teach Arjuna, whether it was knowledge or ignorance, pure *bhakti* or something else. So he made Krishna brush aside all else and say: "Abandon all duties and come to Me, the only refuge." He later made Arjuna also say that he had forgotten what he had been taught. The Lord replied that He, too, did not always remember the discussion and said that He would teach something new. And so He taught another *Gita,* which no one remembers.

The *Gita* was not the first work which advised us to seek refuge in the Lord. How, then, can we end our restless yearning? We must look inwards, not outwards, to discover the way. If we look outwards, where should we search? If God, on the other hand, is not outside of us but inside, how may we look inwards? How shall we blow up the big rock that lies across our way as we look inwards? To seek God means to sink into ourselves, that is, to renounce all activities. Since, however, it is not possible to renounce all activities, we should engage ourselves in as few activities as possible, reduce ourselves to the utmost insignificance. To seek God is not a Herculean task, as the world may think it is; all that is necessary is to make oneself humble and yoke the mind to work every minute for the welfare of the atman. It is we who obstruct ourselves in this effort. What should we do to overcome the obstructions? This is the first thing taught in the science of yoga.

Can procreation for *yajna* be described as consistent with *brahmacharya?* Yes, it can. In it, however, the desire for progeny is more important than concern for *yajna.* Whereas the world simply cannot go on without non-violence practised as *yajna,* we cannot say that procreation is essential. If the *smritis* say, nevertheless, that *brahmacharya* is possible for a householder, they use the term *brahmacharya* in a restricted sense which we have completely rejected in our discussions.

Besides, there is one more argument. If destruction is violence, creation, too, is violence. Procreation, therefore, involves violence. The creation of what is bound to perish certainly involves violence.

The *Mahabharata* is a unique work and in it the *Gita* has a unique place. Describing a physical battle, it gives an account of an invisible fight and shows through it that in the physical battle not only those who lose but even those who win are defeated. The five or six who survived lived as though they were dead. Dhritarashtra becomes miserable, and so does Kunti. We see in the Swargarohana Parva the fate which meets the five brothers and Draupadi. They die one after another. Yudhishthira, too, is hardly able to reach the end of the journey.

And, therefore, Vyasa says that what they got from their victory was no better than dust.

This does not mean that we should stop striving. In one sphere, Fate is all powerful, and in another *Purushartha. Purushartha* means striving, and supreme *purushartha* means escaping from the pairs of opposites. Living in the world of opposites is no better than collecting dust with our hands. It is, however, the purpose of the *Gita* to show that every particle of dust can become as valuable as a jewel in certain conditions. The three *gunas* are aiming arrows at you from all sides. If you remain unmoved as they pierce you, you can win. Those arrows may fall on the body and on the atman dwelling in the body, but, let them fall as long as they may, what harm can they do me so long as my atman is awake?

What is the condition under which this may be so? To explain who can understand this problem, Shri Vyasa gave the *Arjunavishadayoga*. Arjuna here stands for the atman seeking knowledge. So long as the intellect is not aroused by circumstances, it will not feel the desire for knowledge. The *Gita* is not for the intellect so long as it remains ensnared by worldly allurements. Is the *Gita* for students? It is for all those who have faith, such faith that they wish to be Arjunas A student who believes the statement of his teacher that India is 1,900 miles in length and 1,500 miles in breadth will not take up a rod and start measuring the distances. He takes the statement on trust. Similarly, when the teacher tells the pupils in the first standard that the earth is round, an intelligent pupil will believe him and start arguing with another who holds that it is flat. The pupil who is convinced of the truth of the statement will not question it.

Such a pupil will also take on trust statements concerning dharma, which is also a kind of geography, as he does those about the physical science of geography. He will exercise his curiosity in regard to many problems, but some things have to be accepted on trust. For instance, the definition of a straight line. Afterwards, such things become clear as day-light. The years of student-life are a time when one should take things on trust. Why students, even grown-up people take things on trust. We have no choice but to have faith in the ultimate things which remain unexplained by reason. A student's reason is virgin, and it is not taxed much. As its happens and acquires light and power, he goes on solving problems with its help by repeatedly putting questions, bowing humbly to the teacher as he does so. The only condition is that the pupil should feel curiosity and be eager to know.

That is why Chapter I is called *Vishadayoga*. The term means the path which unites one to God through despondency. If we wish to be filled with exclusive devotion to God, to win *moksha*, we should go through despondency. Someone told me: "Cannot we see God through fasting? Is it not right that we should punish the body severely if we feel all the time distracted by evil thoughts?" "There are," he said, "so many *bawas* in the country. Some of them lie on spikes in the fierce sun and derive great contentment; surely they cannot be thinking evil thoughts at that time?" We shall find such persons in Europe too. Fakirs also have that experience. There have always been people in the world who did *tapas* and theirs is not a crazy notion. I have merely put before you my humble view. I do not ask you to do such things. Our aim is to mortify the mind, to teach it patience in order to purify it. Fasting and similar lashes are sufficient for that. If we could be certain that we would always succeed in our aim by fasting, everyone would fast.

Do you think there are only a few in this world who seek knowledge? There are many such. People suffer a great many hardships to secure worldly things; do you think, then, that nobody would come forward to suffer being pierced with a nail in the neck for this purpose? I have seen persons who stabbed themselves with a knife as they begged for a piece. If people can do this to themselves for a piece, why should they not do it for a throne? But that path is not easy. We have a middle way open to us, which is the only one worth following. But there is a point and that is that we should have a burning aspiration in this direction. We should have the same impatience and yearning for *moksha* which lustful men and women display for the gratification of their lust. Let us renounce our yearning for worldly things and cultivate yearning for *moksha* instead.

The first condition for one to be like Arjuna is that one should feel a burning aspiration. People start making distinctions between "mine" and "others". There is no doubt about whether we may kill or not. We know that we may not kill. The eternal law is not the law of killing. Arjuna did not have the strength to follow that independent law, and merely asks how he could bring himself to aim his arrows at Drona and Bhishma. In this way he made the false distinction between "his" and "others" and declared that he would not fight. But he is a mature man. He does not decide impulsively while sunk in darkness. He is all love for

Krishna. Sinking with nervous fear, he asks Krishna to solve his problem. It is only when we feel nervous like him that we shall be cured. We shall not de cured tili we feel a crisis. The experience is like the pangs of childbirth. Arjuna's experience is that which overwhelms one when one feels born again; may all of us have this experience. If the feeling endures, we would he saved.

In Chapter II, we see that the seeker should be eager. A person gets knowledge only when be suffers so much for it that his body becomes completely wasted and seems as if it would pass away any moment. We learn the same lesson from the story of *Gajendramoksha* and the narratives about Draupadi and others. When one has suffered so much, one gets knowledge and one's reason becomes purified. When Pilgrim felt that he was surrounded by fire on all sides, be ran without worrying about his wife and children. When we have such a feeling, we may say that our reason has become purified, and all veils will then be lifted. Arjuna's heart is in the right place, but it is enveloped in ignorance and, therefore, it cannot help him to decide.

So Krishna explains the distinction between atman and the body. He advances one argument to convince Arjuna, till he is overwhelmed by it. Arjuna was worrying so much about the body; he should now worry equally for the atman. Krishna explains to him that the two things are distinct. The atman neither kills nor is killed. It is the body which perishes. Arjuna should know that in any case it will die, and should not worry about it. But this was only an argument. What should Arjuna actually do? "If you do," Shri Krishna tells him, "what I ask you to do, you will have no cause to repent. Even if you make only a moderate effort, it will be rewarded. You should take my word that what you do, however small, will bear fruit." What type of person is he who works without worrying about the result? To answer this question, Shri Krishna describes the characteristics of such a person in Chapter II itself.

The description creates so much interest in Arjuna, who was yearning for knowledge, that he feels eager to hear further. He has no inkling yet of *bhakti*. One cultivates it only when one forgets everything else. Mira was filled with *bhakti* when she realized that having seen the light of the sun and the moon, she did not need the light shed by a glow-worm. If such a person still needs to do karma, it is only for serving others and not for his own sake. A *bhakta* may do exactly what we do, but his reason will show him how to do it in a different manner. And so the Lord explains how to do karma, and thereafter He explains the secret of *bhakti*. Understanding that, one's attachment to the body falls away, the atman becomes stronger and awakens more fully day by day, and ultimately one sees it in a divine vision.

When Arjuna becomes utterly weak, his intellect is awakened. Shri Krishna then tells him: "Your intellect by itself will not serve you. You will need to do yoga, karmayoga." Tilak Maharaj has demonstrated this with many convincing arguments. He has shown that the intellect needs, as it were, to take a partner to itself and be a householder. When Arjuna asked Shri Krishna to explain to him the characteristics of the person practising both forms of yoga, the latter enumerated the characteristics of a *sthitaprajna*. This confused Arjuna. Would such a person be a man of karma or a *jnani?*

In Chapter III, therefore, Sri Krishna explains the meaning of karma Noone can live at all without karma. Mirabai begged of the Lord that she should think on Him with every breathe she took. We do not breathe consciously, but do so instinctively. A healthy person does all karmas with detachment in the same manner as he breathes. Karma may be a sign of health and it may also be a sign of disease. For instance, the manner in which a person suffering from asthma breathes indicates that he has a disease. This is also true of a man who feels suffocated. Similarly, one's karma may be a sign of health in some other person, but not in oneself. After this, Shri Krishna gave the example of Janaka and others. Citing His own example, He said that He, too, had to work and keep the machine going. He could not so much as stretch His limbs for rest. Arjuna could sleep, Shri Krishna said, but He could not. Even then, He was always detached.

If we follow this example, our intellect would retain its power till we are a hundred, or rather it would grow in strength with years. But human beings are attached to sense pleasures. If they were not, they would always attain perfect knowledge in course of time. If our experience is to the contrary, let us not pay attention to that. We are imperfect human beings and deduce imperfect principles from our imperfect experience. There should be, therefore, some flaw somewhere if experience tells us otherwise. Look at a fruit. As it grows bigger, it becomes more juicy and richer. The date has fallen off the tree and dried, but how sweet it is! Similarly, the intellect of a person who does not violate God's law should ripen and grow with years. In actual experience, however, we find that as a person grows older, he or she declines in strength and intelligence. Such a person has been a lover of gross pleasures in his life.

For an ordinary person, Chapter III is as valuable as a silver pot. It is extremely useful.

We have seen that God does not cease from karma even for a moment. How, then, can we win *moksha?* The reply was that the body should be left to do its karmas, that the atman was not involved in them. This teaching has been altogether misinterpreted by immoral people. But, truly speaking, it is easy enough to understand that the bond of the body itself involves karma. If there were no body, there would be no need to do karma, and God having no body He has no need to do karma. But the Lord says that, even though He has no body, He does not cease from karma. He should, therefore, be thought of as having one; for this entire visible creation is His body. When we think of Him as having no body, He is a Formless Reality. If the atman realized that the body does its karma, it will be free from the bond of the latter.

How can one feel that it is the body which goes on doing certain karmas? The body cannot do karma without the ego. Without the atman, the body itself can do nothing. This is one more problem. This makes the atman a doer. It means, then, that the atman, joined to the ego, dwells in the body and does things. What we should do then was explained in Chapter III. "Service of others brings holy merit to one, and through harassment of others one incurs sin." We may unhesitatingly do what is most for the benefit of others. We shall, of course, assume that the person doing that will be as detached from it as he can be. When we take the least credit for such work, it will be done with the most efficiency. A person walking with his natural speed of a mile an hour will outdistance another running at a speed of sixty miles, for the former will have his joy in his atman, whereas the latter will be full of doubts His running will on the whole serve no purpose.

If our work is free from egotism, though our speed may be slow we are certain to reach the goal. Let us by all means work in the spirit of *yajna* and for the benefit of others. All that we should concern ourselves with is whether it is the body or the atman that we serve. To say that man is born for service of others is true in one sense only, because all his work is prompted by self-interest. If this self-interest is the interest of the atman, then one's work is for the benefit of others. All the activities of such a person will be prompted by the motive of service.

Hence, the Lord concluded this part of the argument with the verse, "Better one's own duty, bereft of merit". That means that, be one's own dharma what it is, even if it is seemingly without merit, it is better than another's which may have greater merit in it. Arjuna was attracted by the dharma of other people, and therefore, the Lord told him that, however good it was, it was not this dharma. Dharma well performed cannot be another's, for in fact such dharma cannot be well performed. Only one's own dharma can be well performed. The truth is that ultimately Arjuna will have to renounce both his own dharma and that of others, but he cannot have that *moksha* right now. *Swadharma* is what is natural to one. For him who works without egotism, his dharma lies clear before him. It grows and expands on its own. We can with satisfaction perform only our dharma, that which lies before us.

We are deluded if we think that we can do teaching better than the work of cleaning lavatories which may have been assigned to us. We do as much good by cleaning lavatories as we would by teaching. From one point of view, the former is certainly without merit. What is cleaning lavatories in comparison with studies? The Ganga stands nowhere in comparison with the sea. The Ganga's dharma is to let boats sail over her, the sea's to let ships sail over it. The Ganga's dharma may seem to have no merit, but that is her true dharma. When we may that a dharma may be, or may seem to be, devoid of merit, "may be" is used ambiguously to mean "may seem to be". From one point of view a certain task may be better than another, and yet for us the latter is superior.

This truth is the source of the idea of *varna*. Today all the four *varnas* have forsaken their functions, and yet we believe in the idea, for it helps to have an ideal even if it is no more than an ideal. Anyone who wishes to become free from the body has no choice but to believe in *varna,* that is, in his own natural work. The Lord, therefore, told Arjuna that his work was to kill, and asked him to do it as *yajna,* without making a distinction between kinsmen and others. The words *viguna* and *svanushthitat* have an equal and like force.

As I have told you, the *Gita* is a big knowledge-feast, it is the very *amrita* of knowledge. I must have had some point in saying that. Many can memorize the verses. It is something within the power of both a god and a demon. I have suggested memorizing in order that you may make the right use of the *Gita* thereby, and not to enable you to make a show of your knowledge of it. If you know the verses by heart, you will get a little electrical energy from them at some hour of the day. You will think of some verse or other, and it will save you. These verses are like oxygen. For those who read the *Gita* with faith, it is like the fabled wish-yielding tree. It can end all of our threefold sufferings. We may not see such a result in this life, but our faith should not be shaken on that account. If the result does not come, the reason will be deficiency of our own effort and not want of truth in the idea itself. It is only if we read the *Gita* in this spirit that it will prove the *amrita* of knowledge.

How should we define *swadharma?* The *varnashrama* had its origin in this idea. It is not peculiar to Hinduism, but prevails all over the world. In view of this, it is necessary to consider what *swadharma* means. In Chapter XVIII, we were even told that following one's *swadharma* one attains perfection; that is, **following one's *swadharma* one attains equality with all. In this transitory world, we see equality nowhere. No two leaves are equal. But the *Gita* shows the way to equality.**

Swadharma, though devoid of merit, is better than *paradharma*, so much so that, if need be, one should prefer to die while doing one's *swadharma*. The reason is that *paradharma* may prove dangerous. We should be careful about this. No-one should do work which belongs to another, for that may be dangerous. Suppose that there is a powerful minister in a country. Asquith was superior in authority to the commander-in-chief of the army, but his dharma was only to issue orders and it was for the latter to give effect to them. Obeying his orders, the commander-in-chief would order the army to march to the battlefield. Suppose Asquith became vain and himself wanted to lead the army; if he did that, the country would be destroyed. The minister is of course next to the king in authority, but his taking upon himself this *paradharma* would be fraught with danger.

Now think of the commander-in-chief. Suppose he wanted to rise to a higher position of authority and to become a minister, so that he might order the next commander-in-chief. If he did, there would be a great struggle for power in the country and it would be destroyed. The commander-in-chief would lose the position he already enjoyed, without getting the one he wanted. One more condition is also essential. The commander-in-chief should do his work, and the minister his; neither is superior or inferior to the other. This requires a sense of dharma on the part of both. If they have it, neither would feel superior or inferior to the other, for each would do his own dharma well and earn 100 per cent marks.

In God's court, one's attitude to work will be given the highest importance. No one there will take into account who was superior and who inferior in status and authority. One should never believe that one's own dharma is superior and another's inferior. Or rather, one should believe that one's dharma is the best for one. Take the example of a mother's attitude to her child. If the latter is ugly, the mother will shower all the greater care on it and will quarrel with anyone who slights it. In the same way one's own dharma helps one to win *moksha*. The *Mahabharata* contains many examples of this truth. In Tulsidas's work, too, Guha and Shabari were devoted to God as they did their own work, and so attained the supreme state.

Varnashrama had its origin in the idea of *swadharma*. We do not see today the true idea of *varna*. It is limited now to restrictions about interdining and inter-marriage. The idea of *varna* is not peculiar to Hinduism. Such dharma which was peculiar to one society would become narrow, and one need not die for it. If our dharma is universal and valid at all times, one should be ready to die for it. *Varna* does not consist in customary practices regarding interdining and inter-marriage; the division of society into *varnas* is a division of functions. The idea of pollution by touch was a later accretion. The distinctions of *varna* prevail all over the world. We find them in every country. Most parents have to think what they will do about their children when they grow up, and the boys and the girls, too, have to think about their future. Exercised over these problems, we sacrifice our interests in this world and our welfare in the next. Worried by them, we lose sight of our means of delivery.

Can anyone else show us what our *swadharma* is? Doing *swaharma* does not mean the freedom of the individual and subordination of society. If a man seeks *moksha* and still believes that he is independent, he will utterly fail in his aspiration. One who seeks *moksha* behaves as society's servant. To win *moksha* means to merge in the sea. To attain that state means to be one with an infinitely vast sea. We are but germs in society. That word "germs" signifies our subordination to it. We are, in truth, free in such subordination. Our duty is what society assigns to us. Of three persons who work together, one is bound to be the leader. A commander-in-chief must consult the minister in certain matters; and likewise the minister, too, should consult the former in some other matters. The definition *of swadharma* then, is that one must do the work assigned to one by one's superior. From this, we shall by and by rise to a higher stage.

How is that in this *Gita* which is concerned with *moksha* we are asked to do work which may have no great significance, and to concern ourselves with *swadharma?* Can we win *moksha* in this manner? Yes, we can. In the *Mahabharata* there is Tuladhar's story. The Brahmin in search of knowledge got it from a butcher. The devotee whom Mahadev Desai mentioned was a potter, and Bhojo Bhagat was a cobbler. In saying, "better is death in the discharge of one's duty," Shri Krishna has not laid down a principle very difficult to follow. The idea of *swadharma* involves restrictions on oneself. *Swa* means that which one has been able to digest. If we are not able to digest what we eat, many disturbances in the system will follow and we would get diseases. If, observing others round us consuming *dudhapak* and growing fat, we also eat it, we would come to grief. *Swadha,ma* indeed helps everyone to win *moksha.*

But, till we have won it, what should we do as human beings living in these physical bodies? If we understand the body's dharma and do it, we shall have to voluntarily accept subordination in order that we may become perfectly ourselves. It is to God that we have to subordinate ourselves. Can we hope that, because we recite *antarmama* everyday, God who is asleep in our hearts will awake? To wake Him, we shall have to seek someone's help. *Swadharma* means the work which falls to our lot from hour to hour. We should do the work assigned to us by others. We have to submit ourselves to our conscience, but what will a person do if he has no conscience? When we have eliminated the "I" from us, then will God take the place vacated, by it. We have to accept subordination for His sake.

Having accepted a job anywhere, we should do it with single-minded devotion and sense of duty; we should do it even if this work which falls to our lot is unattractive to us, repels us or smells of violence. If in a world like ours full of violence, such work falls to our lot, we must do it. A task of this kind fell to the lot of Harishchandra. When he raised his sword to kill his wife, he had no violence in him. Did he wish ill to his wife? His heart was filled with compassion. The poet says that he had hardened his heart, but in truth he had hardened only his hand. If we were painters, we would not draw him with a face distorted by a feeling of aversion. If he had in fact raised his sword with reluctance on his face, we would have to say that he was overcome by ignorant attachment and that, having risen so high, at last he fell; this blot would have remained on him. We cannot imagine any sign of suffering on his face.

Following his example, we should do with perfect devotion and without hesitation any duty which falls to our lot it is best, in the first instance, not to take up a task, but, having taken up one, we must not forsake it. Consider, for instance, a large black ant whose feet, if stuck in jaggery, will not let go their hold of it; they remain stuck to it. Not to forsake the task undertaken, that is but the definition of satyagraha itself. Everyone, from a child to an old man, should cling to the task undertaken till he or she breaks. This is internal meditation, this is Vedanta. Of course, the work done in this spirit should be dedicated to God. We should be totally absorbed in any work which we may be doing. If such absorption is inspired with a selfish interest in work, it will bring about our fall, and if with a sense of dedication to God it will lift us up.

The next question is: if noone can escape doing karma, what is the difference between the karma of a wise man and that of an ignorant man? The former performs *yajna* for others, the latter works for himself. If we do karma as *yajna* it would be as if we did no karma. Shri Krishna then advanced the argument of society's good, and told Arjuna that he should work on without wasting a single moment in idleness, should work on without concern for the "I" and dedicating to God all that he did.

How does it happen that though trying to act in this way, man sometimes commits sin? If, in doing *swadharma* we follow our own wishful inclinations, do it in pride, we are not doing *swadharma*. What is the reason that, though most people in the world do their *swadharma,* the pile of sins in the world remains as huge as ever?

With Chapter III the *Gita* ends. It need not have been followed by anything more. Even in the third Chapter, there are five or six verses which are really important. The rest of the *Gita* is intended to explain more clearly what has been said in the first three chapters.

Shri Krishna tells Arjuna, in reply to his question, that desire and anger ride on our two shoulders. If they are with us while we do our *swadharma,* then we gain nothing. Can we say that many of those who enter the Councils act unworthily? They do it to serve others. But their action is prompted by desire, by the aim of getting the better of the Government; there is anger behind it and, therefore, it is not right. Desire and anger are blood-brothers. They dwell in the senses and the mind. We can, therefore, overcome them only by subduing these. Hence it is that the way to *moksha* is said to lie in becoming free from attachments and versions. This is the reason why we are advised to become free from them. If we are enslaved by something, is there anything we would not do for its sake? Vishvamitra did hard *tapas*, but afterwards he felt that his *tapas* was superior to Vasishtha's; from that arose desire, which provoked anger. One should understand this with one's reason at any rate and move as slowly as a snail; one may then work on without fear of any kind.

In Chapter III, Shri Krishna explained the supremacy of karma. After explaining that, if we wish to practise yoga through karma, we should dedicate to God every karma which we do, He explained what other things should accompany karma. It should be enriched with knowledge. Let us think about the path of knowledge and the path of karma. Anyone who follows the former exclusively becomes heartless; he who follows the latter exclusively becomes dull in mind. For the right choice of karma we should combine the methods of both the paths. Both are excellent, but neither can be practised without the other. Is there anything as humble as a stone, or anything which does as much karma as it does? How utterly dedicated to God is its karma? It goes on working for ever in the same, unchanging manner; but, as a mere piece of stone, it never wins *moksha*. A stone should cease to be a stone and should become Ahalya, should come alive. On the one hand, we should be as inert as a stone; and, on the other, we should become the very image of knowledge, and this in such manner that noone can say whether the person is a man of karma or of knowledge. Then will his *purushartha* be complete. Where *jnana* and karma unite, *bhakti* will follow as a matter of course. For the moment, we have seen that there should be a combination of the two. When we have understood the meaning of both, we shall see no difference between *sankhya* and yoga. That is the substance of Chapter IV.

Hathayogis believe Chapter VI to have been written for them. Their belief is that it was written because *hathayoga* has a place in the practice of yoga. I do not share this view, though I admit that *hathayoga* has some utility. We should avail ourselves of all possible means which help in realization. It is said about the purely physical processes described in *hathayoga* that those who go through them will attain self-realization. Jnanadeva went riding on a wall to receive someone who was coming to see him riding a lion. But what then? He thereby brought yoga into discredit. These processes do not necessarily take one to God. The secret of rising towards God lies in the mind. In this very Chapter there is the verse: *Uddharedatmanatmanam natmunamawasadayet.* That is, this chapter teaches the importance of controlling the self. Mortification of the body is also as much for the control of the mind as for the control of the self. Anyone who practises these processes, knowing that they help control of the mind, will certainly derive much profit from them. We have not taken them up because we have not met anyone who knows them. We have been visited by many who believed in them and recommended them to us: but none who knew them. Hence I have done nothing in that field. But I do have them in my mind. I mention this thing so that, if you come across a sadhu who is like me a seeker, you should avail yourselves of his services. Our bodies have become very weak. If we know these physical processes very well, they would be found to be far more effective exercises than what they teach in England.

The sixth chapter of course discusses the importance of rules. It also explains the means of doing karma in a disinterested spirit. *Jnana* signifies the knowledge of man who knows the Shastras and the term yogi means one who knows the science of karma. This chapter explains the conditions which must be fulfilled before we can do karma in a disinterested spirit. It is not possible to do karma in that spirit without control of the spirit. Those who control themselves from hour to hour, only they can work in that spirit. Thieves, robbers and immoral men never talk about doing karma in a disinterested spirit. Many persons use the *Gita* to justify their actions. But disinterestedness is a state of the mind, and such a state can never be cultivated without effort and without self-control. One whose left hand does not know what his right hand does, such a one knows what it is to be equal-minded. Our yardstick is the ability to see others as ourselves. We should think whether we should be happy if others did to us what we do to them. Disinterestedness can never be cultivated without a spirit of renunciation. That is the true meaning of Chapter VI.

•

The *Bhagavad Gita* is divided into three parts: six chapters for the syllable *tat,* six for *twam* and six for *asi.*

In Chapter VI, Shri Krishna explains the means of controlling the senses. In the seventh chapter, he discusses the distinction between *jnana* and *vijnana. Vijnana* means knowledge of particulars. *Jnana* embraces God's *para prakriti,* and *vijnana* relates to His *apara prakriti.* Chapter VIII discusses further what is included in *vijnana.* The last verse in Chapter VII says that he who performs the three types of sacrifice, *adhiyajna, adhidaiva* and *adhibhuta,* goes to the Lord. Discussing *akshara,* Shri Krishna explained that one should meditate exclusively on that, for one becomes like that on which one meditates. He explained *adhidaiva* to mean that He was the *Parabrahman,* supreme above all, and asked thy, since this was so any one should seek to please other deities lower or higher.

It is God alone that one should worship and serve. But what does serving God mean? Shri Krishna said that He was both the invisible Reality and the visible world. If so, the karma which we do is also done by Krishna. If He is the master of the show, can we believe that we do anything? As the dirty water which falls into the Ganga is purified, so we should believe that sins we commit are committed by God, for he who harbours no sinful thoughts cannot commit sin. Anything to which motion is imparted retains it for some time. If we fell a tree, for some time the leaves would remain green, but they would soon begin to wither. If a person has overcome both his conscious and unconscious desires, they will not rise again.

In Chapters VII and VIII, Shri Krishna explains what creation is and describes the visible world and the nature of karma, and shows that everything exists in God. Why does He lay so much stress on the necessity of doing karma in a disinterested spirit? These two chapters sufficiently explain the reason. A person who has plunged into water goes on swimming in it, but the latter is in no way concerned. Similarly, God is a sea of compassion. This too, however, is merely a conception of our mind. Truly speaking, **God is neither a generous-hearted Being nor a sea of compassion. It is in such a God that we live and move.**

Chapters IX and X are to be taken together. Shri Krishna says: "I dwell in all creatures, hence do all things for my sake." And so He said: "On Me fix thy mind, to Me bring thy devotion." In Chapter X Arjuna asked Shri Krishna to show him His divine powers. The stream of *bhakti* which flows from Chapter VII onwards gathers volume from chapter to chapter. Shri Krishna shows Arjuna His divine powers and urges him again and again to dedicate everything to God. All the four chapters lead us towards *bhakti*. Chapter IX, especially, is about *rajavidya* and *rajaguhya*. It is really a great support for persons like us given to a life of sin. Even the most sinful person is promised help and support. **The *Gita* would not approve anyone running down *mantras* from the Vedas. It says, on the contrary, that even the most sinful man will be saved if he dedicates everything to Shri Krishna. This knowledge is *guhya* only so long as it has not touched the heart.**

Shri Krishna showed His cosmic form to Arjuna and explained to him that it could be seen, not by those who had studied the Vedas and gained other like qualifications, but only by those whose hearts were steeped in *bhakti*. What a vision it must have been! My enthusiasm for the *Gita* grows day by day. I agreed to talk about the *Gita* and explain its meaning, and I liked the idea; but my pleasure in the discussion has grown from what it was when I started. I get daily more absorbed in it. We, who are given to self-indulgence, cannot always taste this joy. The real joy comes from *bhakti*, that is, it is spiritual. This interest is growing because it is like savouring food which is digested more and more completely from day to day, and it influences our conduct accordingly. Such is my state of mind.

I feel that in this chapter the *Gita* reaches its highest point. We take twelve minutes to recite it, so that we are likely to feel tired by the time we have come half-way. If we let ourselves sink in it, we should be saved. Shri Vyasa has described the vision so vividly that we feel as if we see it with our own eyes. Beholding it, we wonder what our own place in this universe is. It is nothing. It is as small as a grain of dust. Where are we in this universe of stars, suns and planets? If a hair could speak, it would describe its place thus: "I have value so long as I am a part of the body, separate me from it and my value is lost. The essence of life in me cannot vanish; as for the material substance, even the vast universe is transient, existing only as name and form." We are nothing, compared with that visible manifestation of God, this vast universe. Being what they are, whom can we kill? Even if we kill anyone, we too shall die simultaneously. As we understand this more and more, we should become steeped ever more fully in *bhakti*.

❑❑❑